TEACHING READING, WRITING, AND STUDY STRATEGIES

Teaching Reading, Writing, and Study Strategies

THE CONTENT AREAS

Third Edition

H. Alan Robinson
Hofstra University

Allyn and Bacon, Inc.
Boston   London   Sydney   Toronto

Previous editions were published under the title *Teaching Reading and Study Strategies: The Content Areas*, copyright © 1978, 1975, by Allyn and Bacon, Inc.

Title page photos. Left: top, Anthony Taro; middle, Talbot Lovering; bottom, National Education Association.

Library of Congress Cataloging in Publication Data

Robinson, H. Alan, Date–
  Teaching reading, writing, and study strategies.

  Rev. ed. of: Teaching reading and study strategies.
2nd ed. c1978.
  Includes bibliographies and indexes.
  1. Language arts (Secondary) 2. Education, Secondary
—Curricula. I. Title.
LB1631.R54 1983   428.4′07′12   82–16359
ISBN 0–205–07938–5

Printed in the United States of America

10 9 8 7 6 5 4 3 2 1—88 87 86 85 84 83

To Ann H. Robinson, con amor

Contents

Preface

This book is intended for use by undergraduates as well as graduates enrolled in reading, writing, or language arts methods courses focused on the secondary school. Some college and university instructors used the earlier editions in courses developed to help instructors in a college reading improvement program. A number of college and university instructors have indicated that parts of the earlier volumes were useful for students concerned with intermediate levels and the middle school. Although the major focus is on the secondary school, all of these possible uses have been considered in planning this updated third edition.

This volume, like the earlier editions, is also directed to content area classroom teachers and reading/language arts specialists in secondary schools. Educators in middle and intermediate schools will also find the strategies in the book useful. The volume includes the basic ingredients of a reading-writing-study program across the spectrum of disciplines represented in the overall school curriculum.

In addition, the book has been used as a text in in-service courses conducted in/or by school systems. It may also be used as a reference tool by individual reading/language arts specialists and content area teachers interested in specific techniques, strategies, and/or content areas.

Some learning disabilities and special education teachers, especially those concerned with mainstreaming, indicated that the second edition was useful to them. Additional aids in this third edition should enhance the book's value for them. Moreover, postsecondary teachers in vocational/technical programs have indicated that the earlier editions helped them with many of their immediate teaching problems. Perhaps some of the additional information in this volume will help them plan overall strategies.

Writing strategies have been highlighted and expanded in this edition for three reasons: (1) today's high school students need direct assistance in improving their writing skills; (2) increasing evidence points to the value of interrelating reading and writing instruction; and (3) my own recent experience working with students and teachers on procedures for improving writing strategies has given me enough confidence to focus on some of the techniques that seem most promising.

In addition to the back index, a content area index following this preface has been provided as a guide to readers who want specific information relating to a given content area. Readers of the second edition found it to be a useful tool.

The text is divided into four parts. Part A, "Prologue" (Chapter 1), provides the setting and conceptual framework related to the learner, the curriculum, and the processes of reading and writing. Part B, "Strategies for All Content Areas," comprises Chapters 2 through 6; and Part C, "Strategies for Specific Content Areas," Chapters 7 through 11. Part D, "Epilogue" (Chapter 12), concentrates on suggestions for developing lifetime readers and writers. Indeed, reading-writing-study strategies are of little value if not applied throughout life to solve problems, to provide enjoyment in teaching and learning, and to enhance one's own abilities.

Each chapter opens with a diagram or preorganizer, to prepare the reader for the major propositions and concepts as interrelated in the chapter. In addition to selected readings and notes, each chapter concludes with questions and/or related activities meant especially to provide practice with, or to extend knowledge of, the suggested ideas.

Emphasis is placed on the specific teaching and learning of significant study strategies used in the various content areas.* Reading and writing are conceived of not as separate strands of the school curriculum but as integral, interwoven aspects of the total curriculum. The book is essentially pragmatic, although some parts do describe the psycholinguistic, conceptual framework. Most of the methodology is the result of my thinking over a number of years and my analysis of many materials within the disciplines of the secondary school curriculum. I am grateful to several of my doctoral graduates and students for the ideas they have contributed.

The ideas in this volume are based on the belief that reading and writing strategies related to various types or patterns of writing should be taught to youngsters from the outset. Although some approaches are useful to all content areas, in my opinion the strategies should be taught in *each* content area despite some repetition. I believe that students learn best when the strategies are integrated with the structure of the given content. Reading and writing are not subjects to be taught first and then applied to the content areas. One must have a content to begin with, and the nature of that content—the ideas and structure—interacts with reading and writing strategies in different ways. There is no one reading or writing process; we engage in somewhat different processes, depending on the nature of the learner at a given time, the nature of the material, the purposes for reading, and the nature of the given learning situation. As one of my doctoral graduates, Robert Pehrsson, said, "The reading process is different when we start at page one and when we start at page fifty."

The following general procedures are discussed in this book, and are useful

---

* Additional approaches to study in the secondary school may be found in the companion volume to this book, *Improving Reading in Every Class*, 3rd ed., by Ellen Lamar Thomas and H. Alan Robinson (Boston: Allyn and Bacon, 1982).

for all secondary school teachers whose students use reading and writing to learn about their disciplines: evaluation of individual study strategies, readiness for study, vocabulary strategies, comprehension and readability strategies, and discourse functions. Primarily, however, the instructor must strive to guide each learner toward independence in unlocking and building upon the ideas within a given content area.

I hope that improvements made in this third edition will extend its usefulness. I have already begun a file of changes and additions to be accomplished in the fourth edition. Readers are welcome to make suggestions.

A sincere "thank you" is due to all who reviewed the previous editions in their entirety or in part and shared their comments with me. I am grateful, too, for the excellent reviews of the third edition while in manuscript form. Many suggestions were incorporated into the final publication, and others have been stored for the next edition.

H.A.R.

Content Area Index

The indexes at the back of this book direct the reader to a variety of topics. The content area index that follows is different. The headings reflect the various content areas: English, science, driver education, and so on. The function of this index is to guide you to all the parts of this book and to related parts of its companion volume* that offer help in improving reading in your particular content area. Page numbers in parentheses preceded by T-R refer to the companion volume cited below.

You will find under each content area heading three subheadings: *Specific Approaches*, *Related Approaches*, and *General Approaches*. Under *Specific Approaches* for the content area of science, for example, you will find specific strategies, examples, and procedures especially designed for science. *Related Approaches* will guide you to strategies, examples, and procedures discussed under a variety of topics directly applicable to science. *General Approaches* will lead you to broader background information that may be applied to science as well as to other content areas.

The reading specialist, the language arts consultant, the curriculum coordinator, or the college student preparing to specialize in one of these fields may wish to peruse the book from cover to cover. On occasion, however, any reader should find the content area index useful in meeting specific needs or in giving particular assistance to content area teachers who are ready to help students fuse reading-writing-study skills and course content.

Teaching Reading in Every Class, 3rd ed. unabridged hardback version, by Ellen Lamar Thomas and H. Alan Robinson (Boston: Allyn and Bacon, 1982).

Content Area Index

Part A
PROLOGUE

Chapter 1, "Reading-Writing-Study Strategies and Today's Youth," is the prologue for this book. Like subsequent chapters, it begins with a preorganizer—a diagrammatic overview of the important interrelated concepts discussed in the chapter. Chapter 1 sets the stage for the rest of the volume by concentrating on specific kinds of information related to society, the mass media, the learner, the processes of reading and writing, and the curriculum. Thus the chapter provides a conceptual framework for the reading-writing-study program in the secondary school as viewed by the author.

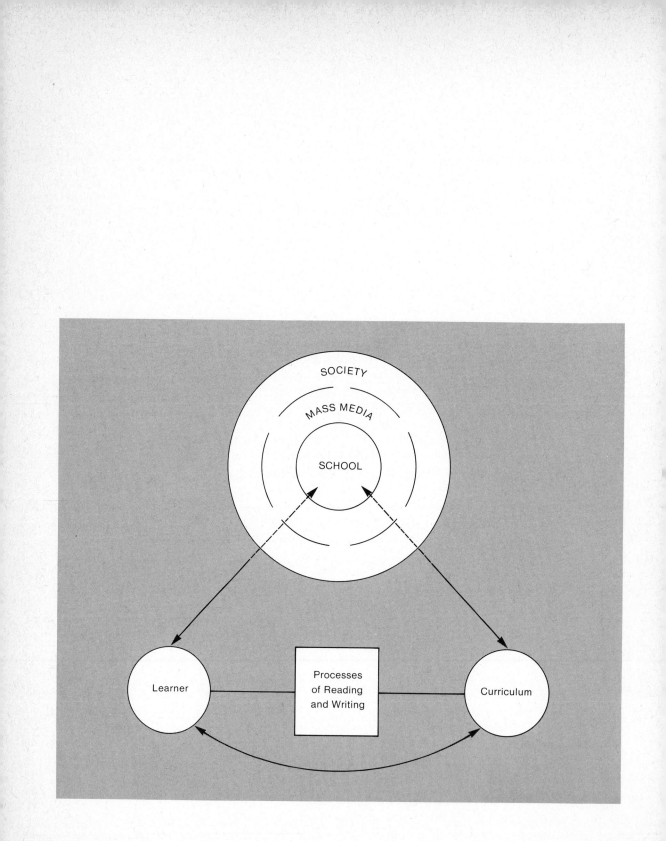

1

Reading-Writing-Study Strategies and Today's Youth

We teachers are faced with the necessity of helping to train participants in a rather unknown future. We are confronted with the awesome responsibility of assisting in the development of future citizens who can think individually, critically, and creatively. At the same time, we must strive to teach students to work together harmoniously and conscientiously in order to learn problem-solving behaviors that may one day make the difference between survival and the end of our world as we know it. Hence, the major goal of the secondary school must change from disseminating knowledge to developing learners who can unlock and generate ideas independently.

As teachers and students are bombarded with new knowledge and reorganizations of the old, and as new realms of knowledge emerge at a rapid pace, it becomes increasingly difficult to conceive of teaching or learning a subject in a given amount of time through the use of a certain textbook or even a host of other materials. When one thinks rigorously about teaching or learning all the ideas in a given discipline, it becomes obvious that even in the past, when things were slower, not everything was learned, or could be learned, within the classroom or with a given set of materials. Today, without question, learning is partial in any content area.

Teachers, no matter how well trained, cannot be the source of all wisdom. If instructors tried to keep up with all the new ideas and reinterpretations of ideas in a discipline, they would have to spend a multitude of hours each day in study. In all probability, if teachers lectured at breakneck pace in every class period during the entire year (presuming the students could incorporate the information), probably only a small percentage of the ideas about a specific subject could be stated.

In fact, because the school and its teachers cannot possibly be responsible for all the learning needed by today's students, the National Panel on High School and Adolescent Education recommended, among other suggestions, that (a) the conceptually inadequate and practically unattainable goal of developing comprehensive high schools be replaced with the more practical goal

3

of providing comprehensive education through a variety of means including the schools; (b) educational programs be inaugurated for the joint participation of adolescents and interested and qualified adults in the community and designated as Participatory Education; and (c) the basic role of the high school as society's only universal institution for the education of the intellect be reemphasized.[1]

By casting off all the extraneous activities and responsibilities that have accrued through the years, the Panel believes, the resources of the high school can be concentrated in the areas of maturing intellectual competency such as learning to write clear prose, becoming proficient in the arithmetic of handling and budgeting money, learning to use the resources of the public library, and to assemble information from a variety of sources germane to an area of personal and community concern. These and more are essential skills susceptible to school training. The Panel is cautiously in agreement that rationality, orderly inquiry, the patient accumulation of skills, the ability to test ideas, the capacity for measuring current experience against the insights provided by literature and history, the rare and wonderful teacher who can become the right mentor and model, all are more likely to occur in a formal school than in any other "arranged" learning environment or within the tribal occasions of "peer groups." Directing the focus of the high school's efforts on them, however, will come only with the reduction in the "global" goals of secondary education.[2]

If indeed the high school can succeed in refocusing and narrowing its goals, it must still consider seriously its dissemination and presentation systems. "Most of its values deserve to be cherished, but their articulation and application in contemporary life seem alien to many students who acquire informal but powerful collateral education via television, the other media, their peers, and other groups with whom they associate in the community."[3]

TELEVISION AND ALLIED MASS MEDIA

From a physiological viewpoint, television viewing may have a deleterious impact on reading because the two activities involve different brain functions. In most right-handed people and some left-handed people, visually presented material is apparently processed primarily by the right side of the brain in a global fashion. Printed material or complex verbal or mathematical sequences seem to engage primarily the left side of the brain. Although reading involves both visual and cognitive processes, some researchers have expressed concern that television viewing is enhancing a strong preference for, or reliance upon, global visual representations. As a result, children, and later adults, will probably be less patient at making the effort required to process auditory verbal material, such as teachers' lectures, or to deal with reading material. Males appear to be more differentiated in right and left brain functioning than are girls which may account for the fact that boys are much more likely to have reading problems than are girls. Research indicates that boys watch more television than girls and are therefore exposed to more visually oriented material in which the verbal component is presented very rapidly. It is possible that this visual emphasis tends to increase boys' difficulties in developing verbal skills. In addition to studies on hemispheric differences, research on the amount of brain activity suggests that there is more extensive and diffuse brain activity during reading than during television viewing.[4]

From a sociopsychological vantage point, television and allied media play a tremendous role in the lives of most students and teachers. Students are bombarded with experiences of all kinds in dramatic fashion, differing usually from the organized, compartmentalized, somewhat dull high school curriculum. They find it difficult to adjust to the daily six-hour interruption in their lives. In fact, it would seem that students who have difficulties in school gain little from the school experience and rely instead on television for their "learning."[5]

While some observers might argue that more learning takes place through the mass media than in schools, an important question remains as to how much of this learning is really "educative." One can learn a great deal which is imbalanced, misleading, and even incorrect, as well as much which is important and insightful. What is the mix of educative and noneducative learning from mass media? And what is the task of schooling in a media-situated world? The fact that young people learn so much from the media means that today's adolescent exists in an educational environment fundamentally different from that of all but his immediate predecessors.[6]

Seemingly, because this bombardment of mass-media experiences is so temporal and unorganized, many students have developed incomplete and hazy concepts. Teachers find it necessary to help students mobilize their ideas as they approach problem-solving situations. In addition, many students have made little use of writing and reading independently. Teachers in all content areas find it essential to be teachers of reading, writing, and study procedures related to their disciplines. A recent statement by a number of professional and educational organizations has emphasized the need and the fact:

The interdependence of skills and content is the central concept of the essentials of education. Skills and abilities do not grow in isolation from content. In all subjects, students develop skills in using language and other symbol systems; they develop the ability to reason;

they undergo experiences that lead to emotional and social maturity. Students master these abilities through observing, listening, reading, talking, and writing *about* science, mathematics, history and the social sciences, the arts and other aspects of our intellectual, social and cultural heritage. As they learn about their world and its heritage they necessarily deepen their skills in language and reasoning and acquire the basis for emotional, aesthetic and social growth. They also become aware of the world around them and develop an understanding and appreciation of the interdependence of the many facets of that world.[7]

Clearly most students in today's world will not become readers and writers by learning the skills taught in the elementary grades or in the high school English class alone. An all-out schoolwide emphasis is needed if reading, writing, and study procedures are to compete in any measure with mass-media forms of learning.

THE LEARNER

Added to the problems of learning content reading, and writing is the fact that not all students are prepared to soak up the ideas offered. To the chagrin of the instructor who comes to the classroom ready to share knowledge, the students have varying degrees of experience. Suddenly and dramatically a new teacher realizes that even the bits of knowledge selected to be imparted cannot be understood, digested, evaluated, and utilized by all the students. The teacher faces learners who not only have differing social and linguistic backgrounds but also learn in different ways; hence, adjustments must be made in the teaching/learning situation to make contact with varied experiences, backgrounds, and modes of learning. In fact, if any relationship at all is to be established, the teacher will find it essential to learn about the learner.

Adolescents and preadolescents demonstrate a wide range of individual differences; indeed, it is difficult to draw generalizations and conclusions about all young people as a group. On the other hand, some behaviors and characteristics appear frequently. Girls, for example, tend to mature faster than boys. Adolescents of either sex may range from awkwardness to coordinated activity, from extreme interest to disinterest, or from cooperativeness to rebellion within a single day, hour, or minute. These changes occur in relation to the people with whom they interact, the situation, and the task. As adolescents move to "break the apron strings," they make a concerted effort to permit their peer group, rather than the adults in their environment, to dictate behavior.

Adolescents will, however, interact with and accept the advice and guidance of teachers who try to understand their moods and who treat them with dignity. Sometimes because of a history of frustration and poor treatment, it may take a long time to obtain their trust. Adolescents appreciate warm affection and a good sense of humor. Given these ingredients, they will accept the structure of a learning situation and constructive criticism when deserved As young adolescents advance in age and/or maturity, they need less obtrusive guidance and look for opportunities to take on more responsibility for their educational programs. Secondary school curriculum planners should be providing many more opportunities for student participation in decisions about what is studied and how programs are structured.

Although this book focuses on reading, writing, and study strategies, I feel the most important teaching techniques are based on *understanding* and *respect*. Students from all backgrounds, as well as students speaking varying dialects or languages, can be taught to read, write, and study if they find themselves accepted, encouraged, and given reasonable opportunities to succeed. As a prelude to specific instruction in reading, writing, and study strategies, consider the following points:

1. *The cultural patterns of a group or groups within the classroom should be studied, understood, and respected.* Time spent in learning about and understanding group behavior patterns and backgrounds will pay off. You will find yourself able to establish the kind of group empathy instrumental as a base for enlarging oral communication and enhancing students' interactions with written communication. Once a group believes you are honestly attempting to understand and respect its traditions, goals, and interests, communication lines open up—cognitively and affectively.

2. *The behaviors of individuals within the classroom should be studied and understood.* It is time consuming and often complicated to do "case studies" of students in a typical secondary school setup. However, case studies will bring results in terms of your relations with students. At least try to conduct "mini-case studies" of those students who seem to present the most crucial problems. Try to learn why they behave as they do, what they like, what they fear, what interests they might have, and how you can capitalize on some of the knowledge you gain as you work with them. Case studies applied to one individual often help as you begin to look at another individual. Gates said that the conducting of comprehensive case studies with youngsters has transformed many teachers "from routine operators to insightful artists."[8] The result of a case study will help you and the learner understand and respect each other—the basic ingredients of instruction.

3. *A learner's dialect should be understood and respected.* Language is used (normally) to communicate meaning. Students are adept at obtaining meaning from their dialects, the languages they hear and use in their daily living with peers and adults in their social community. If you try to understand and respect their dialects and do not deprecate them, students will be able to express their thoughts. By studying their dialects and learning what is part of a given dialect system, you will know when and how communication problems are generated.

If the dialect is denigrated and not understood, the learners will stop using language almost completely in the classroom or will cease to use it for positive communication and will look for ways of using it in negative behavior. In any case, they will most likely make little conscious effort to learn the changes in the rules presented by the dialect used in school and business—often referred to as "standard English."

If students are given many opportunities to use language as an expression of meaning and to search for meaning in the language of others, they will gradually learn to cope with standard English, which represents a dialect needed to gain upward mobility in society. Without doubt, transitions to standard English usage must be made; otherwise, the school fails in its task.

4. *Materials to be read should be selected on the bases of relevance and significance in relation to student needs and the demands of society.* Reading should satisfy immediate and relevant goals as much as possible. Abstract or distant goals may be viewed with greater zeal once immediate goals are satisfied. The messages students are asked to understand should have pertinence in terms of solving problems, supplying enjoyment, and enhancing ability. If students are being asked to read material they cannot possibly understand and/or material for which you cannot establish relevance, the material should be replaced and perhaps the curriculum should be reevaluated.

5. *Instruction should be essentially purposeful and task-oriented, that is, focused on the nature of the job to be accomplished rather than on a writing or reading skill to be taught.* Example 1.1 illustrates this task-oriented focus.

In Example 1.1, students *are* given help in reading-writing-study strategies, but the emphasis is placed on the task—on the need as viewed by the student.

Example 1.1   *Task-Oriented Instruction*

Patrice needs to learn how to fill out employment blanks, since she has her working papers and is eager to obtain a part-time job. In this situation the instructor should not say, "Oh, you have to learn how to read details and main ideas. I have a good workbook for you to use." Obviously, aid should be given in accurately filling out actual employment blanks. Doing this involves reading and writing strategies of tremendous and immediate importance to Patrice.

Budd demonstrates difficulty in following the directions of a science experiment when left on his own. Again, the instructor will not say, "Here are some exercises in finding sequence. Complete them." Instead, the teacher will give help with sequential order in the reading of that experiment and perhaps some other experiments. At some point the teacher might introduce other material, even structured workbook or kit material, for reinforcement. But then, to help Budd succeed with the given task, both the teacher and Budd would return to the actual material that threatened him.

At the secondary school level in particular, there is no sequence of skills to be introduced. When reading tasks appear, strategies should be marshalled to tackle them. As the National Council of Teachers of English Commission on Reading has noted:

> Indeed one danger in the "back to the basics" call . . . is that it can encourage the separation of the teaching of reading from the teaching of content. The result can be the teaching of reading as an isolated process rather than as a means for the communication of information, ideas, and experiences. *It is easy to forget when we become concerned with "the basics" that our best learning occurs when we are performing real and significant tasks.* [9]

Such emphasis should result in realistic goals or objectives related to accomplishing tasks rather than in the ridiculous notion, prevalent in some areas of education today, that reading instruction can be reduced to hundreds of behavioral objectives or competences. With emphasis on tasks rather than on individual skills, even the nature of reading tests can change. We can begin to assess strengths in handling vital reading and writing tasks rather than in coping with such nebulous concepts as "finding main ideas," "noting details," or "making inferences." I am not suggesting that some of these strategies should not be employed; rather, I am suggesting that they are part of a cluster of skills needed to accomplish a task—useful at different times in different ways. When the emphasis is on how to do the task, students will unconsciously make use of varied combinations of those skills as they solve their problems and accomplish their tasks. Competence testing or criterion-reference testing is a strong concept *if* the assessment is concerned with the success of the overall task and not with the tiny, insignificant parts of the task.

Although there is no guarantee of, and certainly no formula for, success, it seems reasonable to assume that if instructors will focus on guiding their students to gain independence in coping with ideas through writing and reading, more adequate learning should take place in a given content area. The independent learners, the students who have learned the techniques for unlocking ideas, can fend for themselves in the acquisition of knowledge and will learn more and more to depend on the teacher as a guide, a question formulator, a reactor, an evaluator, and someone with whom a meaningful dialogue can be maintained.

THE PROCESSES OF READING AND WRITING

On the surface, reading and writing appear to differ fundamentally in that reading processes involve reception and writing processes involve production. However, the difference is not that clear-cut or clean-cut. Both rely heavily on the organized networks (schemata) of experiences with life and language that already exist in the learners' heads. Neither successful reading nor successful writing can take place without "relevant prior knowledge," which Frank Smith calls *nonvisual information.*[10]

Smith defines visual information as the print before the eyes of the reader, and nonvisual information as "information we already have in our brain that is relevant to the language and to the subject matter of what we happen to be reading. . . . Nonvisual information is anything that can reduce the number of alternatives the brain must consider as we read. . . . Whenever readers cannot make sense of what they are expected to read—because the material bears no relevance to any prior knowledge they might have—then reading will become more difficult and learning to read impossible."[11]

As in reading, purposeful and successful writing depends on the ideas one is able to organize in one's head prior to the act of writing. Organized ideas related to a topic mobilize both reading and writing processes.

READING PROCESSES

Prior to the act of reading, students have developed both well-structured and partially structured arrays of information, ideas, and attitudes in their memory banks. Any reading task will be influenced by these arrays. The mature reader tries to read as objectively as possible, but this "objectivity" is always shaped to some extent by the ideas and attitudes stored in memory. Comprehending involves an interaction between the reader's background and the author's background. In addition, the reader brings to the comprehending his or her present status in terms of mind set, feelings, reading situation, and the like. Langer considers reading an idiosyncratic process activated by the individual reader's specific circumstances.[12]

Whatever the purposes for reading—broad or singular, self-imposed or external—parts of the arrays stored in memory are retrieved and mobilized as readers view the graphic representations of authors' particular ideas and attitudes. Readers then select, reject, and finally attempt to integrate into their own arrays what they are able to gain from their interaction with those particular authors. (The less distance between authors and readers, the easier the integration process becomes.) Tierney, Bridge, and Cera, although working with younger children, found that "reading comprehension for both good and poor readers is both constructive and abstractive regardless of whether the construction/abstraction occurs during reading, recall, or both."[13] In subsequent reading experiences, readers make use of their expanded and often reorganized arrays of ideas to solve problems, answer questions, and further increase their knowledge.

Readers in the secondary school frequently need the teacher's aid in selecting the reading process that will meet their needs in carrying on a particular kind of dialogue with authors. Readers assigned a chapter will often require guidance in establishing familiarity with the material by surveying or previewing prior to study. If they must find a particular event in a chapter or an encyclopedia article, they will usually need to be taught to skim and scan and then to stop and read carefully when they find the event. If they are asked to read a contract, they must learn to develop the habit of reading word by word and then rereading. One of the teacher's tasks is to help the reader develop some of these flexible processes for reading suited to the nature of the material and the purposes involved. Example 1.2 suggests how you might monitor your own reading processes.

Example 1.2 *Monitoring Your Own Reading Processes*

A student in your class has asked about the difference between *nuclear fission* and *nuclear fusion*. No one in the class, including you, seems to know the answer. The student has tried to find the answer in other sources without success. You promise to find the answer and report back to the class.

With your reading purpose now established, you search your mind for any information you may possess. At first you feel you have none. As you do some further thinking, however, you realize that you know what nuclear energy is and you know that the generation of nuclear power involves certain processes. You are hazy about the processes, but you suspect fission and fusion are among them. Hence, you have tapped your slight array of information stored in memory as you now search for the answer. You also remember that a junior high science text you reviewed recently contained some information about fission and fusion. Armed with purpose and some background, you now proceed to find and read the information.

As you read, you select the information that will answer the question. Fortunately, the author's writing style is clear and straightforward, the vocabulary is understandable, and you have enough background knowledge so that the "distance" between you and the author is minimal. You are able to obtain the answer and utilize the information to help your student. Undoubtedly you will now fuse what you have learned with whatever else you know about nuclear energy in your memory bank—ready for a withdrawal when another related problem comes along.

Inexperienced readers or readers who perform poorly in particular situations may have trouble because too great a distance may exist between author and reader. On the other hand, some poor readers are victims of teaching that has emphasized the mechanical aspects of reading rather than the important concept of the search for meaning. Too much attention on "phonics" or phonographological cues at the expense of syntactic and semantic cues places such readers at a disadvantage. In a review of studies of the reading comprehension processes of good and poor comprehenders, Golinkoff found good readers flexible and constantly searching for meaning.[14] She found poor comprehenders word-bound and quite inflexible.

If we continue to emphasize "phonics" beyond all other means of coping with meaning, we will continue to put poor comprehenders in more of a bind. We will tie them further to word-by-word reading at the expense of meaning. Of course, learners who need help in reading can often profit from direct instruction related to phoneme-grapheme relationships, *but* only as part of an overall strategy for attacking unknown units in print. Context clues, both semantic and syntactic, ought to be initial priorities. And when phoneme-grapheme instruction is undertaken, it should focus on the problem the reader has within the context of the reading matter—not outside it. I remember a time when I was coordinator of a university reading clinic and one of my instructors did not want to release an eighth grader who was now functioning well with eighth- and ninth-grade materials because "he didn't know his phonics."

WRITING PROCESSES

Dictionaries define writing as the physical act of forming symbols; but when we speak of writing in the secondary school, we are speaking of a composition that begins in the head of the writer. Although students "write" when they fill in blanks and respond to questions with short answers or individual sentences, writing in this text refers to the composing process and editing the results of that process.

Writing, in relation to strategies of study, should be used not only to report on knowledge but also to learn, to reinforce learning, and to extend knowledge. Unless a teacher has demonstrated otherwise, the students' primary foci are on meaning: *Does this communicate with my audience? Does it say what I want it to say?* Too often the teacher is the only audience and the student learns to write to satisfy the teacher. Often this *teacher-as-audience* writing slights full development of ideas in favor of emphasis on the mechanics of writing. When we put the emphasis from the start on complete sentences, *good* sentences, correct spelling, proper grammar, and so on, we swerve the student away from the main purpose of writing—the communication of ideas. "When we create writing situations with atypical audiences, we destroy the normal intention to communicate, and thus undermine in fundamental ways the whole learning process."[15]

Writing as a strategy for study in middle and secondary schools should consist of three parts: prewriting, writing, and postwriting or editing.

> *Prewriting* is the time during which information is gathered and ideas [are] played with. It may include reading, talking, and simply thinking about a topic. Sometimes it includes an incubation period when initial thoughts are set aside and allowed to coalesce without conscious attention. . . .
>
> The *writing* stage of the composing process is the time when

the topic is developed on paper. Getting started on the writing stage is often difficult and painful, producing many false starts and discarded openings. At this stage the concern is with the ideas the writer wants to express, laying out an argument and its implications, or the basic scenes and storyline in fiction. Not infrequently, these ideas will change in the process of writing about them, and successive drafts will be needed before the various sections of the writing will be fully consonant and supportive of one another. . . .

　　The third stage described in studies of the writing process is that of *editing*, polishing what has been written to share with a wider audience. This is the stage for attention to mechanical errors, spelling, punctuation, usage, handwriting. It can also be the stage for fine-tuning for a particular audience or to achieve a particular tone.[16]

There are, of course, back-and-forth movements between the writing stage and the editing stage. Editing in itself often sparks new ways of presenting ideas. The important point is that students realize writing takes much time and effort before it is ready for an audience.

In this text, writing is explored primarily in relation to study—in tandem with reading. Much emphasis is placed on function and purpose in relation to the demands of the various content areas. In all cases, however, instructors should support, encourage, and interact with their student composers during prewriting; help them clarify their ideas during writing; and, once ideas are clear and communicative, assist them in editing their final or next-to-final drafts. The more students feel that their writing must communicate purposefully with audiences other than or in addition to the teacher, the more chance there is for them to strive toward excellence.

THE CURRICULUM

As already suggested, reading and writing are not subjects but processes we use for communication, enjoyment, and learning. The processes change somewhat from task to task depending on the given situation, the nature of the learner, the nature of the task, and the complexity of the task for that particular learner. An *act of reading* is an attempt to reconstruct an author's message. When the semantic and syntactic structure of the message matches the semantic and syntactic knowledge organized in the head of the reader, comprehension is probably rapid and accurate. As the distance between the reader's experiential, emotional, and linguistic background and that of the writer increases, comprehension becomes difficult and slow. An *act of writing* is an attempt to construct a message for someone else to read. When the purpose and audience are hazy, the message usually does not communicate well.

For these and other reasons, it is imperative that subject-matter specialists in each classroom guide students in reading, writing, and study tasks. The ideas of a discipline are entwined with the language used to express those ideas. And it is not only the learner with problems who needs the assistance of the classroom teacher; "good" readers and writers also need help to develop background for the more complex tasks ahead.

Obviously there are numerous other ways of learning, in school and out. And these other ways—viewing, listening, speaking, interacting, contemplating—are highly significant. Demands for reading and writing competence on the part of all learners are, and will continue to be, increasing and varied. The amount and level of such competence will be determined by the needs of the learners, the demands of society, and the requirements of the secondary school curriculum.

It is hoped that the secondary school curriculum will be well integrated with the needs of the learner and the demands of society. At present the blend is by no means adequate. Although multilevel materials and multimedia programs are more evident than before and many teachers are cognizant of changes that need to be made, most often simply a textbook and a limited number of supplementary print and nonprint materials are used in secondary school instruction.

Although secondary school teachers are frequently aware of the expanded choice of materials available, they do not usually consider themselves responsible for teaching reading, writing, or study strategies. They tend to feel that these abilities should be taught elsewhere, by someone else. Often these attitudes are the result of unfamiliarity with the processes and the techniques of teaching study strategies or, indeed, many of the other communication skills. And yet, when one observes classroom teachers in the secondary school, it becomes obvious that many are deeply committed to helping students learn to communicate—to share their ideas and receive and digest the communications of others.

A major reason why secondary school subject-matter specialists feel they know nothing about study strategies is that reading and writing in a content area are not set apart from the subject itself. Reading, writing, and study are unconsciously considered part of the learning of a discipline, and the instructor finds it difficult or impossible to separate content from the learning process. Certainly reading or language arts specialists are aware that reading cannot be isolated from content. On the other hand, reading specialists sometimes appear to believe that content and reading tasks should be taught separately or perhaps side by side rather than together. Reading specialists must be particularly sensitive to the classroom teacher's concept of reading, for a reading or language arts program at the secondary school level cannot exist or claim success unless teacher and specialist cooperate.

Secondary school teachers *do* know something about communication skills and *do* teach many of these skills, often inadvertently. But there is usually no planned, continuous program in reading, writing, or study skills. As Artley suggested after surveying trends and practices in secondary reading:

Subject teachers have been reluctant to assume responsibility for teaching the reading-study skills characteristic of their area for several reasons. In the first place, pre-service training courses have apparently failed to include content dealing with the competencies in need of development for effective reading in science, mathematics, or history. Teachers have also assumed that the teaching of reading involves the addition of something extra to an already overloaded course outline rather than being an inherent part of the teaching process—a *way* to teach rather than *something* to teach. Studies indicate that it is possible to effect reading improvement if teachers are willing to try and if they have adequate help and supervision. [17]

The reading-writing-study program in a secondary school, then, functions in each classroom that has materials to be studied. A secondary school study program simply cannot exist as part of a dichotomous curriculum—a strand in which reading, writing, and study strategies are taught *before* application in the content areas. Teaching, learning, and application must take place simultaneously where and when needed. As Artley summarized in his survey of trends and practices:

> The approach with recognized promise is one providing for the close integration of reading and study with the teaching of the various content areas. Since the teaching of content assumes that the learner will need to purposefully select, comprehend, organize, evaluate, and apply ideas, generalizations, and principles—all of these being reading competencies—the close alliance of subject matter and reading is a natural and an obvious one. [18]

Thus, a secondary school *reading-writing-study* program, should be considered the complete set of skills and strategies needed by each student to contend with the vast array of materials to be digested during the school career. *Skills* are the individual tools needed to contend with the writer's message—for example, locating relevant details, making an inference, noting a graphological pattern, or recognizing relationships among words. *Strategies* are the steps to be taken to satisfy a particular task, most often necessitating the clustering of a group of skills. For example, the strategy of learning the steps in a process discussed in a science textbook calls for grouping a number of skills: (1) slow, cautious reading; (2) differentiation of overall concept or introductory remarks from specific steps; (3) recognition of each step; and (4) recognition of the sequence of steps.

Each classroom teacher in the secondary school who uses printed materials as an instructional tool should learn to analyze the reading and writing tasks most pertinent to curriculum needs and should help students develop or perfect strategies for accomplishing the tasks. Such analyses will include the vocabulary, comprehension, readability, and organizational strategies described in this book.

TRANSFER OF LEARNING

Many teachers assume that reading and writing skills can be taught in isolation or with a single type of written material and then *applied* in other situations. Such an assumption is not supported by studies of transfer of learning. We know that transfer is not accomplished easily except by the highly motivated or the very gifted. We know that a strategy or even a single skill taught in a given situation has the greatest chance for successful application if it is used in another situation similar to the one in which it was taught. If the strategy is used in a different environment without much practice in positive reinforcement, it is unlikely to be successfully utilized in a new situation.

Many of our secondary school students have had a long history of problems with transfer and have lacked guidance. Probably many are *exposed* to certain study skills or strategies in a particular situation and then are never helped to make necessary adaptations in other learning environments. Most students have learned how to read and write narrative or literary materials with some degree of adequacy, but they have rarely been directly helped to deal with varied expository materials in the subjects taught. Example 1.3 shows how a teacher can help students in the transfer of learning.

Example 1.3   Helping Students Transfer Learning

Michael was a great success when it came to finding main ideas in workbook and kit materials containing short narrative or very simple expository passages. He was "checked off" on a progress form as having learned main ideas. However, when he was asked to find major points in typical content area materials, he could rarely do so. Teachers wondered why he couldn't apply what he had learned. Was he dull?

Ms. Herber, his tenth-grade biology teacher, decided to investigate. She asked him to find the major point or main idea in a few simple passages from a workbook used to teach reading skills. He scored 100 percent. Next she asked him to write down the main point in two paragraphs from the science text. He succeeded with one. Then she asked him to find the major idea in a section of the science text. He failed.

They talked about his performance, and Ms. Herber saw that he could not automatically transfer something learned as a rather isolated "reading" skill to the fusion of skill and content in science. In fact, he didn't make any connection in his own mind between finding the main idea of a paragraph in the workbook and the task of finding and writing down the major idea in science material.

Ms. Herber and Michael set up a graduated series of tasks all involving location of major ideas in science materials. The tasks were pertinent to the ongoing work in the classroom, so the goal was not learning how to find the main idea but rather learning the major scientific concepts. He succeeded.

In this book, transfer is not assumed for the teacher or the student. In many instances it might appear that a given strategy could have been learned as a *common* strategy—to be applied by the learner in another situation. Certainly there are common approaches to study tasks that teachers will want to help students use with particular content, and those strategies are described in this volume. On the other hand, many strategies are so tied to writing style and content, as well as to the experiences of the learner, that they must be taught in each content area. Many strategies are inseparably entwined with the content and the purpose of the moment. Hence, in the interest of executing transfer of learning for the reader of this book, some aspects of a given strategy are used in one situation and then used again, but within the framework of given types of writing within given content areas. Instructional materials in numerous subjects have been carefully analyzed in the preparation of this volume, and techniques have been tailored to the particular kinds of materials within the various areas.

Strategies for helping students with study problems belong essentially in each content area classroom. The reading, writing, and study program should permeate every strand of the school curriculum. Granted, there will be some learners who need special help outside the classroom as well as within. But, in the main, if curriculum changes are made to suit the needs of the individuals in a school, the classroom teacher will share with the learner the major responsibility of developing effective study strategies was within a given subject area.

QUESTIONS
AND
RELATED
ACTIVITIES

1. Look back at the chapter-opening diagram (preorganizer). Does it include all the important concepts discussed in the chapter? Does it show how each part relates to the others? Sketch a more representative postorganizer if you think the preorganizer is lacking. If you think the preorganizer is satisfactory, explain why in a paragraph.

2. Do you agree with the concept of reducing the global role of the secondary school? Would you consider such a reduction a "return to the basics"? Write a paragraph of agreement or disagreement and share your views with others.

3. After considering the reading and writing processes described in the

chapter, have you formulated your own definitions of reading and writing? Either write your definitions or map them out in a diagram or flow chart. Compare your responses with those of your classmates or colleagues.

4.   Think of a specific procedure you can use to transfer a reading or writing strategy you helped students learn in one situation to a different context. Try it out. Why did it work or not work?

SELECTED READINGS

Anders, Patricia L. "Dream of a Secondary Reading Program? People Are the Key." *Journal of Reading* 24 (January 1981):316–20.

Applebee, Arthur N., and others. *A Study of Writing in the Secondary School.* Final Report, NIE–G–79–0174. Urbana, Ill.: National Council of Teachers of English, September 1980.

Burr, Miriam. "What the Classroom Teacher Looks for in Leadership." In *Roles of the Administrator and Parent in the School Reading Program*, edited by David L. Shepherd, pp. 38–40. Proceedings of Hofstra University Reading Conference, pt. I. Hempstead, N.Y.: Hofstra University, 1966.

Harker, W. John, ed. *Classroom Strategies for Secondary Reading.* Newark, Del.: International Reading Association, 1977.

National Panel on High School and Adolescent Education. *The Education of Adolescents.* HEW Publication, no. (OE) 76–00004. Washington, D.C.: U.S. Government Printing Office, 1976.

Palmer, William S. "Defining Reading in Proper Perspective." In *Applied Linguistics and Reading*, edited by Robert E. Shafer, pp. 2–11. Newark, Del.: International Reading Association, 1979.

Smith, Frank. *Understanding Reading*, 2nd ed. New York: Holt, Rinehart and Winston, 1978.

NOTES

1.   National Panel on High School and Adolescent Education, *The Education of Adolescents*, HEW Publication, no. (OE) 76–00004 (Washington, D.C.: U.S. Government Printing Office, 1976), pp. 10–14.

2.   Ibid., pp. 13–14.

3.   Ibid., p. 1.

4.   Diana M. Zuckerman, Dorothy G. Singer, and Jerome L. Singer, "Television Viewing, Children's Reading, and Related Classroom Behavior," *Journal of Communication* 30 (Winter 1980):167. Reprinted by permission.

5.   Jackie S. Busch, "Television's Effects on Reading: A Case Study," *Phi Delta Kappan* 59 (June 1978):668–71.

6.   National Panel, *Education of Adolescents*, p. 95.

7.   "The Essentials of Education: A Call for Dialog and Action," *Reading Research Quarterly* 16 (1981):325.

8.   Arthur I. Gates, "Characteristics of Successful Teaching of Reading," in *Reading: Seventy-Five Years of Progress*, ed. H. Alan Robinson, Supplementary Educational Monograph, no. 96 (Chicago: University of Chicago Press, 1966), p. 15.

9. National Council of Teachers of English, "Back to the Basics: Reading," *Slate* 1 (October 1976):1.

10. Frank Smith, *Understanding Reading*, 2nd ed. (New York: Holt, Rinehart and Winston, 1978), p. 5.

11. Ibid., pp. 40–41.

12. Judith A. Langer, "An Idiosyncratic Model of Affective and Cognitive Silent Reading Strategies" (Doctoral dissertation, Hofstra University, 1978).

13. Robert J. Tierney, Connie Bridge, and Mary Jane Cera, "The Discourse Processing Operations of Children," *Reading Research Quarterly* 14 (1978–79):566.

14. Roberta M. Golinkoff, "A Comparison of Reading Comprehension Processes in Good and Poor Comprehenders," *Reading Research Quarterly* 11 (1975–76):623–59.

15. Arthur N. Applebee and others, *A Study of Writing in the Secondary School* (Urbana, Ill.: National Council of Teachers of English, 1980), p. 10.

16. Ibid., pp. 145–46.

17. A. Sterl Artley, *Trends and Practices in Secondary Reading*, ERIC/CRIER Reading Review Series (Newark, Del.: International Reading Association, 1968), p. 110.

18. Ibid., p. 108.

Part B
STRATEGIES FOR ALL CONTENT AREAS

Chapters 2 through 6 focus on teacher and student strategies and learnings applicable to most content areas. Monitoring and assessment procedures described in Chapter 2 are concerned with both process and product. Chapters 3 through 6 present techniques and strategies that can be utilized by students on their own but initially are best directed by the teacher.

Teachers should be sure to integrate direct group instruction with individualized instruction if students are to become independent learners. Direct instruction serves a purpose for the group in terms of introduction of procedures, directed guidance of strategies essential for all students, and overall reinforcement. Individualized instruction, however, is essential for those students who need additional guidance, who learn at a slower or faster pace, or who need special strategies at special times. Most examples used in these chapters are samples of actual classroom activities and events.

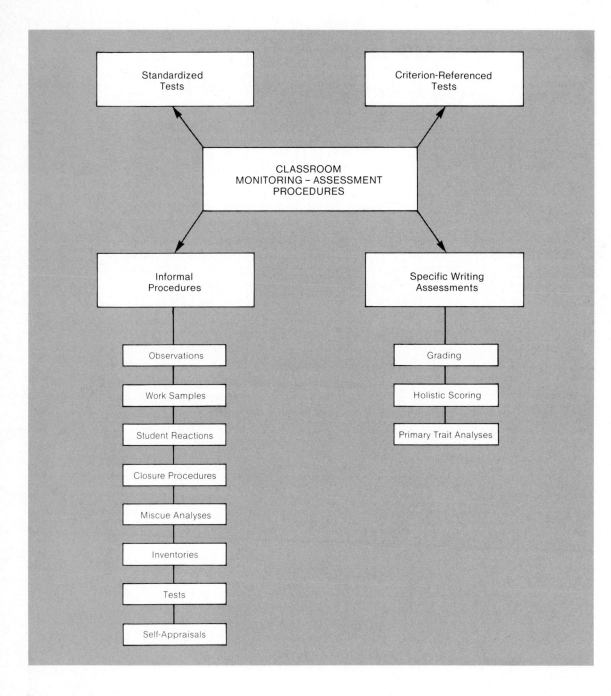

2

Monitoring and Assessment Procedures in the Classroom

Monitoring is the process of observing and noting strengths and needs during writing and reading activities. It involves the processes of both reading and writing as they are taking place as well as their products (a piece of written work or a written or oral response to a reading assignment). Monitoring is a part of, and an aid to, learning and teaching.

Assessment is a measurement of products in an attempt to ascertain competence in reading or writing. It includes standardized as well as less formal means of measurement. Assessment is particularly useful at the beginning and end of a cycle of instruction, although establishing assessment checkpoints during a broad cycle of instruction is also helpful.

Some readers may feel that this chapter should be read toward the end of the book, particularly for beginning teachers who need to learn more about the teaching and learning strategies in subsequent chapters. Although the point may be well taken, my intent in placing it here is to acquaint teachers with the need to monitor and assess as integral parts of instruction from the start. Some content area teachers may feel they have little time for monitoring and assessment—*they need the time for teaching*. However, in my view, and in the view of an increasing number of content area teachers, they cannot afford *not* to take the time to monitor and assess. Teaching time is wasted on students who cannot deal with specific study strategies. Once they remove some of the obstacles in reading and writing, students become comprehenders and utilizers of content.

STANDARDIZED
TESTS

Standardized tests of reading are of limited help to the classroom teacher, for they report the products of very specific types of behaviors usually not closely related to required student performance in a subject-matter classroom. Results on standardized tests should not be used to make decisions about the overall ability of students or their ability to read or write in a given area. Other monitoring and assessment information is needed to give substance to the picture.

Not only do standardized tests contribute little knowledge about performance in the classroom, they also contribute to the lowering of "ego strength" for many students. Placement in a stanine or percentile, of even in a percentile range, only serves to suggest that a given student always reads at or within some given statistical level. Grade-equivalent scores are even worse—the labeling of a secondary school student as a 5.6 or 7.9 or even 13+ reader simply does not make sense and is certainly not functional.

The concept of reading or writing at any particular level is at best an average of peaks and valleys on a given test or over a variety of classroom tasks. "Level" will change, depending on the test, the task, the environment, the student's interest, and so on. Some writers in the field of reading feel that the level a student achieves on a standardized reading test is usually indicative of a frustration level in reading. This may be so. But it might be more accurate to say that we really don't know what the level indicates for a given student other than some average of performance at that time on certain reading tasks. These tasks are usually far removed from the type of reading expected in the usual classroom setting. In addition, it may be, as Asher hypothesized, that "achievement test passages function as low-interest material."[1]

> The statistical basis of such scores is straightforward enough, but those reported to be "below grade level" are left with a false sense of failure and low achievement. The eternal struggle to bring everyone "up to grade level," laudable though it sounds, is doomed from the start because it is inherent in a norm-referenced, standardized reading test that 50 percent of the children taking it will be below grade level. Schools so fortunate that all of their pupils are at or above grade level simply mean that elsewhere, where the health and social welfare of the children may not be so favorable, there will be schools almost all of whose children will "fail." While we believe that teachers and schools have important and lasting effects upon children's reading abilities, we also know that socioeconomic factors have a strong influence.[2]

Several professional educational organizations have suggested a moratorium on norm-referenced standardized testing. Other organizations, such as the National Council of Teachers of English, although not calling for a moratorium, stress the need for

> new processes of assessment that are more fair and effective than those currently in use and that more adequately consider the diverse talents, abilities, and cultural backgrounds of children.[3]

Buros, in the preface to the *Sixth Mental Measurements Yearbook* (1965), stated:

Unfortunately, the rank and file of test users do not appear to be particularly alarmed that so many tests are either severely criticized or described as having no validity. Although most test users would probably agree that many tests are either worthless or misused, they continue to have the utmost faith in their own particular choice and use of tests regardless of the absence of supporting research or even of the presence of negating research.[4]

In the introduction to volume I of the *Seventh Mental Measurements Yearbook* (1972), Buros said: "At least half of the tests currently on the market should never have been published. Exaggerated, false, or unsubstantiated claims are the rule rather than the exception."[5]

THE TEACHER'S ROLE

Under these circumstances, how should a classroom teacher view standardized tests? Should assessment through standardized techniques be abandoned? Houts responds by saying:

No one should interpret the current controversy over standardized tests as an effort to abandon assessment. Rather, it is an effort to develop assessment procedures that are more in keeping with a new set of educational and social assumptions that we as a society are working on: that the purpose of education is not to sort people but to educate them; that in a knowledge society we need to expose as many people to education as possible, not to exclude them from it; that human beings are marvelously variegated in their talents and abilities, and it is the function of education to nurture them wisely and carefully; and, not least, that education has an overriding responsibility to respect and draw on cultural and racial diversity. Assessment of students must begin to reflect that philosophy, and that is the true reason for the current call for test reform and an end to IQ testing.[6]

If standardized tests are to be used in a school system or in a given classroom, the following steps should be taken as part of the selection process:

1. Consult these sources:
The *Mental Measurements Yearbooks*, compiled and edited by Oscar K. Buros. Teachers should consult The *Eighth* and earlier yearbooks when necessary. Yearbooks contain reviews of tests by experts who have examined the tests quite carefully. Published by the Gryphon Press, Highland Park, New Jersey.

Reviews of Selected Published Tests in English, edited by Alfred H. Grommon, 1976. Suggests questions to be asked in test selection and evaluates over fifty widely used English tests. Published by the National Council of Teachers of English.

Common Sense and Testing in English by the Task Force on Measurement and Evaluation in the Study of English, edited by Alan Purves, 1975. Discusses tests and lists criteria for selection and interpretation. Published by the National Council of Teachers of English.

Testing in Reading: Assessment and Instructional Decision Making by Richard Venezky, 1974. Discusses assessment procedures and use of results. Published by the National Council of Teachers of English.

Reading Tests for Secondary Grades, edited by William Blanton, Roger Farr, and J. Jaap Tuinman, 1972. Published by the International Reading Association.

2.   If there is a vocabulary or word knowledge subtest, choose a standardized reading test only if the words in this particular subtest are presented in context. The practice of having students read an isolated word and then try to find another isolated word to match is a far cry from measuring vocabulary power. Emphasis should be placed, as much as possible, on examining strengths in using strategies to unlock ideas across a language context. In the same light, do not choose tests of the "mechanics of written English" as assessments of writing ability. They do play a role, but the teacher must still assess the major aspects of "unity, organization, and word choice."[7]

3.   Although measuring comprehension is a difficult task, be sure that the emphasis in the comprehension section of a standardized test is also on examining strengths in using strategies to unlock ideas. If multiple choice is used, be certain that a wide range of thinking processes is tapped and that the forced choices are all sensible and plausible. The use of a closure procedure (filling in blanks within the running context) is a promising technique for measuring readers' ability to use many language skills in their search for meaning. However, it should not be the only method of measuring comprehension. A closure procedure may not be tapping the readers' abilities to synthesize and integrate what they read. Using several techniques for measuring comprehension within the same test might be an interesting way to learn more about the readers' search for meaning as well as the product of that search.

4.   Examine several tests that seem suitable. Look carefully to be sure that the material in a reading test is representative of what students are asked to read within the secondary school curriculum. Be sure the content is not too distant from the background of the youngsters to be tested; if it is, you may be testing lack of background experience rather than ability to read. Consider the way the material is presented. The written discourse should represent at least some match between both the readers and the material they have been accustomed to reading.

5.   Try to choose tests that describe norms or populations somewhat equivalent to yours. If this is impossible, or even if the norms seem somewhat satisfactory, consider the possibility of developing local norms.

6.   Although the validity (and there are many kinds) of a test is often complex to ascertain, be sure that the test publisher offers evidence of validity. Do not jump into administering a new test with the publisher's promise of information to come. The information may not be available for a long time *and* it could be unsuitable.

7.   Do not choose a test when reliability is questionable. An unreliable test means that you cannot trust it or its alternate forms to give consistent results over administrations.

Should standardized norm-referenced tests be used? With all the criticism levied at them in recent years, they will undoubtedly be improving. They can be used with a great deal of caution and with the realization that they measure particular kinds of performances in particular ways. They largely measure some type of product rather than process. They do not permit adequate evaluation of any individual's ability. And certainly at the secondary school level a score of 4.5 or 37th percentile or 6th stanine has little relationship to overall performance, since students are asked to read and write at many "levels."

To a limited extent, standardized tests can provide rough, initial information, particularly for the instructor who is meeting a new class. Even though there is no such thing as a level for students in the secondary school, an individual score shows where a given student stands on that test in relation to other students. Although the score itself might be different on another test, the student would probably stand in approximately the same place in relation to peers. Hence, although there will not be a one-to-one correspondence between the kind of ability measured on the test and the reading and writing in a classroom, the teacher learns that a variety of needs ought to be provided for. The teacher might also be able to plan in advance some study techniques that will help poorer readers and writers cope with some of the essential but complex material.

Although subtest scores are often unreliable, an overview of subtest results frequently helps the instructor form tentative suppositions about the possible strengths and weaknesses of some students. Very high vocabulary and comprehension scores with a low speed score might suggest to the English teacher that Gregory could be reading some materials at too low a rate for efficiency. The math instructor, on the other hand, might feel that Gregory might do very well, for speed reading is usually a detriment in math. Subtest scores on a standardized language arts test offer some information to the teacher, although a punctuation score is far from an assessment of effective writing.

In some circumstances even an analysis of individual test items is useful. Once, while working with a young man from Iran who had a very high score in vocabulary but a fairly low score in comprehension on a particular standardized reading test, I discovered that numerous terms used in our classroom materials were unknown to him and appeared to be at the root of his comprehension problems. I held a conference with him, with standardized test in hand, and found that he had memorized synonyms for words without really knowing many of their meanings.

CRITERION-REFERENCED TESTS

Scores on the norm-referenced, standardized tests previously described are used to compare an individual or group to a group mean—a standard established for all individuals in a given grade at a given time. Criterion-referenced tests establish a standard for achievement (80 percent, or seven right out of ten, and so on). *Mastery* at the standard level permits students to move on to the next learning step; inability to achieve the standard usually indicates need for additional instruction before moving on.

Criterion-referenced tests are tied to more specific objectives than norm-referenced tests.

> Now, the norm-referenced test may include items which would logically fit into each of the objectives corresponding to a subtest in the criterion-referenced test; but the norm-referenced test sums across all those items to yield aggregate scores for only a few areas. Put another way, a norm-referenced test and a criterion-referenced test might consist of exactly the same fifty items. But the criterion-referenced test might have ten subtests of five items each, whereas the norm-referenced test would have two subtests of twenty-five items each. [8]

Criterion-referenced tests that are tuned to instruction are probably more useful to a classroom teacher than are norm-referenced tests. Surely knowing that a student is able to recognize cause-effect relationships eight or nine times out of ten is more useful to both teacher and learner than knowing the student achieved 40th percentile or 7th stanine or 7.4. On the other hand, these tests must be subject to the same evaluative criteria as norm-referenced tests: validity, reliability, and appropriateness of test and test items for your population. We also cannot assume that *mastery* on one test in one situation relieves us of responsibility for helping students continue to develop competence in a given skill area.

INFORMAL PROCEDURES

Fortunately, as a teacher, you are in a position to collect many samples of student performance over a long period of time. Hence, you need not rely on one particular test or one particular assessment procedure. Because you are in a position to collect many samples of behavior on a particular student, you are likely to get a reliable estimate of how that student is performing on a particular task— main ideas, for example (remember that the more items used to make an assessment, the more likely it is to be reliable).[9]

"Informal measurement can be the heart of diagnostic teaching since it can be done regularly and frequently in the classroom setting and can be used to quickly and effectively emulate a number of classroom reading [or writing] situations."[10] Informal procedures can pinpoint strengths and needs in specific reading-writing-study strategies directly related to the use of materials in a given content area. Such monitoring can be continuous rather than done at a given point during the school year. However, special emphasis placed on informal procedures at the start of a term or new unit, during the instructional period, and at the conclusion of a piece of work is particularly useful. Information gained may be utilized for differentiating instruction, carrying on corrective procedures, and planning for future activities. One of the great values of informal procedures is that small pieces of work can be assessed at once so students note rather immediate success or begin corrective strategies before they are lost beyond repair. Another, perhaps obvious, value is that study behaviors are analyzed in fusion with the materials used in the content area rather than in the *isolated* context of a formal test. As Kress suggested:

> In a very real sense, the master teacher gives a group informal test with each lesson that he teaches in the classroom. Diagnosis is an integral part of his teaching because he realizes that without it he cannot know *what* and *how* to teach. Only when he feels that he still lacks necessary information about a student's grasp or application of certain skills and abilities does he feel it is necessary to rely on individual tests.[11]

A number of informal procedures are process-and-product-oriented. They are used to look at both what the reader is doing during the reading act and what *information or idea* the reader has gained from the reading. In addition, as suggested by Goetz and Armbruster, "teachers should realize that different students may interpret the same text differently and that tests must be designed to reveal not only whether or not a student has understood, but *what* that student has understood."[12]

OBSERVATIONS

General, unrecorded observations of reading, writing, and study behaviors in the classroom are of some value in identifying students who appear to have few or no problems as well as those who have many. But, like the standardized test, such observations can help to identify only gross strengths and weaknesses and possibly succeed in assisting the instructor to place students on some sort of performance continuum, at least in relation to the task performed at the time of observation.

To be most meaningful, observations should be made in relation to the objective(s) of a given instructional situation. Students should be observed as they work independently, as they respond to questions formulated by the teacher, and as they interact with their peers. The teacher should concentrate on one or at most a few students at one time and record dated impressions. In this way the instructor is able to compare observations for given students over time while coping with specific reading and writing tasks. The instructor then has a product—dated written comments—to view in conjunction with other evaluative evidence.

WORK SAMPLES

Dated samples of written work can assist the instructor in gathering additional information and maintaining a running record of progress. The instructor will want to decide on the size of intervals for dating such work and to include compositions of all kinds as well as written responses to reading assignments. Such monitoring is certainly useful for the teacher and is also valuable as a self-monitoring device for students.

STUDENT REACTIONS

Written Response.   Techniques that seek to probe specific areas, such as attitudes toward reading and writing, study habits, and experiential background, are often valuable tools to use with a class, a smaller group, or even an individual. If such techniques are to be used in the typical departmentalized secondary school, interdepartmental agreement must be reached on where, how, and when such assessment will be conducted and or how results will be communicated to all instructors concerned; otherwise, needless duplication may take place.

Clearly the following techniques are subject to the conscious and unconscious wishes of the student. Students and instructor will need to develop "a mutual relationship of trust and respect."[13]

Reading Autobiography.   A reading autobiography is, of course, a written account of a student's reading experiences. (It could be done orally if a student's writing ability is very poor and if the teacher can manage the time.) It gives the student a chance to vent feelings about reading and may give the teacher definite suggestions about what direction to take with a given student. Strang presented some interesting and specific procedures.[14] She cited an autobiography that consisted solely of specific questions such as:

	Yes	No	
1.	___	___	Do you remember the name of the first book you ever read?
2.	___	___	As a child, did you prefer books that were illustrated?
3.	___	___	Do you like to have the radio or record player . . . [or TV] . . . on while you read?
4.	___	___	Did you learn to read before you came to school?[15]

Strang also suggested that specific directions and guiding questions be provided for the autobiography that is to be written in essay form. The reading autobiography in essay form, of course, can also serve as an assessment of composing ability and writing style.

Daily Schedule or Diary Record. The schedule or record is a way of obtaining information about books being read, about time spent in study, and about the kinds of activities that occupy a student's daily life. Strang pointed out that "for accuracy's sake [the student] is asked to make entries all during the day, not to try to remember at the end of the day just what happened in the morning."[16] Strang provided detailed information and an example of this technique in her book *Diagnostic Teaching of Reading.*

Projection. Students and teacher must develop extremely good rapport before such a technique can be used if meaningful and valid responses are to be made. The technique is projective—that is, the student is presented with a stimulus that permits free response and seeks to have the student record information about his or her inner feelings and personality structure. The technique should be used selectively when such information might be helpful in viewing the total picture or in getting at an area that appears to be significant for a given student or group of students. Strang, McCullough, and Traxler presented an example of a sentence-completion test. Here are a few of the items:

When I have to read I _____
To me, books _____
I like to read about _____
When I read math _____
For me, studying _____
I'd read more if _____[17]

However, Vaughan points out that such affective instruments may have questionable validity.[18] Responses should only be "trusted" in light of different types of data amassed over time.

Oral Response. Granted, the classroom teacher, particularly in a departmentalized secondary school, has little time for individual, structured meetings with students; but there are times when such meetings are essential, especially if a student is having problems and is not very communicative in informal situations. The following two techniques are sometimes useful.

Interview.   A structured interview, in which the instructor asks the student to respond to a set of questions designed to elicit needed information not gained earlier, can be very revealing. Usually the student who has been hesitant to respond in writing or orally in group situations will react and answer questions orally in a one-to-one interview.

Retrospection.   Immediately after students have read a selection and completed any written assignment related to it, they can be asked a series of questions probing into the processes used in comprehending the material and organizing ideas for completion of the assignment. Such questions might include:

1.   What did you do when you came across a word unfamiliar to you?
2.   Did you have any purpose in mind when you did the reading? If so where did this purpose come from?
3.   How did you decide which were the most important ideas?
4.   Did you read the whole thing at approximately the same rate of speed? Why or why not?
5.   Why did you organize your essay in this way?

IN-PROCESS INDICATORS OF READING COMPREHENSION[19]

Although several of the general informal procedures presented earlier focus on process (the thinking and feeling strategies that occur during a study task), tests of reading comprehension usually focus on product (the information or ideas remembered after reading). Closure procedures and the miscue analysis technique permit both in-process and product monitoring of reading comprehension.

Closure Procedures.   Closure procedures are based on the concept of *gestalt*— the need of an organism to complete something that appears incomplete. There are several ways of using closure to monitor or assess a student's ability to interact with an author; the best methods for middle school and above seem to be the maze technique and the cloze procedure.

Maze Technique.   In the maze technique, developed by Guthrie and others, every fifth or tenth word is deleted from a passage and three alternative words are substituted for each deleted word.[20] The substitutions include the correct word, an incorrect word from the same form class, and an incorrect word from a different form class. Students circle the correct answer, and scores may be computed on the basis of percentage correct. Passages are usually not shorter than about two hundred words. Ideas about scoring criteria vary, but I have found that somewhere between 65 to 80 percent correct demonstrates adequate understanding of the passage, at least for classroom-constructed maze assessments.

In the maze exercise shown in Example 2.1, every tenth word is deleted, rather than every fifth, since the material was new, complex, and technical for the secondary school students who responded to it.

Example 2.1   *A Maze Exercise*[21]

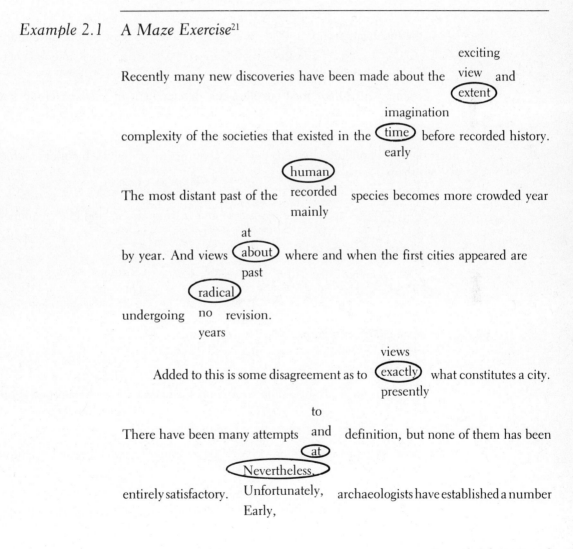

Recently many new discoveries have been made about the [view / exciting / (extent)] and

complexity of the societies that existed in the [(time) / imagination / early] before recorded history.

The most distant past of the [(human) / recorded / mainly] species becomes more crowded year

by year. And views [(about) / at / past] where and when the first cities appeared are

undergoing [(radical) / no / years] revision.

Added to this is some disagreement as to [(exactly) / views / presently] what constitutes a city.

There have been many attempts [and / to / (at)] definition, but none of them has been

entirely satisfactory. [Unfortunately, / (Nevertheless,) / Early,] archaeologists have established a number

Example 2.1 (continued)

Example 2.1 *(continued)*

truly

of characteristics which, it ⟨is⟩ generally agreed, mark true urbanization. They

has

existed;

include permanence of records;   specialization of skills and functions among

⟨settlement;⟩

define

the inhabitants who, about   some extent, need to draw on the surrounding

⟨to⟩

inhabitants

regions ⟨for⟩ their food supplies; the development of a characteristic style

beneath

⟨of⟩

during building; the erection of communal or public buildings, which

urban

limits

⟨presupposes⟩ appreciable resources and a work force; and the attainment

is

building   ⟨need⟩

after   a certain size. All of these factors do not contribute to exist at once

⟨of⟩   skill

⟨regarded⟩

for a community to be erected as urban.

resources

⟨after⟩

The great advance in prehistoric research began on   the Second World

development

building

War. In the case of carbon–14 ⟨dating⟩ techniques, which enable scientists

and

⟨remarkable⟩

to date ancient sites with little accuracy, it was a by-product of nuclear

species

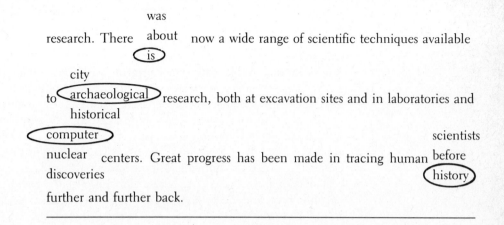

research. There $\overset{\text{was}}{\underset{\bigcirc\text{is}}{about}}$ now a wide range of scientific techniques available

to $\overset{\text{city}}{\underset{\text{historical}}{\big(archaeological\big)}}$ research, both at excavation sites and in laboratories and

$\big(computer\big)$ scientists

$\overset{\text{nuclear}}{\underset{\text{discoveries}}{}}$ centers. Great progress has been made in tracing human $\overset{\text{before}}{\big(history\big)}$

further and further back.

In responding to the maze exercise, students should be cautioned to use a pencil with a good eraser or an erasable pen; they may want to change some of their answers, as the redundancy of information and language suggests reinterpretations. Although the maze technique is useful as one type of comprehension assessment, its chief value to the learner stems from the discussion of responses with teacher and peers. All develop insights about their strategies for comprehending the message. Students discover that the sense of language contributes to understanding almost as much as do the interrelated meanings of the words.

Cloze Procedure. The creator of the cloze technique or procedure, Taylor, suggested that every *n*th word be deleted from the passages students are asked to read.[22] (In practice, every fifth word is usually deleted, although there seems to be a growing tendency to increase the number of words between deletions—consistently—when concepts are particularly dense.) Usually the first sentence of the passage is left intact, and sometimes the last sentence. Students are asked to fill in the deleted words; they may retrace their steps and erase when desired. The objective is to find out how much background knowledge students possess about a topic and, especially, whether they are capable of making connections between ideas as they utilize the syntax of the sentences.

In using the cloze procedure as a *monitoring* device, there is no right or wrong. The teacher is looking for students' strengths in processing this type of information. Synonyms are perfectly acceptable. To learn more about how the student is reading, the following questions should be considered: (1) Is the student searching for meaning? (2) Does the student make use of syntactic and semantic cues in trying to figure out the deleted words? (3) What procedures must be used in the teaching situation to help certain students learn to make connections between ideas within and across sentences?

Example 2.2   A Cloze Exercise[23]

One might ask as well about the increasing amount of violence that pervades American life. Why, after the Surgeon _____ report to Congress in _____ on violence in television _____ nobody appear to listen? _____ exhaustive report, undertaken by _____ group of social scientists _____ requiring three years and _____ to complete, warned that "_____ overwhelming consensus is that _____ violence does have an _____ effect on certain members _____ society." The Surgeon General _____ "immediate remedial action" and _____ the members of Congress _____ "these conclusions are based _____ solid scientific data and _____ on the opinion of _____ or another scientist." Nevertheless, _____ has been business as _____ in television land because _____ pays off where it _____. Parents who turn the _____ attempting to avoid the _____ find that difficult. One social scientist who studies TV programs estimated that by the time the average child is 15, he or she will have witnessed somewhere between 13,000 to 14,000 televised killings!

Some of the blanks (all kept the same size in order to eliminate space cluing) can be filled in because students are aware of logical word sequence. Some can be filled in because normal redundancy may enable students to pick up semantic clues within the material. Others can be filled in only when the learner has prior knowledge about the particular topic. Depending on the situation, information can be gained by doing the following:

1. Have the student attempt to fill in all the blanks and discuss the results. Both you and the student draw conclusions about why some of the responses would not be accurate for that particular blank.

2. Have the student fill in only those blanks he or she feels are possible— in light of the student's background. Discuss the responses.

3. Provide the missing words in scrambled fashion and have the student insert them. Discuss the responses. (In Example 2.2, the exact words in correct order are: *General's, 1972, did, That, a, and, $1,000,-000.00, the, televised, adverse, of, urged, reminded, that, on, not, one, it, usual, violence, counts, dial, violence.*)

In using the cloze procedure as an *assessment* device to determine comprehension of an author's message, both exact answers and synonyms should be accepted as correct answers. Since comprehension is an interactive, constructive process, it is unfair to accept only exact words. The synonyms may elucidate how the reader is thinking. The only time when nothing but exact words are acceptable is when large groups are reacting to cloze as a readability procedure (pages 134–135 and 141–142).

Closure procedures can also be utilized by leaving out specific words to view students' strengths and needs. For example, rather than the every-5th-or-*n*th-word technique, a group of important content words—for example, *violence*, *television*, and *scientist*—may be left out. Or connectives could be omitted, such as *and*, *nevertheless*, and *or*. Pronouns or certain verbs may be deleted also. Each technique will help the teacher to learn more about specific strategies employed by youngsters as they process material.

Miscue Analysis. Secondary school students should rarely be asked to read out loud without specific purpose and preparation. A valid exception is to have students, on a one-to-one basis, read orally in order to find out more about the strategies they might employ when reading silently.

Yetta M. Goodman and Carolyn L. Burke developed a procedure called the *Reading Miscue Inventory*.[24] Although the material is aimed largely at an elementary school population, the miscue analysis technique, once learned, can be applied to all materials and all students. The *Inventory* is based on Kenneth Goodman's concept that students miscue, or deviate from the expected responses, during reading for a variety of reasons.[25] In the traditional sense, these miscues might appear to be synonymous with *errors*, but there is a distinct conceptual difference.

> In such standardized oral reading tests as the *Gray Oral Reading Test* or the *Gilmore Oral Reading Test*, for example, mispronunciations and other types of word recognition errors are added up; results are based on the number of errors—a *quantitative* assessment. In the *Reading Miscue Inventory*, the miscues, or deviations from the expected responses, are classified in relation to specific questions about the reader's strategies in handling language and ideas. The assessment is largely *qualitative*.[26]

The full *Reading Miscue Inventory* is time consuming; thus secondary school teachers may want to use it only for specific students. Hittleman's modification of the *Inventory* saves times and helps teachers learn a great deal about the reading strategies of students.[27] Hittleman's steps are summarized below with a few adaptations; for further clarification, turn to the original *Inventory* and/or the original Hittleman modification.

1.   Record on tape a student reading orally from a selection that is difficult but not frustrating. Do not have the student stop reading until she or he has made at least twenty-five miscues. If the student does not make twenty-five miscues during the first hundred words or so, find a more challenging selection. (Miscues consist of word substitutions, insertions, omissions, word reversals, repetitions, and incorrect intonation in terms of the author's presentation—not as a penalty for someone's accent or dialect.)

2.   When the oral reading is completed, keep the recorder on and ask the student to retell the selection or aspects of the selection. Use an outline you

have prepared in advance so you may follow the recitation. Have the student retell without assistance first but use prodding, general questions if all the essential information is not offered. Once the retelling is done, turn off the recorder and dismiss the student.

3.   Mark miscues on a copy of the selection you have prepared for this purpose. (This marking may be done while the student is reading and then confirmed when the tape is replayed.)

heavy   ball   reloaves

a. Substitutions: "The moon is a ~~heavenly body~~ that ~~revolves~~ around the earth."

b. Insertions: "Why does the grass ∧ *always* seem greener on the other side of the fence?"

c. Omissions: "The creatures were ⟨not⟩ covered with an outer shell as you would expect." (Circled word was omitted.)

d. Word reversals: "The first essential for such an enormous

base   level

structure was an absolutely ~~level base~~."

e. Repetitions:

    1. Correction of miscue: "The moon is a <u>heavenly</u> body." heavy ⓒ

        <u>reloaves</u> ⓡ

    2. Repetition of uncorrected miscue: "It revolves around the earth."

    3. Repetition that changes correct response: "It was a trembling ⟨ch⟩ <u>tremendous</u> earthquake."

f. Intonation miscue: "They followed that path ✗ ?"

4.   Analyze substitutions first to determine the extent of the student's phonographological cues and knowledge of grammatical functions. Ask the following questions of each miscue:

Question 1: Does the miscue look like the word in the text?

Question 2: Does the miscue sound like the word in the text?

Question 3: Does the miscue retain the same grammatical function as the word in the text (noun for noun, verb for verb, etc.)?

5.   Ask the following questions of all sentences containing one or more miscues. All sensible language is acceptable, irrespective of dialect or accent.

Question 4: Is the sentence as finally produced an acceptable and grammatical sentence (irrespective of other sentences)?

Question 5: Does the sentence as finally produced have an acceptable meaning (irrespective of other sentences or the author's intended meaning)?

6. Ask the following question of each sentence containing one or more miscues:

Question 6: Does the sentence as finally produced change the meaning of the selection? If expository, consider major propositions and supporting arguments. If narrative, consider plot and theme.

7. Tally *yes* or *almost yes* responses to the first five questions for each miscue and convert to percentages. Examples: If Teresa substituted fifteen times, and twelve of these miscues looked like the word in the text, her graphic similarity score—in response to question 1—is 80 percent. If of Jonathan's twenty-five miscues only fourteen were grammatically acceptable, in response to question 4, his grammatical acceptability score is 56 percent.

8. In relation to question 6, tally the number of *no meaning changes* for miscue sentences and convert to a percentage.

9. Score the retelling record. (Don't be afraid of subjectivity; this is an insightful analysis not a standardized test.) For narrative material, as suggested by Y. Goodman and Burke, you can allot fifteen points for recall of characters, fifteen for character descriptions, twenty for theme, twenty for plot, and thirty for recall of specifics. For expository material, you might allot fifty points for recall of major propositions, thirty for supporting arguments, and twenty for recall of important specifics. Such scoring may be adjusted in relation to purpose, nature of the material, etc.[28]

After learning how to analyze miscues, the knowledge and attitudes gained can be easily transferred to a variety of readers and reading situations. Every student does not have to be given a formal reading inventory. Notice how the tenets of the *Reading Miscue Inventory* are used in very informal ways in Example 2.3.

Retrospection—asking students to think about their reading performance and report it—may be coupled with a miscue analysis. Although retrospection has many limitations, Raisner found it useful as she asked her group of academically underprepared college students to talk about their miscues when their reading was played back.[29] Such retrospection also seems useful in combination with the responses on a closure exercise.

Dialect and Language Differences. In any assessment of oral reading, teachers must distinguish between variant pronunciations due to dialect or language differences and miscues due to inadequate reading strategies. Teachers

---

Example 2.3   A Miscue Analysis

Actual Passage

> Segregation in Birmingham was dying despite the confusion and violence. A white city businessman asked: "Are the Negroes I see around town walking a little straighter these days?" And Birmingham, wrote Dr. King, "was a fuse—it detonated a revolution that went on to win scores of other victories."[30]

Christopher's Version

> Segregation in Birmingham was dyin' (I mean *dying*) in spite of the confusion and violence. A white city businessman asked: "Are the blacks I see around the city walkin' (I mean *walking*) a little straighter today?" And Birmingham, said Mr. King, "was a bomb—it detonated (I meant *fuse* not *bomb*) a circulation that went on to win a high score in victories." (No, wait a minute that says "went on to win scores of other victories." I don't understand that part. Oh, wait a minute, *scores* probably means *lots*. Oh, it's a *revolution* not *circulation*)—a revolution that went on to win scores of other victories.
>
> As a result of the miscue analysis and student Christopher's accompanying retrospection, we learn that Christopher doesn't permit much meaning change. A strength appears to be his search for meaning in what he reads. He corrects both for meaning and for what he seems to have learned as *correct* pronunciation (*dying* and *walking*). He replaced *despite* with *in spite of* and made no correction, as the meaning was quite unchanged. He said *blacks for Negroes* because he was used to saying blacks and it made perfect sense as a substitution.

---

working with students who speak in a dialect (black English, for example) or a combination of English and another language should acquire sufficient knowledge of the dialect or language to avoid penalizing students unjustly for variant pronunciations.[31] Teachers need to learn the differences between dialect or dominant language-based miscues and those derived from problems that may, indeed, interfere with comprehension. Most of the research in the field supports the thesis that dialect and dominant language-based miscues do not, as such, interfere with reading comprehension.[32]

INVENTORIES

Inventories may be administered to an individual or a group. At the secondary level, inventories are most often given to the whole class *prior to instruction*—

at the beginning of the school year or when new materials are to be used. An inventory is usually administered to students who are late entrants or who show signs of having extreme difficulty and need to interact with the instructor on a one-to-one basis.

With an inventory a teacher attempts to survey the students' strengths and needs in using the important writing and reading strategies considered essential in a particular content area. Such inventories may be used in connection with a textbook, a supplemental book, a reference book, a periodical article, a chapter in a book, or a passage from any one of these materials.

The traditional informal reading inventory (IRI) is of limited use in the middle school and high school. Information about independent, instructional, or frustration level based on a graded series of passages has little applicability in content area classrooms. If, however, a teacher desires to use such an inventory, I suggest careful perusal of the excellent review of commercial informal reading inventories by Jongsma and Jongsma.[33]

Secondary Reading Inventories.   Vaughan and Gaus proposed a secondary reading inventory (SRI) in which several selections on each of four levels would be utilized: grades 5 and 6; 7 and 8; 9 and 10; and 11 and 12.[34]

> Within each of these four levels of an SRI would be five selections based on a variety of material from which adolescents are most often required to learn. These categories of material include (1) fiction, (2) factual narration (e.g., biography, or historic description), (3) social studies exposition, (4) scientific description and exposition, and (5) problematic or directional exposition (e.g., math word problems or vocational "how to" material). Additionally, in order to provide a diagnostician with an opportunity to assess the difference between a student's comprehension when left to read the material independently and the student's comprehension when aided by some intervening instructional assistance, each selection might be divided into two parts. In effect, the framework of the proposed SRI would consist of 20 passages, with five selections on each of four levels.[35]

Vaughan and Gaus also suggested that the SRI include an interest inventory consisting of annotations of the selections to be read. Students are asked to rank selections in their preferred order. The ranking can be followed by an interview for additional insights, and postreading interviews can be held to see if preferences have changed.

After assessing comprehension of the passages, a teacher will want to decide on the maximal instructional level for the student; according to Vaughan and Gaus, the effect of the instruction should also be assessed. The second part of each selection might be read following an instructional sequence guided by specific reading purposes.

Vaughan and Gaus advised that a discussion of key vocabulary terms after a comprehension check could serve to unlock some problems. The Vaughan-

Gaus description of the SRI should be studied for further details not reported here.

Specific Content Area Inventories.   Inventories related to specific content areas yield useful insights into study strategies for content area teachers. One such inventory, based on a history text but applicable in form to most subjects, may be found in its entirety in a book by Strang and Bracken.[36] The inventory in Example 2.4, also based on a history text, was developed by a history teacher and Jerome Flescher, a reading consultant.[37]

Example 2.4   *An Inventory Related to World History*[38]

THE PAGEANT OF WORLD HISTORY

Group Inventory

General Directions

This is *not* a test that you can fail. As an inventory, this is a measure of your ability to use your textbook and to understand the information contained within it. The results of this inventory may indicate ways for you to learn how to do a faster and better job with your reading assignments in social studies.

Some directions will be given to you orally, and some are written in this inventory. *Follow all directions carefully.* Write *all* answers on the answer sheet provided.

I.   Locating Information
Directions: Place your pencil on the desk. When you are given the signal to begin, you are to locate the page (or pages) on which the answer to each of the following questions is found in your textbook. Write the page number (or numbers) in the space provided on the answer sheet. When you have finished the questions in this section, put your pencil back on the desk. *Do Not Go On To The Next Section.*
1.   Who was John J. Pershing?
2.   Where is Uganda?
3.   Where is Mount Sinai?
4.   What was Mount Olympus?
5.   What was the Japanese social structure before World War II?
6.   How did imperialism cause war?
7.   How did the Mogul Dynasty rule India?
8.   How were the Dutch involved in the African slave trade?
9.   What is meant by the "scientific revolution"?
10.   When were American military advisors first sent to Viet Nam?

II.   Map and Graph Interpretation
Directions: Turn to page 602 and refer to the graph on that page for questions 1 and 2.

    1.   By 1925, how many millions of people were there on earth?
    2.   How many times will the world population have increased from 1900 to 2000?

Directions: Turn to page 174 and refer to the map on that page for questions 3, 4, and 5.
    3.   Who ruled Gascony in the twelfth century?
    4.   Who governed the major portion of Flanders after 1550?
    5.   What portion of France was ruled by the English in 1550?

III.   Vocabulary in Context
Directions: Turn to page 584. Find the paragraph in the left column which begins "In Poland the Soviet Union . . . ." Write an appropriate, brief definition for each of the following words:
    1.   force
    2.   lost
    3.   puppet
    4.   condemned
    5.   checking

IV.   Study Reading
Directions: Read pages 584–86. Make notes. Then close your book and keep it closed. However, you may use the notes you made to help you answer these questions. [The questions that follow are on another sheet of paper distributed after the book is closed.]

Write your answers in the space provided below each question on this sheet.

At what latitude was Korea divided at the end of World War II?
1a. _____

What was the date of this division?
1b. _____

When did the Korean War end?
1c. _____

Where was Korea divided at the end of the war?
1d. _____

Who was the supreme commander of the U.N. troops?
2. _____

What was the significance of the Korean War?
3. _____
_____
_____

Why did President Truman replace the American commander?
4. _____
_____

Example 2.4 (continued)

Example 2.4 (continued)

Why did the Chinese Communists attack the American forces in Korea?

5. _____

_____

Answer Form

Name _____ Date _____

Teacher _____ Social Studies Period _____

THE PAGEANT OF WORLD HISTORY

Group Inventory

I. Locating Information

    1. _____

    2. _____

    3. _____

    4. _____

    5. _____

    6. _____

    7. _____

    8. _____

    9. _____

   10. _____

II. Map and Graph Interpretation

    1. _____

    2. _____

    3. _____

    4. _____

    5. _____

Do Not Write in This Box

I   ___%   _ / _

II   Gr___   Mp___

III   Voc___

IV   Comp___

   1a   Detail   ___

   1b   Detail   ___

   1c   Detail   ___

   1d   Detail   ___

   2   Detail   ___

   3   Main Idea   ___

   4   Main Idea   ___

   5   Inference   ___

III. Vocabulary in Context

    1. force _____

_____

    2. lost _____

_____

    3. puppet _____

_____

    4. condemned _____

_____

    5. checking _____

_____

Example 2.4 (continued)

IV.   Study Reading   Time _____
      Write your notes below:

_____

For Articles.   A fine example of an inventory related to the reading of a scientific article in a journal was presented by Strang in 1945;[39] an abstract of this inventory may be found in Strang, McCullough, and Traxler.[40] The journal article inventory in Example 2.5 is used with upper high school students in Hofstra University's Reading Clinic. (The inventory was developed by Sidney Rauch and Harold Tanyzer.)

_____

Example 2.5   *An Inventory Related to a Scientific Article*[41]

A.   *Students are presented with the following article and asked to read it silently at their own speed. They inform the examiner when they have finished the reading.*

THE AMERICAN DESERT

1.   To the ordinary air traveler winging across the U.S. Southwest, the great American desert still seems an arid and forbidding waste of sand, dry lake beds and jagged rock mountains. But to the observant, a careful look reveals surprising signs of a new civilization rising among the ocotillos and greasewood. Thin asphalt ribbons stretch across the sand, linking black and white dots of clustered homes, blue bands of irrigation canals and rectangles of bright green new farms. From California's southern coastal ranges inland 375 miles to the central Arizona cities of Phoenix and Tucson, the searing desert, long a shunned part of the U.S.'s land surface, is filling up. Today, thousands of pioneers are moving in, claiming a brand-new empire in which to build new homes, farms, businesses and a whole new way of life.

2.   To the ill-equipped and the unwary, the desert can still be a savage and treacherous foe. But to the man who comes to the desert with caution and respect, the forbidding area has much to offer: fabulous mineral riches, water so pure that it tastes like distilled water, incredibly fertile farmland and a growing season 365 days long. Above all, the desert offers the restless migrants from city stress a combination of peace, solitude and a fresh start on a new frontier. "There are three ways of life now," says Indio (Calif.) publisher Ole Nordland, "The city, the farm, and the desert."

Example 2.5 (continued)

Example 2.5 (continued)

3.   *Mass Migration.*   Ever since the Spaniards first explored the region in the 16th century, man has been able to promote a cautious friendship with the great deserts of the Southwest. Springs and river water from the Colorado, Mojave, Verde, Salt, and Gila gave rise to settlements and small farming districts. Deep wells supported a slowly growing population, clustered along well-traveled desert highways in a few centers—Tucson, Phoenix, Las Vegas, Barstow. In the mountains, miners hammered away at sun-baked mineral vaults, and on the sandy desert floor men learned to irrigate and raise truck crops, cotton, dates and citrus trees.

4.   But within the past 15 years, so casually that the nation at large was scarcely aware of the change, man discovered how to live comfortably almost anywhere he chose on the desert. From the old centers, suburbs began mushrooming out through the mesquite and yuccas. Long fingers of civilization stretched along brand-new desert highways, reaching toward new cities that sprang up among the saguaros and Joshua trees.

5.   Behind the push was one of the greatest migrations the world has ever known. Since 1940, more than 5,000,000 newcomers have moved into the Far West; 200,000 are still arriving in California each year. They flow into Los Angeles and the main cities of the Southwest and, in search of more space and freer living, push on through the populated centers and out over the desert. . . .

6.   Great areas of the desert have turned green with new water wells and hundreds of miles of new irrigation canals. The fertile soil and year-round growing season give desert agriculture an intensity and diversity undreamed of by the Midwest dirt farmer. In California's rich, 650,000-acre Imperial Valley, grains, cotton, lettuce, sheep, flax, cattle and carrots can be raised side by side. Farmers change their crops to meet changing market conditions, and when water is needed, a telephone order brings it sluicing through laterals from the All-American Canal, which stretches 80 miles to the Colorado River. . . .

7.   Farther north, on the Mojave Desert, rancher Stoddard Jess has built one of the desert's tidiest agricultural arrangements. His chief crop is turkeys, 55,000 birds or more each year, and better than 100,000 poults. In a complex of fresh-water ponds, he raises a million rainbow trout from fingerlings. The trout fatten on entrails from the dressed turkeys and on worms grown as a crop on the ranch. Water from the ponds irrigates fields of corn, and the turkeys are turned loose to fatten on the corn.

8.   *Out of the Submarines.*   The desert influx got its first big push with World War II. The military services and aircraft industry, seeking space for maneuvers and testing, as well as the desert's clear, dry weather and year-round sunshine, were the first to move out in expansive style. They sank hundreds of wells, established mushrooming service installations: Edwards and George

Air Force Bases in the Mojave, the U.S. Naval Ordnance Test Station near Inyokern, the Army's Camp Irwin at Barstow, Marine Corps depots and bases at Mojave, Barstow, and Twenty-nine Palms, and other big bases at Las Vegas and in the Arizona Desert around Tucson and Phoenix. At Frenchman Flat, 70 miles north of Las Vegas, the AEC set up its nuclear-weapons test site.

9. Where the military pioneered, citizens followed in vigorous and increasing waves. People who looked for a healthy climate, pleasant living, new opportunities, and the freedom of elbow space found them in the desert. Modern technology was ready to help combat the desert's age-old barriers. A dozen years before, old settlers slept in wet sheets or went to bed in "submarines," welded metal boxes over which cooling water was pumped during the night. Now, at war's end, there was modern air cooling and refrigeration. In homes, offices, and resorts, men found they could live, work and play in air-conditioned comfort and move about in air-conditioned cars. Big machines and modern techniques met other problems, from the drilling of deep wells and the mass production of swimming pools to the erection in double-quick time of whole towns, planned to order.

10. In Arizona, guest ranches once advertised desert seclusion. Now surrounded by housing developments and shopping centers, they are eying distant locations, wondering how far to retreat to avoid still another move. As the settlers push out of Los Angeles, buying up one desert tract after another, realtors bulldoze farther and farther into the desert.

11. *Big Dreams.* With the increasing pool of skilled workers, payrolls are swelling at desert plants and industries. The wartime installations, now permanent, compete for workers with newer desert arrivals such as the $50 million complex of chemical and metal plants at Henderson, Nev. Aircraft workers, fleeing the smog and traffic of Los Angeles, find work with North American, Lockheed, or Northrop at new assembly and testing plants on the Mojave.

12. Other immigrants are finding new starts in real estate, insurance, farming and stock raising. Mojave Desert realtors obligingly indoctrinate home buyers in the business of poultry raising, sell them the equipment along with their new homes, even arrange the buying (on credit) of chicks and feed and the marketing of the grown product. Today, a new housing project near Lancaster claims to be the most concentrated poultry raising area in the U.S., with every backyard a crowded chicken run.

13. More spectacularly, the new desert book is studded with examples of settlers who have come up fast and furiously:

Near Victorville, Calif., George McCarthy was trying to make ends

Example 2.5 (continued)

Example 2.5 (continued)

meet by running a small guest ranch. Two years ago he sold a piece of Mojave Desert land that had cost him $180. His price: $250,000. Today he is subdividing 3,300 acres that cost him less than $1 an acre into half-acre tracts to sell for $2,000 apiece.

Del E. Webb, once a Phoenix carpenter, became a builder, grew with the desert boom, is now a multimillionaire contractor and developer, with interests ranging from oil to part ownership of the New York Yankees.

In Arizona's Paradise Valley, where Frank Lloyd Wright and his students at nearby Taliesin West design homes for desert living, realtor Merle Cheney bought 6,000 acres of land for as low as 25¢ an acre, now sells it at prices up to $3,000 an acre.

In Apple Valley, Calif., Long Beach oilmen Newton Bass and Bernard Westlund developed 26,000 acres of desert land they bought in 1946 for an average of $50 an acre into a plush resort, now use 90 salesmen and a fleet of radio-controlled cars to sell half-acre lots for as much as $11,500. . . .

14.   *No Place but Here.*   Water has always been the limiting factor to the desert's growth. There are few places on the desert where a man, for a price, cannot sink a well and bring up water. But the price is sometimes prohibitive, and the water table is going down. The Colorado is tapped for domestic and industrial use in Nevada's Clark County, for irrigation in the Yuma area of Arizona and (via the long All-American and Coachella Canals) in the Imperial Valley and the Coachella Valley, and for domestic consumption in Los Angeles. As the area grows and demand increases, men will have to find new sources of supply. When that time arrives, area officials hope that scientists will have learned how to convert sea water into fresh water at an economic price.

15.   Meanwhile, the desert, offering many things to many men, is still attracting increasing numbers of new settlers. Some, like Tucson businessman Larry Sierck, who migrated from Davenport, Iowa, five years ago and is still in his 30's, came for the opportunities of the fresh new land. Others, like William Bentham and his wife, who left Los Angeles when Bentham got ulcers in his city job, come for the healthy climate and the pleasant living. Today the ulcers are gone and the Mojave Desert location has turned into valuable property. "But hell," he says, "if we sold, where would we go, Sudie and me? I don't want to go any place but here."

B.   *After reading the article, students are presented with the following set of questions spaced so they might write answers on the paper. With the exception of question number one, students may sometimes be permitted to refer back to the text—depending on the purpose(s) of the examiner and the observed ability of the student.*

1. What is the title of this article?

2. Write a one-paragraph summary of the selection answering the question, "What did the author say?"

3. Using the following skeleton outline, fill in the three main ideas and as many supporting details as necessary to adequately complete the outline.
   I.   Change in the American Desert: Past and Present.
   II. Reasons for Change in the American Desert.
   III. The Future of the American Desert.

4. In all probability this article was written by
   A. An Army Recruiting Officer
   B. Arizona's Chamber of Commerce
   C. U.S. Government Agricultural Office
   D. Southwestern Real Estate Bureau
   Defend and support your choice.

5. Explain the following statements:
   A. "To the ill-equipped and the unwary, the desert can still be a savage and treacherous foe."
   B. "Modern technology was ready to help combat the desert's age-old barriers."
   C. "But to the observant, a careful look reveals surprising signs of a new civilization rising among the ocotillos and greasewood."

For Chapters. Since comprehension is what we learn from our reading minus what we knew before we started, a simple way of determining prior knowledge of a chapter is to raise the questions often placed at the end of a chapter *before* the chapter is read. Responses to such questions can help you evaluate the readiness of individuals for the reading of the chapter (see Chapter 3). This type of inventory permits individualization of assignments to be planned, particularly when a single text is used for the entire class.

A comprehensive, teacher-structured inventory of a chapter takes time to construct; but once constructed, it can be used for a number of years. The format of the inventory in Example 2.6, although designed for a chapter in a biology book, could be used in most any content area. This particular inventory (slightly adapted) was designed by a biology teacher and a reading consultant.[42]

For Passages. Viox, in her excellent booklet *Evaluating Reading and Study Skills in the Secondary Classroom*, presented the inventory in Example 2.7, based on a passage in a homemaking text.[43]

*Example 2.6   An Inventory Related to a Biology
Textbook Chapter* [44]

ELEMENTS OF BIOLOGY, CHAPTER 6

Name _____   Date _____

Thought questions (to keep in mind as you read but *not* to be answered until you have finished the chapter).

Why do we study simple one-celled animals?

How does an understanding of one-celled animals help you explain how human skin grows?

A human being has been described as a group of cells that are cooperating. Explain this idea—in what ways are the cells cooperating?

Survey the chapter.

Skim each section of the chapter as numbered below until you find the information needed. When you have located the information you think will provide an answer to the question, read that material carefully. Write each answer on this worksheet.

6.1   What is meant by *phyla* (*fy*-luh)? _____

Define:
　　Vertebrate: _____
　　Invertebrate: _____

6.2   _____ are the group of _____ representing the simplest animals known. Although they are only _____ cells, they have the ability to _____, _____, _____, and _____.

6.3   The simplest animal of the Protozoa group is the _____ (_____). It has _____ _____ shape.

6.4   What does the ameba have in common with the higher animals?
_____

How does the ameba *reproduce*? _____
　　Asexual reproduction is _____
　　Reproduction by *fission* is when _____ new cells are formed from a _____ parent.

6.5   The *paramecium* has developed a division of labor within its single cell to _____ _____ functions.

6.7   Why is the *euglena* especially interesting?

_____

6.10   Certain cells in a colony of *volvox* are _____ cells. Other cells are called _____ cells.
       When a sperm cell centers an egg cell, it forms a _____ _____ cell, called a _____.

6.11   Now see if you can answer the three thought questions posed at the beginning of this inventory.
       I.   _____
       II. _____
       III. _____

Example 2.7   *Inventory Related to a Homemaking Textbook Passage*[45]

Purpose: To find out if pupils can read and understand recipes.

Directions to teacher: The following test is based on the text *Teen Guide to Homemaking* by Barclay and Champion (McGraw-Hill Book Co., 1961).

Directions to student: It is very important for a good cook to be able to read and understand recipes without help. To find out how well you can do this, turn to page 447 in your text. Study the recipe for tuna fish casserole. Then answer the following questions:

1.   What is meant by "1 can cream of celery soup, *undiluted*"?
2.   What is the first step in preparing the casserole?
3.   Why must you add the noodles gradually?
4.   Why must you stir the noodles as they are cooking?
5.   What is a colander?
6.   How would you prepare the onions?
7.   To what do you add the soup, milk, tuna fish, peas, salt, pepper and noodles?
8.   How should you prepare the casserole dish before putting the ingredients into it?
9.   At what temperature should you bake the casserole? For how long?
10.   What can you do to vary the recipe?

INFORMAL TESTS

Informal teacher-made tests are not as comprehensive as inventories and usually focus on a single skill or on a cluster of related skills. (In some of the professional literature, however, no distinction is made between informal inventories and informal tests.) Sometimes the express purpose of an informal test is to ascertain students' abilities in putting general strategies or skills to work in the framework of a content area—for example, the strategy of using context clues in arriving at word meanings in a science passage; at other times a skill may be quite specifically tied into the content area—for example, reading and following directions on a worksheet in industrial arts.

Many fine examples of specific informal teacher-made tests in a large variety of content areas may be found in *Evaluating Reading and Study Skills in the Secondary Classroom*[46] and in Thomas and Robinson.[47] Example 2.8 is a *rate of reading* test that can be utilized in many content areas.

Example 2.8

Exploring Rate of Reading Study Material[48]

A study task that students are often called upon to perform is to read study-type material and master its contents thoroughly. To explore the rates of students on this type of reading, select a passage representative of the material they will be expected to read and comprehend thoroughly, a passage not less than 1,000 words in length. Prepare short-answer questions, perhaps ten of these.

Have the students take your "homemade" test in class, following these directions: "When I give the starting signal, please read this passage carefully. Be sure you understand and remember the information. You will be asked to answer questions after you finish reading. Use the method of reading that will enable you to achieve maximum comprehension. As soon as you finish, look up at the board to learn the time that has elapsed. Divide (the number of words in the passage) by the figure you see on the board to learn the number of words you read per minute."

As the students are reading, write on the board, at quarter-of-a-minute intervals, the elapsed time in minutes. To make the division easier for the students, write the elapsed time in decimals instead of fractions—"3 minutes," "3.25 minutes," "3.5 minutes," "3.75 minutes," and so on. After a student has finished reading and has recorded his or her rate in words per minute, hand the student the comprehension questions. As you examine the results of this test, your students' words per minute and their degree of comprehension on a typical passage, you should find that you now have deeper insights into how rapidly they can handle their day-to-day assignments that call for thorough study.

SPECIFIC WRITING ASSESSMENTS

Reading and writing go together as naturally as do listening and speaking. The content teacher can and should incorporate writing as an integral part of classroom learning without trying to teach writing "skills" or unduly burdening himself with papers to read and correct. The important thing is to give students writing experience in all content areas.[49]

Concentration on writing in English classes does not provide enough quantity or consistency for students in departmentalized learning situations. Students must learn to expect writing standards across the curriculum—in every content area in which writing is used for learning and responding. Such planned activity, of course, presents a problem in terms of time to teachers who are already overworked. The two questions and answers that follow are designed to provide some help to content area teachers eager to assist their charges develop into competent writers:

1. *Must I grade every paper for writing expertise as well as for content?* Sometimes you may want to give a separate grade for success in written communication and another grade for content. Or you might want to establish a rating scale, known to students, and use a numerical rating for written communication ability. (See the suggested scales that follows.) The major thrust, however, should be to develop your students' understanding that content and expression of ideas are fused. Your assessment is based on not only the accuracy and depth of the ideas but also on how well those ideas are organized and communicated. It is often profitable to have students write for their peers, who, assisted by a rating scale or evaluative criteria of some kind, can give valuable feedback. Such interchange is useful for both the reader and the writer.

You will probably want to differentiate between composing and responding. In *composing*, the students are organizing their own ideas and setting them down as lucidly as possible in order to communicate those ideas. In this situation you (and their peers) will want to help them with their first draft to be sure it communicates the ideas well. The best technique here is to ask questions about meaning, not about technical problems. The time for straightening out technical problems that still exist is when writing the second or third draft (or even later drafts). Many technical problems are taken care of as students attempt to make subsequent drafts communicate.

In *responding*, students write short or long answers to questions you pose. Here, as above, the major emphasis is on meaning; however, your concern will be with correctness of the answers in response to your questions. If answers are required to be complete sentences or paragraphs, you will want to maintain the concept that you are monitoring writing expression through placing stress on coherence and clarity. Not every written response needs a writing grade, but students should become aware that the quality of written expression is always considered in every content area.

2.   *When I do mark papers for writing expertise, and how can I do it without spending an inordinate amount of time on each paper?* Overcorrection is as bad as paying no attention to written-expression ability. Students become frustrated and hardly know how to proceed when every fragment, run-on, spelling error, and punctuation problem is marked. Students are usually helped most by a planned program throughout the year that considers their progress in writing. For such a program, *holistic scoring scales* and *primary trait analyses* seem most functional.

Holistic Scoring.   "Holistic scoring procedures assign a single score to a written exercise which purports to summarize the overall quality of the writing."[50] Although specific strengths and needs cannot be pinpointed, generalizations can be made over time and progress can be noted. Ratings are never based on any one aspect of an essay but must always take into consideration content, organization, style, expression, and mechanics.[51] The two holistic scoring scales given below seem particularly useful. Smith, Smith, and Mikulecky presented six-point scale in Example 2.9 as a means of monitoring and assessing students' writing.

Example 2.9   A Diagnostic Framework[52]

1 = Minimal communication: The writer gives only a few simple utterances which he [she] does not attempt to develop in any way. Writing is extremely brief.

2 = Some development of communication: The writer expands the number of statements and achieves some complexity but lacks evident organization or an overall idea of what he [she] wants to get across. Writing is still quite brief.

3 = Some development and organization of communication: The writer is achieving order and completeness at the sentence level but still lacks a clear grasp of overall structure. Writing is rather brief.

4 = Evidence of abstraction along with orderly presentation: The writer includes interpretive comments of his [her] own along with a coherent presentation of information. Writing now seems complete.

5 = Communication that combines orderly presentation of information, development of ideas, interpretation beyond a concrete level, and strong overall organization: The writer can provide cohesive sentences organized into paragraphs (for longer writing assignments). Overall organization

shows a clear beginning and end with a well-developed body. Writer has produced a complete and organized statement.

6 = Communication that includes the criteria of number 5 along with originality of expression or idea, or a polished writing style that adds clarity and personality to writing.[53]

The same authors added the following suggestion:

Perhaps the individual student is the best possible source for reducing the teacher's chore in correcting compositions and for increasing the learning done by the student. If each student had his [her] own set of criteria for proofreading or reviewing his [her] own writing, he [she] could be asked to reread his [her] paper and mark on it the number of the scale that seems to represent what he [she] did. The teacher could then glance at it quickly to see whether it achieved the level that the student had given it. If the teacher agreed, the evaluation could stand and both would know what must be done next time to achieve a higher number on the scale. If the teacher disagreed, they could confer or the student would have to review and rewrite (or scale down) to achieve the level he [she] had posted.[54]

McCaig reported on a districtwide plan for the evaluation of student writing. The example he provided for grades 9 and 10, shown in Example 2.10, seems useful as a guide in content area classrooms.

Example 2.10   *Interpretation Guide for Levels of Writing*[55]

Level 1 . . . Not competent

Either the content is inadequate for the topic selected, or deficiencies in the conventions of written expression are so gross that they interfere with communication.

Level 2 . . . Not competent

The student can express a message which can be readily understood, which contains adequate content for the selected topic, and which demonstrates at least marginal command of sentence sense.

The writing, however, is grossly deficient in one or more of these skills, judged by standards appropriate for high school:

Example 2.10 (continued)

Example 2.10 (continued)

Spelling

Usage

Punctuation and capitalization

Level 3 . . . Marginally competent

The student can compose a completed series of ideas about a topic with a minimum of gross deficiencies in spelling, usage, or punctuation, judged by standards appropriate for high school.

The writing, however, does not contain at least one competent paragraph or is not competent in one or more of these skills, judged by standards appropriate for high school:

Sentence sense	Usage
Spelling	Punctuation and capitalization

Level 4 . . . Competent

The student can compose a completed series of ideas about a topic with basic skills at a level appropriate for high school and with at least one competent paragraph.

The writing, however, does not demonstrate all of the characteristics of highly competent writing:

Good overall organization	Good sentence structure
Competent paragraphing	Good vocabulary
Regular use of transitions	Appropriate use of subordination
Interpretive meaning (as opposed to literal writing)	

Level 5 . . . Highly competent

The student can compose a completed series of ideas about a topic with basic skills at a level appropriate for high school and with these characteristics of highly competent writing:

Good overall organization	Good sentence structure
Competent paragraphing	Good vocabulary
Regular use of transitions	Appropriate use of subordination
Interpretive meaning (as opposed to literal writing)	

The writing does not, however, demonstrate thesis development and does not contain critical or creative thinking.

Level 6 . . . Superior

The student can compose a completed series of ideas about a topic with excellent basic skills, with the characteristics of highly competent writing, with adequate thesis development, and with at least one passage demonstrating critical or creative thinking.

The passage of superior writing, however, tends to be an isolated example.

Level 7 . . . Superior

The student can compose a completed series of ideas about a topic with excellent basic skills, with critical or creative thinking, and with a sustained vitality and richness of expression.[56]

Primary Trait Analyses. "Primary trait procedures identify specific aspects of writing ranging from mechanical grammar and punctuation to variables reflecting the exercise's logical organization, form or creativity."[57] Primary trait analyses are valuable as pressure reducers for both students and content area teachers. Teachers can tell students what aspects of a piece of writing they will assess at a given time. Students are then freed from being concerned about every aspect of the writing and can concentrate on just one, two, or three areas. This type of concentration helps students improve in specific areas faster than does the "shot-gun" approach. Some of the traits listed in McCaig's interpretation guide above can be major focuses in primary trait analyses.

SELF-APPRAISAL

Some teachers tend to be leary of self-appraisal techniques, and indeed a number of students probably cannot or will not, in particular situations, evaluate their needs and/or strengths seriously. Alvin, a perfectionist, may find it impossible not to find and explore weaknesses even though his performance is far above average. Doris, who knows, or thinks she knows, that she will be penalized for admitting that she finds it difficult to read portions of a textbook, will try to cover up the inefficiency. But there is little doubt that both students would be willing and even eager to evaluate their own performances (1) if they knew that their teacher, Mr. Roberts, was sincerely interested in them and eager to help; (2) if Mr. Roberts did not make self-appraisal a competitive exercise but a valid part of the total evaluation process; (3) if the self-appraisal were private and individual; (4) if the appraisal focused on a small and visible segment of the curriculum; (5) if what was being appraised were comprehensible, relevant, and significant enough to Doris and Alvin; and (6) if the self-appraisal led to either a better understanding of themselves and the way they function or to a more successful or secure experience in the next unit of work.

Several of the techniques already discussed in this chapter can serve as techniques for self-appraisal. A structured interview or an informal conference may often result in student self-appraisal. (Strang stressed the possibilities of capitalizing on a variety of evaluation techniques for self-appraisal.)[58] The following three aspects of self-appraisal may be used in conjunction with many forms of evaluation.

Free Response.   The value of self-appraisal is brought to the attention of an individual, small group, or class. The self-appraisal is focused on one area, such as vocabulary development, study skills, rates of reading, or problems of reading a textbook in industrial arts. Some guiding questions are suggested by the teacher or student(s). Then students are asked to discuss, in writing or orally, their strengths and weaknesses in the particular area. Strang formulated directions for such introspective study, shown in Example 2.11, and presented two sample responses.

Example 2.11   *Directions for Free-Response Self-Appraisal*[59]

HOW I READ!

Should you like to discover how you actually read, watch yourself as you read. It may not be easy at first, but you will soon find it interesting and helpful. After you have made some discoveries about your reading process, you may wish to share them with the rest of the class and discuss ways to improve.

Directions

Select a story, article, or section at least three pages long from a school book. As you read your selection, try to observe what you do as you read. For example, do your eyes move backward over the line of print? If so, why? Do they ever miss a line? Do you look at every single word? Do your eyes mover faster than your mind? Do your thoughts wander? Where do they wander? Do you think of the meaning of each word or group words in phrases and thoughts?

When you have finished your reading, write down immediately everything you noticed about your reading. You may be surprised at what you discover about your own reading.

Strang reported responses to the analysis above by a superior reader and a poor reader:

A superior reader wrote: "When I read, my eyes follow the lines and sometimes go a few lines ahead of what I am reading. I don't look back. I don't get help on words. I don't read every word but I don't skip any lines. I read all the way through the article without stopping."

A very poor reader made this analysis: "Sometimes I miss a line. I look at almost every word. My eyes move faster than my mind can read. Sometimes my thoughts wander. Sometimes I think about what I read. I usually read too fast. I don't often think about the ideas in the lesson I am reading. I don't concentrate on my reading."[60]

Structured Questions. Questions that zero in on a particular area are formulated by the instructor. Such questions may be utilized in interviews and conferences, in directed reading autobiographies, and as an inventory calling for written responses. Thomas and Robinson presented some questions in the area of vocabulary development: "What do you do when you're studying an assignment and meet an important new technical term?" "Have you ever consciously done anything to build your vocabulary? If so, what methods have you used?"[61] They also proposed the following questions to see "whether students have acquired the concept of rate adjustment and can identify some of the factors involved: 'Do you use the same rate of reading in most of your assignments? If you shift your rate, what considerations cause you to do so?'"[62]

Strang pointed out that it may be necessary to differentiate questions, depending on the nature of the student. For *successful readers* she suggested such questions as: "Do you skim material before reading it in detail?" "Do you summarize material after you read it?" "Do you raise questions when reading and then read to find the answer?" "Do you immediately reread sections of your assignment which are not clear?" "Are you careful not to skip graphs, tables, and charts when you read your assignment?" For *poor readers* she suggested: "Why do you want to read better?" "What advantage would it be for you to be a better reader?"[63]

Self-Rating Checklists. Evaluation checklists can be developed for specific reading tasks in a host of content areas. Thomas and Robinson presented a *Self-Evaluation Checklist for Reading Directions* particularly structured for students in a typewriting class but suggested its adaptability for several other subjects. This checklist is shown in Example 2.12.

Example 2.12   *Self-Evaluation Checklist for Reading Directions*[64]

Name _____   Period _____   Date _____

This checklist is intended to focus your attention on any need areas and point the way to improvement. Your teacher, too, will evaluate you.

Example 2.12 (continued)

Example 2.12 (continued)

Consider how you stand on each of the points below, then rate yourself from 1 to 10 in the space before the numeral.

Points to Consider

_____ 1. Do you focus full attention on directions in whatever format you find them—itemized lists with numerals, brief directions out in the margin, directions inserted right into the copy, etc.?

_____ 2. At the end of an especially difficult step, do you stop, reflect, and reread, if necessary, to make sure you understand just what you are to do?

_____ 3. Do you make sure you understand the meaning of unfamiliar key terms?

_____ 4. Do you examine the photographs and drawings?

_____ 5. Are you moving in the direction of independence in handling directions largely on your own?

_____ 6. Are you gradually eliminating errors due to superficial reading of directions?

_____ 7. Are you gradually eliminating redoing practices because of superficial reading?

Now that you have considered your specific strengths and weaknesses, give yourself a general rating on the scale below. Place a single check mark at the appropriate point on the scale.

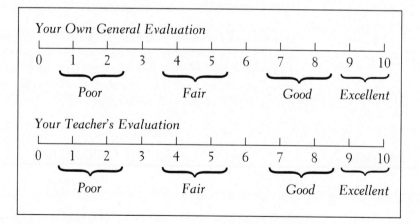

Set Your Own Goals

What general rating do you hope to attain before the next evaluation? Place numeral here: _____.

QUESTIONS
AND
RELATED
ACTIVITIES

1. What is the difference between monitoring and assessment? How do they overlap?

2. How can you ascertain what a student has gained from his or her reading beyond, or divergent from, your expectations?

3. How can affective or highly subjective instruments demonstrate some measure of validity?

4. Construct an informal inventory for an article or a chapter on content area material similar to that used in a specific content area classroom. Emphasize those reading and writing strategies you deem important for success in handling the material.

5. The self-evaluation checklist in Example 2.12 focuses on the reading of directions. Develop—with students if you like—another self-evaluation checklist focused on another important reading strategy. You might also want to develop a self-evaluation checklist for writing tasks.

6. Use holistic criteria to assess two or three writing tasks. You may wish to modify or add criteria, depending on your purposes.

SELECTED
READINGS

Bimes, Beverly J. "Total School Writing: A Working Approach to Writing Problems." *Today's Education* 70 (April–May 1981):40GS–41GS.

DeFord, Diane E.; Lorelie Meeker; and Ernest B. Nieratka. "An Effective Screening Profile in Reading for High Risk Students." *Viewpoints in Teaching and Learning* 56 (Spring 1980):65–73.

Farrell, Edmund. "The Vice/Vise of Standardized Testing: National Depreciation by Quantification." *Language Arts* 54 (May 1977):486–90.

Lehr, Fran. "Testing Reading Comprehension at the Secondary Level: Informal Measures." *Journal of Reading* 23 (December 1979):270–73.

MacGinitie, Walter H., ed. *Assessment Problems in Reading*. Newark, Del.: International Reading Association, 1973.

Page, William D., and Gay Su Pinnell. "Assessing Reading for Meaning." In *Teaching Reading Comprehension*, pp. 81–104. Urbana, Ill.: ERIC Clearinghouse on Reading and Communication Skills and National Council of Teachers of English, March 1979.

Page, William D., and Richard T. Vacca. "Overt Indications of Reading Comprehension: Product and Process Considerations." In *New Perspectives on Comprehension*, Monograph in Language and Reading Studies, no. 3, edited by Jerome C. Harste and Robert F. Carey, pp. 49–63. Bloomington: School of Education, Indiana University, October 1979.

Robinson, H. Alan, "Testing Reading: Product Versus Process." *Reading Teacher* 26 (December 1972):303–4.

————, and Ellen Lamar Thomas, eds. *Fusing Reading Skills and Content*, pp. 23–24, 39–43, 75–76, 105–6, 131–32, 165–68, 187. Newark, Del.: International Reading Association, 1969.

Ruth, Leo (for the SLATE Steering Committee). "Standardized Testing: How to Read the Results." *Slate* 2 (March 1977).

Schell, Leo M. *Diagnostic and Criterion-Referenced Reading Tests: Review and Evaluation.* Newark, Del.: International Reading Association, 1981.

Schreiner, Robert. *Reading Tests and Teachers: A Practical Guide.* Newark, Del.: International Reading Association, 1979.

Searle, Dennis, and David Dillon. "Responding to Student Writing: What Is Said or How It Is Said." *Language Arts* 57 (October 1980):773–81.

Sims, Rudine. "Miscue Analysis: Emphasis on Comprehension." In *Applied Linguistics and Reading*, edited by Robert E. Shafer, pp. 101–11. Newark, Del.: International Reading Association, 1979.

Smith, Sharon L. "Retellings as Measures of Comprehension: A Perspective." In *New Perspectives on Comprehension*, Monograph in Language and Reading Studies, no. 3, edited by Jerome C. Harste and Robert F. Carey, pp. 84–99. Bloomington: School of Education, Indiana University, October 1979.

Strang, Ruth. *Diagnostic Teaching of Reading.* New York: McGraw-Hill, 1964.

————, and Dorothy Kendall Bracken. *Making Better Readers*, pp. 60–75, 82–85, 222–33. Boston: D.C. Heath, 1957.

Strang, Ruth; Constance M. McCullough; and Arthur E. Traxler. *The Improvement of Reading*, 4th ed., pp. 151–211. New York: McGraw-Hill, 1967.

Thomas, Ellen Lamar, and H. Alan Robinson. *Improving Reading in Every Class*, 3rd ed., pp. 12–13, 15–16, 40–41, 51–52, 158–59, 203–6; (abridged ed., pp. 10–11, 13–14, 34, 45–47, 138–39, 171–74). Boston: Allyn and Bacon, 1982.

NOTES

1. Steven R. Asher, "Topic Interest and Children's Reading Comprehension," in *Theoretical Issues in Reading Comprehension*, ed. Rand J. Spiro, Bertram C. Bruce, and William F. Brewer (Hillsdale, N.J.: Lawrence Erlbaum Associates, 1980), p. 530.
2. Slate Steering Committee of the National Council of Teachers of English, *Slate* 1 (October 1976):1–2.
3. North Dakota Study Group on Evaluation of the National Council of Teachers of English, reprinted in *Slate* 2 (November 1976):3.
4. Oscar Krisen Buros, reprinted in *Slate* 2 (November 1976):4 (from preface of 1965 *Sixth Mental Measurements Yearbook*).
5. Oscar Krisen Buros, *Seventh Mental Measurements Yearbook*, vol 1 (Highland Mysteries (Pleasantville, N.Y.: Reader's Digest Association, 1979), p. 142.
6. Paul L. Houts, "Behind the Call for Test Reform and Abolition of the IQ," *Phi Delta Kappan* 57 (June 1976):673. © 1976, Phi Delta Kappan, Inc.

7. Roger A. McCaig, "What Your Director of Instruction Needs to Know About Standardized English Tests." *Language Arts* 54 (May 1977):495.

8. P. David Pearson and Dale D. Johnson, *Teaching Reading Comprehension* (New York: Holt, Rinehart and Winston, 1978), p. 214.

9. Ibid., p. 218.

10. Kenneth Kavale, "Selecting and Evaluating Reading Tests," in *Reading Tests and Teachers: A Practical Guide*, ed. Robert Schreiner (Newark, Del.: International Reading Association, 1979), p. 24.

11. Roy A. Kress, "Identifying the Reading Difficulties of the College-Bound Student," *Vistas in Reading*, Proceedings of the Annual Convention of the International Reading Association, vol. 11, pt. 1, 1966, pp. 257–61.

12. Ernest T. Goetz and Bonnie B. Armbruster, "Psychological Correlates of Text Structure," in *Theoretical Issues in Reading Comprehension*, ed. Rand J. Spiro, Bertram C. Bruce, and William F. Brewer (Hillsdale, N.J.: Lawrence Erlbaum Associates, 1980), p. 217.

13. Ruth Strang, "Diagnostic Teaching of Reading in High School," *Journal of Reading* (January 1965):153.

14. Ruth Strang, *Diagnostic Teaching of Reading* (New York: McGraw-Hill, 1964), pp. 76–84.

15. Ibid., p. 76. Reprinted by permission.

16. Ibid., p. 92.

17. Ruth Strang, Constance M. McCullough, and Arthur E. Traxler, *The Improvement of Reading*, 4th ed. (New York: McGraw-Hill, 1967), pp. 172–73.

18. Joseph L. Vaughan, Jr., "Affective Measurement Instruments: An Issue of Validity," *Journal of Reading* 24 (October 1980):16–19.

19. The term and concept "in-process indicators of comprehension" was borrowed from William D. Page and Richard T. Vacca, "Overt Indications of Reading Comprehension: Product and Process Considerations," in *New Perspectives on Comprehension*, Monograph in Language and Reading Studies, ed. Jerome C. Harste and Robert F. Carey (Bloomington: School of Education, Indiana University, October 1979), pp. 54–59.

20. John T. Guthrie and others, "The Maze Technique to Assess, Monitor Reading Comprehension," *Reading Teacher* 28 (November 1974):161–68.

21. Slightly adapted from May Veber, "The World's First Cities," in *The World's Last Mysteries* (Pleasantville, N.Y.: Reader's Digest Association, 1979), p. 142.

22. Wilson L. Taylor, "Cloze Procedure: A New Tool for Measuring Readability," *Journalism Quarterly* 30 (Fall 1953):415–33.

23. Frank T. Kane, *Justice in America* (Boston: Allyn and Bacon, 1977), p. 112.

24. Yetta M. Goodman and Carolyn L. Burke, *Reading Miscue Inventory* (New York: Macmillan, 1972).

25. Kenneth S. Goodman, "Analysis of Oral Reading Miscues: Applied Psycholinguistics," *Reading Research Quarterly* 5 (Fall 1969):9–30.

26. Nila Banton Smith and H. Alan Robinson, *Reading Instruction for Today's Children*, 2nd ed. (Englewood Cliffs, N.J.: Prentice-Hall, 1980), pp. 60–61.

27. Daniel R. Hittleman, *Developmental Reading: A Psycholinguistic Perspective* (Chicago: Rand McNally, 1978), pp. 113–32.

28. Adapted from Smith and Robinson, *Reading Instruction*, pp. 61–62. By permission of Prentice Hall, Inc., Englewood Cliffs, N.J.

29. Barbara Raisner, "Reading Strategies Employed By Non-Proficient Adult College Students as Observed Through Miscue Analysis and Retrospection" (Doctoral dissertation, Hofstra University, 1977).

30. Alfred Jamieson, *Minorities and Politics* (Boston: Allyn and Bacon, 1977), p. 85.

31. Walter J. Lamberg, "Assessment of Oral Reading Which Exhibits Dialect and Language Differences," *Journal of Reading* 22 (April 1979):609–16.
32. James L. Laffey and Roger W. Shuy, eds., *Language Differences: Do They Interfere?* (Newark, Del.: International Reading Association, 1973).
33. Kathleen S. Jongsma and Eugene A. Jongsma, "Test Review: Commercial Informal Reading Inventories," *Reading Teacher* 34 (March 1981):697–705.
34. Joseph L. Vaughan, Jr., and Paula J. Gaus, "Secondary Reading Inventory: A Modest Proposal," *Journal of Reading* 21 (May 1978):716–20.
35. Ibid., p. 718.
36. Ruth Strang and Dorothy Kendall Bracken, *Making Better Readers* (Boston: D. C. Heath, 1957), pp. 223–32.
37. Reproduced with the permission of Jerome Flescher, reading consultant, Newfield High School, Selden, N.Y.
38. Gerald Leinwand, *The Pageant of World History* (Boston: Allyn and Bacon, 1967).
39. Ruth Strang, "Scientific Method in Reading Science," *Science Education* 29 (March 1945):72–77.
40. Strang, McCullough, and Traxler, *Improvement of Reading*, pp. 167–69.
41. "The American Desert, 1955," *Time* (July 25, 1955), pp. 44–53. Reprinted by permission from TIME, The Weekly Newsmagazine, copyright Time Inc.
42. Reproduced with the permission of Jerome Flescher, reading consultant, Newfield High School, Selden, N.Y.
43. Ruth G. Viox, *Evaluating Reading and Study Skills in the Secondary Classroom*, Reading Aids Series, ed. Vernon L. Simula (Newark, Del: International Reading Association, 1968). Reprinted with the permission of Ruth G. Viox and the International Reading Association.
44. William M. Smallwood, Ida L. Reveley, and Guy A. Bailey, *Elements of Biology*, revised by Ruth A. Dodge (Boston: Allyn and Bacon, 1965).
45. Ibid., pp. 37–38.
46. Ibid., pp. 14–18, 20–25, 31–33, 42–46, 48–51.
47. Ellen Lamar Thomas and H. Alan Robinson, *Improving Reading in Every Class*, 3rd ed. (Boston: Allyn and Bacon, 1982), pp. 24–26, 203–5 (abridged ed., pp. 171–74).
48. Ibid., pp. 203–4 (abridged ed., p. 172).
49. Carl B. Smith, Sharon L. Smith, and Larry Mikulecky, *Teaching Reading in Secondary School Content Subjects: A Bookthinking Process* (New York: Holt, Rinehart and Winston, 1978), p. 338.
50. Leslie Hendrickson, "Procedures and Results of an Evaluation of Writing," *Educational Evaluation and Policy Analysis* 2 (July–August 1980):19.
51. John C. Mellon, *National Assessment and the Teaching of English* (Urbana, Ill.: National Council of Teachers of English, 1975), p. 23.
52. Smith, Smith, and Mikulecky, *Teaching Reading*, pp. 334–38.
53. Ibid., pp. 334–35. © 1978 by Holt, Rinehart and Winston. All rights reserved. Reprinted by permission of Holt, Rinehart and Winston.
54. Ibid., pp. 336–37.
55. Roger McCaig, "A District-Wide Plan for the Evaluation of Student Writing," in *Perspectives on Writing in Grades 1–8*, ed. Shirley Haley-James, (Urbana, Ill.: National Council of Teachers of English, 1981), p. 7.
56. Ibid., p. 22.
57. Hendrickson, "Procedures and Results," p. 20.
58. Strang, *Diagnostic Teaching of Reading*, pp. 75–96.
59. Ibid., pp. 86–87. Reprinted by permission.

60. Ibid., p. 87.
61. Thomas and Robinson, *Improving Reading*, 3rd ed., p. 11 (abridged ed., p. 13).
62. Ibid., p. 203 (abridged ed., p. 171).
63. Strang, *Diagnostic Teaching of Reading*, pp. 87–88. Reprinted by permission.
64. Thomas and Robinson, *Improving Reading*, 3rd ed., pp. 372–73. Reprinted by permission.

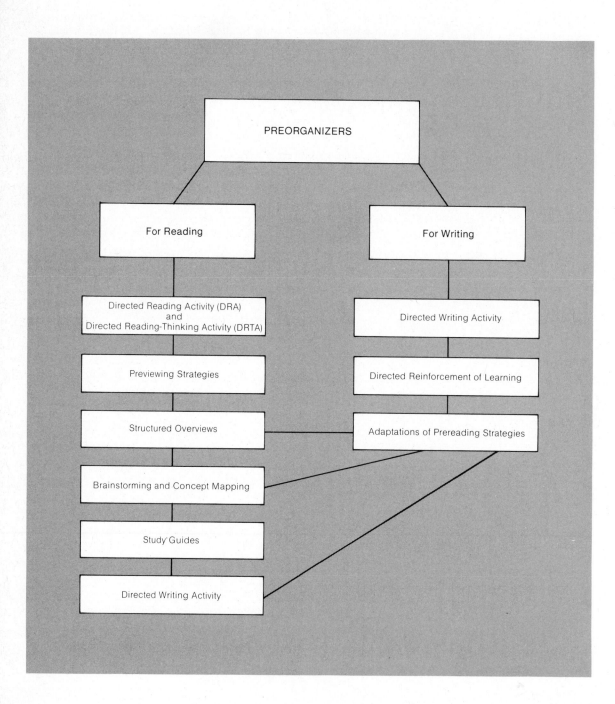

3
Prereading and
Prewriting Strategies

As early as 1660 Hoole, in his *New Discovery of the Old Art of Teaching School*, admonished that when a student was to read a chapter in the Scriptures, the teacher should "acquaint him a little with the matter beforehand, for that will entice him to read it, and make him more observant of what he reads."[1]

Since that time, intermittently, educators have been concerned with preparation or readiness for reading. Usually this preparation has been applied to basal reading lessons in the elementary grades, although some of the strategies have permeated lessons with other textbooks in the middle school and, to some degree, in the junior and senior high schools. In the main, however, few preparatory steps have found their way into content area classrooms. Unfortunately the major approach to a textbook chapter still appears to be: "Read pages 24 through 43 and come to class tomorrow with answers to the twelve questions at the end of the chapter."

In composing or composition writing, practices of the past seem dismal with regard to preparatory steps. There is little evidence of much activity beyond assigning a topic, possibly clarifying it, and—at times—beginning the writing in class. In a recent study of writing in the secondary school,

> the amount of time devoted to prewriting activities averaged just over 3 minutes. That included everything from the time the teacher began introducing the topic until the first student began to write. Those 3 minutes were spent writing the essay topic on the board, or passing out and reading through a dittoed assignment sheet, followed by student questions about task dimensions: "How long does it have to be?" "Can I write in pencil?" "Do I *have* to do this?"[2]

The teacher's role in reading and writing tasks is more important *before* the actual activity begins than during or after the activity. Helping readers marshall and organize what they know about a broad topic in advance improves comprehension in reading and production in writing. The discourse-processing theorists (theorists concerned with the ways readers comprehend text) speak of *schemata* as the organization of prior knowledge about a multitude of "objects, situations, events, sequences of events, actions and sequences of actions."[3] A *schema* (singular of schemata) "is a data structure . . . representing the generic concepts stored in memory."[4] When a reader or writer possesses a schema that can be activated to accomplish a reading or writing task, the teacher may not be needed at all or may be needed simply to stimulate the activation. But when a student does not have a schema to bring to the task (or has only an incomplete or inadequate one), then the teacher must help the student build a schema prior to the study task. The prospective reader or writer will be unsuccessful without a cognitive map. In most study situations, reading and writing tasks should not be initial activities for most students. Prereading and prewriting strategies should precede the actual reading and/or writing task.

PREORGANIZERS

In this chapter prereading and prewriting strategies aimed at developing and/or activating schemata are called *preorganizers*. The notion of a preorganizer was first introduced by Ausubel. He used the term *advance organizer* as a passage or statement to be read by a learner in advance of material to be studied.[5] The passage or statement was to be written at a higher level of generality than the material to be studied. In this way it could provide what Ausubel called an "ideational scaffolding" for the information to be studied and could mobilize related concepts already established in the learner's schema.[6]

In this volume I use the term *preorganizer* to include any structured prewriting or prereading activities undertaken to build, strengthen, and activate schemata. Teachers will find it most necessary to develop preorganizers (1) where students are to study material that is particularly complex and beyond their present experience; (2) when the material to be read is poorly organized; (3) when the assignment is new or difficult; (4) when the form and/or content of a composition to be written is abstract or new.

Of course, in the interest of developing independent learners, it behooves the instructor to move as fast as possible toward assisting students in developing their own preorganizers. The remainder of this chapter considers both teacher-directed and student-directed preorganizers for approaching reading and writing tasks.

PREORGANIZERS FOR READING ASSIGNMENTS

DIRECTED READING ACTIVITY

A directed reading activity (DRA) at the secondary school level usually consists of the following steps: (1) preparation for reading, (2) guided silent reading, (3) rereading when needed, (4) skill development, and (5) independent reinforcement or practice activities.[7] The first two steps act as preorganizers. In the preparation step students discuss the title and hypothesize about the possible content of the selection to be read. The teacher introduces, in some type of context, some of the key words or phrases to be met in the reading as a means of both helping students understand them and enhancing prediction about content. The teacher, sometimes with the aid of the students, sets specific purposes for the reading. In step 2 the teacher, again with the collaboration of students, directs students to find the answers to specific questions as they read. Although students may play a role in generating some of the ideas and questions, the teacher orchestrates and conducts.

DIRECTED READING-THINKING ACTIVITY

In a directed reading-thinking activity (DRTA), students glance through the selection and then hypothesize about the content.[8] (In the beginning stages, the teacher may instruct students unused to generating their own predictions from text how to survey material and how to generate questions.) After students have stated their hypotheses, they must defend them to the best of their ability. Following this discussion, students read to affirm their predictions. They may stop and reevaluate their hypotheses. Although there is a resemblance between the DRA and DRTA, the DRTA is largely directed by the students themselves.

PREVIEWING OR SURVEYING

As an aid to proficiency in using the DRTA and as a preorganizer standing on its own merit, previewing (sometimes called surveying) is of great value. It helps students to see the forest before the trees—that is, to become conscious of text structure and content. It stimulates hypothesis making. The teacher will want to direct the previewing steps carefully and over time before asking students to use previewing independently. Nevertheless, the ultimate goal is to have students preview on their own when preparing to study. Previewing is most useful with expository materials, although it also serves a purpose with some narrative material—other than O. Henry–like short stories.

Previewing may be defined as an organized preliminary look at the material to be studied, whether it be an entire book, a chapter, a section, or an article. The instructor should always use the strategy in introducing a new book or periodical and should keep on using it with chapters and other study-reading assignments until students take on the task rather automatically and independently.

Previewing a Book.   At the beginning of the school year or whenever an instructor plans to introduce a new book to the group, time should be taken to have students become familiar with it. A session or two spent exploring the terrain provides a "set" for purposeful reading. When considering a new text, in addition to teacher evaluation, a session of exploration with a group of students might demonstrate the suitability or lack of suitability of the text for those students or students similar to them.

Title.   Frequently a brief stop to consider the title of a book is useful, for students can review related information that they may possess. Also, many titles have subtitles that help to delineate the subject. Sometimes the subtitle carries little additional meaning, as in *Mathematics: A Modern Approach*; sometimes the subtitle is specific about the plan of the book, as in *French: An Oral Approach*; and at times a subtitle might even define the subject of the book broadly, as in *Biology: An Inquiry into the Nature of Life*.

Preliminary Material.   Noting the date of publication or revision assists students in realizing what information might not be included, which is particularly important in history and science texts. Information about the authors can be perused rather quickly just to assure the readers that the book has been written by experts. Students should read the preface to learn as much as possible about the author's objectives, the overall contents of the book, and the organizational plan. Occasionally, a special students' preface will emphasize organizational aids of value in reading the book.

Table of Contents.   Readers should be helped to realize that a table of contents provides a broad map that, when surveyed, gives a pretty good picture of the book. When a table of contents is divided into units, they can see how each of the chapters within a unit relates to it. Most tables of contents also have some descriptive information about each chapter, which students should note. When first getting students used to understanding the importance of a table of contents, the instructor may ask them to answer several questions that can be handled without reading further in the book. The total table of contents or a section such as the one in Example 3.1 may be used for this purpose.

Introductions.   Writers often clue readers into what they consider most significant through the use of introductions to units and chapters. Often questions are raised that permit the reader to focus on major concepts. At times, especially as an introduction to a chapter, an example is cited to dramatically place the writer's overall message in clear view at the outset. Occasionally a picture is used with some verbal material to introduce the major idea. More frequently, a unit or chapter is succinctly summarized, which permits readers to gain an understanding of "what the book is all about" as they preview each unit and/or chapter.

Typographical Aids.   Print size and style are useful aids in previewing. Large, bold unit and chapter titles are helpful, as are the headings of each section. In surveying a book, paying attention to other subheadings would normally be too time consuming and probably not very profitable; however, the reader should heed the headings, usually at the ends of chapters, that are standard for a given book. Frequently, such stock headings as "Questions" and "Vocabulary" are useful to glance through, even if just to realize what the writers consider important.

Example 3.1 *Previewing a Table of Contents*[9]

Unit VI   Evolution

Possible questions:
1.   What are the major topics in this unit?
2.   Why do you think the unit contains topics?
3.   Will you learn about the process of evolution? Beginning on what page?
4.   You probably already know something about evolution. Which subtopics seem to introduce topics that may be new to you?

Graphics.   Figures, tables, pictures, and the like, may contribute useful information during the previewing of a book. It does not pay to attempt to preview all the graphic displays, but the instructor might pick out a few ahead of time that seem valuable in terms of the overall concepts being developed or that are particularly stimulating. For example, in *Biology: An Inquiry into the Nature of Life*, Figure 26–5, reproduced here in Figure 3.1, is a representation of primate evolution—"a human family tree."[10] A moment or two spent perusing the figure places the chapter "The Human Species" into perspective and makes the reader aware that the text will delve further into the matter.

Summaries.   Reading a biology textbook is not the same as reading an O. Henry short story. The preview should contribute as much information as possible to make subsequent study more purposeful and comprehensible. There

Figure 3.1   Previewing a Figure

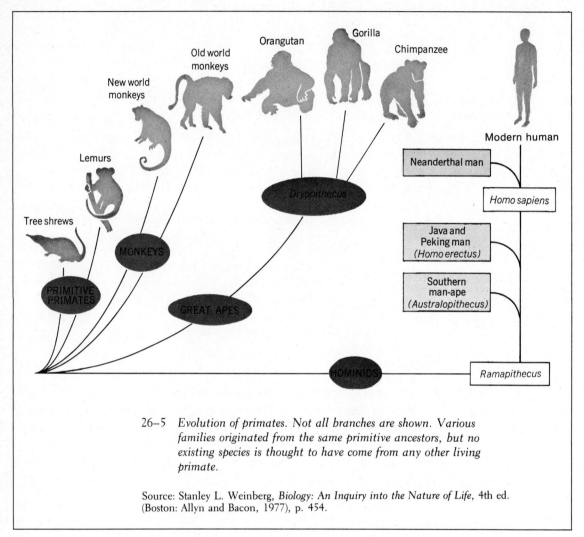

26–5   *Evolution of primates. Not all branches are shown. Various families originated from the same primitive ancestors, but no existing species is thought to have come from any other living primate.*

Source: Stanley L. Weinberg, *Biology: An Inquiry into the Nature of Life,* 4th ed. (Boston: Allyn and Bacon, 1977), p. 454.

is no need for an element of surprise. Therefore, the more summaries the students can pinpoint when previewing a book, the more useful the preview procedure will be.

Textbook writers frequently place summary paragraphs or sections at the ends of chapters and/or units. If, in a teacher-directed survey, the summaries are in both places, attention should be focused on unit summaries, for the purpose is to provide an overall introduction to the book; too many summaries could block retention of major ideas. If the summaries are not placed in con-

Figure 3.2   Previewing a Figure

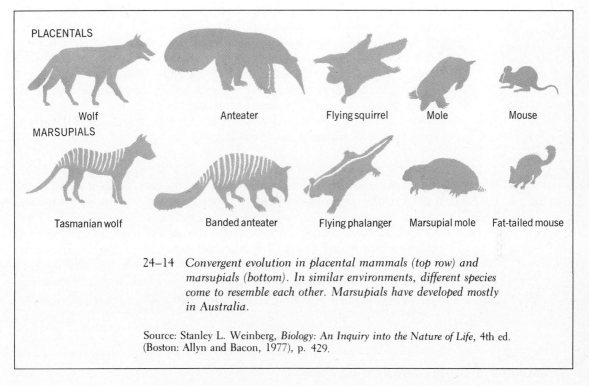

PLACENTALS

Wolf   Anteater   Flying squirrel   Mole   Mouse

MARSUPIALS

Tasmanian wolf   Banded anteater   Flying phalanger   Marsupial mole   Fat-tailed mouse

24–14   *Convergent evolution in placental mammals (top row) and marsupials (bottom). In similar environments, different species come to resemble each other. Marsupials have developed mostly in Australia.*

Source: Stanley L. Weinberg, *Biology: An Inquiry into the Nature of Life*, 4th ed. (Boston: Allyn and Bacon, 1977), p. 429.

sistent locations, the teacher should find a few to help readers synthesize some of the ideas as well as to point out that when they preview by themselves, they need to be on the lookout for summaries. Sometimes a "summary" is in reality a conclusion, where the opinions of the writers and factual information are intermixed; instructors will want to help students recognize such writing patterns and learn to separate facts from opinions.

Terminal Aids.   Readers should be directed to the concluding parts of the book. The use of such elements should be emphasized, for they may become particularly valuable in independent study. Most books will have indexes; many will have glossaries; others—math books especially—will have useful tables. Students who do not know how to use these aids, as well as those who rarely turn to them, should receive guidance in the form of specific exercises in order to be "turned on" to their significance.

During the preview period, students can be presented with brief problems that will give them more insights into what the book has to say and at the same time will accustom them to using some terminal aids. For instance, in the biology book that has been used as an example, one of the questions at the end of the chapter "The History of Life" can be used as part of the preview situation: "Using plant and animal examples, explain what is meant by convergent evolution." The question necessitates use of terminal aids while it also causes exploration of a major concept. In seeking the answer, students will find that the index does not list "Convergent evolution," but that the term is defined in the glossary. They will find that looking under the entry "Evolution" in the index will bring them to the subtopic "convergent." They can then read the short section about convergent evolution on page 429 of the text and study the accompanying figure (24–14) shown here in Figure 3.2 (page 73), prior to formulating their response to the question.[11]

Previewing a Chapter or an Article.   Directing the previewing of a unit shorter than a book is similar in many ways to directing the previewing of a book: think about the title; read introductions; use typographical aids; peruse graphics; and read summaries or conclusions. However, experience in previewing a book will not automatically "transfer" to the chapter or article level. Readers need to become indoctrinated into the important procedure of intelligent survey prior to study. Example 3.2, based on the text *Earth, Science*, serves as an illustration of a guided preview through a chapter.[12] A review of the steps in previewing, with an example from a social studies text, may be found in Thomas and Robinson.[13]

Example 3.2   *Previewing a Chapter*

Ms. Baxter, while teaching an eighth grade science class, realized that some of her students considered natural resources to be unlimited, despite the current anxieties voiced in the mass media and elsewhere. She provided each student with a copy of *Earth Science* (Challenges to Science program, McGraw-Hill) and guided the previewing of Chapter 15, "The Future of Our Natural Resources." She planned to have them study the chapter following the preview for further intensive study in class.

There was some discussion of the title in relation to their earlier informal discussions of what a number of students had called "the make-believe energy crisis." Students raised several questions, which Ms. Baxter placed on the blackboard as possible purposes for study—to search for the answers. A two-paragraph introduction read by all students appeared to dissolve the "make-believe" hypothesis immediately by facing students with the reality of the problem. In the introduction the authors also established two purposes for studying the chapter. In thumbing through the chapter, the students discovered that there were two main headings—one a statement "Population" and the other a question "How Do We Use Our Natural Resources?". They discussed the possible reasons for and meanings of those headings. Under the question they also noted three subheadings—"Metals," "Fossil fuels," and "Other energy sources"—and talked them over. They considered the meaning of *fossil fuels* and found they knew more about the topic than they had realized at first glance.

They spotted a question in the running context within the section "Other Energy Sources" and agreed that some possible solutions would be offered. Within that section they also noted words in dark bold type. Some of the students felt they had some knowledge about the terms, but all realized they would have to read carefully to be sure of the meanings of *nuclear fission, breeder reactor,* and *nuclear fusion.*

One student suggested that the line graph accompanying the small section headed "Population," along with its caption, was frightening as it showed what could happen without controls on population growth. Other students could not understand what that meant; all decided that the section and the graph needed to be studied carefully when they read on their own.

Ms. Baxter asked the group whether the information at the end of the chapter was helpful as a preview aid. The three terms the students had already noted were listed under "Key Words." Students agreed that it would be worthwhile to check such a section when reading a chapter on their own to be sure they had noted the same terms the authors wanted to pinpoint. They felt that the section of questions headed "Check Your Facts" raised some questions they hadn't thought about that could be added to their study guide—purpose-setting questions listed on the board, which each student wrote in a notebook. The students especially like the section at the end of the chapter headed "Applying What You Have Learned." They felt it was good to have read those questions in advance of study, for it led them to do more thinking about the content.

The instructor might even discuss rates of reading with students following the preview. Students should be helped to realize that they can vary their rates of reading in terms of purpose. There is no need to study at a snail's pace if they can pick up the essential ideas rather quickly. On the other hand, students will want to slow down as they arrive at each exercise to be sure that the directions are clear. They will, of course, also want to "slow down to a walk" when they do not understand something; they ought to know that it is perfectly sensible to reread a complex statement and even, if they need to do so, to read it out loud if that strategy helps.

The two approaches that follow, *ReQuest* and *PRep*, are variations of previewing particularly useful at a chapter or an article level. They do not require investigation of text structure but put a great deal of desirable emphasis on helping students tap their prior knowledge in an organized fashion.

THE REQUEST PROCEDURE

In the "ReQuest" procedure, students read the first sentence in a selection silently and take turns asking the teacher questions about that sentence.[14] Then the teacher also asks questions, thereby serving as a model of good questioning. Students may go on using the same procedure for several sentences until they can answer the following: "What do you think is going to happen in the rest of the selection? Why? (That is, what have you read that allows you to make a guess?)"[15] Students then read to confirm or reject their predictions.

PRE-READING PLAN

In the "Pre-Reading Plan" (PRep), the teacher selects a word, phrase, or picture about a key concept in the material to be studied.[16] Group discussion is encouraged through three steps:

1. The teacher says: *Tell us anything that comes to mind when* (you hear this word, see this picture, and so on). Students are each given a turn to contribute an idea, and responses are written on the board.

2. Each student is then asked: *What made you think of* (his or her given response)?

3. Students are then told to consider all the ideas and asked: *Based on our discussion, have you any new ideas about* (the word, the picture, and so on)?

STRUCTURED OVERVIEW

In the preorganizer known as a structured overview, as reported by Earle, key vocabulary is "arranged to show relationships among the terms and the relationships of the vocabulary to the structure of the disciplines."[17] Teachers are instructed to:

1. Select every word used in the unit that is necessary to the students' comprehension.

2. Take the word list and arrange the words to form a diagram that shows the relationship among ideas in the unit as well as their relationship to the semester's work.

3. On the first day of studying the unit, draw the diagram on the chalkboard. While doing this, explain why you arranged the words as you did and get the students to contribute as much information as they can.

4. Throughout the unit, as it seems appropriate and comfortable, refer to the structured overview. It may be helpful to sketch portions of it on the chalkboard. The object here is to aid the students in their attempt to organize the information in a meaningful way.[18]

Vacca discussed a structured overview constructed by Joseph Janoch, a ninth-grade social studies teacher in Lyons Township High School, LaGrange, Illinois.[19] In Figure 3.3, Vacca pointed out: (1) the hierarchy of major concepts,

Figure 3.3   A Structured Overview

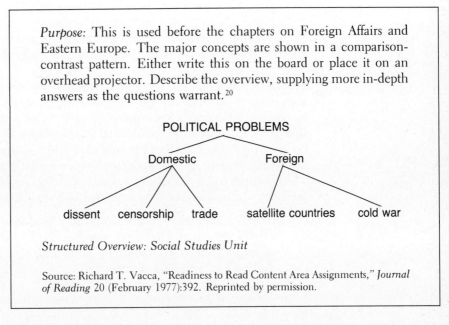

Purpose: This is used before the chapters on Foreign Affairs and Eastern Europe. The major concepts are shown in a comparison-contrast pattern. Either write this on the board or place it on an overhead projector. Describe the overview, supplying more in-depth answers as the questions warrant.[20]

POLITICAL PROBLEMS

Domestic   Foreign

dissent   censorship   trade   satellite countries   cold war

Structured Overview: Social Studies Unit

Source: Richard T. Vacca, "Readiness to Read Content Area Assignments," *Journal of Reading* 20 (February 1977):392. Reprinted by permission.

(2) the connections between the concepts as presented in the selection to be read, and (3) the comparison pattern expressed implicitly in the structured overview. He suggested that "the structured overview provides a visual map, a network, that permits students to see the relatedness of the important concepts in an overall unit or specific reading assignment to be studied."[21]

BRAINSTORMING

Brainstorming requires a group situation. Students in the group contribute ideas about a topic (the subject of subsequent reading) stimulated by teacher questions, titles or headings from the selection, excerpts that are interesting, or experiences with nonprint materials. (Langer's PRep is also an example of brainstorming, at a highly structured level.)

Headings.   Occasionally the title of or a heading in a selection will command attention by its unusualness or significance. If the heading can be used profitably to focus attention on what is to be read, the teacher may write it on the board or point to it in the selection. Frequently, it may be the title of the material to be read.

For example, in a seventh-grade social studies textbook, a chapter was entitled "The Ship of State Is Launched." Even a brief discussion of this title focuses attention and clarifies the intent of the chapter. A question often serves the same purpose—for instance, "What Is Disease?" used as a heading in a tenth-grade biology textbook. The first subheading, "Misspellings We Are Born With," in a chapter about spelling might focus the high school students' attention on the chapter. Such headings are worth some discussion time, for the ensuring reading will be more purposeful and profitable.

Excerpts.   Often an excerpt from a selection, particularly from literature, is interesting or different enough to capture the groups attention. It is frequently an opening statement or short paragraph, but it may actually be taken from any part of the material to be read or studied. Sometimes the instructor may write the excerpt on the blackboard or may read it to the group. It can then be used as a taking-off place for developing readiness to read and/or to study the selection. The following passage from an essay was placed on the blackboard and left there for a day; Curiosity certainly was piqued and attention focused:

> He was an undersized little man, with a head too big for his body—
> a sickly little man. His nerves were bad. He had skin trouble. It was
> agony for him to wear anything next to his skin coarser than silk.
> And he had delusions of grandeur. [22]

Nonprint Materials.   A pertinent, outstanding still picture (mounted or projected), a concrete object, or a brief filmstrip often serves to provoke interest and provide a stimulus for reading. For instance, a gilded apple sitting on the teacher's desk for a couple of days was responsible for much of a group's anticipation related to reading "Midas."

On occasion, particularly if the reading and/or study to be accomplished is comprehensive and significant, instructors might use excursions, classroom visitors with related experience, full-length movies, television programs, and recordings. They must be careful, however, that the readiness does not become weightier than the reading. Certainly if a great deal of study was to be made in the science of formation and effects of hurricanes, a motion picture or television program concerned with the topic would be useful as a readiness tool.

Nonprint experiences are often useful to poor readers, who may frequently be operating out of a limited experiential background. These focusing techniques permit weak readers to strengthen their abilities in the reading-study situation.

The term *nonprint* may even now be a dated concept. With the advent of the videodisc, which can be projected on a television screen, we already have a viable intermix of picture and words. One can see a film and read a book projected from the same disc. Even television presents words as well as pictures. Hence, the reader is able to get ready to accomplish a difficult reading-study job by using a combination of print and nonprint materials that can be used to give purpose and meaning to the assignment.

Concept Maps.   As indicated above, brainstorming will yield responses from students that teachers will want to write on the chalkboard in some organized way. Concept maps permit an organization of all the ideas without the con-

Figure 3.4   Forming a Concept Map

In preparation for reading a short expository selection entitled *Hound Dogs*, students looked at pictures of hounds and contributed their own ideas to a concept map. Notice the teacher did some rough organizing as the concept map developed on the chalkboard.

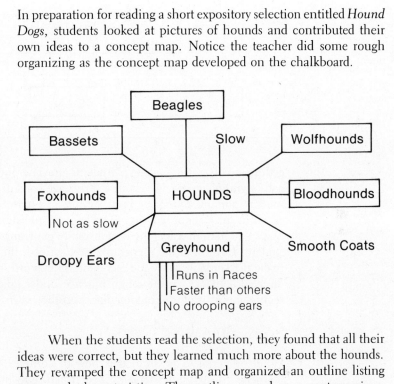

When the students read the selection, they found that all their ideas were correct, but they learned much more about the hounds. They revamped the concept map and organized an outline listing types and characteristics. The outline served as a postorganizer, replacing any need for specific comprehension questions from the teacher.

straints of a formal outline. Concept maps (sometimes called semantic maps,[23] semantic organizers,[24] or semantic webbing[25]) are similar to structured overviews but allow for more random ideas from the group. They seem extremely useful in permitting the group to see relationships among concepts and to make predictions about the selection. Student's search for confirmations or rejections of their ideas in addition to gaining ideas contributed by the author. (The diagrams at the beginning of each chapter in this book are types of concept maps.) The situation described in Figure 3.4 involved a group of "slow learners" in the ninth grade.

CONSTRUCT PROCEDURE

In the "ConStruct" procedure, Vaughan combines previewing, a type of structured overview, and concept mapping as a first step in study.[26] (His total pro-

Figure 3.5   A Graphic Overview

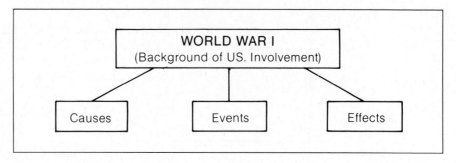

cedure involves three steps.) Students preview and construct what Vaughan calls a *graphic overview*, which at this stage consists of the major topic and the most important subtopics. The example in Figure 3.5 is Vaughan's. Students go on in subsequent readings to add details and subdetails to the concept map.

Vaughan transfers the responsibility of organizing the concept map to the student. In most of the preorganizers described, the teacher's aim should be to make the students study-independent. They need careful introductions, many directed activities, and enough practice under guidance before they will feel secure about using the preorganizers on their own.

STUDY GUIDES

When material to be studied is new or complex, and particularly for "slow learners," study guides lend needed structure to the material. "A study guide is a teaching aid written by the teacher to be used by the student to assist the student in developing reading skills for the purpose of enhancing comprehension of textual material."[27]

Authors of professional materials categorize study guides in different ways. The "types" described in Example 3.3 seem useful, as I see it:

Example 3.3   *Types of Study Guides*[28]

Process Guide

As viewed by Karlin, this type of guide "provides children with a 'teacher' who offers suggestions on how to read the material. It calls their attention to the skills they might need in order to resolve difficulties and makes them aware of skills they might otherwise ignore."[29]

For example, in this paragraph about chimpanzees (only a small portion of the text children might ordinarily study), Karlin suggested duplicating questions and comments on strips of paper that could be lined up with the text:[30]

You may have seen chimpanzees on television or at a zoo. These primates are taught many tricks and are very smart. Chimpanzees are not monkeys but are apes. Apes do not have tails, but monkeys do. Apes have larger brains and are smarter than monkeys. There are four kinds of apes, two from Asia and two from Africa. The chimpanzee is from Africa. Chimpanzees live in bands of as many as 30. They are good climbers and can swing from limb to limb, but spend most of their time on the ground. They build nests in trees to spend the night. Chimpanzees mostly eat plant foods, but will eat smaller animals, termites, and eggs. In one part of Africa, chimpanzees have been seen to hunt, kill, and eat colobus monkeys.[31]

a contrast

Who are they?

important details

The word but is a signal. What does it tell you?

Content Guide

Karlin suggested that another broad type of study guide could be called the content guide. This type of guide focuses attention on the content and establishes purposes for reading. It could also be used in place of teacher-directed discussion following a reading. "In that case, children would respond to the items in the guide after they have read the chapter or section."[32] Or, as Karlin demonstrated in a discussion of such a guide, the guidesheet could have purpose-setting questions *as well as* response questions following reading.

For a selection about chimpanzees and other apes, the guide might read like this:

Read question number one, answer it on your paper, and then go to number two, three, and four. The page and paragraph numbers for each question are in parentheses.

1. How are chimps similar to and different from human beings? (page 271: paragraphs two, three, and seven)
2. How do apes communicate? Is there a chimpanzee language? (page 272: all paragraphs but the last one)

Example 3.3 (continued)

Example 3.3 (continued)

3.   Compare the orangutan, the chimpanzee, and the gorilla. (pages 272–74: last paragraph on p. 272 through first paragraph on p. 274)
4.   What makes you think chimpanzees are intelligent? (page 271 through first paragraph on page 274)

After reading the selection and answering the four questions, do one of the following:

1.   Draw a picture of the chimpanzee accompanied by a paragraph describing the chimpanzee. Make sure the paragraph includes any details you couldn't manage to show in the picture.
2.   Write a newspaper article with the headline, *Chimps Talk!* Be sure you are perfectly clear so your reading audience knows exactly what you mean.
3.   Organize a chart with four headings: Human Beings; Chimpanzees; Orangutans; Gorillas. List the characteristics of each in detail. You may need to use some of your own knowledge about human beings.

Individualized Guides

In this type of guide, the types of questions suggested for content guides may be used, but they are not directed toward the content of a given selection or book. The teacher suggests a number of references at a range of readability levels that contain similar information. Pupils may refer to one or more books or magazines, suggested by the teacher, which may be found in the classroom or in the school library. Teachers may want to suggest to some pupils that they try certain references suited to their abilities. Pupils are at liberty to find additional references that speak to the questions.

Alternative Guide Formats

Most guides feature specific questions for pupils to answer, as above. There are several interesting alternatives.

A study guide may be introduced through a closure technique:

You are going to read about three types of apes. The chimpanzee is most like the _____ being. Chimps seem to "speak" a _____ and appear to be quite _____. Learn about the _____ and its closeness to humans. Then learn how the orangutan and gorilla _____ differ from the _____ and from human beings.

The closure technique may also be used effectively as a response procedure following the reading: Example—The chimp shows its _____ by learning

many tasks and by learning how to communicate through a type of
_____.

. . . , Herber decried the use of direct questions for pupils who did not have the experience to bring to the material.[33] For such pupils, types of statements suggested by Herber might be utilized in a study guide prior to reading. For example:

> *Read each of the three statements below. Then read the material about chimpanzees and apes. Check each statement you believe to be true according to what the material stated. Defend each answer on your paper—those you believe to be true according to the material and those that you do not feel are true.*
>
> _____ 1. Chimpanzees and monkeys are the same.
> _____ 2. Chimpanzees eat smaller animals, termites, and eggs.
> _____ 3. Chimpanzees eat colobus monkeys.

DIRECTED WRITING ACTIVITY

My directed writing activity, as a preorganizer for reading, consists of the following steps: (1) Choose a major concept from the selection to be read and have students use brainstorming, concept mapping, and/or organized notes to indicate their knowledge and pinpoint their questions. (2) Ask students to write a paragraph or more indicating what they feel their present organized knowledge about the major concept consists of. (3) Have students form teams for peer conferences to review each other's paragraphs and to ask for, or suggest, clarifications. Emphasis should be placed on content, not mechanics, or writing. (4) Then have students read to confirm or reject their predictions and to look for new information.

PREORGANIZERS FOR WRITING ASSIGNMENTS

DIRECTED WRITING ACTIVITY

The directed writing activity may be used as a preorganizer (only step 1 is the preorganizer) for writing in this way: (1) Review two or more major interrelated concepts that have interlaced and permeated class activities over a period of time. Use brainstorming, concept mapping, and/or organized notes to have students share their knowledge. (This may also be done by one student or a team of students independent of the teacher.) (2) Drawing on their knowledge—organized in some form—ask students to compose a first draft demonstrating their ability to highlight and integrate the major ideas. (3) Have students review each other's essays intent on learning more from the compositions of others while asking questions if points in the compositions are not clear. (4) Have students share a second draft with peers and the instructor in an effort to make the composition as clear as possible. Content and mechanics should now be considered. (5) Ask students to submit the third and final draft to the instructor.

DIRECTED REINFORCEMENT OF LEARNING

Although a major effort should be placed on using writing as a creative learning tool, there are times when it serves a vital reinforcement role. Directed reinforcement of learning is a replacement for individual questions at the ends of chapters or on worksheets. Directed reinforcement of learning might be considered a way of checking on a student's comprehension of a given reading, listening, or viewing assignment.

The steps are as follows: (1) In one of the ways suggested elsewhere in this chapter, have students tap (usually with direction) their schemata in preparation for reading a selection, listening to a lecture, or viewing a visual or audiovisual presentation of some kind. (2) Assign one or more writing-composing tasks to be completed after the reading, listening, or viewing. Tasks may vary from asking students to complete a paragraph from a topic sentence you provide to having students write a short essay comparing two points of view emphasized in the material. (3) Although only the first two steps serve as the preorganizer, the next step would be to have students complete the writing tasks. This type of writing would be evaluated by the teacher only on the basis of clarity of thought, organization, and adequacy of content—not on mechanics.

ADAPTATIONS OF PREREADING STRATEGIES

Some of the strategies suggested in this chapter as preorganizers for reading can easily and beneficially be adapted for writing. Langer's *Pre-Reading Plan (PRep)* can become a prewriting plan unattached to a reading selection. The structured overview (pages 76–77) can be built in relation to a writing rather than a reading task. Brainstorming and concept mapping (pages 77–78) are naturals, of course, for prewriting advance organizers. Writing assignments that deal with new, complex, or abstract ideas—as such reading-study tasks—demand thoughtful advance organizing.

QUESTIONS
AND
RELATED
ACTIVITIES

1. Define *schema* and *schemata* as you understand the terms.

2. Choose one of the preorganizers for reading and develop a lesson based on material used in your classroom or material available to you related to the age of youngsters you plan to teach.

3. Choose one of the preorganizers for writing and develop a lesson based on a topic relevant and of probable interest to students you teach or plan to teach.

SELECTED
READINGS

Barron, Richard, and Rose Cooper. "Effects of Advance Organizers and Grade Level upon Information Acquisition from an Instructional-Level General Science Passage." In *Diversity in Mature Reading: Theory and Research*, edited by Phil L. Nacke, pp. 78–82. Twenty-second Yearbook of the National Reading Conference, 1973.

Bean, Thomas W., and Rick Pardi. "A Field Test of a Guided Reading Strategy." *Journal of Reading* 23 (November 1979):144–47.

Daigon, Arthur. "From Reading to Writing." In *Reading Through Content*, edited by Richard T. Vacca and Judith A Meagher, pp. 117–20. Storrs: Reading-Study Center, University of Connecticut, 1979.

Estes, Thomas H., and others. "Three Methods of Introducing Students to a Reading-Learning Task in Two Content Subjects." In *Research in Reading in the Content Areas: First Year Report*, edited by Harold L. Herber and Peter L. Sanders. Syracuse, N.Y.: Syracuse University Reading and Language Arts Center, 1969.

Hansell, T. Stevenson. "Increasing Understanding in Content Reading." *Journal of Reading* 19 (January 1976):309–10.

Homer, Cynthia L. "A Directed Reading-Thinking Activity for Content Areas." In *Reading Through Content*, edited by Richard T. Vacca and Judith A. Meagher, pp. 104–9. Storrs: Reading-Study Center, University of Connecticut, 1979.

Karahalios, Sue M.; Marian J. Tonjes; and John C. Towner. "Using Advance Organizers to Improve Comprehension of a Content Text." *Journal of Reading* 22 (May 1979):706–8.

Lange, Bob. "Making Sense with Schemata." *Journal of Reading* 24 (February 1981):442–45.

Langer, Judith A. "Facilitating Text Processing: The Elaboration of Prior Knowledge." ERIC ED 188171, 1980.

Lewis, Jill S. "Directed Discovery Learning: Catalyst to Reading in the Content Areas." *Journal of Reading* 22 (May 1979):714–19.

Lexier, Kenneth. "Concept Learning in the Content Classroom." In *Reading Through Content*, edited by Richard T. Vacca and Judith A. Meagher, pp. 51–59. Storrs: Reading-Study Center, University of Connecticut, 1979.

Luiten, John; Wilbur Ames; and Gary Ackerman. "A Meta-Analysis of the Effects of Advance Organizers on Learning and Retention." *American Educational Research Journal* 17 (Summer 1980):211–18.

Manzo, Anthony V. "Guided Reading Procedure." *Journal of Reading* 18 (January 1975):287–91.

———. "The ReQuest Procedure." *Journal of Reading* 13 (November 1969):123–26, 163.

McClain, Leslie J. "Study Guides: Potential Assets in Content Classrooms." *Journal of Reading* 24 (January 1981):321–25.

Robinson, H. Alan, and Ellen Lamar Thomas, eds. *Fusing Reading Skills and Content*, pp. 14–15, 32–33, 67, 75–76, 108–9, 134, 148–49, 159, 178–79. Newark, Del.: International Reading Association, 1969.

Rumelhart, David E. "Schemata: The Building Blocks of Cognition." In *Theoretical Issues in Reading Comprehension*, edited by Rand J. Spiro, Bertram C. Bruce, and William F. Brewer, pp. 35–58. Hillsdale, N.Y.: Lawrence Erlbaum Associates, 1980.

Simmons, John S.; Robert E. Shafer; and Gail B. West. *Decisions about the Teaching of English*, pp. 53–63. Boston: Allyn and Bacon, 1976.

Smelstor, Marjorie, ed. "A Guide to Teaching the Writing Process from Pre-Writing to Editing." ERIC ED 176274, 1978.

Thelan, Judith. "Reading Textbooks: Close Encounters of the Worst Kind?" In *Reading Through Content*, edited by Richard T. Vacca and Judith A. Meagher, pp. 10–18. Storrs: Reading-Study Center, University of Connecticut, 1979.

Thomas, Ellen L., and H. Alan Robinson. *Improving Reading in Every Class*, 3rd ed., pp. 15–19, 53–74, 128–32, 164–67, 227–34, 264–73, 360–63; (abridged ed., 13–17, 47–57, 121–25, 153–58, 222–31, 295–98). Boston: Allyn and Bacon, 1982.

Tutolo, Daniel J. "The Study Guide: Types, Purpose and Value." *Journal of Reading* 20 (March 1977):503–7.

Vacca, Richard T. "Readiness to Read Content Area Assignments." *Journal of Reading* 20 (February 1977):387–92.

Vaughan, Joseph L., Jr. "The ConStruct Procedure Fosters Active Reading and Learning." Unpublished paper. February 1981.

NOTES

1. Charles A. Hoole, *New Discovery of the Old Art of Teaching School* (London: J.T. Crook, 1660; reprint ed., Syracuse, N.Y.: C.W. Bardeen, 1912, p. 52); cited by Nila B. Smith, *American Reading Instruction* (Newark, Del.: International Reading Association, 1965), p. 34.
2. Arthur N. Applebee and others, *A Study of Writing in the Secondary School*, Final Report NIE–G–79–0174 (Urbana, Ill.: National Council of Teachers of English, September 1980), pp. 106–7.
3. David E. Rumelhart, "Schemata: The Building Blocks of Cognition," in *Theoretical Issues in Reading Comprehension: Perspectives from Cognitive Psychology, Linguistics, Artificial Intelligence, and Education*, ed. Rand J. Spiro, Bertram C. Bruce, and William F. Brewer (Hillsdale, N.J.: Lawrence Erlbaum Associates, 1980), p. 34.
4. Ibid.
5. David Ausubel, "The Use of Advance Organizers in the Learning and Retention of Meaningful Verbal Material," *Journal of Educational Psychology* 51 (October 1960):267–72.
6. Francine Deitsch, "The Effect of Advance Organizers on Children's Processing of Text Structure" (Unpublished paper, Reading Department, Hofstra University, 1981), p. 109.
7. Emmett Betts, *Foundations of Reading Instruction* (New York: American Book Co., 1946).
8. Russell G. Stauffer, *Directing Reading Maturity as a Cognitive Process* (New York: Harper & Row, 1969).
9. Stanley L. Weinberg, *Biology: An Inquiry into the Nature of Life*, 4th ed. (Boston: Allyn and Bacon, 1977), pp. ix–x.
10. Ibid., p. 454.
11. Ibid., p. 429.

12. Robert L. Heller and others, *Earth Science* (New York: Webster Division, McGraw-Hill, 1973), pp. 229–305.
13. Ellen L. Thomas and H. Alan Robinson, *Improving Reading in Every Class*, 3rd ed. (Boston: Allyn and Bacon, 1982), pp. 173–76; (abridged version, pp. 153–57).
14. Anthony V. Manzo, "The ReQuest Procedure," *Journal of Reading* 13 (November 1969):123–26, 163.
15. Ibid., p. 125.
16. Judith A. Langer, "Facilitating Text Processing: The Elaboration of Prior Knowledge," ERIC ED 188171, 15, no. 11, November 1980.
17. Richard A. Earle, "Reading and Mathematics: Research in the Classroom," in *Fusing Reading Skills and Content*, ed. H. Alan Robinson and Ellen Lamar Thomas (Newark, Del.: International Reading Association, 1969), p. 164.
18. Adapted from Earle, "Reading and Mathematics," p. 166.
19. Richard T. Vacca, "Readiness to Read Content Area Assignments," *Journal of Reading* 20 (February 1977):387–92.
20. Ibid., p. 392.
21. Ibid., p. 392.
22. Deems Taylor, "The Monster" in *Modern American Essays*, ed. Sylvia Z. Brodkin and Elizabeth J. Pearson (New York: Globe Book Co., 1967), p. 253.
23. P. David Pearson and Dale D. Johnson, *Teaching Reading Comprehension* (New York: Holt, Rinehart and Winston, 1978), ch. 3.
24. Robert S. Pehrsson, "Semantic Organization: An Approach to Teaching Deaf Children How to Process Written Language" (Doctoral dissertation, Hofstra University, 1979).
25. Glenn Freedman and Elizabeth G. Reynolds, "Enriching Basal Reader Lessons with Semantic Webbing," *Reading Teacher* 33 (March 1980):677–84.
26. Joseph L. Vaughan, Jr., "The ConStruct Procedure Fosters Active Reading and Learning" (Unpublished paper, February 1981).
27. Daniel J. Tutolo, "The Study Guide: Types, Purpose and Value," *Journal of Reading* 20 (March 1977):503.
28. Reprinted by permission from Nila B. Smith and H. Alan Robinson, *Reading Instruction for Today's Children*, 2nd ed. (Englewood Cliffs, N.J.: Prentice-Hall, 1980), pp. 375–77.
29. Robert Karlin, *Teaching Elementary Reading: Principles and Strategies*, 2nd ed. (New York: Harcourt Brace Jovanovich, 1975), p. 264.
30. Ibid.
31. Neal J. Holmes and others, *Science: People, Concepts, Process* (New York: Webster Division, McGraw-Hill, 1974), p. 172.
32. Karlin, *Teaching Elementary Reading*, p. 265.
33. Harold L. Herber, *Teaching Reading in the Content Areas*, 2nd ed. (Englewood Cliffs, N.J.: Prentice-Hall, 1978), p. 194.

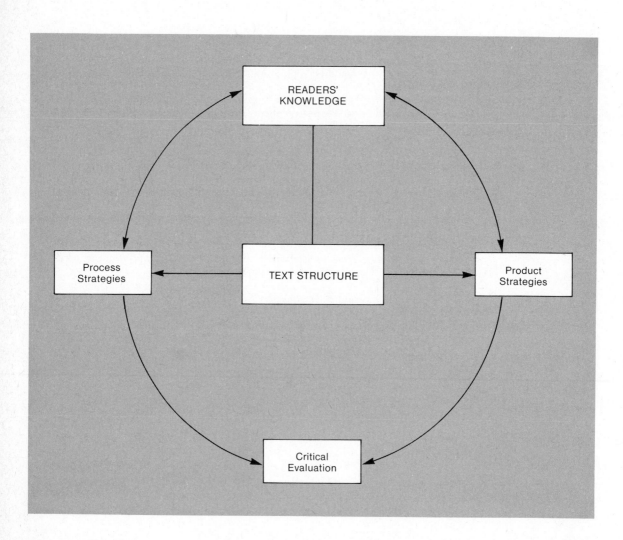

4

Comprehension Development and Comprehension Strategies

"Meaning is the starting point of the reading process as well as its end-product. . . ."[1] In each content area discussed in this book (Chapters 7–11), comprehension is emphasized as an interaction between reader and author or between writer and audience. In fact, certainly at this level, the term *reading* is synonymous with comprehending or discourse processing. Reading does not take place unless understanding is involved.

Comprehension is not a simple concept. It always involves memory—whether relatively short-term or over a long period. Since readers bring their backgrounds to what they read, comprehension involves not only an interaction but a construction or reconstruction of the author's message based on ideas the readers already have in their heads. The result is rarely the same for all readers unless the product is a given fact. The goal, of course, is understanding; but readers will have different ways of interpreting ideas. There is no absolute accuracy.

The key point here is that teachers often fail to realize that what is considered an appropriate understanding is likely to vary from context to context, that "accuracy of understanding" is relative. That is, criteria for "accuracy" should be considered a function of reader and text characteristics, as well as purposes of reading. It seems, then, that teachers need to understand that a "word-perfect" rendition of a text is rarely required and seems difficult to justify for any reading situation. When readers interact with text, they will and should acquire some information that was stated in the text and some information that they generate. Certainly there are situations for which it may be reasonable to expect a reader's understanding to remain close to the text; for example, when following a set of directions to build something. Alternatively, there are other situations for which it may be appropriate to expect a more personal interpretation; for example, when reading literature or poetry.[2]

**READERS'
KNOWLEDGE**

Tierney and Spiro pointed out three types of reading situations that necessitate different teaching strategies: (1) lack of background experience, (2) overreliance on prior knowledge, and (3) overreliance on the text.[3] *Lack, or inadequacy, of prior experience or knowledge* can make certain textual materials "unintelligible" for given readers. In this reading situation, teaching strategies—as suggested by Tierney and Rand and in Chapter 3 of this volume—should help to build appropriate knowledge and experience prior to reading or "provide an analogy by which the readers can build such backgrounds for themselves."[4]

Overreliance on prior knowledge is frequently the problem of gifted readers and others who possess a great deal of knowledge about the text to be read. They often assume they know all without interacting very much with the author. Tierney and Spiro suggest the following teaching strategies:

> In these situations, a teacher has several options: to alert the students to the need to read the material carefully; to have the students read the material in conjunction with carrying out some activity, the successful performance of which is dependent on careful reading; to provide the students with strategies such as outlining and note-taking for carefully reading the text; to alert the students to their own level of understanding and maybe to ways to monitor that understanding; or to force the students to construct an understanding, for example, through questioning their ideas.[5]

Overreliance on the text is often a problem for readers when the content is supposed to be very precise and they fear depending, to some extent, on their own knowledge. Overreliance may also be related to learning tasks that emphasize specific answers to factual questions. Here teachers ought to encourage "reader-text interaction either through discussion or through appropriate vicarious experience prior to, during, or after reading."[6]

**TEXT
STRUCTURE**

The structure or organization of the material to be read is a vital aspect of comprehension, since comprehension is an interaction between reader and author. Research tells us that "among texts, those that are more highly organized or more congruent with the reader's knowledge and expectations are better remembered."[7]

> Experimental psychologists have noted that readers' comprehension of text is very similar to the structures in the text itself. Ask people to recapitulate what they read in a story and they will tend to do so with the same structural form as the story, rather than with the same words or even "their own" words. Readers not particularly familiar with the genre scheme and discourse structure of a text, with the

grammar of the story, will not only fail to comprehend aspects of the text but will recapitulate what they did understand in forms closer to their own structures.[8]

Children appear to learn "story grammars" early, probably from listening to and viewing numerous stories over a number of years. A story grammar is "an idealized internal representation of the parts of a typical story and the relationships among those parts."[9] Or, as Smith defines story grammars:

> They are the framework upon which various characters, plots, motives, and resolutions are linked together in related episodes and represented in ways that will be intelligible. If a story makes sense to us, if it *sounds* like a story, this is not just because the story is appropriately told but also because we know the appropriate way in which stories are told, at least in our culture.[10]

Meyer, Brandt, and Bluth found good and average ninth-grade readers more sensitive to text structure than poor ninth-grade readers.[11] It would seem that for those students who have inadequate "story grammars" or who find a given story complex, instruction in story components might serve a useful purpose.

Developing adequate schemata for the structures in texts (other than the basic story) is another matter. The genre of literature (see Chapter 9) and the large variety of structures in other content areas present problems even for good readers. In addition, sometimes the material is poorly organized and hence contributes another hurdle to understanding. One approach to helping students understand the structure of such textual materials is to focus on the structure in a given content area text both prior to and during study of the text.

Just as in a story grammar, students need to learn that most chapters in texts have a text grammar consisting of three major components: (1) a short *beginning*, which introduces the major idea(s) to be developed in the bulk of the chapter and possibly hints at the way that information will be organized; (2) a lengthy *development* of several interrelated major ideas; and (3) a *conclusion*, which often summarizes major points and sometimes includes viewpoints of the authors. Students should be helped to build this schema even though they will meet some very poorly structured discourse. Kintsch and Kintsch add the notion that students need to develop *purpose schemata*, plans for coping with the specific purposes designated for reading given material.[12] Teachers need to help students build schemata for dealing with the kinds of questions they generate and the types of purposes they set for reading.

Some attention should also be given to the types of paragraphs or groups of paragraphs found within the structure of the text. Usually the basic unit for presenting meaning—certainly in content area texts—is the paragraph. This structural unit is an aid to the reader. At its best, it signals the beginning and end of one well-supported major idea; at its worst, it breaks up the mass of print into a more manageable unit.

Theoretically, a series of paragraphs should "add up" to a well-organized message the writer wishes to communicate. But sometimes individual paragraphs are not well constructed; sometimes more than one point is developed in a given paragraph—intentionally or unintentionally. Of course, perfectly constructed paragraphs, each opening with a topic sentence, completely supported, without diversions, are not always developed. In fact, reading perfectly structured paragraphs that all open with clearly stated topic sentences would be a bore. Nevertheless, whether the paragraphs are well organized or not, the reader trained to be on the lookout for specific functions of paragraphs as guideposts to meaning will have gained additional strategies for effective reading.

Aside from much of the literary material read in English classes and by individual students for enjoyment, most of the discourse read within the school curriculum is expository; hence, the greatest number of paragraphs have the function of explaining and informing. Such paragraphs present the steps in a process or sequence; state a chronology of events; give instructions for performance; present and relate causes and effects; cite problems and solutions; raise questions and give answers; state a group of details related to a previous paragraph; develop generalizations; and so on. In numerous cases the reading of such explanatory paragraphs must be coordinated with the reading of graphs, charts, tables, diagrams, and pictures presented on the same page or on a nearby page.

In all content areas, a substantial number of paragraphs function as definers. They, too, are usually expository in nature, but their purpose is to define a word, a group of words, or a larger concept. A smaller number of paragraphs within all content areas serve the significant functions of introducing ideas, forming transitions from one group of ideas to another, and summarizing and/ or concluding a discussion. Narrative and descriptive paragraphs are found occasionally within the framework of expository writing but, of course, are most often found in specific genres of literary composition. Persuasive paragraphs are generally found in editorials, essays, and primary source materials often used in history texts.

Knowledge of paragraph functions will not, of course, automatically result in expert reading, nor will the reader find that all paragraphs follow formulas. However, such knowledge should help readers to boost comprehension and develop a "feel" for the atmosphere or environment in which the message is communicated. Application of knowledge about paragraph structure is another tool for readers in setting purposes for what they are reading or about to read. Suggestions for developing some consciousness about various paragraph types may be found in the "Questions and Related Activities" section of this chapter.

COHESIVE TIES

In addition to the overall structure of texts or parts of text, specific language units used by authors to connect ideas are important to the reader in her or his attempts to comprehend. In fact, the absence or sparseness of such units—usually resulting in text that is more implicit than explicit—often causes comprehension problems for the poor reader, for the good reader attempting to process complex text, and for the bilingual reader who needs such signposts in a second language.

Halliday and Hasan define many types of cohesive ties.[13] Two types are discussed here, as they seem to need conscious attention when secondary school students are confronted with their content area textbooks. I have labeled these two types as *connectives* and *referents and antecedents*.

Connectives.   Rodgers introduced a discussion of conjunctive connectors in the following interesting way:

> Two men are talking casually; one mentions that he is going on vacation. Several ideas come into the mind of the second man: burglaries of empty homes are on the increase; the police are advising people to lock all doors and windows securely, leave a light burning and the radio playing, stop all deliveries, have a neighbor check the house at intervals.
>
>   What is the second man going to say? Is he going to advise his friend that, *"If* you don't want your house burgled, *then* . . ."? Or will he say, "Do these things, *otherwise* . . ."? Perhaps he speaks from experience and will say, *"Because* I didn't . . ."; alternatively, perhaps he did take precautions, *but*, *however*, *despite* doing so his house was still burgled. The information content of the man's comments is known to us—what we lack are the words that signal the relationships which he sees among his ideas. We know the pieces of his argument—what we do not see yet is the pattern into which his ideas will fall. We will not know the shape of that pattern until he gives us the words that signal those relationships—words which we may term *"connectives."*[14]

Connectives are keys to improving the precision of a student's comprehension. Specific instructional time should be devoted to the functions of major connectives. In a study of twelfth-grade science and social studies textbooks, Rodgers ranked (by frequency) the most common connectives in each subject area:[15]

Connective	Geography	History	Chemistry	Biology	Physics
but	1	1	1	1	2
if	9	5	2	2	1
however	3	8	5	3	8

Connective	Geography	History	Chemistry	Biology	Physics
when	2	12	6	9	4
because	5	9	11	8	3
thus	7	4	7	4	14
as	8	6	10	7	6
although	4	3	12	11	11
since	15	10	3	6	12
while	11	2	14	10	13
therefore	14	16	13	14	5
for example	12	—	4	5	9
also	10	—	9	16	10
then	13	13	—	13	7
so	6	—	15	20	15
yet	16	14	17	17	—
perhaps	19	19	16	18	—
that is	18	—	18	19	—
even	—	7	—	12	—
until	—	11	19	—	—
in fact	20	15	—	—	—
such as	—	—	20	15	—

Note: Connectives pertinent to a particular subject area entered the ranking in this order: geography—where (17); history—meanwhile (17), whether (18), despite (20); chemistry—if so (8); physics—in other words (16), so that (17), on the other hand (18), consequently (19), furthermore (20).
Source: Adapted from Denis Rodgers, "Which Connectives? Signals to Enhance Comprehension," *Journal of Reading* 17 (March 1974):464.

Type of Signals.   Students should be helped to learn that although connectives have little or no meaning themselves, they are used to signal certain kinds of messages. The following classifications, sometimes overlapping, are useful to the learner if time and energy are put into thought and practice.

Go Signals.   Go or *coordinating* connectives inform readers that they are going to meet another equivalent idea that will continue the same line of thought. For example: "At the zoo they visted the elephants *and* then they went to the bird house." Some of these connectives are called *sequence signals*, for they join a number of coordinate ideas. For example: "At the zoo *first* they visited the elephants and *next* the bird house." The most common go signal is **and**. Others include:

first, second, third, etc.	in addition
next	similarly
not only . . . but also	moreover
more than that	at the same time
furthermore	also
likewise	

Caution Signals.   A number of connectives tell the reader to read the next point but to get ready to stop and pay especially careful attention to it. These connectives are conclusion and summary signals; they are of vital importance to the reader and are obviously so marked by the writers.

thus	hence
therefore	in conclusion
consequently	in summation
accordingly	in brief
in retrospect	as a result

Caution signals are particularly visible, for they either begin a sentence or are marked with punctuation on either side. For example:

1. *In conclusion*, then, the four principal parts of a verb (infinitive, present participle, past, and past participle) can help you form six tenses.

2. The secrets of photosynthesis are still not completely known; *hence* the problem must be attacked through the collaborative efforts of physicists, biochemists, and cytologists.

Turn Signals.   A group of connectives warn readers that they are about to read a different view, an opposing idea, or a change in the direction of the discussion. For instance: "The senator talked about human rights, yet he voted against the civil rights bill." The most common turn signal is **but**. Others include:

yet	otherwise
on the contrary	in spite of
nevertheless	although
meanwhile	despite
notwithstanding	conversely
on the other hand	however

Stop Signals.   Another group of connectives signal the reader to stop and pay careful attention to what follows, for it is of special significance. These connectives appear to reflect a quality of certainty and authority. For example: "*Undoubtedly*, the most important advancement in Renaissance Europe was the Gutenberg printing press." Others include:

without question	without precedent
significantly	unquestionably
without doubt	absolutely

Relationship Signals.   Numerous words and phrases—in fact, some of those already named—are useful connectives to remember as signals that point to relationships of time (finally, while, when, soon); space (beside, there, here); cause and effect (because, since, so that); degree (above all, many, less); or condition (if, unless, though).

Some connectives are particularly useful to recognize as indicators of writing patterns. In the two sentences that follow, the connective *that is* clearly plays a major role in telling the reader that the prior point will now be explained:

The President is responsible for our *foreign policy*. That is, he is responsible for the way our nation conducts its relations with the other nations of the world.[16]

Two other connectives, *for instance* and *for example*—used often in this book—always signal the reader that an illustration of some type is about to be presented.

Strategies for Connectives.   The following principles, among others, can help guide students as they learn to use connectives in improving their reading comprehension:

1. Time needs to be planned for working on frequent and complex connectives in each subject area. Direct and consistent instruction should be given.

2. Along with direct instruction, incidental aid must be administered on an individual basis, for students often differ in their abilities to handle certain of the more abstract connectives.

3. Instruction followed by wide reading permits students to meet the connectives over and over again so that natural reinforcement takes place.

4. In working with connectives, all instruction must be done in relation to context, or else the work is meaningless. Memorization of connectives helps little because function, not form, is the issue.

5. Instruction should be followed by many opportunities for practice so

that students can become effective and independent users of connectives as signals for meaning.

Referents and Antecedents.   Referents are words (often pronouns but not necessarily so) that substitute for, and relate to, other words in the text (the antecedents). For instance, in the example below, *It* is the referent and *Status* is the antecedent. The referent and antecedent form a cohesive tie and are utilized to promote comprehension.

> *Status* is an intangible thing. *It* will come to the elderly when they have meaningful and well-defined roles.[17]

Although the cohesion between referent and antecedent seems to enhance comprehension, some students appear to have problems understanding such relationships in the formal discourse of content area text materials. They need to have their consciousness raised—that is, they need directed practice. Such practice is important, particularly for the poor reader who typically reads word by word or sentence by sentence. Here is an opportunity to help readers use the ties that will allow them to interrelate ideas. Conscious analysis of text will enhance understanding and begin to create independence in utilizing such ties. In analyzing the following materials, for example, a teacher might ask: "Who are *these people?* What are *contact lenses?* Who or what are *They?*"

> A hundred million Americans—more than a third of the population—have visual problems that require correction. Most of *these people* wear glasses. But eight million wear *contact lenses.*
>   *Contacts* are little plastic discs that fit over the cornea of the eye. *They* can be made of hard or soft material.[18] [Italics added.]

Numerous examples of referents and their antecedents will be found in the instructional materials used by students. Many incorporate whole ideas discussed in previous paragraphs. In the following example, the antecedent is the total sentence before the referent (much information about the public's chance to make laws had been discussed in previous paragraphs):

> About twenty states give the public a chance to make laws when the legislature fails to act. *This* is done by means of the initiative and referendum.[19]

PROCESS STRATEGIES   Comprehension is best developed by noting and discussing the interactions between reader and author either during (if feasible) or immediately following the process of reading. Closure procedures, retrospection, and aspects of miscue analysis appear to be the best comprehension process strategies available at present.

CLOSURE PROCEDURES

Closure procedures, introduced in Chapter 2 as useful assessment and monitoring devices, are even more functional as instructional procedures focused on comprehending. Jongsma reported that "the literature appears to indicate that cloze instruction is more effective at improving reading comprehension than other aspects of reading proficiency."[20] (Note: Taylor's cloze procedure[21] of deleting each *n*th word—usually each fifth—has been broadened by many researchers and writers to include any type of related deletion system. I choose to refer to *closure* as the general term and *cloze* as specific to Taylor's concept.)

Cloze.   Bortnick and Lopardo suggested techniques for working with closure procedures as instructional tools. Their suggestions are given in Example 4.1.

Example 4.1   *Instructional Closure Techniques*[22]

As a group activity, or on a one-to-one basis or small group activity, the teacher instructs students to read silently an entire cloze passage which has been specifically prepared for them. Reading the cloze passage in its entirety will help the students to make maximum use of redundant information and contextual cues *throughout* the passage when they later attempt to fill in the cloze blanks. Reading through the cloze passage also fosters the habit of reading the material before and after the deletion. . . .

After the cloze passage has been silently read, it can be read aloud, sentence by sentence, either by the teacher or a student. Students can then suggest words which might fit into the blanks. All semantically and syntactically acceptable responses are taken but students are asked to offer reasons for their choices. Offering the reason is one of the most important aspects of the instruction since it encourages an understanding of the structure of the language and provides the teacher with a considerable amount of information on the instructional needs of students. For example, the student who replaces a noun in a verb slot or a present tense verb in a past tense verb slot is in need of particular type of instruction. Through examination of student responses, the teacher becomes sensitized to students' peculiar instructional needs.

Through discussion and direct instruction, the teacher helps the students decide on acceptable responses and to eliminate unacceptable ones. Reasons for acceptance or elimination are taught and/or discussed. It is not necessary to discuss every item in a passage. The teacher may pick certain deletions for discussion which suit the purpose of the lesson and students.

The cloze passage with possible correct responses is then compared with the original, unmutilated passage. In this comparison, discussion and teacher guidance will focus on whether meaning is affected by the acceptance of certain responses. For example, it can be pointed out that the insertion of the word *automobile* for *car* does little or nothing to change the meaning of a passage.

On the other hand, the substitution of the noun *bike* for *book*, although syntactically acceptable, most probably would affect the meaning of the passage. In using the cloze procedure to teach context, the teacher repeatedly points out the cues which immediately surround the blank as well as cues which may appear at the beginning, middle, or end of the passage.

Further Benefits

Other kinds of information can be pointed out in the comparison of the cloze and original passages, depending upon the purpose of the instruction.

Certain words (noun, adjective markers) in the immediate environment of the deletion cue the reader.

The position of words in a sentence gives certain cues: a deletion that is the first or last word in a sentence limits the possibilities of choice.

The redundancy of language within the passage cues the reader: often a deletion at the beginning of the passage is clarified by later redundant information in the passage.

The teacher should lead students to understand that activities utilizing cloze passages involve strategies that will be of value to them in their independent reading. Reading strategies (such as those described above) need to be carefully delineated for students. Moreover, students will need many opportunities to apply and practice these strategies. Simply having students complete cloze passages does not teach the strategy but gives practice in what has already been taught.

After the comparison and discussion of the cloze and original passages, students can independently follow the same procedures on a different passage. Passages of different levels and length can be prepared to meet the reading needs of a wide range of students.

After the teacher sets the purpose for the particular cloze passage, the activity can be summarized in terms of directions to the students as follows.

Read through the entire cloze passage silently.

Reread the cloze passage, writing in words you think fit the blanks.

If you can, try to offer your reasons for your choices for these blanks: (teacher selects certain items). "It sounds right" is a good reason in many cases.

Compare your choices with the original passage.

Be prepared to discuss both passages.

Op-In. Robert S. Pehrsson, Idaho State University, devised the Op-In procedure (still in an experimental stage), in which clauses are deleted from every other sentence in a passage. According to Pehrsson, evidence shows that focusing on larger chunks of language than in typical closure procedures seems to result in students gradually coming closer to the authors' messages. In this procedure, deletions follow the complete subject. In the example shown here, portions that would be deleted are in italics:

> Some animals use their teeth for protection. Dogs and wolves *have long, sharp teeth with which to defend themselves*. Rats, woodchucks, mink, and weasels also have sharp teeth. These animals use *teeth in attacking other animals*. The teeth of some animals have developed into large tusks. Elephants and boars *have tusks*. The tusks of an elephant or of a wild boar are greatly feared by their enemies.[23]

Selective Deletions.   Jongsma, in his review of "cloze instruction research," concluded that "selective deletions which are focused on particular contextual relationships have a greater instructional effect than random deletions."[24] Selective deletions permit teachers to focus on certain aspects of language that they wish to highlight. For example, words defined in the material can be deleted; hence, students must locate the definitions and then attempt to replace the appropriate deletion or its synonym. Or certain markers or connectives may be deleted, and students can be asked to figure out which are missing and why.

The connective exercise in Example 4.2 serves a double purpose. It not only is functional as a way of learning more about the roles of connectives, but in addition it enables students to think in greater depth about paragraphs that introduce a chapter they are about to read.

In any type of closure activity, students inexperienced at dealing with the technique should be given a great deal of guidance at first. They soon learn. Pencils or erasable pens should be used, and students should be encouraged to erase responses if subsequent reading seems to make earlier responses inadequate. And, as stated earlier, discussion of responses is the most important part of instruction. Reasons given by students for their insertions provide continuing instructional information for the teacher and dictate the structure of future closure procedures.

RETROSPECTION[25]

When students are asked to think about their own reading strategies and the reasons for their successes and failures in coping with a particular passage, they are using *retrospection*—looking back at what they did and examining their own mental processes. With this technique, of course, there is always the danger that pupils will not be able to verbalize or will verbalize what they think is expected, but the value seems worth the risk. The more experience students obtain in using the technique, with continuous positive reinforcement from peers and teacher, the more adept and honest they become. Retrospection was

Example 4.2   *A Connective Exercise*[26]

WHICH CONNECTIVE?

Some of the connectives in the social studies passage below have been deleted. Fill in the blanks with appropriate connectives chosen from the list which follows. Think carefully about the type of signal the connective represents and how it fits into the context. We'll discuss your reasons for making specific choices once you have completed the assignment.

yet	as a result
while	after
when	and

At the time this unit begins, Great Britain and France had each built strong empires in America. France controlled the St. Lawrence Valley and a great V-shaped area in the central part of North America, _____ England's colonies were nestled along the east coast. The two nations became rivals in the New World and elsewhere, _____ fought four long and bloody wars. _____ , France lost its land in America. Why did these nations go to war? How did France come to lose its land and power in the New World?

_____ the French had been defeated, Great Britain was the world's most powerful nation. The English looked forward to years of peace. _____ only 12 years after the French wars, quarrels between Great Britain and its colonies grew into yet another war. How could this happen so quickly? Why did the colonies go to war?

_____ the war was over, a new nation had been born. The United States faced a big problem—it needed strong government. How was this problem solved?

---

urged as a vital part of the instructional sequence in using the closure procedures described earlier. It may also be used in the following ways, among others.

1.   Miscue analysis, described as an assessment and monitoring technique in Chapter 2 (pages 37–40), may be used instructionally. Have a student read a short passage orally and record the miscues. Show the passage to the student again, after the initial reading, and point out a few of the miscues— one at a time. Ask the student why she or he thinks they were made. Guide the student in developing better strategies. An alternative is to record the reading on tape. Play the recording as the student looks at the passage again. Have the student spot miscues and attempt to give reasons for them.

2.   Present students with a specific learning task involving reading. After

they are finished, give them a duplicated answer sheet to check against their own answers. Allow time for them to think through the similarities and differences. Now have them discuss the answers and challenge or defend them. Get them thinking about *why* they responded in certain ways. Help them, over time, to generalize strategies for tackling certain types of problems.

3.   Have students predict in writing (a) the next or final step in a sequence they have read; (b) the ending of a short story; (c) the outcome of an event; or (d) the solution to a problem. Discuss the predictions and the bases on which they were made. Emphasize that there is no right or wrong answer and do not supply a teacher or author answer at this point. Stress must be placed on the reasoning of the students. They are, of course, free to revise and question their own responses in the group discussion. Once students have established a good feeling about working together on predictions—without deprecating one another—then the teacher might introduce the next step, ending, outcome, or solution as written by the author. Now they must think through the author's reasoning process and compare with their own. Again, right or wrong is not the issue!

PRODUCT STRATEGIES

Although *process strategies* probably help to develop comprehension much more than *product strategies* do, there are times, of course, when responses to reading are called for and necessary. Typically questions have been used to elicit responses, but other means are also available. Specific graphic responses as well as overall postorganizers offer particular success to the poor reader who finds it difficult to cope with another organized linguistic task after reading a complex passage. Such "product strategies" also provide a way of allowing bilingual youngsters to respond without having to think through all the linguistic nuances in a second language.

QUESTIONS

Questions both guide and limit comprehension. Well-framed questions related to the ability of the learner can enhance learning. Teachers must be concerned with the task the question is imposing and whether the student is able to cope with that task. As Herber said, "To be able to answer questions, one must be able to apply the reading skill or skills implicit in the relationship between the questions and the content."[27]

Instructors should consider what aspect(s) of the reading-thinking processes they want to tap when tests and examinations are structured. Undoubtedly the multiple-choice test is making different demands on the reader than the essay question. Two factors need to be taken into consideration: (1) the kind of questioning that best fits the nature and purpose(s) of the task and (2) the type of thinking that the test is to focus on and the reasons for that choice.

Differing weights may be placed on the results of different kinds of evaluation. In all probability, an essay question that calls for high-level thought and organization is a more complex task than filling in the blanks or regurgitating content through answering a host of short-answer questions. In the instructional situation, outside of formal measurement procedures, instructors should examine their own use of questioning in day-to-day teaching. Although many types of questions are needed and will be utilized in a classroom, efforts should be made to create questions that call for synthesis, integration, organization, evaluation, and creative utilization. The abilities of specific youngsters to cope with differing types of questions should be evaluated. Structured guidance in moving from regurgitation to digestion and expansion can only increase the students' repertoire and aid reading comprehension.

Questions may be used as a means of moving from one level of thinking to the next. As Guszak and others have indicated, teachers tend to emphasize recall questions at the expense of other types of questions that can extend thinking.[28] Guszak suggested that teachers determine what kinds of thinking outcomes they want to develop in advance of a lesson. Then they should determine what is best for an individual, for the type of material, and for the goal(s) of instruction. Questions should be tried out first to see if they are ambiguous. He classified questions as:

> *Recognition*—location of information;
>
> *Recall*—usually relating small pieces of factual information;
>
> *Translation*—regurgitation;
>
> *Conjecture*—making a cognitive leap, anticipating an event or conclusion;
>
> *Explanation*—infer, provide a rationale;
>
> *Evaluation*—judgment of worth, value, and the like.

Lucking found a taxonomy of questions useful in helping students move from one level of thought to the next in an orderly fashion after reading a short story.[29] Hierarchically ordered questions move from testing knowledge to evaluation. The following questions in Lucking's taxonomy are based on "A Mother's Tale," a short story by James Agee, from a collection about the environment and the future (*Eco-Fiction*, John Sandler, ed. New York: Washington Square Press, 1973):

> *Knowledge*—What event is taking place as the story opens? What do the calves want to know?
>
> *Comprehension*—Can you summarize the story that she tells them?
>
> *Application*—How would you apply this tale to her uncertain feelings about humans?

Analysis—What motivates her to tell the tale even though she is not sure it is true?

Synthesis—What might be other situations where a mother might have this kind of concern for her son?

Evaluation—Do you think the mother is presented in a sympathetic manner?[30]

Pyrczak and Axelrod and others have demonstrated that often "comprehension questions" do not test understanding of a given passage.[31] Some questions may be so passage-*independent* that students can answer them on the basis of their general knowledge bank. Other questions may be worded in such a way that the correct answer becomes obvious through the use of logic alone. Hence, some students may not have to read in order to get correct answers. This is perhaps a laudable use of their knowledge and reasoning power, but hardly a way of determining reading comprehension.

Even though some students' preknowledge bank may be extensive, questions should be worded so that students must use the ideas presented by the authors. When creating multiple-choice questions, teachers should attempt to make the answer choices equivalent in length, parallel in structure, sensible and relevant in content, and as passage-dependent as possible. Based on a study focused on the passage dependence-independence of factual and inferential questions, Duffelmeyer concluded:

> The blame for passage independence does not lie in the question's type. Instead, it lies in the item writer's ability to eliminate the influence of the information that the examinee brings to the passage, due either to the selection of material ill-suited to measure comprehension or to lack of skill in constructing questions.[32]

GRAPHIC RESPONSES

Depending on the reading task accomplished, responses need not always be in the form of written sentences or paragraphs. Often a graphic response can demonstrate certain kinds of relationships better than a written response can. And, as indicated earlier, it might be a less threatening and even more suitable response for many learners. Here are two examples:

1. A group has read a selection detailing U.S. budget expenditures for 1982. The teacher may ask specific questions eliciting the information, of course, but another option is to have the students construct a pie graph. Students could be given choices: answer specific questions; write a paragraph about the expenditures; or draw a pie graph.

2. Students have read about the major events leading to the modern use of television. A time line response may be more fitting than any type of written response alone.

POSTORGANIZERS

Postorganizers highlighting important ideas and interrelationships among ideas permit students to reconstruct what they have read. Postorganizers, in reality another type of graphic response (but one I feel warrants highlighting), usually take the form of a diagram or map. They are similar to the concept map preorganizers illustrated in Chapter 3 (pages 78–80) and at the beginning of each chapter of this book. It is frequently profitable to construct a concept map preorganizer before reading and then modify it as a preorganizer following reading. Figure 4.1 is an example of one student's postorganizer.

Note that Brenda added her feeling to the postorganizer—something she would not normally do in a written response. Brenda is a slow learner who has been mainstreamed into a junior high school reading class. She felt much more comfortable without the syntactic constraints of formal composition or sentence

Figure 4.1   A Postorganizer

Brenda has just finished reading about her favorite topic—diamonds. During this reading she learned that there are four types of diamonds and she learned something about each type. She formulated this postorganizer:

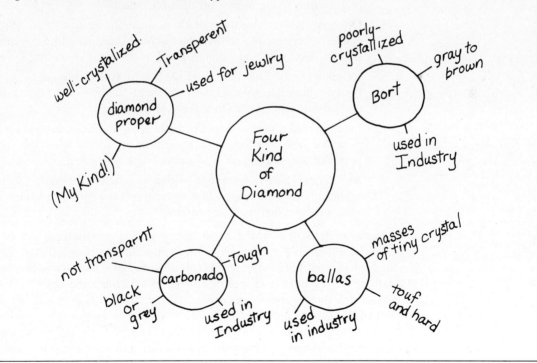

structure. Brenda's postorganizer was assessed on the basis of what she comprehended; spelling errors and inconsistencies in capitalization were not rated.

CRITICAL EVALUATION

Opinions and feelings, as in Brenda's postorganizer, interact with facts and ideas in all reading situations. In addition, however, readers will need to be helped to evaluate what they read. Of course, they are evaluating on their own, but the teacher plays a major role in helping them to evaluate critically. Critical evaluation (called critical reading by some authorities) requires the reader to develop a set of standards or criteria on which to base evaluation. It involves the withholding of judgment, the sorting of arguments, the weighing of evidence, and the ability to be flexible.

The list of questions that follows, adapted from Thomas and Robinson's Check List on Critical Evaluation, probably includes all considerations that are important in the critical evaluation of a piece of writing:[33]

1. Do students note the publication date and realize its importance in relation to events and the writer's attitudes?

2. Do they attempt to appraise the writer's qualifications when feasible?

3. Do they ask, "What evidence supports this statement? Is it opinion? Is the writer trying to pass off opinion as fact?"

4. Do students ask, "Are the writer's implications reasonable in light of evidence presented? Are the writer's conclusions based on the information developed and supported within the piece of writing?"

5. Do students suspend judgment? Do they resist the impulse to accept the first plausible solution to a problem, holding on to that information but waiting for other possible solutions?

6. Do they read widely and deeply, looking for and welcoming different points of view? Do they understand how to proceed when the viewpoints of authorities and/or researchers are in conflict?

7. Are students able to recognize writing designed to persuade—a conscious attempt on the part of a writer to get the reader to believe an idea, accept a fact, or buy a product?

Students should be helped to use the preceding questions as criteria on which to base their evaluations. Once these questions become habitual tools, the reader will find it almost impossible to utilize what is read without critical evaluation. All the criteria cannot be applied to all written messages but even the use of one or two encourages critical thought and, it is hoped, wiser utilization of the writer's message.

Example 4.3, excerpted from a large travel brochure, should immediately bring to mind question 7. The material is no different from the persuasion or propaganda used by many companies competing for business; however, the

Example 4.3   A Message to Be Critically Evaluated[34]

Since all airlines charge the same fares to the same places, you should choose an airline on the basis of what it *gives* you—rather than what it costs you.

The most important thing Pan Am has to give you is *experience.* After all, we are the most experienced airline in the world. And because we've been flying longer than anyone else, we know more about what you want from a trip and how to see that you get it.

Just look at the record. We opened up more of the world to air travel than all other airlines combined. . . .

As for in-flight service, we probably know more about pampering passengers than anyone—simply because we've been doing it longer. . . .

In our offices—which today number 235 in 122 cities in 79 countries around the world—you'll find dedicated people who have been brought up in the outstanding tradition of Pan Am experience.

reader must recognize it for what it is. Questions 1 through 4 may also be considered and answered as follows:

1. The publication date is current, and this is most important in terms of the present planning of trips.

2. There is no evidence about who wrote the brochure, but one is sure to know that they are expert writers of persuasive materials and are paid by the airlines.

3. Although one cannot do a reference check on each piece of writing, it seems obvious (and of course this is usually true of persuasive types of writing) that much of the discourse is opinion unsupported by facts—and the writers do try to make most of it appear to be factual. (*Experience* leads to much knowledge and superior performance—as does the *record!*)

4. Implications and conclusions appear to be rampant, with little supporting evidence.

PROPAGANDA DEVICES

Three of the illustrations in Figure 4.2 relate to specific propaganda devices often used in varied advertising campaigns. Students, however, must become aware that clever propaganda techniques can also be used to persuade them to believe or to act in certain ways in regard to voting, human relationships, and the like. Students should be alert to questioning writing that seems to be aimed at influencing them. Their questions should be framed in relation to the six types of propaganda devices illustrated in Figure 4.2.

Figure 4.2   Propaganda Devices

FIGURE 1–4.   *Students should detect these and other propaganda devices and note their proposed effect. Source: From* American Civics, *Second Edition, by William H. Hartley and William S. Vincent, copyright © 1974 by Harcourt Brace Jovanovich, Inc., p. 246. Reproduced by permission of the publisher.*

Source: Ellen L. Thomas and H. Alan Robinson, *Improving Reading in Every Class*, 3rd ed. (Boston: Allyn and Bacon, 1982), p. 118.

QUESTIONS
AND
RELATED
ACTIVITIES

1.   Formulate your own definition of reading comprehension based on your own thinking, the information in prior chapters of this book, and the illustrations in this chapter.

2.   Why is readers' knowledge a part of comprehension?

3.   Why is text structure a part of comprehension?

4.   Select sentences and passages from material to be studied and have students figure out referent-antecedent relationships. Once students begin to realize the importance of clarifying the relationship under your guidance, they will begin to use the strategy on their own. For example, in a social studies book, you might choose a clear-cut paragraph to be read and discussed. Then introduce the beginning of the next paragraph, which, in the example shown below, states: *This rapid growth* . . . . Students need to be sure they understand what the antecedent of that phrase is in order to process the forthcoming material. Often they look for the meaning only in the preceding sentence when the relationship may encompass a larger chunk of the material. Note all the details that a reader must marshall in this passage:

> Not all of California's wealth was dug from the earth by prospectors and miners. The sudden rise of San Francisco's population created new problems. Thousands of newcomers needed food and shelter. Banks and express companies were needed to keep and move the gold. Warehouses had to be built to store cargoes for ships. Some pioneers discovered that selling tools, groceries, and liquor to the miners at high prices was more profitable and less dangerous than prospecting. They could charge such high prices at first because goods were extremely scarce. The profits these businessmen made were then reinvested in still larger businesses.
>
> *This rapid growth* also increased the variety of occupations needed to keep the community running. . . .[35] [Italics added.]

5.   Have students use the strategies of introspection and retrospection—that is, have them think about what they are doing and what they have done. For example, ask them to read the following paragraph from a geometry text:

> Hereafter, whenever we speak of two lines, or two planes, we shall always mean that the lines or planes are different. That is, when we speak of two things, we shall always mean that there are indeed two separate items. But if we say merely that P and Q are points, we mean to allow the possibility that $P = Q$.[36]

When students are asked to read the paragraph above, they might be cautioned that each of the sentences begins with one or more words signaling the reader that something in particular is to happen. Have them find the words. Have them decide the roles each connective plays. They might write down their answers and/or discuss the ideas in class.

6.   Prepare worksheets containing contrasting paragraph types taken from student texts. You could ask certain kinds of questions directed toward increased understanding of paragraph functions. For example, if a transitional and summarizing paragraph were put on the worksheet, some questions might be:

a. Which paragraph is transitional? How do you know?
b. Which paragraph is a summarizing paragraph? How do you know?
c. In the transitional paragraph, which sentence(s) refers back to material already covered? Which refers to material about to be introduced?
d. In your own words, and as briefly as possible, state the essential information summarized in the summarizing paragraph.

7. Note the preorganizer for this chapter. After reading the chapter, would you diagram a postorganizer in the same way? If not, diagram your own. If you feel the preorganizer is suitable as a postorganizer, use the ideas and organize an alternative format.

SELECTED READINGS

Altick, Richard D. *Preface to Critical Reading*, 5th ed. New York: Holt, Rinehart and Winston, 1969.

Cameron, Jack R. "Read Critically—or Join the Mob." *Journal of Reading* 12 (October 1968):24–26.

Eller, William, and Judith G. Wolf, compilers. *Critical Reading: A Broader View*. Newark, Del.: International Reading Association, 1972.

Gerhard, Christian. *Making Sense: Reading Comprehension Improved through Categorizing*. Newark, Del.: International Reading Association, 1975.

Grant, Patricia L. "The Cloze Procedure as an Instructional Device." *Journal of Reading* 22 (May 1979):699–705.

Guthrie, John T., ed. *Cognition, Curriculum, and Comprehension*. Newark, Del.: International Reading Association, 1977.

———. *Comprehension and Teaching: Research Reviews*. Newark, Del.: International Reading Association, 1981.

Henry, George H. *Teaching Reading as Concept Development: Emphasis on Affective Thinking*. Newark, Del.: International Reading Association, 1974.

Herber, Harold L., and Joan B. Nelson. "Questioning Is Not the Answer." *Journal of Reading* 18 (April 1975):512–17.

———. *Teaching Reading in Content Areas*, 2nd ed. Englewood Cliffs, N.J.: Prentice-Hall, 1978.

Hunkins, Francis P. *Involving Students in Questioning*. Boston: Allyn and Bacon, 1976.

Jones, Margaret B., and Edna C. Pikilski. "Cloze for the Classroom." *Journal of Reading* 17 (March 1974):432–38.

Jongsma, Eugene A. *Cloze Instruction Research: A Second Look*. Newark, Del.: International Reading Association, 1980.

Karlin, Robert. "Developing Comprehension Skills in the High School Student." In *Teachers, Tangibles, Techniques: Comprehension of Content in Reading*, edited by Bonnie S. Schulwitz. Newark, Del.: International Reading Association, 1975.

Kintsch, W., and E.H. Kintsch. "The Role of Schemata in Text Comprehension." *International Journal of Psycholinguistics* 5, no. 2 (1978):17–27.

McCallister, James M. "Using Paragraph Clues As Aids to Understanding," *Journal of Reading* 8 (October 1964):11–16.

McKenna, Michael C., and Richard D. Robinson. *An Introduction to the Cloze Procedure*, rev. ed. Newark, Del.: International Reading Association, 1980.

Meyer, Bonnie J.F.; David M. Brandt; and George J. Bluth. "Use of Top-Level Structure in Text: Key for Reading Comprehension of Ninth-Grade Students." *Reading Research Quarterly* 16, no. 1 (1980):72–103.

Pearson, P. David, and Dale D. Johnson. *Teaching Reading Comprehension*. New York: Holt, Rinehart and Winston, 1978.

Robinson, H. Alan. "A Plan for Helping Teachers Relate Reading and Writing Instruction." In *Reading and the Language Arts*, edited by H. Alan Robinson, pp. 224–27. Supplementary Educational Monograph, no. 93. Chicago: University of Chicago Press, December 1963.

Schleich, Miriam. "Improving Reading Through the Language Arts in Grades Nine Through Fourteen." In *Reading and the Language Arts*, edited by H. Alan Robinson, pp. 39–41. Supplementary Educational Monograph, no. 93. Chicago: University of Chicago Press, December 1963.

Simons, Herbert D. "Reading Comprehension: The Need for a New Perspective." *Reading Research Quarterly* 6 (Spring 1971):338–63.

Smith, Frank. *Comprehension and Learning*. New York: Holt, Rinehart and Winston, 1975.

Soltis, Judith M., and Susanna W. Pflaum. "The Effect of Instruction in Connectives on Reading Comprehension." *Reading World* 19 (December 1979):179–84.

Spiro, Rand J.; Bertram C. Bruce; and William F. Brewer. *Theoretical Issues in Reading Comprehension*. Hillsdale, N.J.: Lawrence Erlbaum Associates, 1980.

Thomas, Ellen L., and H. Alan Robinson. *Improving Reading in Every Class*, 3rd ed., pp. 49–125 (abridged ed., pp. 43–117). Boston: Allyn and Bacon, 1982.

Thorndike, Robert L. "Reading as Reasoning." *Reading Research Quarterly* 9, no. 2 (1973–74):135–47.

Whaley, Jill F. "Story Grammars and Reading Instruction." *Reading Teacher* 34 (April 1981):762–71.

Wheat, Thomas E., and Rose M. Edmund. "The Concept of Comprehension: An Analysis." *Journal of Reading* 18 (April 1975):523–27.

NOTES
1. Constance Weaver, "Using Context: Before or After?" *Language Arts* 54 (November/December 1977):883.
2. Robert J. Tierney and Rand J. Spiro, "Some Basic Notions About Reading Comprehension: Implications for Teachers," in *New Perspectives on Comprehension*, ed. Jerome C. Harste and Robert F. Carey, Monograph in Language and Reading Studies, School of Education (Bloomington: Indiana University, 1979), p. 134.
3. Ibid., pp. 134–35.
4. Ibid., p. 135.
5. Ibid.

6. Ibid.
7. Ernest T. Goetz and Bonnie M. Armbruster, "Psychological Correlates of Text Structure," in *Theoretical Issues in Reading Comprehension*, ed. Rand J. Spiro, Bertram C. Bruce, and William F. Brewer (Hillsdale, N.J.: Lawrence Erlbaum Associates, 1980), p. 216.
8. Frank Smith, *Understanding Reading*, 3rd ed. (New York: Holt, Rinehart and Winston, 1982), p. 64.
9. Jean Mandler and Nancy Johnson, "Remembrance of Things Parsed: Story Structure and Recall," *Cognitive Psychology* 9 (January 1977):111.
10. Smith, *Understanding Reading*, 3rd ed., p. 64.
11. Bonnie J.F. Meyer, David M. Brandt, and George J. Bluth, "Use of Top-Level Structure in Text: Key for Reading Comprehension of Ninth Grade Students," *Reading Research Quarterly* 16, no. 1 (1980):72–103.
12. W. Kintsch and E.H. Kintsch, "The Role of Schemata in Text Comprehension," *International Journal of Psycholinguistics* 5, no. 2 (1978):27.
13. M.A.K. Halliday and Ruqaiya Hasan, *Cohesion in English* (London: Longman Group Ltd., 1976).
14. Denis Rodgers, "Which Connectives? Signals to Enhance Comprehension," *Journal of Reading* 17 (March 1974):462–63. Reprinted by permission of the author and the International Reading Association.
15. Adapted from Rodgers, "Which Connectives?" p. 464.
16. William H. Hartley and William S. Vincent, *American Civics*, rev. ed. (New York: Harcourt Brace Jovanovich, 1970), p. 74.
17. William E. Cole and Diana K. Harris, *The Elderly in America* (Boston: Allyn and Bacon, 1977), p. 21.
18. Julius B. Richmond and others, *You and Your Health*, Book 8 (Glenview, Ill.: Scott, Foresman, 1977), p. 77.
19. Smith, Tiegs, Adams, *Your Life As a Citizen* (Lexington, Mass.: Ginn, 1976), p. 217.
20. Eugene A. Jongsma, *Cloze Instruction Research: A Second Look* (Newark, Del.: International Reading Association, 1980), p. 23.
21. Wilson L. Taylor, "Cloze Procedure: A New Tool for Measuring Readability," *Journalism Quarterly* 30 (Fall 1953):415–33.
22. Robert Bortnick and Genevieve S. Lopardo, "An Instructional Application of the Cloze Procedure," *Journal of Reading* 16 (January 1973):297–99. Reprinted by permission of the authors and the International Reading Association.
23. Nila B. Smith, *Be A Better Reader*, Level A, Basic Skills Edition (Englewood Cliffs, N.J.: Prentice-Hall, 1977), p. 41.
24. Jongsma, *Cloze Instruction Research*, p. 23.
25. The section on *retrospection* is somewhat adapted with permission from Nila B. Smith and H. Alan Robinson, *Reading Instruction for Today's Children*, 2nd ed. (Englewood Cliffs, N.J.: Prentice-Hall, 1980), pp. 214–16. Reprinted by permission of Prentice-Hall, Inc.
26. Revised by William E. Gardner, *Story of Our America* (Boston: Allyn and Bacon, 1977), p. 97.
27. Harold L. Herber, *Teaching Reading in the Content Areas*, 2nd ed. (Englewood Cliffs, N.J.: Prentice-Hall, 1978), p. 193.
28. Frank J. Guszak, "Questioning Strategies of Elementary Teachers in Relation to Comprehension," in *Reading and Realism*, ed. J. Allen Figurel, Proceedings of the International Association, 1968, pp. 110–16.
29. Robert A. Lucking, "A Study of the Effects of a Hierarchically-Ordered Questioning Technique on Adolescents' Responses to Short Stories," *Research in the Teaching of English* 10 (Winter 1976):269–76.

30. Ibid., p. 271.

31. Fred Pyrczak and Jerome Axelrod, "Determining the Passage Dependence of Reading Comprehension Exercises: A Call for Replications," *Journal of Reading* 19 (January 1976):279–83.

32. Frederick A. Duffelmeyer, "The Passage Independence of Factual and Inferential Questions," *Journal of Reading* 24 (November 1980):133.

33. Ellen Lamar Thomas and H. Alan Robinson, *Improving Reading in Every Class: A Sourcebook for Teachers* (Boston: Allyn and Bacon, 1972), pp. 265–66 (abridged ed., p. 203).

34. *Pan Am's World—Latin America* (Boston: Pan American World Airways, 1973), p. 3.

35. Revised by Gardner, *Story of Our America*, p. 97.

36. Edwin E. Moise and Floyd L. Downs, Jr., *Geometry*, 2nd. ed. (Reading, Mass.: Addison-Wesley, 1971), p. 63.

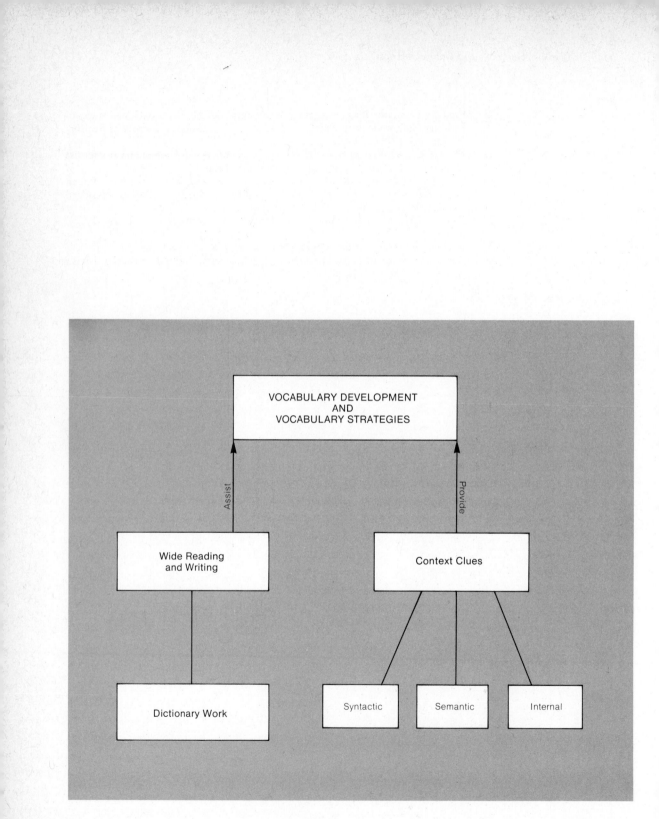

5
Vocabulary Development and Vocabulary Strategies

The current cry of "back to the basics" has caused a return to or intensified continuance, in some classrooms, of having students memorize given lists of words each week. This procedure has failed in the past and does not promise to succeed in the future. Rather than *back to the basics*, we should finally *get to the basics* and make an all-school effort to help students cope with contextual vocabulary needs in each classroom. Certainly students should be assisted in learning essential and technical vocabulary—when needed to deal with specific content area tasks. But at the same time, emphasis should be placed on strategies for aiding students to unlock and generate ideas independently. Planned lessons in each content area classroom should be developed that focus on *how* to make use of context to figure out hazy or unknown language units. While composing, students should be helped and encouraged to make use of clear, familiar context as an aid in defining technical or complex language units for their readers.

Do not expect the English or reading teacher to do the whole job. Technical vocabulary and vocabulary strategies need to be learned within the framework of each content area if memory is to be given a chance to store meaningful components of ideas in an organized, retrievable manner.

As an extension of Chapter 4, this chapter places major emphasis on context clues as aids for unlocking meaning (when reading) or as clarifiers of meaning (when composing and writing). Hence, vocabulary strategies become another tool of comprehension. Vocabulary development and strategies are treated separately in this chapter as a matter of emphasis, for the meanings of words are essential, although certainly not sufficient, ingredients for comprehension.

One of the techniques suggested in Chapter 3 was having the teacher focus attention on a few important words, phrases, or clauses undefined by the writer and probably unknown to the prospective reader. The teacher will also want to stand ready during or following a reading assignment to assist individual students to understand language units they could not grasp. Also, the instructor may be of great help as an interactor while students are searching for more precise, more picturesque, or varied ways of expressing ideas in subsequent drafts of their compositions.

But the most important vocabulary strategies are those an instructor helps students develop for their independent use. Direct work on vocabulary development is a significant aspect of any type of language instruction. Intensive practice and dictionary work, however, should *not* be done immediately before or during a reading or writing activity. Such intensive instruction intrudes on the task at hand. Some brief discussion of stopper words or key words in reading and writing (pp. 35–37) may be useful at times. Generally speaking, vocabulary development—extensive and/or intensive—is appropriate *following* a discussion of a reading or writing assignment or at another time when vocabulary is concentrated on as a specific lesson.

Throughout this chapter I have used the term *language units* in perhaps an overzealous desire to communicate the fact that, in discourse processing (comprehending), we decode language (comprehensible units of speech), not usually solitary words. Hence I feel that vocabulary development must stress the acquisition and extension of words and groups of words in larger contextual language frames than isolated lists of words. In vocabulary training, emphasis should be placed on learning the varied meanings of words that appear frequently enough in a variety of contexts to pay dividends to the learner.

> While current research demonstrates the importance of such factors as a reader's perspective on a text . . . and text structure . . . , it is also clear that word knowledge is a requisite for reading comprehension: people who do not know the meanings of very many words are most probably poor readers.[1]

Thus the focus here is on unlocking meaning, not on pronunciation. Although it may be necessary to help some students in the secondary school with phoneme-grapheme relationships, it is dangerous and destructive to overemphasize them or to use them as *the* strategy for attacking language units. We must keep in mind and heart that secondary school students use an intermix of the dialect they use outside of school and the dialect preferred in the classroom. Emphasis on *correct* pronunciation at the expense of a search for meaning defeats the purpose of instruction. It is a difficult task to learn the pronunciation or meaning of language units unfamiliar to the learner. But if the printed language unit is already part of the learner's speaking or listening vocabulary, the task is quite easy.

Vocabulary instruction must take place within the framework of context, not isolated from it. As Smith, Goodman, and Meredith point out:

> An unfamiliar use of a familiar word or phrase may cause a learner problems because in his or her dialect that usage may be incorrect. Mere manipulation of lists of words is not a solution to these vocabulary problems. Relevance becomes a key word here. Relevant instruction and relevant materials capitalize on the language and

experience of each learner. Vocabulary differences between cultural groups reflect differences in cultural experiences. One is not a deficient example of the other.[2]

DEVELOPING
READING AND
WRITING
VOCABULARIES

All "normal" middle school and high school students have at least four vocabularies: listening, speaking, reading, and writing. A common core exists among them, but usually listening is the most expansive. Depending on many factors in the learning and experiential background of the student, reading or speaking is the next widest. Writing is almost always the most meager of the vocabularies.

The task in this chapter is to concentrate on reading and writing vocabularies, with more emphasis on reading. Fortunately, stress on one vocabulary modality appears to have a degree of transfer to the other. Hence teachers should make every effort to include both reading and writing as activities in the direct teaching of vocabulary strategies.

THROUGH WIDE READING AND WRITING

Although direct and indirect instruction in vocabulary acquisition is the teacher's important and continuing responsibility, there is no replacement for wide and varied reading and writing. Students who spend enough time in the world of words and who think about what they are reading and writing cannot help but increase their individual language banks. Since most words in a language are used over and over again, students will become familiar with the most commonly used words and expressions, although, without instruction, familiarity may not always lead to mastery of meaning. Instructors can help readers become aware of the less frequently used language units by suggesting readings of interest and/ or pertinence beyond the basic instructional materials—followed by direct instruction.

In addition to encouraging wide reading/writing and suggesting or even guiding trips to the school library, the establishment of a classroom library collection can be a boon to vocabulary development. Students can rather painlessly reinforce and extend their vocabularies through a multitude of immediately available materials.

THROUGH DICTIONARY WORK

Dictionaries also play a vital role in vocabulary development. Without doubt numerous students enter junior or senior high school with little knowledge of how to use dictionaries or thesauri. Assuredly their problems cannot be solved by lamenting the fact; any teacher of any subject who wants students to build their vocabularies must take the time to give assistance.

Three factors need to be considered: (1) the nature of the dictionaries, (2) the students' knowledge of dictionaries, and (3) the students' practice in using dictionaries. Dictionaries are often difficult to use because they are beyond the students' reading levels and because the definitions sometimes contain words unknown to the reader. Teachers need to step in at this point and clarify. They should try to provide a variety of dictionaries at various levels in any content area classroom. Students should also be guided in surveying dictionaries to learn what they have to offer. Practice, sometimes extensive, must be given with the pronunciation guide of a dictionary so that a student can "take a stab" at the pronunciation of an unknown word. But students must be brought to realize that even though most of the entries in the dictionary are single words, their concern is rarely with single, isolated words. They must bring the content—phrase, clause, sentence, paragraph—*to* the dictionary, for most words are adequately defined only within their verbal environments. Note the following example:

> The corn *field* has been harvested.
>
> All nations hope they can find more oil *fields*.
>
> Are you going to study the *field* of science?
>
> Man, he can really *field* that ball!
>
> Are they going to *field* their third-string fullback?
>
> This is the range of its magnetic *field*.

Exercises with common words, even technical words (such as *magnetic field*), increase word power and hence comprehension. Working with the *depth* of word meanings for given language units is at least as significant as working with breadth—knowledge of individual meanings for a host of language units.

Although all learners should know how to make use of dictionaries, one cannot depend on a dictionary as the major means of gaining vocabulary competence or looking up unknown words or expressions. A reader/writer cannot possibly keep referring to a dictionary every time he or she is uncertain about a language unit. Aside from losing the train of thought, it is downright boring and "turns off " the unmotivated adolescent. As *readers*, students need to learn to use dictionaries as *one* tool if the context in something they are reading cannot be of enough assistance in a particular circumstance. Along with other references, a dictionary may also be of use to them *as writers* when they are searching for ways of clarifying a concept they want their readers to understand.

CONTEXT CLUES

Specific and carefully guided work in vocabulary development and in the acquisition of vocabulary strategies is of particular importance with slow learners or mainstreamed youngsters. Frequently their reading and writing vocabularies are exceptionally weak, so they may need continual reintroductions and reinforcements. Teachers should not be misled, however, into isolating words or working with word lists. These students need "mental hooks" to hold onto—

they must learn words in contextual settings. Learning is sometimes facilitated by spending some time on *contrasting* words in different settings or circumstances. Note the following example:

> His two roommates in the hospital were in very different stages of recovery from operations. John, whose operation was two days ago, was now alert and and even *energetic*. He was practically doing all of the body-building exercises he did at home. Pete, on the other hand, was *lethargic*. He spoke little and moved little. However, he had returned from the recovery room only a few hours ago. What could you expect!

Learners should never be presented in initial learning situations with words or longer language units that have similar characteristics, like *too, to,* and *two; affect* and *effect; they're, there,* and *their.* Simultaneous and isolated presentations of such words will ensure lifetime confusion.

Although gifted learners can often remember and integrate isolated vocabulary instruction, they too learn best when instruction considers the total context of language. And many gifted learners do need help with vocabulary development. Giftedness in itself does not ensure knowledge or independent mastery.

> The very characteristics that distinguish the gifted from other learners and should determine the scope and sequence of the language arts often act as deterrents to the type of experiences with which gifted learners are presented and the degree of progress they achieve. . . . Language arts experiences and expectations . . . , however, are sometimes related to characteristics of giftedness as if those characteristics were absolute, constant, and possessed only by gifted persons. Consequently, curriculum experiences and expectations . . . are tailored to a stereotypical description of giftedness rather than to an analysis of the entry skills, abilities, and interests of the individual gifted student.[3]

All students, in different ways, must learn strategies for unlocking meanings and generating meanings. The context clues that follow are important strategies for students to internalize over time.

The term *context clues* is sometimes used as an oversimplification of a group of vital strategies for vocabulary development. Often the term is used to indicate a vague and general way of searching the words surrounding an unknown word to see if the reader can guess at the meaning. Such an endeavor rarely pays off. On the other hand, knowledge and trained application of such knowledge about semantic interrelationships, syntax, and clues within words (frequently called *structural elements*) will result in understanding most of the time.

Granted, the use of context clues does not always unlock meaning, particularly when the reader's experience does not match that of the writer, when a piece of writing is poorly organized, and/or when the writing lacks redundancy. At such times the reader must resort to an external authority—the dictionary, a peer, or the teacher. If the student is forced to rely frequently on an external authority in attempting to study given material, the teacher should find a replacement closer to the reader's present language ability.

Although the remainder of this section deals with specific types of context clues, students will need assistance in synthesizing the strategies into an overall attack. Simply knowing that a noun marker is *a, an,* or *the,* for example, will not assist the learner sufficiently. Once students have mastered some of the following strategies, they should begin putting them together as an overall approach to making use of the environment in which the unknown or hazy language unit is embedded.

The information and strategies discussed should not be introduced to students for their memorization. No lasting effects for use in unlocking ideas independently will come of trying to have students master this body of information. Instead, the teacher should master the information and through practical, relevant classroom work eventually lead students to incorporate these strategies into their existing strategy networks.

The syntactic, semantic, and internal context clues discussed can never be used in isolation. They are organized in separate categories for emphasis and as an aid to understanding their individual qualities. Students should be assisted in developing context clue strategies by gradually putting them to use in an integrated, synthesized approach.

USE OF SYNTACTIC CONTEXT

Patterns and Functions of Words.   Learners need to be assisted in using their knowledge of syntax (grammatical principles) to reduce the number of possible alternatives for an unknown language unit in a given context. Just through awareness of the order and function of words in sentences, a reader can eliminate a host of improbable meanings of the unknown language unit. For example, assume that the learner understands the following message reasonably well, except for the word *truculent:* "His truculent criticism of your painting betrayed some jealousy." Before considering any other strategies, the learner knows that the word is not the name of something (noun or subject) or an action (verb) just by looking at its position in the sentence. Its position indicates that it must be describing the subject *criticism* and hence is an adjective. Now the choices of meaning have been at least grossly delimited. Students should be urged to become conscious of patterns and functions of words as an initial means of approaching unknown language units.

Inflectional Cues.   By being aware of inflectional cues and their consistency, students can delimit the range of possibilities for an unknown language unit.

Consider the following example: "Mrs. Ames *scrounged around* the empty lot for sharp objects." Some students have heard the expression "scrounged around" but have never really been certain of its meaning. Before turning to *meaning* clues in the sentence, learners already know that the event took place in the past just by noting the inflectional ending "d" added to *scrounge*. In addition, through knowledge of sentence patterns, learners conclude that *scrounged* must be an action (verb) indicating what Mrs. Ames did.

Inflectional changes, both external (such as *d, ed, ing, s*) and internal (such as *mouse* to *mice*), are useful as initial context clues in placing limitations on possible choices.

Markers. For most secondary school students, capital letters and punctuation marks automatically serve as contextual aids; however, many students make little conscious use of language markers in ascertaining the meaning of unknown language units. A brief introduction to langauge markers, with a succinct review now and then, gives students another strategy for beginning to evaluate the unknown or the unclear language unit.

There are "a small number of words in English that have little or no meaning but perform key functions as structure cues. In a major language study, Fries found that 154 structure words made up fully a third of the total volume of language."[4] Function words include articles, auxiliary verbs, prepositions, and conjunctions. Once students are directed to function words as syntactic markers of meaning, they have added to their repertories another strategy for delimiting the possible alternatives for the unknown language unit. Although the awareness of syntactic markers must be built over time, teachers can raise students' consciousness by selecting a small section from a content area text and asking students to indicate the markers and their functions.

A *noun marker* is usually an article (the, a, an), a cardinal number, or a possessive (his, her, its, and our). The existence and position of the marker indicate that a noun follows: (1) "A radiometer is *an* instrument for detecting and measuring small amounts of radiant energy." (2) "*Their* centrifugal box produced yarn in *ten* seconds."

A *verb marker* (such as was, had, will) indicates that a verb follows: "They *were* jubilating about his amazing recovery."

Phrase markers (prepositions) are useful in identifying the function of an unknown language unit: "The acts of a government official are subject *to* judicial review."

Clause markers frequently help the reader identify the unknown language unit because they often signal specific kinds of meaningful actions. For example, *since, when, if, that,* and *because* are common clause markers. Notice how the phrase and clause markers in these two sentences begin to help the reader understand the difficult language units: (1) "A *prolegomenous statement* is particularly useful **if** the rest of the book is complex." (2) "**Since** the water could not *permeate* the dam, the valley was saved."

USE OF SEMANTIC CONTEXT

Although never freed of the constraints of syntax, the utilization of semantic clues appears to be the best way to understand an unknown or hazy language unit met within a context. Unless the unit is formally defined within the context, the unlocking of meaning may not be absolutely precise but will usually suffice to enable the reader to decode the writer's message. When a more precise definition is required, the reader should turn to an external authority source, such as a dictionary or the teacher.

It is also necessary to turn to an external source when a careful scrutiny of context does not yield meaning. Occasionally the context can be misleading. For example, in reading "The long distance runner was *enervated* when she finally reached the finish line," one high school student thought the runner was very nervous at the end of the race—a reasonable guess in light of the structure of the word, the structure of the sentence, and the possible gamut of meanings. But for that student the context was misleading.

The following sentences also provide little help through context: "They had an in-depth discussion of *philately* that lasted well into the night. Their interest in the subject was so keen that they were unaware of the passage of time." The reader does recognize that *philately* is the name of something that can be discussed in depth and with interest, but it could mean almost anything. Fortunately for the reader and for the writer who seeks to clarify, context usually does provide assistance. The context clues that follow are useful for readers in unlocking difficult language units and for writers in clarifying meaning.

Types of Clues.   The types of context clues described here are among the most common and useful, based on my own study and the reports of others.[5] Students should receive practice in recognizing and using these clues as vocabulary strategies and, in the long run, as tools for overall comprehension.

Statement of Meaning.   A forthright statement is frequently employed to elucidate the meaning of a language unit the writer feels might be misconstrued by or be unknown to the reader. Writers normally reserve such statements of meaning for language units they consider particularly significant. Occasionally the language unit will be marked with an asterisk or superscript number and formally defined in relation to the context as a footnote or in a glossary. More frequently, the following techniques are used:

Statement in parentheses
   John's *recapitulation* (review of the major points on both sides through a brief summary) of the Watergate debate, which finally concluded after three hectic days in civics class, was masterful.

Statement in apposition
   Glandular fever, **or** infectious mononucleosis, is a serious disease.

He caught more *flounder*, flatfish other than sole, than any of the amateur fishermen.

An *object lesson*—concrete illustration of a principle—was obviously learned by her today.

The term he used was *struggle for existence*, **that is,** the competition in nature among organisms to maintain themselves, survive, and produce others in a given environment.

Formal definition

A *micropyrometer* **is** an optical instrument to measure the temperature of small glowing bodies.

Subsequent statement

We must all soon learn how to compute in the *metric system*, which is used in a large number of countries. **It is** a decimal system of weights and measures universally used in science.

Students trained to spot statements of meaning will find it easy and satisfying to quickly locate statements in parentheses and in apposition, for they are assisted by the typographical aids of parentheses, commas, and dashes as well as by the words *or* and *that is*. Also, they will begin to notice that writers present many more formal definitions (frequently introduced by **is**) than they ever realized.

Exercises similar to the one in Figure 5.1 may be used as consciousness-raising activities by employing sentences and passages from the students' texts.[6]

Definition by Example. At times writers use examples alone to clarify a meaning, although more frequently definition by example is used in combination with a statement of meaning. The combination is common in science and mathematics texts when writers are eager to emphasize and make precise certain significant concepts. Exercises similar to the one in Figure 5.1 can be developed with the following examples—as well as with all the other types of context clues:

1. Trees, animals, and the sea are examples of *nature*.

2. The *mass* of a rock—like the weight of a car—can be computed.

3. Your body has several *organ systems*. For example, you have several organs that work together to perform digestion.[7]

Readers should be cautioned to pay attention to examples, for their very specificity often clarifies meaning when the more general statement fails. They need to appreciate the fact, however, that writers (particularly of expository materials) utilize examples as support for major concepts and are not usually focusing on the example itself. Nevertheless, from the readers' standpoint, the examples may be of tremendous importance in helping them learn how to make

Figure 5.1   A Statement-of-Meaning Exercise

The following example shows you how to set up an answer sheet and illustrates the correct answers for the first three items. Study the first three items and the answers to be sure you understand. Then read item 4. Find the word in *italics* and write it on your answer sheet, next to the number 4 and under the heading "Words." Next find the signal(s) and write it under the heading "Signals." Find the definition of the word in italics and write it under the heading "Definitions." Then, do items 4 through 10 in the same way.

WORDS	SIGNALS	DEFINITIONS
1. cacao	is	tree whose seeds are made into chocolate
2. foundations	are	bases on top of which houses are built
3. timid	—	shy and easily frightened
4.		

1. A *cacao* is a tree whose seeds are made into chocolate.

2. The workers came to put in *foundations* for the two new houses. These are the bases on top of which houses are built.

3. A *timid* person is someone who is shy and easily frightened.

4. The *city-state* (a small independent state made up of a city and the territories around it) was common in ancient Greece.

5. Of the forty-eight connecting states, Florida is the only one that is a *peninsula*. It is a point of land almost surrounded by water.

6. In the early days, citizens of a town were known as *burghers*.

7. Ancient scribes perfected the art of *calligraphy*. This skill, beautiful handwriting, has never been improved upon.

8. Now came the crisis! It—the point at which a change must come for better or for worse—needed to be faced calmly and with courage.

9. The inside of a building is called its *interior*.

10. For centuries England was ruled by an *aristocracy*. That was a class of people born into families with high rank and noble titles given them by a king.

use of the major concept in future coping situations. In math and science, for instance, problems to complete based on a given principle or theorem may best be faced after a review of specific examples.

Definition by Synonym.   A synonym is a word or brief expression close in meaning to the unknown or hazy language unit. Synonyms are used rather commonly, and readers should be on the lookout for them. Two problems are involved, however, especially if the synonym is a single word: (1) A synonym must be known to the reader or else it will fail to serve its purpose. (2) A synonym never represents the exact meaning of the unknown language unit. At times it will be close enough to provide adequate meaning, and the reader may move ahead. At other times it may not suffice, and then, of course, the reader will need to resort to an external authority for clarification. But in spite of the drawbacks, definition by synonym is more often than not a useful contextual aid. Here are a few examples:

After linking verbs
   To malign is to slander an innocent person.

   Indian paintbrush is a type of showy herb that grows in the southwestern United States.

After the word **or**
   Wapiti, or elk, have very large, spreading antlers.

Definition by Experience.   Comprehending what one reads suggests that the reader is able to carry on a meaningful dialogue with the author. The background—linguistic and experiential—the reader brings to the page becomes a contextual aid. In the absence or even presence of more structured and obvious context clues, readers should be encouraged to search through their experiences for keys that will unlock meaning. Note these examples:

Life experience
   The basketball game was a *fiasco*, with our team scoring 21 points to their 104.

Vicarious experience
   The heart attack victim was *resuscitated* through the use of mouth-to-mouth breathing.

Language experience
   He took upon himself—yes, he *appropriated*—the entire responsibility for raising money for the class gift.[8]

Definition by Similarity.   Although the reader is not assured of a precise meaning, similarity clues are useful, for known words or ideas are matched with the unknown or hazy language unit. Sometimes figures of speech, particularly similes and metaphors, are keys to unknown units. In example 1 below, a simile is used to define the word *idle*:

1. Day after day, day after day,
    We stuck, nor breath nor motion;
    As idle as a painted ship
    Upon a painted ocean.[9]

2. In his fight for India's independence, Mahatma Gandhi followed the teachings of the American writer Thoreau; and in his work to gain rights for Black people, Martin Luther King was also Thoreau's *disciple*.[10]

3. The scientist discovered the whole *skeletal system* of a dinosaur. It had almost as many bones in it as an elephant's bone structure.[11]

Definition by Contrast.   In using contrast to get an idea of the meaning of an unknown language unit, the reader may need to refer backward or forward. Sometimes a subsequent contrasting idea will unlock the meaning of a word or phrase skipped temporarily for lack of certainty about it; more frequently, however, the reader will find that retrospection is most helpful. At times the contrast will be between two words or brief expressions (antonyms); at other times contrast is developed by explanation, description, or example:

> Although Mr. Manson guzzled liquor in great quantities every evening, his *sobriety* was without question during the business day.
>
> The *flaccid condition* of his body is unlike that of Jim, who now exercises daily, watches his diet, and has become thin and wiry.
>
> When the light brightens, the pupils of the eyes contract; when it grows darker, they *dilate*.[12]

Reflection of Intent, Mood, Tone or Setting.   Harmony and inference are the key words in using this type of context clue! The reader must infer a feeling that harmonizes with the overall context. In some ways this is the easiest context clue of all, for it is primarily at the affective level and does not normally rely on deep thought. Precise understanding of the unknown language unit rarely results, and if the experience of the reader in no way matches that of the writer, the results can be disastrous. At times, high-level thinking does intermingle with feelings, especially when the intent being conveyed is rather subtle:

> The starchiness in his voice and the scowl on his face warned us that father was in a *captious* mood. Absolutely nothing suited him! Dinner was too late—the meat was too cold—the coffee was too hot![13]
>
> Such a poor, old, gray-haired man as leader! To ask him to serve us again is to murder him. How can we impose ourselves as his worthless children upon such a *paternal creature*?[14]

In the first example above, both the mood and the setting contribute to providing the reader with a reasonable meaning for *captious*. In the second example, if taken at face value, the tone would appear to present *paternal creature* as a kindly, old, fatherly man; however, one would need to be aware of the larger context. If the intent were to draw sympathy with a plea to let the gentleman retire, that is one thing. On the other hand, if a politician was using a sarcastic tone with the intent of forcing retirement, the meaning would change radically.

Students need concentrated practice with the various types of semantic context clues if they are to develop each as a strategy. They must have enough guided involvement so that they will make use of a given strategy at the appropriate time. When readers must turn to new materials and their experiential backgrounds are not close to matching those of the writers, renewed guidance may be necessary and desirable.

USE OF INTERNAL CONTEXT

Sometimes clues within words can help to unlock the meaning of a word, especially when used in collaboration with syntactic and semantic clues. Teachers in each content area should consciously help students learn prefixes and roots that occur commonly enough so that they become meaning clues. I agree with Courtney, however, that too much attention should not be placed on internal clues, for they can be misleading to the learner who is not a Greek or Latin scholar.[15] Emphasis must be placed on high-yield prefixes, roots, and some suffixes when relevant to specific content areas and always in connection with syntactic and semantic context. Thomas and Robinson suggest the following strategy:

1. Students examine the word for familiar parts.
2. If they recognize a part as familiar but do not know its meaning, they try to think of other words in which the part appears, then reason out the meaning of the part.
3. Returning to the context, they combine contextual clues with the structural to try to work out the word's meaning.
4. They check with the dictionary when necessary. With repeated success experiences in the classroom, students should come to apply their techniques of structural analysis habitually.[16]

Each teacher needs to develop a list of productive word parts most pertinent to a given content area. A roughly graded list by Thomas and Robinson may serve as a reference point.[17] Also, Dale and O'Rourke present comprehensive lists of common prefixes and derived words, common suffixes and derived words, and common roots and derived words.[18]

RELATED ACTIVITIES

1. Build a classroom library collection with books and materials at a variety of reading levels and focused on a variety of topics related to the units you have been studying, are studying, and will be studying. Encourage students to choose books or other materials to take home and to read in class. Part of a period set aside weekly for reading such materials, and your availability to chat and help with questions, will do much to encourage wider reading in your content area. You will also find that students will begin to handle the vocabulary of the subject with greater facility. (See Chapter 12 also.)

2. Provide some time for students to examine the dictionaries available in the content area classroom. Discuss what they have to offer and how they should be used. Select some sample sentences and short paragraphs from the textbook(s) and help students conclude that the context must be brought to the dictionary in order to find the appropriate meaning. For example, in one science textbook, students are confronted at the end of each chapter with the heading *"Applying What You Have Learned."* Unless the teacher has explained the meaning of the heading, many students may never be certain of its meaning. The heading can be taken to the dictionary to find the meaning of *apply(ing)* as it is used. One unabridged dictionary contains thirteen definitions; a student dictionary may contain about five. Students enjoy searching for the "right" meaning in directed activities and learn an important strategy.

3. You will want to help students with the various types of syntactic and semantic context clues described in the chapter. The first step should be to review the material being used in your given content area and note the clues that are most prevalent. Examine the material with students as they meet the specific types of clues. When you find a particularly useful passage, put it on a transparency and show it on an overhead projector. (Save it as an example for next year's class.) Conscious attention to context clues as a part of study strategy pays off in strengthened individual study.

4. Try the following technique for assisting readers to make use of strategies by concentrating on intersentence and intrasentence factors. Patrick McCabe, who is responsible for this material, calls the technique: *Vocabulary Building Through the Reduction of Uncertainty or How to Help Students Avoid the Garden Path.*[19] He borrowed the "garden path" concept from a theory by Garrett.[20] Another investigator, Mackay (in a discussion of Garrett's theory) suggested that one of the "garden path" postulates "is that we derive or process only one meaning or structure of an ambiguous sentence, without following the alternative path or derivation at all. If it turns out that the remaining context of the sentence does not fit this reading, the individual has been led down the garden path and must go back and start from scratch again."[21]

McCabe introduces the technique as a training device to help students formulate numerous guesses regarding a word, and through the use of subsequent information, to get them to disambiguate the meaning of the word in the particular context. Here is an example of the material he uses:

> There were three girls sitting at the counter all together, but there were four of us guys. These girls were dressed in the height of fashion with purple and green wigs on their heads and make up to match (colors around the eyeglasses and their *rot* painted). Then they had long, black very straight dresses. They kept looking our way and I nearly felt like saying (out of the corner of my *rot*, that is) that we should all go off to the party.
>
> . . . . So we scattered and went down the road and there we found what we were looking for, a *malenky* jest to start off the evening. There was an old schoolmaster who was walking down the street with books under his arm. He looked a *malenky* bit *poogly* when he *viddied* the four of us like that coming up so quiet and polite and smiling, but he said, "Yes, What is it?" in a very loud teacher like voice, as if to show he wasn't *poogly*. I said, "Hello, How are you?"[22]

Students enjoy figuring out *rot, malenky, viddied,* and *poogly,* and at the same time learn a great deal about the use of context clues as a potent strategy for unlocking meaning. McCabe usually leaves three or four spaces between each line in the passages and numbers each of the target words. When the student encounters one of the words initially, there may be three or four possible definitions because, at that time, many hypotheses regarding which meaning to assign may be logical. However, as the reader progresses, certain of the initial possibilities are no longer viable and can be discarded. The spaces between the lines allow the reader to write several guesses and then go back and cross them out as the meanings of certain target words become clear. The reader actively learns to reduce uncertainty.

SELECTED
READINGS

Anderson, Richard C., and Peter Freebody. "Vocabulary Knowledge." In *Comprehension and Teaching: Research Reviews,* edited by John T. Guthrie, pp. 77–117. Newark, Del.: International Reading Association, 1981.

Dale, Edgar. *The Word Game: Improving Communications.* Bloomington, Ind.: Phi Delta Kappa Educational Foundation, 1975.

————, and Joseph O'Rourke. *Techniques of Teaching Vocabulary.* Palo Alto, Calif.: Field Educational Publications, 1971.

Deighton, Lee C. *Vocabulary Development in the Classroom.* New York: Bureau of Publications, Teachers College Press, Teachers College, Columbia University, 1959.

Jones, Don R. "The Dictionary: A Look at 'Look It Up.'" *Journal of Reading* 23 (January 1980):309–12.

Kaplan, Elaine M., and Anita Tuchman. "Vocabulary Strategies Belong in the Hands of Learners. *Journal of Reading* 24 (October 1980):32–34.

Petty, Walter T.; Curtis P. Herold; and Earline Stoll. *The State of Knowledge About the Teaching of Vocabulary.* Champaign, Ill.: National Council of Teachers of English, 1968.

Piercey, Dorothy. *Reading Activities in Content Areas*, abridged ed., pp. 5–30, 100–2, 106. Boston: Allyn and Bacon, 1976.

Rauch, Sidney J. "Enriching Vocabulary in the Secondary Schools." In *Fusing Reading Skills and Content*, edited by H. Alan Robinson and Ellen Lamar Thomas, pp. 191–200. Newark, Del.: International Reading Association, 1969.

Stieglitz, Ezra L., and Varda S. Stieglitz. "SAVOR the Word to Reinforce Vocabulary in the Content Areas." *Journal of Reading* 25 (October 1981):46–51.

Thomas, Ellen Lamar, and H. Alan Robinson. *Improving Reading in Every Class*, 3rd ed., ch. 2. Boston: Allyn and Bacon, 1982.

NOTES

1. Richard C. Anderson and Peter Freebody, "Vocabulary Development," in *Comprehension and Teaching: Research Reviews*, ed. John T. Guthrie (Newark, Del.: International Reading Association, 1981), p. 110.

2. E. Brooks Smith, Kenneth S. Goodman, and Robert Meredith, *Language and Thinking in School*, 2nd ed. (New York: Holt, Rinehart and Winston, 1976), p. 64.

3. Sandra N. Kaplan, "Language Arts and Social Studies Curriculum in the Elementary School," in *The Gifted and the Talented*, The Seventy-eighth Yearbook of the National Society for the Study of Education, ed. A. Harry Passow (Chicago: University of Chicago Press, 1979), p. 162.

4. Smith, Goodman, and Meredith, *Language and Thinking*, p. 272.

5. Wilbur S. Ames, "The Development of a Classification Scheme of Contextual Aids," *Reading Research Quarterly* 2 (Fall 1966):57–82; A. Sterl Artley, "Teaching Word-Meaning Through Context," *Elementary English Review* 20 (February 1943):68–74; Lee C. Deighton, *Vocabulary Development in the Classroom* (New York: Bureau of Publications, Teachers College Press, Teachers College, Columbia University, 1959); Constance McCullough, "Context Aids in Reading," *Reading Teacher* 11 (April 1958):225–29; Roger J. Quealy, "Senior High School Students Use of Contextual Aids in Reading," *Reading Research Quarterly* 4 (Summer 1969):512–33; Earl F. Rankin and Betsy M. Overholser, "Reaction of Intermediate Grade Children to Contextual Clues," *Journal of Reading Behavior* 1 (Summer 1969):50–73; Louise C. Seibert, "A Study on the Practice of Guessing Word Meaning from Context," *Modern Language Journal* 29 (April 1945):296–322.

6. Adapted from Oliver Andresen, Leitha Paulsen, and H. Alan Robinson, *Social Studies Word Clues 3: Building Vocabulary through Context* (New York: EDL/McGraw-Hill, 1981), pp. 1–3, 7–8, 10.

7. Adapted from Joel Hillman and H. Alan Robinson, *Science Word Clues 3: Building Vocabulary through Context* (New York: EDL/McGraw-Hill, 1981), pp. 24, 27.

8. Ellen Lamar Thomas and H. Alan Robinson, *Improving Reading in Every Class*, 3rd ed. (Boston: Allyn and Bacon, 1982), p. 23 (abridged version, p. 22).

9. Edgar Dale and Joseph O'Rourke, *Techniques of Teaching Vocabulary* (Palo Alto, Calif.: Field Educational Publications, 1971), p. 33, with special thanks to Coleridge.

10. Andresen, Paulsen, and Robinson, *Social Studies Word Clues* 2, p. 35.
11. Hillman and Robinson, *Science Word Clues* 2, p. 35.
12. Thomas and Robinson, *Improving Reading in Every Class*, 3rd ed., p. 23 (abridged version, p. 22).
13. Ibid., p. 25 (unabridged version), with special thanks to Leitha Paulsen.
14. Artley, "Teaching Word Meaning," p. 71.
15. Brother Leonard Courtney, "Methods and Materials for Teaching Word Perception in Grades Ten Through Fourteen," in *Sequential Development of Reading Abilities*, Supplementary Educational Monographs, no. 90, ed. Helen M. Robinson (Chicago: University of Chicago Press, 1960), p. 43.
16. Thomas and Robinson, *Improving Reading in Every Class*, 2nd ed., p. 41.
17. Ibid., pp. 49–55.
18. Dale and O'Rourke, *Techniques of Teaching Vocabulary*, pp. 326–60.
19. Included with the permission of Patrick McCabe, Coordinator of the Graduate Program in Reading, Herbert H. Lehman College of the City University of New York.
20. Merrill F. Garrett, "Does Ambiguity Complicate the Perception of Sentences?" in *Advances in Psycholinguistics*, ed. Giovanni B. Flores d'Arcais and Willem J.M. Levelt (New York: American Elsevier, 1970), pp. 48–55.
21. Donald G. Mackay, "Mental Diplopia: Towards a Model of Speech Perception at the Semantic Level," in *Advances in Psycholinguistics*, ed. Giovanni B. Flores d'Arcais and Willem J.M. Levelt (New York: American Elsevier, 1970), p. 79.
22. Adapted by Patrick McCabe from Anthony Burgess, *A Clockwork Orange* (New York: Ballentine, 1971), pp. 10–11, 12–13.

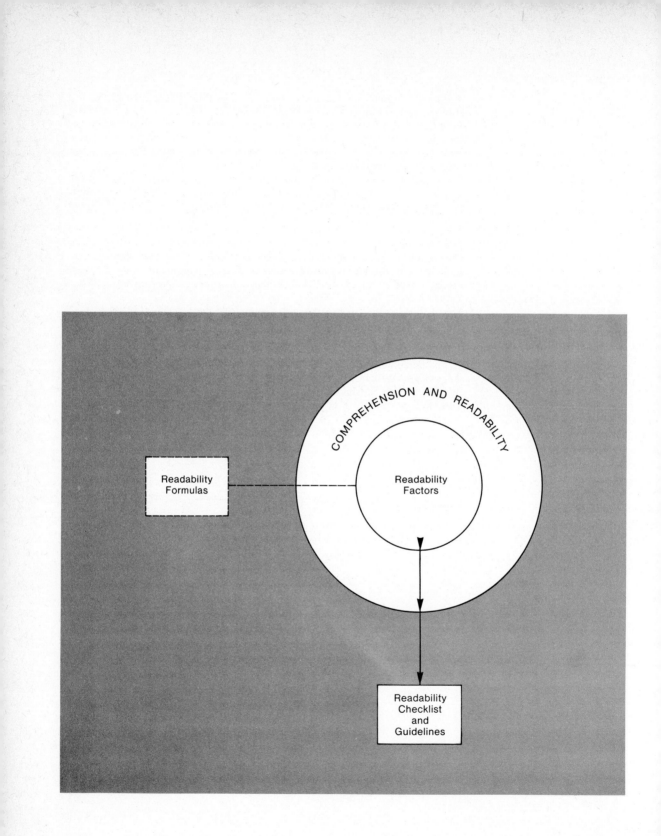

6
Readability Assessment

COMPREHENSION AND READABILITY

There seems to be little question that comprehension and readability are intricately linked. Readers without organized background experiences related to the concepts within the text will find the material difficult to process. Material that is poorly organized, unattractive, unclearly written, or linguistically distant from the intended readers will not be comprehended easily or well. On the other hand, reducing vocabulary load in some way and shortening sentences in text will not—in themselves—ensure readability or comprehension. Oversimplified text without explicit relationships in the text may result in poor or limited comprehension. "When sentences and vocabulary are oversimplified, cohesion is lost. As a result, comprehension becomes more difficult because the reader must infer the missing information."[1]

Marshall suggested that the term *readability* be replaced by the term *comprehensibility*:

> Since comprehension is the process of dealing with meaning, readability and comprehensibility are not interchangeable terms. Instead of determining the readability of textbooks, educators should be determining their comprehensibility.[2]

Marshall's terms might also be applied to student writers. The postwriting stage is when the emphasis is usually on editing, "polishing what has been written to share with a wider audience."[3] During this stage of writing, most of the attention has been traditionally placed on "the mechanics of writing." Although the mechanics have some importance, the major stress should be placed on comprehensibility—"Is what I am writing understandable to my audience?" As Applebee and others have said, "It can . . . be a stage for fine-tuning for a particular audience or to achieve a particular tone."[4]

READABILITY FORMULAS

Thorndike's *Teacher's World Book*, published in 1921, was ostensibly the first contribution to a concept of readability.[5] In this study, as in others to follow, emphasis was placed on the number of "difficult" words in a selection to indicate readability for a given group of readers. The concept of "word difficulty" was based on relative frequency of appearance on a list of words. Lively and Pressey constructed the first readability formula based on the premise of word difficulty in terms of frequency.[6] Subsequent researchers looked at a variety of other factors they thought might be related to readability—number of polysyllabic words or number of syllables in a passage, number of phrases of varying types, number of personal references in a passage, syntactic complexity of sentences, and so on—although vocabulary difficulty (relative frequency of appearance on a list) and sentence length emerged as the two factors most often considered. A *Formula for Predicting Readability* by Dale and Chall is used frequently in the secondary school; vocabulary difficulty and sentence length are the two factors considered.[7] Fry's formula is also often used as a quick way of estimating readability; it is based on sentence length and number of syllables in a passage.[8] More recently the Raygor Readability Estimate has been added to the list of quick appraisal techniques; in this formula long words (rather than syllables as in the Fry formula) are counted as a consideration of difficulty.[9]

Although these formulas and methods of ascertaining readability appear to have some limited value in roughly placing selections on a continuum of difficulty, they are very unsatisfactory. They do not take into consideration the changing concepts of words today as used in a variety of contexts; for example, the word *jet* is considered a difficult word (beyond fourth-grade level) in the "familiar word" lists of two readability formulas. Also, since the words are on lists, it is impossible to know which meaning of a word is considered easy or difficult; clearly it is the total context in the continuous discourse that will illuminate meaning. *The race horse wore a cooler after the race* can only be interpreted through one's experience and/or context clue expertise, although most high school students can pronounce the word *cooler* and have some preconceived notions about its meaning. In some of the formulas, it would seem that pronounceability rather than comprehensibility is determined.[10]

As Marshall pointed out, "still another flaw with readability formulas is that they do not account for the relationship between the content in the book and the knowledge of the reader."[11] Shortening sentences, using "easier" words or words with fewer letters or syllables, and other such mechanical treatments of the material can result in "vaguely defined concepts and a disjointed string of simple sentences."[12] The material can be labeled "more readable" based on the standards of a given readability formula but certainly not on the basis of comprehensibility to the reader.

Although not conveniently organized with charts and standard scores, Bormuth's cloze readability procedure is an improvement over others. It does include the individual reader and, within its limitations, helps one gain information about the semantic and syntactic strengths and weaknesses of a given reader. It also provides a scale for arriving at a readability level. The construction of cloze passages are described on pages 35–37 of this book. Bormuth found that scores falling between 44 and 57 percent on a cloze test indicated that students were able to handle the material with supervised instruction. Scores above 57 percent indicated that students could read the material on their own with adequate comprehension. For specifics in conducting readability tests using the cloze procedure, consult Bormuth's clear explanations in *Elementary English*.[13] (Bormuth counts only exact word responses in his readability procedure.)

READABILITY FACTORS

Hittleman suggests:

> Readability might not be an absolute entity inherent within a written passage and measured by a scale or index but might be relative to a "moment" at which time the reader's emotional, cognitive, and linguistic backgrounds interact with each other, with the topic, with proposed purposes for doing the reading, and with the author's choice of semantic and syntactic structures.[14]

In light of Hittleman's comment and other evidence about "comprehensibility," it seems naïve and detrimental to students to attach a grade level to books and consider them "readable" for all students at that level. As Campbell states:

> The problem of matching reader with appropriate text in the content areas is far more complex than merely applying a readability formula to the text and a reading test to the reader. It is comparatively simple to establish which factors influence comprehension of a subject-specific text and to make judgments about suitability of vocabulary, purpose of the text, usefulness of the content, layout, logical structure of information which can be linked to the reader's real world knowledge, difficulty of syntax, and the adequacy of explanation of subject-specific words and concepts. Presumably teachers are aware of this, yet many students are still being confronted with a text which is unsuitable for them.[15]

On the other hand, this misfit between student and text is understandable. Trying a book on for size with students and/or using the Bormuth formula as well as considering a multitude of factors that can influence comprehension is a big job. Individual teachers must certainly find it time consuming to attempt to match all books and all readers. Certainly, however, in textbook selection and evaluation, care must be taken since so much time, effort, and money are involved.

Perhaps suggesting some of the major factors involved in readability-comprehensibility might be useful in guiding textbook selection and evaluation. The following factors appear to be paramount (no ranking is intended); appropriate credit is given to sources in the "Notes" section of this chapter:

1. Main ideas are always remembered better than details, no matter where the main ideas occur in the text.

2. Main ideas can be used to organize information best when they are explicitly stated and familiar.

3. Repeated words are remembered better than words used only once,

and repeated information is remembered better than novel information.

4. Information explicitly related to other information is remembered better than unrelated ideas.

5. The distance between a pronoun and its referent affects comprehension of both the pronoun and its content.

6. Information in the text is remembered better when it is tied to the reader's prior knowledge.[16]

7. Vagueness and ambiguity (excessive use of indeterminate qualifiers such as "rather" or "any number of " and probability words such as "might," "possibly," or "sometimes") hamper understanding and hence readability.

8. Irrelevant, unrelated digressions and unnecessary restatements get in the way of understanding.

9. Readability is improved when content texts contain sufficient and clear examples that illustrate rules and/or principles.[17]

10. Information is best remembered when sentences in the continuous discourse are cohesively related through the use of such explaining links as "because," and "if . . . then."[18]

11. Readability is enhanced by highlighting and defining important technical words clearly and in a variety of contexts likely to be meaningful and familiar to readers.[19]

12. Attractive, well-organized text is a vital factor in promoting memory and understanding.

13. Unimportant ideas should be written as briefly as possible without the use of vivid examples.

14. The relationship between examples and important ideas should be tight.

15. Important principles should be stated positively, never negatively.

16. Important points should be enumerated.

17. Semantic labels should be attached to important concepts.

18. Technical terms should be highlighted in some way.

19. Straw men (discussions of minor importance that appear to divert the reader from the significant issues) should be indicated as such.[20]

READABILITY CHECKLIST

The checklist by Irwin and Davis presented in Example 6.1 seems to be a step in organizing what we know about text and the reader in some systematic way to assess readability.[21] The first five items (A–E) focus on the relationships between the background of the reader and the text information according to Irwin and Davis. Items F through H are concerned with concepts, and I through L deal with factors associated with comprehension in a number of research reports.[22] M and N are self-evident. (I would not include the results of a readability formula, for I think it is meaningless in light of the other fine evidence that this checklist is able to assemble.)

Irwin and Davis discuss the difficulty of categorizing in terms of their major headings, "Understandability" and "Learnability," but they feel that the *learnability* section of their checklist focuses on "how well the information in a textbook is remembered," as differentiated from *understandability*, or "how well it is understood."[23] The subsections under "Learnability" seem self-evident.

Example 6.1   *A Readability Checklist*[24]

This checklist is designed to help you evaluate the readability of your classroom texts. It can best be used if you rate your text while you are thinking of a specific class. Be sure to compare the textbook to a fictional ideal rather than to another text. Your goal is to find out what aspects of the text are or are not less than ideal. Finally, consider supplementary workbooks as part of the textbook and rate them together. Have fun!

Rate the questions below using the following rating system:

> 5—Excellent
> 4—Good
> 3—Adequate
> 2—Poor
> 1—Unacceptable
> NA—Not applicable

Further comments may be written in the space provided.

> Textbook title: _____
> Publisher: _____
> Copyright date: _____

Understandability

A. _____ Are the assumptions about students' vocabulary knowledge appropriate?

B. _____ Are the assumptions about students' prior knowledge of this content area appropriate?

Example 6.1 (continued)

Example 6.1 (continued)

C. ____ Are the assumptions about students' general experiential backgrounds appropriate?

D. ____ Does the teacher's manual provide the teacher with ways to develop and review the students' conceptual and experiential backgrounds?

E. ____ Are new concepts explicitly linked to the students' prior knowledge or to their experiential backgrounds?

F. ____ Does the text introduce abstract concepts by accompanying them with many concrete examples?

G. ____ Does the text introduce new concepts one at a time with a sufficient number of examples for each one?

H. ____ Are definitions understandable and at a lower level of abstraction than the concept being defined?

I. ____ Is the level of sentence complexity appropriate for the students?

J. ____ Are the main ideas of paragraphs, chapters, and subsections clearly stated?

K. ____ Does the text avoid irrelevant details?

L. ____ Does the text explicitly state important complex relationships (e.g., causality, conditionality, etc.) rather than always expecting the reader to infer them from the context?

M. ____ Does the teacher's manual provide lists of accessible resources containing alternative readings for the very poor or very advanced readers?

N. ____ Is the readability level appropriate (according to a readability formula)?

Learnability

Organization

A. ____ Is an introduction provided for in each chapter?

B. ____ Is there a clear and simple organizational pattern relating the chapters to each other?

C. ____ Does each chapter have a clear, explicit, and simple organizational structure?

D. ____ Does the text include resources such as an index, glossary, and table of contents?

E. ____ Do questions and activities draw attention to the organizational pattern of the material (e.g., chronological, cause and effect, spatial, topical, etc.)?

F. ____ Do consumable materials interrelate well with the textbook?

Reinforcement

A. ____ Does the text provide opportunities for students to practice using new concepts?

B. ____ Are there summaries at appropriate intervals in the text?

C. ____ Does the text provide adequate iconic aids such as maps, graphs, illustrations, etc., to reinforce concepts?

D. ____ Are there adequate suggestions for usable supplementary activities?

E. ____ Do these activities provide for a broad range of ability levels?

F. ____ Are there literal recall questions provided for the students' self-review?

G. ____ Do some of the questions encourage the students to draw inferences?

H. ____ Are there discussion questions which encourage creative thinking?

I. ____ Are questions clearly worded?

Motivation

A. ____ Does the teacher's manual provide introductory activities that will capture students' interest?

B. ____ Are chapter titles and subheadings concrete, meaningful, or interesting?

C. ____ Is the writing style of the text appealing to the students?

D. ____ Are the activities motivating? Will they make the student want to pursue the topic further?

E. ____ Does the book clearly show how the knowledge being learned might be used by the learner in the future?

F. ____ Are the cover, format, print size, and pictures appealing to the students?

G. ____ Does the text provide positive and motivating models for both sexes as well as for other racial, ethnic, and socioeconomic groups?

Readability Analysis

Weaknesses

1. On which items was the book rated the lowest?
2. Did these items fall in certain categories?
3. Summarize the weaknesses of this text.
4. What can you do in class to compensate for the weaknesses of this text?

Assets

1. On which items was the book rated the highest?
2. Did these items fail in certain categories?
3. Summarize the assets of this text.
4. What can you do in class to take advantage of the assets of this text?

The following questions might be used to augment those in the checklist:

1. Are captions under graphs, tables, and diagrams clearly written?
2. When a text refers to a graph, table, or diagram, is that aid on the same page (or a facing page) as the textual reference?
3. Are pictures contemporary (not dated by dress), unless the author's intention is to portray a certain period?[25]
4. Is passive tense used only when essential, since frequent use seems to trouble poor readers?
5. Are the variety of connectives (such as consequently, in spite of, thus, however) used in meaningful ways as important signals to readers?
6. Are relative clauses limited in number in given sentences, clearly written, and clearly attached to referents?

READABILITY GUIDELINES

The following guidelines or procedure, involving self-monitoring by students, also seems promising. It is adapted from Estes.[26] The procedure focuses on determining how many ideas readers see in the text, what those ideas are, what the relative perceived importance of the ideas is, how familiar the ideas are, and how well the ideas are structured as text.[27]

1. Select a textbook passage of 3,000 words or less.
2. Have students read through the passage once.
3. Without trying to define what *an idea* is, have students place lightly penciled slash marks wherever they believe an idea ends and another begins.
4. Ask students to compute the number of their slash marks and add one for the end of the last idea unit.
5. Average the totals each student provides for one overall figure.
6. With an overhead projector and a transparency copy of passage, enter the number (by a show of hands) of students who opt for idea breaks throughout the passage.
7. Now count the most frequently chosen break as number one, the next as number two, and so on through the break that equals the average number.
8. Now students can erase their own marks and put in the breaks agreed upon by the majority.
9. With the group version before them, students should be asked to rate each idea unit on a scale of 1 to 7 (number 7 regarded as most important) in relation to the author's message and intent.

10. Students should then decide individually on the five most important and the five least important ideas. They can then have a group discussion defending their ideas, which should provide all with a good idea of the comprehensibility of the passage and a hint about the total text.

11. Then have students rerate each idea unit on the basis of familiarity or unfamiliarity (scale of 1 to 7). The result is another estimate of comprehensibility, which also suggests how much effort and help will be required to understand the text.

IMPORTANT QUESTIONS TO CONSIDER

Estes raises three important questions teachers need to ask as they select texts for their students:

1. Do the ideas all obviously relate to the subject of the selection? (unity)

2. Are the ideas organized to give *continuous development*? (coherence)

3. Does the text emphasize what it should, given the topic? (emphasis)[28]

We should be searching for texts that unify ideas rather than present a multitude of ideas not clearly related to the topic. We should eliminate the consideration of texts that present a number of irrelevant or disconcerting ideas. We should choose texts that emphasize major ideas explicitly.

> Textbooks might, it would seem, try to say what they mean. It is, after all, in the nature of exposition to do so. Unfortunately, they don't always do so for the people who are assigned to read them.[29]

QUESTIONS AND RELATED ACTIVITIES

1. Why can some material labeled as relatively easy on the basis of a readability formula cause comprehension problems for the reader?

2. Try your hand at preparing a cloze readability passage. Select a passage from material you would like to try out. Leave the first and last sentences intact, but delete every fifth word from the sentences in between. This means your passage will range from about 270 to 280 words. Administer the passage to a group and have them write the answers they believe to be correct in each blank. Spelling does not count, and they may erase whatever and whenever they like. When you review the papers, count only exact word responses as correct. Assign two points to each correctly inserted word. Scores between 44 and 57 percent indicate that comprehension is adequate. Above 57 percent suggests that students can handle the material independently. (Synonyms and other responses may

be accepted in assessment and instructional situations but not for readability purposes as structured by Bormuth. If you do want to accept other responses, only synonyms based on an external criterion, such as a dictionary or thesaurus, should be considered.)

3.   Use the "Readability Checklist" in Example 6.1 (omitting N) to compare two books you deem to be somewhat equal in readability or books that have been given the same readability level on the basis of a standard readability formula.

4.   During the postwriting stage, have students consider the comprehensibility of what they have written for a specific audience and have them edit first on the basis of audience need before considering the mechanics. You might try the same strategy with your own writing.

SELECTED READINGS

Campbell, Anne. "How Readability Formulae Fall Short in Matching Student to Text in the Content Areas." *Journal of Reading* 22 (May 1979):683–89.

Davison, Alice, and Robert N. Kantor. "On the Failure of Readability Formulas to Define Readable Texts: A Case Study from Adaptations," *Reading Research Quarterly* 17, no. 2 (1982):187–209.

Irwin, Judith W., and Carol A. Davis. "Assessing Readability: The Checklist Approach." *Journal of Reading* 24 (November 1980):124–30.

Marshall, Nancy. "Research: Readability and Comprehensibility." *Journal of Reading* 22 (March 1979):542–44.

Pearson, P. David, and Kaybeth Camperell. "Comprehension of Text Structures." In *Comprehension and Teaching: Research Reviews*, edited by John T. Guthrie, pp. 27–55. Newark, Del.: International Reading Association, 1981.

Spiro, Rand J.; Bertram C. Bruce; and William F. Brewer, eds. *Theoretical Issues in Reading Comprehension*. Hillsdale, N.J.: Lawrence Erlbaum Associates, 1980.

NOTES

1.   Nancy Marshall, "Research: Readability and Comprehensibility," *Journal of Reading* 22 (March 1979):543.
2.   Ibid.
3.   Arthur N. Applebee and others, "A Study of Writing in the Secondary School," Final Report NIE–G–79–0174 (Urbana, Ill.: National Council of Teachers of English, September 1980), p. 146.
4.   Ibid.
5.   Edward L. Thorndike, *The Teacher's Word Book* (New York: Teachers College, Columbia University, 1921).
6.   Bertha Lively and Sidney Pressey, "A Method of Measuring the 'Vocabulary Burden' of Textbooks," *Educational Administration and Supervision* 9 (October 1923):226–31.
7.   Edgar Dale and Jeanne S. Chall, *A Formula for Predicting Readability* (Columbus: Bureau of Educational Research, Ohio State University, n.d.).

8. Edward Fry, "Fry's Readability Graph: Clarifications, Validity, and Extention to Level 17," *Journal of Reading* 21 (December 1977):242–52.

9. Alton L. Raygor, "The Raygor Readability Estimate: A Quick and Easy Way to Determine Difficulty," in *Reading: Theory, Research and Practice,"* ed. P. David Pearson, Twenty-sixth Yearbook of the National Reading Conference (Clemson, S.C.: National Reading Conference, 1977), pp. 259–63.

10. Marshall, "Research," pp. 542–44.

11. Ibid., p. 543.

12. Ibid.

13. John R. Bormuth, "The Cloze Readability Procedure," *Elementary English* 45 (April 1968):429–36.

14. Daniel R. Hittleman, "The Readability of Subject Matter Material Rewritten on the Basis of Students' Oral Reading Miscues" (Doctoral dissertation, Hofstra University, 1971), pp. 125–26.

15. Anne Campbell, "How Readability Formulae Fall Short in Matching Student to Text in the Content Areas," *Journal of Reading* 22 (May 1979):688.

16. The first six factors were contributed by Marshall, "Research," p. 543.

17. Factors 7 through 9 are based on discussions by Campbell, "How Readability Formulae Fall Short," p. 685.

18. Factor 10 was generated from remarks by Marshall, "Research," p. 543; Campbell, "How Readability Formulae Fall Short," p. 685; and P. David Pearson and Kaybeth Camperell, "Comprehension of Text Structures," in *Comprehension and Teaching: Research Reviews*, ed. John T. Guthrie (Newark, Del.: International Reading Association, 1981), p. 48.

19. Marshall, "Research," p. 544, and Campbell, "How Readability Formulae Fall Short," p. 685.

20. Points 13 through 19 adapted from Thomas H. Estes, "The Nature and Structure of Text," in *Secondary School Reading: What Research Reveals for Classroom Practice*, ed. Allen Berger and H. Alan Robinson (Urbana, Ill.: National Conference on Research in English and ERIC Clearinghouse on Reading and Communication Skills, 1982), p. 91.

21. Judith W. Irwin and Carol A. Davis. "Assessing Readability: The Checklist Approach," *Journal of Reading* 24 (November 1980):124–30.

22. Ibid., p. 125.

23. Ibid., p. 126.

24. Ibid., pp. 129–30. Reprinted with permission of the author and the International Reading Association.

25. Kenneth C. Krause, "Do's and Don'ts in Evaluating Textbooks," *Journal of Reading* 20 (December 1976):213, contributed the ideas for the first three questions.

26. Estes, "Nature and Structure of Text", pp. 92–94.

27. Ibid., p. 92.

28. Ibid., p. 94.

29. Ibid.

Part C
STRATEGIES FOR SPECIFIC CONTENT AREAS

Chapters 7 through 11 concentrate on specific text structures or patterns found within the instructional materials used in the various subject matter areas. Patterns of writing overlap at times, but differences are evident, as content and context interrelate. To improve comprehension in each content area, specific instruction and practice utilizing the instructional materials of a given area are required for most learners. Teachers will want to introduce the concepts of text patterns to all readers, not just to those considered "poor" readers. As a reading tool, knowledge and use of text patterns in a discipline will increase understanding, for students are then able to set their own purposes for each reading task. Some students may need more intensive directed practice with some patterns of writing than with others.

Strategies for coping with particular patterns are described in detail in the chapters that follow.

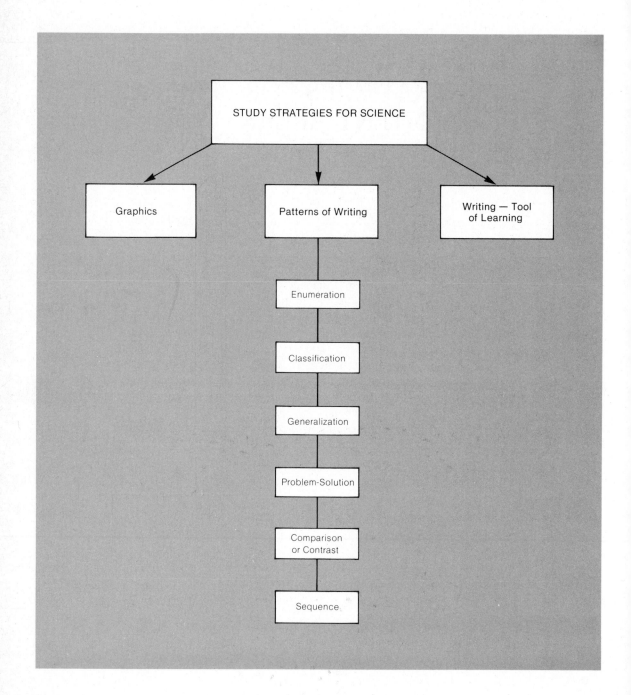

7
Science

No content area appears to be in more of "a state of dynamic change" than science.[1] The condition is neither strange nor unanticipated, for we have been swept with gusto into the age of technology and space travel. We must learn to understand and utilize science not only as a body of information but as a process, a way of attempting to understand our environment and the organisms in that environment.

To help students understand and use the concepts of science, science educators place much emphasis on observation, discovery, inquiry, and involvement. A multitude of scientific activities is offered; laboratory work is stressed. Generally, in both courses of study and instructional materials, fewer topics are covered at one time than in the past, but greater intensity and rigor are applied. A large number of teachers seem to be turning toward other materials, both print and nonprint, but textbooks still appear to be used frequently. Learners acquire much of their knowledge and know-how through reading and writing, whether it be through straight exposition, through exposition integrated with the use of figures and mathematical equations, or through the following of printed directions.

A major task of the reader of instructional materials in science is to understand a host of details that often add up to a generalization, an abstraction, or a theory. The reader must then attempt to comprehend the theory, which frequently necessitates a review and even a remarshalling of the details. Then he or she usually must understand one or more illustrations of how a given theory is tested. Following this, the reader is frequently directed to read a series of instructions aimed at utilizing what has been learned. This attention placed on "learning by doing" *does* actively involve the learner, but it often makes the reading assignment more difficult by asking the learner to fulfill two tasks at once (reading and doing) and by demanding very exact reading in order to have the activity completed accurately. Also, less explanation and more involvement deplete discourse of much of its redundancy. Hence, although the emphasis is on inquiry and not on delivery of information, reading scientific material remains rather complex. And, of course, when the material needs to include more of the language of mathematics, the complexity increases. Especially in the physical sciences, the reading task is complicated by the intertwining of mathematical and verbal language in explaining details, generalizations, and illustrations.

No matter how expert the teaching, how excellent the materials, or how fascinating the activities, a mass of complex reading still faces the solitary reader. Since the reading tasks and the content are so interwoven, *a* role of the high school science teacher is to assist the learner in learning how to pursue knowledge through reading. Also, students can be helped to organize ideas in written form as part of the learning process. The very act of organizing data in written form, as a review and/or reinforcement of what has been read, is a learning tool. In this chapter the nature and organization of materials in science textbooks are considered along with strategies for helping students cope with such materials.

GRAPHICS
In both the physical and the life sciences, graphics are an integral part of the text. In many cases, without graphics it would be impossible to explain fully some processes and concepts. Graphic displays appear to have three major, often overlapping, purposes: (1) to serve as a base or model for actual experimentation or activity; (2) to add information, usually organized details, to ideas initiated through the words in print; and (3) to parallel the running text as a means of further explanation, clarification, and/or expansion.

The diagram in Figure 7.1 must be "read" in conjunction with the passage beneath it. The reader needs to *apply* the explanatory material to the graphic in order to understand the operation of the engine. In addition, the reader is asked to interrelate this information, particularly in the graphic, with the actual movement of valves and pistons in a classroom model. This three-part activity—(1) reading the graphic and the printed material; (2) interrelating the ideas in both; and (3) using the graphic in an activity—is difficult for many students, and persistent guidance by the instructor is often imperative.

In Figure 7.2, information in chart form is added to what has been read. Students need to be guided into realizing that such information must be read and analyzed carefully, for it contributes new information in condensed form.

In Figure 7.3, the reader must be helped to realize that she or he should read both the running text *and* the graphic, for neither presents the whole process alone. Guided instruction in reading and thinking about the caption as well as the labels pays off in understanding. Some students need a great deal of such guidance before they can incorporate the strategy into their own plans of study.

In order to assist certain students in the reading of graphics, captions, and labels, the teacher occasionally may want to isolate a segment of the chapter or selection. Most students should receive some type of structured guidance in attacking graphics, particularly if they have dismissed or only lightly considered such significant material in the past. All students should be introduced by the

*Figure 7.1   Studying a Graphic in the
Physical Sciences*[2]

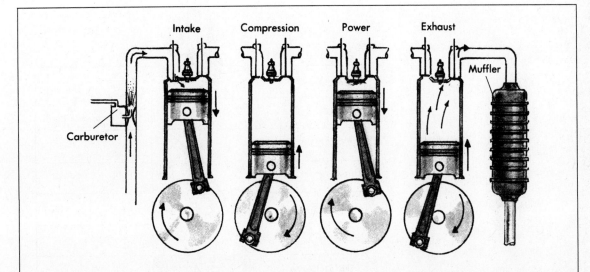

The diagram above shows the four strokes of a four-stroke engine. Refer to this diagram while turning the flywheel of an engine from which the head has been removed. Note the action of the valves and the motions of the piston. Identify each of the strokes.

1. *Intake stroke*. The piston moves downward, producing a partial vacuum inside the engine. The intake valve opens. Air flows into the carburetor, mixes with gasoline vapor, and goes to the engine.

2. *Compression stroke*. The intake valve closes and the piston moves upward. The air and gasoline mixture is compressed above the piston.

3. *Power stroke*. When the piston reaches the top of its compression stroke, the spark plug produces a spark and ignites the fuel. The resulting fire heats the gases to a temperature of about 1300°C (2300°F). The gases expand and push downward on the piston, turning the crankshaft and flywheel.

4. *Exhaust stroke*. The energy of the spinning flywheel starts the piston moving upward again. The exhaust valve opens and burned gases are forced out through the muffler. At the end of the exhaust stroke, the exhaust valve closes, the intake valve opens, and the four-stroke cycle begins again.

Source: Walter A. Thurber, Robert E. Kilburn, and Peter S. Howell, *Exploring Physical Science* (Boston: Allyn and Bacon, 1977), p. 178.

Figure 7.2   Studying a Graphic in the Living Sciences[3]

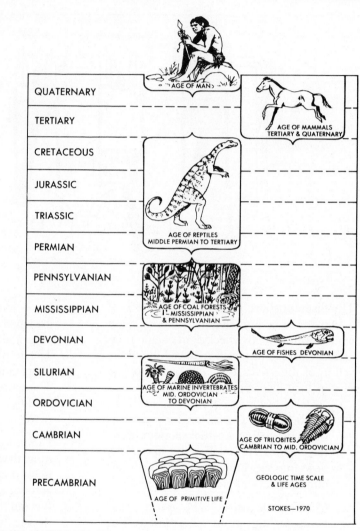

Relation of the great life ages to the standard geologic time scale. The successive ages are strictly informal designations for certain intervals dominated by certain life forms from which they get their names. The ones given here are not universally used, and, of course, others may be designated for additional subdivisions.

instructor to types of graphics not met in their previous reading. (See the activities at the end of this chapter for suggestions related to graphics illustrated here as well as to graphics that may appear in the materials students are using.)

Often students can be encouraged and/or directed to organize their own

Figure 7–3 (continued)

Faunal Succession

A third generalization of the great importance in thinking about the past history of the earth is the *principle of faunal succession*, which is: *Groups of fossil plants and animals succeed one another in a definite and determinable order and each period of time can be recognized by its respective fossils.* Note that this statement does not specify the manner of origin of the different groups of fossils; it is a fact regardless of whether or not organic evolution is true.

The principal of faunal succession was not conceived as an unsupported thoery; it was discovered through the accumulation and study of thousands of fossil collections from all parts of the earth. Anyone who is interested can repeat the process of collection and comparison if he wishes, as long as he is careful to apply the law of superposition to his work. When superposition is taken into account it is always found that the oldest abundant metazoan fossils are the trilobites. An Age of Trilobites can be recognized on all continents. In successively higher and younger rocks we recognize an Age of Fishes, an Age of Coal Forests, an Age of Reptiles, an Age of Mammals, and an Age of Man [see figure]. These terms, of course, pertain to the groups of organisms that were especially plentiful and characteristic during certain periods. Within each of the great "ages" there are numerous minor subdivisions marked, for example, by certain species of trilobites, certain kinds of fish, and so on. That the same succession of ages is found on each major landmass, never out of order and never repeated in the same area, proves uniform worldwide similarity and correlation.

It should be understood that not all fossil-bearing periods are present everywhere. The Grand Canyon, for example, is a magnificent display of rock layers, but it shows only four of the twelve major fossil-bearing periods of earth's history. Records of two of the missing periods were never deposited in this area, but were laid down in southern Nevada a short distance away. Here they are found in proper order "sandwiched" between the formations that are present in the Grand Canyon.

Source: William L. Stokes, Sheldon Judson, and M. Dane Picard, *Introduction to Geology: Physical and Historical* (Englewood Cliffs: N.J.: Prentice-Hall, 1978), pp. 346–47. Reprinted by permission Prentice-Hall, Inc.

graphs and charts as a way of making notes on their reading. Categorizing ideas in this way usually aids comprehension as well as retention. At times, instructors may also ask for diagrams or flow charts as comprehension products in place of the usual written response.

Figure 7.3   Studying a Graphic in the Living Sciences[4]

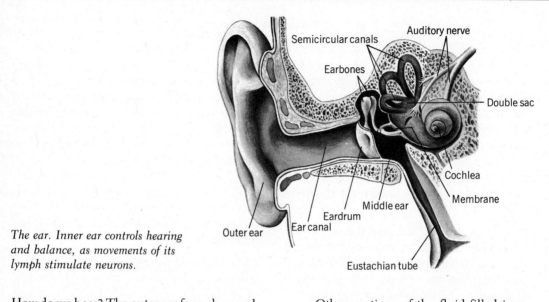

The ear. Inner ear controls hearing and balance, as movements of its lymph stimulate neurons.

How do we hear? The outer ear funnels sound vibrations against the *eardrum*, which separates it from the middle ear. Three tiny earbones carry the vibrations to a similar membrane covering a window that opens to the inner ear.

The complex inner ear, buried in bone, and filled with a lymph-like fluid, is a multiple sense organ. The coiled *cochlea* is the sound-detecting portion. Vibrations in the fluid are transferred to a base membrane, and then to microscopic hairs which respond to certain frequencies. Sensory neurons, fired by the hairs, carry the sensations to the brain through the auditory nerve.

Other portions of the fluid-filled inner ear are concerned with balance. A double sac contains earstones that rest on sensitive hairs and enable us to tell our position. A curious reflex connecting the sacs with the abdomen causes the sinking feeling we feel in a rapidly rising elevator or airplane.

Three *semicircular canals* are set at right angles to each other. Here the rocking of the fluid starts signals conveying a sense of motion. Impulses to the cerebellum initiate reflexes which we use to keep our balance. Unusual movements of the lymph in the canals cause seasickness.

Source: Stanley L. Weinberg, *Biology: An Inquiry into the Nature of Life*, 4th ed. (Boston: Allyn and Bacon, 1977), p. 268.

PATTERNS
AND
STRATEGIES

My own study of contemporary science textbooks used in junior and senior high schools, plus what I have gleaned from the analyses of others, has led me to determine that there are six major patterns of writing or text structures in science: *enumeration, classification, generalization, problem-solution, comparison or contrast*, and *sequence*. Although other patterns are sometimes used, these six appear to be the most common. In addition to explaining the six patterns and presenting examples of each, the following discussion focuses attention on specific strategies for helping the reader unlock the ideas within each pattern of writing. When applicable, some type of written response is emphasized as a tool of study.

ENUMERATION

Examples. The enumeration pattern is sometimes found in single paragraphs, but it most often spans a large section of writing. In this pattern the topic is usually introduced at the outset along with a stated number of descriptions, characteristics, or attributes (subtopics). The reader's task is to locate, understand, and remember the subtopics along with the pertinent information explaining each.

At times the enumeration pattern is mistaken for a main idea or generalization followed by details. In my opinion, this error is responsible for superficial comprehension in many instances. When a main idea is present, it is a broad, significant statement—the major thought the author wants to get across. (See discussion of generalization, pp. 158–159.) Frequently no main idea is present in a paragraph or group of paragraphs, and the major thesis actually consists of a group of related details. In the enumeration pattern, the group of enumerated facts is of major importance, not the broad introductory statement. For instance, in Example 7.1, a passage from a physics textbook,

---

Example 7.1[5] There are two types of waves, *transverse* and *longitudinal*. *Transverse waves are those that cause the particles over which they pass to vibrate at right angles to the direction in which the waves are moving.* We shall see that light and heat appear to be transmitted by transverse waves. Water waves are not true transverse waves but they approximate this type of wave, as is shown when waves move over the surface of a lake. They cause small boats and other floating objects to bob up and down, or to vibrate at right angles to the direction in which the waves are moving.

Longitudinal waves cause the particles over which they pass to vibrate in a direction parallel to the direction in which the waves are moving. Sounds are transmitted through the air by longitudinal waves. As the sound of a bell moves northward, it can be shown that it causes the molecules of the air through which it passes to vibrate in a north-and-south direction.

---

the major information the reader comes away with should include definitions of the two types of waves, not just the concept that there are two types. "There are two types of waves" is an introductory statement that states the topic and facilitates the listing of the important information.

Example 7.2 is the opening paragraph of a large section of a chapter in a biology textbook; it introduces and defines, but its major function is to set the stage for the enumeration pattern of writing:

Example 7.2[6]   **Basic Life Functions**

There are several important functions performed by each living organism which, occurring together, make it possible for these organisms to be alive. These functions include metabolism, growth, responsiveness, reproduction, and adaptation. Dead organisms cannot carry on these functions. Hence, by definition, they are not alive. Nonliving things, such as automobiles and computers, at times may seem to carry on some of these functions. However, they never carry on any of these functions. Thus they are not considered to be alive.

Strategies.   Three steps should be taken for successful reading of the enumeration pattern: recognition of topic; recognition of subtopics; and organization of details related to a subtopic. Steps one and two are quite visible and evident to most readers. Step three, a basic cluster of skills pertinent to many strategies in the reading of scientific discourse, often proves difficult for readers.

Step One: Recognition of Topic.   The topic is the subject about which something is written. It is not the main idea; the main idea usually encompasses the topic with the major, most essential message the writer wishes to convey. Hence, a topic normally names something and does not include a description of it, what it does, or what was done to it.

Readers must be alert to an opening statement that signals the enumeration pattern by naming the topic and indicating the number of subtopics that will be developed. In Example 7.1, the specific number *two* is stated; in Example 7.2, the word *several* is used immediately, followed by the five functions to be discussed in subsequent paragraphs. In either case, once readers find this opening statement, they will be aware of the topic and the pattern of writing.

Step Two: Recognition of Subtopics.   The readers' task is to locate each subtopic as they proceed through the reading. In most cases the job is a fairly simple one, for the writers use such signal words as *first, second,* or *third,* frequently accompanied by a key word such as *characteristic.* Occasionally the student will have to monitor more carefully when less specific signals are used, such as *then, next,* and *finally.* In Example 7.2, each of the life functions mentioned in the introductory paragraph became a heading for the paragraphs to follow.

Students who have difficulty with this pattern of writing should spend time working on steps one and two before proceeding to step three. Once students learn to find and understand the function of an opening statement in this pattern, and when they can recognize each subtopic, they will gain confidence in proceeding, for they will possess a structure or framework in which to operate. A possible step at this point is to have slower learners and/or those students having particular difficulty with the text simply make a list of the functions to be found in the section on basic life functions:

Basic Life Functions
Metabolism
Growth
Responsiveness
Reproduction
Adaptation

They can then use this list as a framework to find specific, important information about each function.

Step Three: Organization of Details Related to Subtopic. After noting each subtopic, readers should return to the first subtopic to read all the information about that subtopic until they note the beginning of the next subtopic. In Example 7.2, the readers will need to proceed to other paragraphs to work on each subtopic and the details explaining each.

The major task in the two paragraphs about waves (Example 7.1) is to find and understand the definitions of the two types of waves. The author has helped by placing each definition in italics. In addition, the reader should find examples of what each type of wave transmits.

Outcome. For Example 7.2, students should come up with an outline including important facts and/or illustrations that explain each of the five basic life functions. For Example 7.1, students could answer in either of two ways:

Types of Waves
There are two types of waves. *Transverse* waves cause the particles over which they pass to vibrate at right angles to the direction in which the waves are moving. Light and heat appear to be transmitted by transverse waves, and water waves approximate this type of wave. *Longitudinal* waves cause the particles over which they pass to vibrate in a direction parallel to the direction in which the waves are moving. Sounds are transmitted through the air by longitudinal waves.

Although most of the information in the students' summary above is verbatim (a necessity dictated by the nature of the information), this type of written response increases organizational ability as well as knowledge of both content and structure.

The second type of response is a type of outline suited to the structure of the information and valuable for just that reason. This outline was organized by a language disabled student:

Types of Waves

1. *Transverse* waves cause particles over which they pass to vibrate at right angles to the direction in which the waves are moving.
   a. Appear to transmit light and heat.
   b. Water waves approximate these waves.
2. Longitudinal waves cause particles over which they pass to vibrate in a direction parallel to the direction in which the waves are moving. Sounds are transmitted through the air by these waves.

Some learners will need help in differentiating between illustrations and important facts. In this pattern of writing, illustrations or examples usually enhance understanding of a point already made rather than introduce a new fact.

Additional examples and discussion of strategies applied to the enumeration pattern appear on pages 187–189.

CLASSIFICATION

Example.   The classification pattern most often spans a group of paragraphs, a large part of a chapter, a chapter, or even several chapters. In this pattern a topic is divided into two or more parts at the outset, followed by subtopics that are grouped under each part. Usually both the divided topic and the subtopics are explained or described. The text is frequently accompanied by a chart in which the authors diagram the classification scheme.

The pattern appears to be most often used in the biological sciences, although it may be found throughout the sciences. Its paragraphs are normally explanatory, although individual paragraphs with other functions may appear as a part of the total pattern.

Example 7.3 introduces a total chapter devoted to this pattern. The four present-day classifications of *reptiles* are presented, and the rest of the chapter describes, explains, and illustrates each of the classes. In some cases, comparisons and contrasts are made (see pages 166–168 in this chapter), but—in the main—the purpose is to set forth clear pictures of each classification.

Strategies.   On the surface the classification pattern appears similar to the enumeration pattern, but it is not. Different thought processes are involved. In the enumeration pattern, the reader needs to locate the topic, then the subtopics, and then the pertinent details related to each subtopic. In the classification pattern, the reader must recognize the divided topic, comprehend

Example 7.3[7]   There are about 6,000 species in the class *Reptilia* today. This may seem like a great many, but it is only a small fraction of the number that inhabited the earth during the Age of Reptiles. Once there were 16 orders of reptiles. Only four orders of reptiles exist today. One of these orders is represented by a single species that is nearing extinction.

Some of today's reptiles are very much like their prehistoric ancestors. Others, called modern reptiles, have become very different. Reptiles are most numerous in the tropics. Some reptiles, however, have migrated to more temperate climates. In fact, reptiles are even found in colder parts of the earth. However, there are no reptile populations in icy regions, high mountains, and the ocean depths. There are about 275 reptile species in the United States.

Rhynchocephalia consists of one species, nearing extincton; *Sphenodon* (tuatara).

Squamata includes reptiles with horny epidermal scales; lizards and snakes.

Chelonia (Testudinata) have bodies with two bony shells; turtles and tortoises.

Crocodilia are large reptiles with elongated skulls the most prominent feature; alligators, crocodiles, gavials, and caimans.

why it is divided, and assign each subtopic to the appropriate part of the divided topic.

Step One: Recognition of Divided Topic.   Frequently in science materials, writers make the topic so obvious that it is impossible to miss. The topic will appear in the title of the chapter or in a heading, usually in boldface type. Much of the time the title or heading will be followed by an introductory paragraph that reiterates the topic, often in the first sentence or two. In Example 7.3, the actual heading that preceded the introductory paragraphs was "Classification of Modern Reptiles." The first of the introductory paragraphs states the number to be described—four. (Instructors working with slow learners should be sure to cement the concept that order and class or classification refer to the same thing.) The information following the second paragraph pinpoints the four orders or classes. The student should now be ready to read to fill in vital information about each of the orders.

Step Two: Recognition and Assignment of Subtopics.   Once the divided topic has been established, a purpose has been established, and the reader is now set to find important descriptive and explanatory information about the first of the divided topics—in this case, *Rhynchocephalia*. After that job has been accomplished, the reader will work in the same way with each of the additional three classes.

Outcome.   A natural outcome of the classification pattern is to have students construct a classification chart if it has not already been provided by the authors of the text. Although a chart is useful, some readers are able to construct one without fully understanding the interrelationships among the ideas. Since this pattern lends itself to clear expository writing, the construction of an essay about the chapter is one way of ensuring some internalization of the classes. Using the reptile example (Example 7.3) and the remainder of the chapter, students can be helped to structure a six paragraph essay: (1) introduction of number and types of classes, (2) paragraph on Rhynchocephalia, (3) paragraph on Squamata, (4) paragraph on Chelonia, (5) paragraph on Crocodilia, and (6) concluding paragraph.

GENERALIZATION

Examples.   The generalization pattern is found frequently, and the generalization takes a variety of forms. In explanatory paragraphs, it is most often a principle, a hypothesis, or a conclusion. In definitional paragraphs, it is sometimes just a statement synthesizing a group of facts. It is always the writer's main idea, major point, or principal thought. It is the broadest as well as the most significant idea the writers wish to convey. Unlike the classification and enumeration patterns, where the subtopics take on major importance, in the generalization pattern the reader is concerned primarily with the one generalization, and subtopics are used only as supporting information.

In the generalization pattern, supporting information is significant, then, not to be organized and retained for its own value, but to explain, clarify, and emphasize the generalization. In science the supporting details may consist of facts and/or illustrations. When the generalization is a conclusion, the supporting information may consist of "proof "; when it is a hypothesis, "evidence" usually follows; when it is a principle or general statement, various illustrations and comparisons are often presented.

In Example 7.4, the generalization is a conclusion stated at the very beginning of the paragraph; the rest of the paragraph provides "proof " for the statement:

Example 7.4[8]   Water is one of man's most useful resources. Man realized its possibilities as a means of transport and built ships; he saw it as a natural defense and entrenched himself behind moats; he understood it as an enemy and set up embankments; he learned to control, direct, and exploit it as a source of fertility and devised systems of irrigation and drainage. Finally, he realized that he could use the water's flow and fall as a source of energy. Its exploitation as an energy source probably dates from about one hundred years B.C. Since that time, many technical advances have been made and many new energy sources have been exploited.

Example 7.5, from a biology textbook, is a unit of three paragraphs concerned with one generalization. In paragraph one, the generalization, in the form of a principle, is stated and restated from the first sentence in italics to the last reexplanation in the final sentence of the first paragraph. Paragraph two is an illustration in the form of an analogy—a rather common style in scientific discourse. Illustrative paragraphs, although hardly patterns in themselves, are frequently part of larger patterns of writing. Paragraph three presents a comparison that is another form of illustration, although this paragraph can stand by itself irrespective of the larger unit. (Comparison-contrast patterns of writing are examined later in this chapter.)

Example 7.5[9] *The speed of an impulse is independent of stimulus intensity.* The conduction of an impulse in any one neuron occurs at one speed regardless of the strength of the stimulation. A single nerve fiber will either respond completely or not at all. There is no half measure. The impulse cannot become larger or smaller or change in any way. Any stimulus—be it electrical, mechanical, or chemical—that can stimulate a nerve will produce an impulse of one strength, traveling at one speed. This is called the *all-or-nothing law of conduction.* The minimum strength of a stimulus that can cause a reaction is called the *threshold intensity.* In other words, no matter how much stronger than the threshold intensity a stimulus may be, the strength of the impulse is constant.

An analogy to this all-or-nothing reaction can be drawn from the common safety match. To light the match, it takes a stroke of a certain intensity, or energy level. This may also be called the threshold intensity. Once this level is reached, the match ignites. A stroke that is several times more "energy-rich" will only produce the same reaction.

The nerve impulse is often compared to a spark traveling along a fuse. It does not lose its intensity as it travels. Unlike a fuse, however, the nerve is not consumed. After a brief rest for recharging, called the *refractory period,* the nerve is ready to operate again.

Example 7.6, from a chemistry textbook, is a definitional paragraph beginning with the generalization in the form of a statement followed by clarification through details and illustrations; the table serves as specific support for the generalization:

Strategies.   The generalization pattern is prevalent in most subject matter areas; hence, students need specific guidance within each of the areas. Some students have great difficulty in grasping generalizations and may need directed teaching of a cluster of subskills before being able to attack the generalizations in science materials. Such students will not learn how to unfold generalizations by getting more and more exercises on finding them; they need help with more funda-

Example 7.6[10]   Formulas for hydrated compounds include the water of hydration following a raised dot after the regular formula. For example, $CuSO_4 \cdot 5H_2O$ is the formula for a hydrate of copper sulfate that contains 5 moles of water for each mole of copper sulfate. The name of the compound is copper sulfate pentahydrate. Such compounds are named just as regular compounds except that the regular name is followed by a word (composed of a prefix followed by the suffix, hydrate) which indicates the relative molar proportions of water and compound. The prefixes used with the suffix, hydrate, are as follows:

Prefix	Moles of Water	Name	Formula
mono-	1	monohydrate	$XY \cdot 1H_2O$
di-	2	dihydrate	$XY \cdot 2H_2O$
tri-	3	trihydrate	$XY \cdot 3H_2O$
tetra-	4	tetrahydrate	$XY \cdot 4H_2O$
penta-	5	pentahydrate	$XY \cdot 5H_2O$
hexa-	6	hexahydrate	$XY \cdot 6H_2O$
hepta-	7	heptahydrate	$XY \cdot 7H_2O$
octa-	8	octahydrate	$XY \cdot 8H_2O$
nona-	9	nonahydrate	$XY \cdot 9H_2O$
deca-	10	decahydrate	$XY \cdot 10H_2O$

mental skills. The steps that follow begin at a rather elementary level; teachers will need to decide at what point individual students need help. I have found that I can also use the steps as an evaluation device to find out the level of the generalization or main-thought maturity of students. Some of the material in the steps that follow is adapted or directly quoted from an article I wrote called "A Cluster of Skills: Especially for Junior High School."[11] The procedure is equally useful in the middle school, in the senior high school, and at the college level.

Step One: Key Words in a Sentence.   The technique of sending a telegram in which each word costs the sender $100 is used to establish the concept of key words as the most important words in a sentence. Students quickly observe that "Arrive LaGuardia Airport New York nine Wednesday evening" states the most important words in the sentence, "I shall arrive at LaGuardia Airport in New York City at nine o'clock on Wednesday evening." They also learn that, for the most part, the same essential words will be chosen by different persons, but experience may cause some people to choose fewer or more words than others. The person who knows New York City or lives there might only need "Arrive LaGuardia nine Wednesday evening."

Students then might be given a host of factual statements growing out of life situations until they are fairly proficient. They should underline the key words in such sentences as "Please be very careful that you do not damage the new desks." Essentially, students will underline "do not damage" or "not damage . . . new desks." At this point some sentences from the content area—in this case, science—should be introduced. They might be asked to underline the key words in such a statement as "For the reaction to take place, it is essential that the reactants reach a very high pressure and temperature." In the dense discourse of science, students will often find it necessary to select more key words than in factual statements growing out of life situations.

Step Two: Key Sentence in a Paragraph. In this step the students first learn that they need be concerned with fewer key words when sentences are treated together in paragraph form. They learn this through the experience of underlining key words in the sentences of short paragraphs. In Example 7.4, the sentences are so closely linked that it is not necessary to keep repeating the subject as one attempts to get the essential message from each sentence. Students might try listing the key ideas (groups of key words) they have found; many will probably begin changing tenses and words in order to organize at the paragraph level. This should be encouraged, for they are proceeding to the next steps independently. A list might be:

Water useful resource

Means of transport using ships

Natural defense as moats

Source of fertility

Source of energy

Students should *add up* the key ideas and decide whether or not one of them represents an overall idea. It happens to be contained in the first sentence of the paragraph. Hence, the generalization, a conclusion, is contained in a key sentence at the beginning. The same is true of Examples 7.5 and 7.6.

Students will, however, meet paragraphs in science where the generalization is stated at the end (in Example 7.5, the generalization is at the end as well as at the beginning), and students should have directed practice with such a structure as well. This often happens when a paragraph or two is used to explain a theory or principle and the theory or principle is not directly stated until the end of the paragraph(s). Practice from one type of paragraph to the next is best done inductively rather than deductively. Students should not be told that they are moving to another type of structure, but should discover this for themselves.

For instance, look at this next example:

Example 7.7   Animals have interesting habits. One of the habits of some animals is to use nature's medicine when they are ill. Deer may eat twigs and the very tender bark of trees. Cats and dogs may eat grass when they are not feeling up to par. Bears often eat different kinds of roots and berries.

Deer eat twigs + tender bark + cats + dogs eat grass + bears eat roots + berries = some animals use nature's medicine when ill. The first sentence in the paragraph serves only an introductory purpose. It may be introducing a series of paragraphs that will deal with interesting habits of animals. It may just be a lead-in the writer desired to use. It is not, of course, the pertinent generalization directly supported by information in the paragraph. In this case, the key sentence, or generalization, is the second sentence in the paragraph.

It is possible for the key sentence to be located anywhere in the paragraph(s); it is even possible for the key idea or generalization to be expressed over a number of sentences. At any rate, students need much experience in searching for generalizations once they have ascertained that this is their task.

With many students it is useful and stimulating to consider the nature of the generalizations found in science materials. For those students who grasp the concepts, an exploration and identification of the type of generalization assists them in evaluating the supplementary information. For instance, a hypothesis should be followed by evidence; a conclusion should be followed by proof; and so on.

Step Three: Main Thought in a Paragraph.   Scientific materials most often state key sentences directly when the generalization pattern is used, but there are times when the generalization must be inferred (a more common occurrence in some other content areas). After students have sustained successful practice in working with paragraphs containing many types of key sentences in a variety of positions, they should be ready for paragraphs or groups of paragraphs without stated generalizations, where they can be responsible for thinking through and providing the generalization.

At this point, students ought to examine paragraphs such as the following ones from a physics textbook:

Example 7.8[12]   As a speeding car makes a sharp left turn, a passenger is forced over toward the right side of the car until pressed up against it. The motion and the force acting on the passenger are explained in this way. When the car begins to make the left turn, the passenger at first continues to move in the original direction of the car in accordance with the law of inertia. However, as the car continues to move toward the left, the straight-line motion of the passenger soon brings him up against the right side of the car, which blocks the continuation of the straight-line motion. At the same time, it exerts a force pushing the passenger toward the center of the car's circular path. This is the centripetal force that now compels the passenger to travel around the turn.

.
.
.

In constructing high-speed roads and turnpikes, engineers bank the road on the turns so that the outside of the road is higher than the inside. This slope of the road resists the inertial tendency of a car to leave the road at a turn and go off on a tangent. In doing so the road supplies the centripetal force needed to keep the car going around the turn.

Now when readers add up the key ideas, they find no overall idea stated by the writers. The student is called upon to supply the generalization by adding up the clues (key ideas) and making an inference. In this case the inference is that force must be applied to a body to make it move in a circular path— centripetal force. The answer can be found by reading further in the text. Students will need a number of directed lessons in order to develop some expertise in supplying generalizations when the writers do not state them.

Additional examples and discussion of strategies applied to the generalization pattern may be found on pages 190–193.

PROBLEM SOLUTION

Examples.   The problem-solution pattern is found frequently in scientific texts, essentially taking four forms: (1) the problem may be clearly stated followed by a solution(s) also clearly stated; (2) the problem may be clearly stated followed by hypothetical solutions; (3) the problem may be clearly stated followed by no solution(s); and (4) the problem may take the form of a question and the solution(s) the form of an answer to the question.

Example 7.9 demonstrates the clear-cut statement of problem and solution in a physics textbook.

Example 7.9[13]   Find to the nearest degree the angle of refraction of a ray of light passing from air into water at an incident angle of 30°.

Solution
From Table 17.1, the index of refraction of water $n_w = 1.33$.

The angle of incidence is $i = 30°$.

From Table 1 in the Appendix, sin 30° = 0.500.

Example 7.9 (continued)

Example 7.9 (continued)

By Snell's law:

$$\frac{\sin i}{\sin r} = n_w$$

$$\frac{0.500}{\sin r} = 1.33$$

$$\sin r = \frac{0.500}{1.33} = 0.375$$

Looking in Table 1 for an angle whose sine is 0.375, it is found that sin 22° = 0.375. Hence, *r* is 22°.

Example 7.10 is the opening paragraph of a chapter section subtitled "How Did Life Originate?" The paragraph presents the problem both in statement and question form; the rest of the section deals with hypothetical solutions:

Example 7.10[14]   Still another major problem for students of the theory of evolution has resulted indirectly from Darwin's work. The problem stems from this aspect of the theory: If all present-day organisms are the modified descendants of previously existing species, all life must have descended originally from one or more primordial species. Thus, the problem is an outgrowth of investigations of all workers who have contributed to the theory and who have thereby helped it achieve wide acceptance. The problem also stems from the logical implications of Virchow's principle that every cell originates from another cell. . . . If there were primordial cells or organisms, how did they originate?

The group of three problems in Example 7.11, from a physics textbook, presents three common forms of statements where problems are initiated and solutions are not given. The reader must provide the solutions. These usually follow a chapter or chapter section that has been devoted to explaining and illustrating such types of problems and their solutions.

Example 7.11[15]

---

1.   Explain how a transistor may be used to amplify a signal such as a weak alternating current.

2.   (*a*) How are the atoms in a ruby laser brought to a selected excited state?
     (*b*) In what two ways can excited atoms return to the ground state?

3. Many of the atoms in a ruby rod laser have been raised to a selected excited state. One of them now drops spontaneously to the ground state and emits a photon in a direction parallel to the axis of the ruby rod. What chain of events does this photon set off that quickly produces a strong beam of coherent light?

Problems 2 and 3 above are stated as questions, a common practice in science materials. The question-answer pattern (see pages 200–202 in Chapter 8) is really another form of this problem-solution pattern.

In Example 7.12, a problem is set up through a question, and the rest of the paragraph is used to answer the question.

Example 7.12[16] Why does it seem to be so much easier to melt ice into water than it is to get an orderly crystalline arrangement of the ice again? It is because temperatures in our environment are more often above the point where water freezes, and because the crystalline pattern in ice is an orderly arrangement, whereas in the liquid state there is no evidence of order. Something about heat disrupts the orderly arrangements of solids and results in a condition of confusion. Depending on the kind of substance, the temperature at which this disorder becomes noticeable is different. This is another way of saying that different substances have different melting points.

Strategies.   The major strategy, of course, is to recognize and understand the problem and then proceed to recognize and understand the solution(s).

Step One: Recognition of Information about the Problem.   Readers should search for all the information they can find that tells about the problem before they proceed to or raise the question(s) that leads to the solution(s). For instance, in Example 7.9 the reader must understand the precise meanings of *angle of refraction*, *nearest degree*, and *incident angle*. In Example 7.10, readers find two statements that give them essential information; the writers use the signal words *the problem stems from*; hence the important information about the problem is contained in sentences two and four. In Example 7.11, obviously all the connections among the individual concepts must be understood before the problem can become clear. Particularly in the third problem, the reader must understand *atoms raised to selected excited state, one drops to ground state and emits photon in direction parallel to axis of ruby rod*, and *strong beam of coherent light*. In Example 7.12, students must be taught to analyze the question to extract all the necessary information: *easier to melt ice into water than to get orderly crystalline arrangement of ice again*.

Step Two: Recognition of the Problem.   Once the information stated is clear in the mind of the learners, they can turn to the actual statement of the problem. In Example 7.9, it now becomes clear that the operational problem statement is: compute the angle of refraction to the nearest degree at an incident angle of 30°. In Example 7.10, although readers are probably quite aware of the problem statement before they reach the sentence at the end of the paragraph, it is nevertheless that question which states the problem. And, in Example 7.12, it is the addition of the *why* to the information about the problem that completes the statement of the problem in question form. In Example 7.11, once the basic facts are understood, the reader uses the operational terms *explain, how, in what two ways,* and *what.* The reader should take the time to be sure the task is clear.

Step Three: Recognition or Execution of the Solution(s).   In coping with this step, the learner is often confronted with the organization of numerical as well as verbal symbols. In Examples 7.9 and 7.11, the solutions are mathematical, whether stated or executed by the student. In Example 7.9, the reader learns that other sources in the text must be tapped in order to solve the problem. The reader of the excerpt on evolution (Example 7.10), who now goes on to search for solutions, will need to bring the question to the context in order to sort out the hypothetical solutions. Much the same strategy is used with the melting points example (7.12), except that all the information is in the single paragraph. Readers must keep referring back to the problem to be sure that they are finding the solutions.

Outcome.   Readers who identify and utilize the problem-solution pattern when they meet it should be able to organize and write notes in a cohesive paragraph utilizing the problem-solution pattern. As above, solutions are not always clear-cut, and readers must sometimes make several inferences. In addition, although a central pattern such as problem solution is evident, the writers may furnish supplementary information that is important and will need to be understood and retained by the reader. Nevertheless, the recognition and written reproduction of whatever clear problem-solution structure is present assists readers in comprehension and leaves them with just a small number of isolated facts to contend with.

COMPARISON OR CONTRAST

Examples.   Actually comparison and contrast are two different patterns, but they are so closely related that students have no difficulty understanding the differences, once the basic concept is clear. A substantial number of paragraphs in science use comparison or contrast to explain ideas or to illlustrate an idea already introduced. In the comparison pattern, relationships are established between similar and dissimilar things or characteristics. In the contrast pattern only differences are considered. Authors may sometimes intermix the classification pattern with comparison and/or contrast.

The excerpt that follows is clearly a comparison pattern. The similarities between the beginning of meiosis and mitosis are stated; then a difference is given.

Example 7.13[17] The process of meiosis begins in very much the same way as mitosis. Here, too, the chromosomes shorten and thicken until the species number of chromosomes emerge from the tangled network. Here, too, each chromosome is doubled because every DNA molecule has duplicated itself. But in meiosis something happens that did not take place in mitosis. Each doubled chromosome is attracted to a very special partner.

In the next excerpt, contrast is evident.

Example 7.14[18] Still another way to differentiate between centripetal and centrifugal forces is to observe that the two forces are never applied to the same object. In the case of the twirling ball, for example, centripetal force is applied to the ball while centrifugal force is applied to the string. In the case of an orbiting space vehicle, centripetal force is applied to the vehicle by the earth's gravity. Centrifugal force is applied to the earth by the moving vehicle.

Strategies. The reader is usually made aware of the comparison or contrast pattern by the writer's signals at the outset. In Example 7.13, the words "in very much the same way" establish the comparison pattern, just as "another way to differentiate" signals the contrast pattern in Example 7.14. Readers need to become accustomed to perceiving such signals.

In the comparison pattern, the task students must be helped to do is evident. They should list similarities on one side of a column and differences on the other. Notes might look something like this:

Beginning of Meiosis

Similarities to Mitosis	*Difference*
Chromosomes shorten and thicken.	Each doubled chromosome attracted to very special partner.
Species number emerge from network.	
Each chromosome is doubled (because every DNA molecule duplicated itself).	

In the contrast pattern, readers should be aware that they are searching for the difference(s) between one thing and another or between one process and another. Only one difference is mentioned between centripetal and centrifugal forces; the signal words *(way to differentiate)* help the reader realize that the difference is "that the two forces are never applied to the same object." The difference is further emphasized by two illustrations: the case of the twirling ball and the orbiting space vehicle.

More examples of the comparison-contrast patterns may be found on pages 196–198.

SEQUENCE

Examples. Most frequently the sequence pattern takes two forms in scientific discourse: (1) explanation of steps in a process, and (2) presentation of steps in an experiment. Students sometimes have difficulty reading this pattern because they are unaccustomed to being held responsibile for such precision in reading. They must be sure they understand each step in its appropriate sequence. They must learn how to isolate the steps from illustrations and additional information. They must learn to look at the interrelationships among the steps.

The example in Figure 7.4 is representative of the type of material readers meet when they attempt to understand the steps in a process.

The examples in Figures 7.5 and 7.6 illustrate the two kinds of experiments that are encountered by readers of science materials. Sometimes the experiments are more complex and include many more activities, but those that follow are exemplary enough. Figure 7.5 is an illustration of the type of experiment that is explained by the writers. Figure 7.6 is an illustration of the type of experiment that the student must read and perform. Both types are used frequently and initially require the same task of the reader.

Strategies. The sequence pattern of writing may seem rather elementary for secondary school students, but it is more complex than would appear on the surface. It must be read slowly and cautiously. Scientific discourse is not meant to be read rapidly under most conditions anyway, but this pattern needs particularly precise reading. The student who misses or misinterprets one small step, whether reading the explanation of a process or reading directions in an experiment, will not understand what the steps led up to and/or will be unable to complete an experiment satisfactorily.

Step One: Recognition of Introduction. Sequence patterns are introduced in a variety of ways. In Figure 7.4, the first paragraph describes the area where swallowing starts, but the steps are not stated until the reader is cued to them by the words *act of swallowing*, which introduce the second paragraph. In Figure 7.5, the first paragraph acts as an introduction and enumerates the materials of the experiment as well. The graphic ties it all together before the

Figure 7.4   Studying a Sequence Pattern[19]

Peristalsis. Successive waves of muscular contraction and relaxation move food along digestive tube from esophagus to colon.

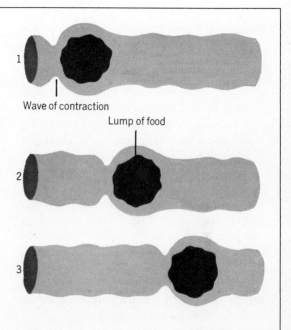

1

Wave of contraction

Lump of food

2

3

Pharynx and Gullet

The *palate* is hard and bony in front, soft in back. It forms the roof of the mouth, and separates the mouth from the nasal cavity. The nose and mouth both lead into the pharynx or throat. Tonsils and adenoids are lumps of lymph tissue in this region.

The act of swallowing pushes food through the pharynx into the gullet. Air on its way to the windpipe also passes through the pharynx, crossing the path of the food. When we occasionally swallow the wrong way, food takes the path of air into the windpipe. We quickly cough it up again.

Normally the tongue prevents such accidents. As it tosses food backwards, it presses on a little flap, the *epiglottis*. Simultaneously the *larynx* (*voicebox* or *Adam's apple*) rises against the epiglottis. This flap closes off the windpipe. For a moment, as food enters the gullet, we stop breathing and talking.

Muscles contract behind the lump of food in the gullet, squeezing it along. As the first group of muscles relax, succeeding groups in turn contract. These waves of contraction, called *peristalsis*, are the means by which food moves through the entire digestive tract.

The lubricating action of saliva helps food pass along the gullet. Peristalsis makes it as easy for us to swallow upside down as sitting in the customary position.

Source: Stanley L. Weinberg, *Biology: An Inquiry into the Nature of Life*, 4th ed. (Boston: Allyn and Bacon, 1977), p. 199.

Figure 7.5   Studying a Sequence Pattern[20]

Faraday Ice-Pail Experiment

The distribution of charge over a metallic conductor can, in part, be demonstrated by an experiment first performed by Michael Faraday in 1810. This demonstration, known as *Faraday's ice-pail experiment*, involves a small metal ball, a hollow metal container such as a tin pail, and an electroscope:

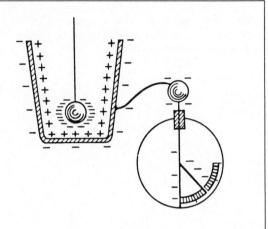

If the ball is charged from another source and then lowered into the pail, the leaf of the electroscope rises. When the ball is moved around inside the pail and even when it touches the inside surface, no change in the potential is shown by the electroscope leaf. After the ball has been removed, the inner surface of the pail and the ball are found to be completely free of charge.

To explain what happens, let the ball be charged negatively and lowered to the position shown. Free electrons in the metal pail are repelled to the outer surface and to the connecting electroscope, leaving positives on the inside unneutralized. When the ball touches the pail, all negatives leave the ball and neutralize an equal number of positives.

The fact that the electroscope leaf remains fixed when the ball is removed shows (1) that there is no redistribution of the negative charges on the outer pail surface and (2) that the number of induced positives is equal to the number of negatives on the ball.

Source: From *Physics: An Experimental Science* by White, White, and Gould, pp. 436–37; © 1968 by Litton Publishing, Inc.

steps in the experiment are delineated. In addition, the heading—containing the word *experiment*—cues the reader to the pattern. Except for the heading "Student Activity," the graphite experiment has little introduction. Here the opening question ("What kind of a conductor of electricity is graphite, the form of carbon used in pencils?") sparks the student into accomplishing the steps while it acts as a type of preorganizer for the specific questions in the last paragraph.

Step Two: Recognition of Steps.   Reading and rereading are necessary to ascertain that each of the steps in the sequence is found, that something considered a step is really a step, and that the order of steps is correct. Particularly for students having problems with this type of reading, it is useful to have them

Figure 7.6   Studying a Sequence Pattern[21]

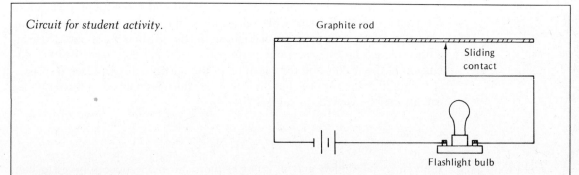

Circuit for student activity.   Graphite rod

Sliding contact

Flashlight bulb

STUDENT ACTIVITY

What kind of a conductor of electricity is graphite, the form of carbon used in pencils? Remove a rod of graphite from a pencil. Connect it in series with a 3.0-volt battery and a flashlight bulb, as in [the figure]. Fix one wire connection to the left end of the graphite rod. Make the other wire connection flexible so that it can be moved from the left to the right end of the graphite rod.

Starting with the movable connection at the left end of the rod, move it slowly to the right until it reaches the right end. What change do you observe in the brightness of the bulb? Remove the graphite rod from the circuit and replace it by a copper wire about the same length and diameter. Note the brightness of the bulb. How does the resistance of the graphite rod compare with that of the copper wire?

Replace the graphite rod in the circuit. Adjust the movable connection so that the filament of the bulb glows a dull red. Heat the part of the graphite rod now in the circuit gently by moving a lighted candle under it from end to end. (*Caution:* Be careful not to overheat the graphite since it will burn.) Note the brightness of the bulb.

How does heat affect the resistance of the graphite rod? Does graphite behave like a metallic conductor or like a semiconductor?

Source: Alexander Taffel, *Physics: Its Methods and Meanings* (Boston: Allyn and Bacon, 1981), p. 615.

write and number each step. They need to be helped to realize that more than one step may be contained in a single sentence and that writers do not always organize their ideas perfectly.

In considering the steps in a process, readers must constantly evaluate the statements they read and ask themselves if they are really reading a step—an action. For instance, in Figure 7.4, there is much extraneous information. If the purpose is to understand the act of swallowing, readers must separate the information from the steps. This is not to say that all the information may be unimportant, but readers should be able to separate the steps in a process from the additional information given.

The steps in an experiment are usually rather clear, particularly when students must execute them. But even so, readers must be sure that they understand each direction. In Figure 7.5 the results and conclusions are given to the reader, but they make little sense unless the reader has understood the sequence of steps. In the case of Figure 7.6, the learners must come to conclusions based on their accurate performance of what they read. Further discussion of the results and the meaning of the results will take place in class.

Additional examples and discussion of strategies applied to the sequence pattern may be viewed on pages 193–196.

WRITING AS A TOOL OF LEARNING

Both in social studies and in science, there are many opportunities to help students learn through writing. Exclusive emphasis on objective tests and short responses not only cripples the thought processes in these disciplines but affords students little opportunity to write. The very organizing of ideas into a cohesive and coherent paragraph or essay helps students internalize important propositions in organized fashion.

In science, particularly, students must understand often complex relationships. Appropriate writing assignments—often using the patterns suggested in this chapter—will aid in clarifying some of those relationships. Creager, who believes that writing is an important tool in biology, cautioned:

> Writing about science poses special problems. To overcome these problems, students should be encouraged to follow these suggestions: (1) define all scientific terms the first time they are used; (2) use active, not passive, voice; (3) anticipate questions the reader might have and try to answer them as you write; (4) write vividly—turn facts into images by using forceful verbs and strong nouns; and (5) offer examples to illustrate ideas.[22]

RELATED ACTIVITIES

1. Using an opaque projector, show one of the graphics with accompanying text in this chapter, or a similar example from one of the texts being used in your students' classes. Focus discussion and activity on interrelating the reading of both running text and graphic. If possible, apply what is read to an actual, moving model. A desirable follow-up activity is to have students read another similar example on a worksheet and demonstrate ability to put what they've read to use.

2. Using either an opaque projector or a worksheet compare Figures 7.2 and 7.3. Have students note the importance of realizing that Figure 7.2 consists of the same kind of reading they did with Figure 7.1, except for application to a model, while Figure 7.3 must be carefully read and studied as *additional*

data. Activities 1 and 2 should be repeated several times, using students' materials, in order to ensure understanding.

3.   Use Examples 7.1 and 7.2 as introductory examples of the enumeration pattern, but continue by finding and/or having students find such patterns in the materials they are using. Have them search for the various introductory phrases that clue them in to the enumeration pattern: *in three respects; several important functions; seven ways of doing; four causes of;* and so on.

4.   Locate a few examples of the classification pattern in student materials and have students organize some type of classification table or chart.

5.   Take students through the strategies for finding key words in a sentence, the key sentence in a paragraph, and the main thought in a paragraph as suggested in the chapter. Apply the strategies to their materials.

6.   Compare the enumeration pattern to the generalization pattern. Start with examples in the chapter, if you like, but continue on to examples in student materials. Have them verbalize, orally or in writing, the major difference between the enumeration statement and the generalization statement.

7.   By using examples in the chapter and/or material in student texts, develop the concept that the problem-solution pattern is particularly useful for helping readers set their own purposes for doing the reading. When the problem is quite specifically stated, either in statement or question form, the readers then know they must read to try to find the solution(s).

8.   You will find many examples of comparison and/or contrast in the materials being used by students. Once the students understand the pattern, have them read and organize charts illustrating the similarities and/or differences.

9.   Students should get a great deal of practice in working with the sequence pattern—particularly in reading the steps of an experiment. The best way to give this kind of assistance is to have the students read the experiment and then carry it out. If this is not feasible, have students ascertain the purpose(s) for the experiment and the materials to be used. Then have them paraphrase the procedures. You may want to have them sketch the procedures if they cannot paraphrase accurately. If the findings are given, have students paraphrase them; if the findings are not given, have the students hypothesize what they would be.

SELECTED READINGS

Bechtel, Judith, and Bettie Franzblau. *Reading in the Science Classroom.* Washington, D.C.: National Education Association, 1980.

DeVito, Alfred, and Gerald H. Krockover. *Creative Sciencing: A Practical Approach.* Boston: Little, Brown, 1976.

Donlan, Dan. "Science Writing: A Call for Continuing Education." *Science Teacher* 42 (December 1975):19–20.

Novak, Joseph D. "Learning Theory Applied to the Biology Classroom." *American Biology Teacher* 42 (May 1980):280–85.

Shepherd, David L. *Comprehensive High School Reading Methods*, Columbus, Ohio: Charles E. Merrill, 1978, ch. 10.

Singer, Harry, and Dan Donlan. *Reading and Learning from Text*. Boston: Little, Brown, 1980, ch. 13.

Stewart, James; Judith Van Kirk; and Richard Rowell. "Concept Maps: A Tool for Use in Biology Teaching." *American Biology Teacher* 41 (March 1979):171–75.

Strang, Ruth; Constance M. McCullough; and Arthur E. Traxler. *The Improvement of Reading*, 4th ed., pp. 323–36. New York: McGraw-Hill, 1967.

Sund, Robert B., and Leslie W. Trowbridge. *Teaching Science by Inquiry in the Secondary School*. Columbus, Ohio: Charles E. Merrill, 1973.

Thelen, Judith. *Improving Reading in Science*. Newark, Del.: International Reading Association, 1976.

Thomas, Ellen L., and H. Alan Robinson. *Improving Reading in Every Class*, 3rd ed., ch. 10. Boston: Allyn and Bacon, 1982.

Zimmerman, S. Scott. "Writing for Chemistry." *Journal of Chemical Education* 55 (November 1978):727.

NOTES

1. Robert B. Sund and Leslie W. Trowbridge, *Teaching Science by Inquiry in the Secondary School* (Columbus, Ohio: Charles E. Merrill, 1967), p. v.
2. Walter A. Thurber, Robert E. Kilburn, and Peter S. Howell, *Exploring Physical Science* (Boston: Allyn and Bacon, 1977), p. 178.
3. William L. Stokes, Sheldon Judson, and M. Dane Picard, *Introduction to Geology: Physical and Historical* (Englewood Cliffs, N.J.: Prentice-Hall, 1978), pp. 346–47.
4. Stanley L. Weinberg, *Biology: An Inquiry into the Nature of Life*, 4th ed. (Boston: Allyn and Bacon, 1977), p. 268.
5. Alexander Taffel, *Physics: Its Methods and Meanings* (Boston: Allyn and Bacon, 1981), p. 265.
6. Ralph P. Frazier and Herbert A. Smith, *The Biological Sciences: Investigating Man's Environment* (River Forest, Ill.: Laidlaw Brothers, 1969), p. 23.
7. James H. Otto, Albert Towle, and James V. Bradley, *Modern Biology* (New York: Holt, Rinehart and Winston, 1981), pp. 469–70.
8. Paul F. Brandwein, Robert Stollberg, and R. Will Burnett, *Energy: Its Form and Changes* (New York: Harcourt Brace Jovanovich, 1969), p. 9.
9. Excerpt from *Biology* by William L. Smallwood and Edna R. Green, p. 482; © 1968 General Learning Corporation. Reprinted by permission.
10. Robert C. Smoot, Jace Price, and Richard L. Barrett, *Chemistry: A Modern Course* (Columbus, Ohio: Charles E. Merrill, 1968), p. 261. Reprinted by permission.
11. *Reading Teacher* 15 (September 1961):25–28. Reprinted with permission of the author and the International Reading Association.
12. Taffel, *Physics*, pp. 140–41.

13. Taffel, *Physics* p. 315.
14. Excerpt from *Biology* by William L. Smallwood and Edna R. Green, p. 228; © 1968 General Learning Corporation. Reprinted by permission.
15. Taffel, *Physics*, p. 615.
16. John H. Marean and Elaine W. Ledbetter, *Physical Science: A Laboratory Approach* (Reading, Mass.: Addison-Wesley, 1968), p. 108.
17. Alvin Nason and Philip Goldstein, *Biology: Introduction to Life* (Reading, Mass.: Addison-Wesley, 1969), p. 509.
18. John E. Williams and others, *Modern Physics* (New York: Holt, Rinehart and Winston, 1968), p. 110.
19. Weinberg and Kalish, *Biology*, p. 199.
20. From *Physics: An Experimental Science* by White, White, and Gould, pp. 436–37; © 1968 by Litton Educational Publishing, Inc. Reprinted by permission of Van Nostrand Reinhold Company.
21. Taffel, *Physics*, p. 615.
22. Joan G. Creager, "An Overture: Teaching Writing Is Every Teacher's Job," *American Biology Teacher* 42 (May 1980):273.

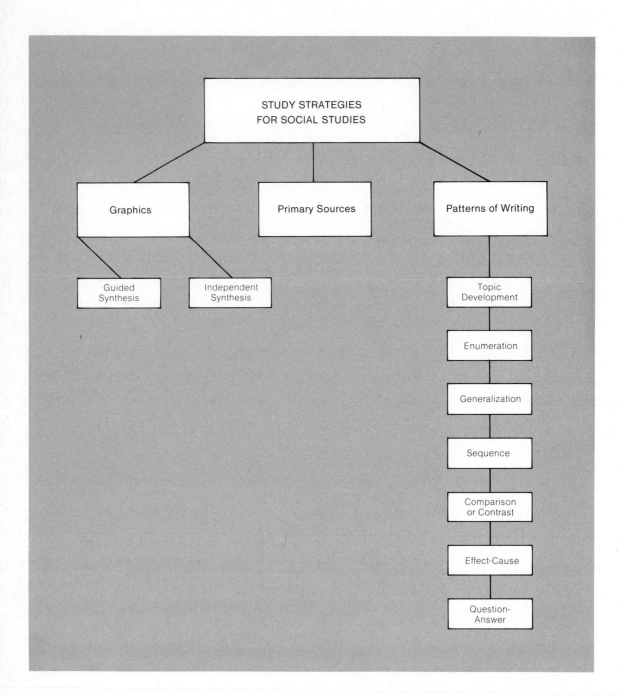

8
Social Studies

From about 1960 through the mid-1970s, the "new social studies" was visible, with its emphasis on inquiry methods, values, and controversial issues. Today the "new social studies" faces an uncertain future: some parents are critical of its processes, and many teachers are uncertain about its methodology. Although some diversity exists in course offerings and approaches, the curriculum is largely governed by commercially published textbooks and reading assignments followed by recitation.[1] There is no question that the textbook is still "the dominant tool of instruction and the focus of testing."[2]

Hence, reading appears to be the major tool for acquiring information across the social studies curriculum. Although there are indications that multimedia materials are being used more commonly and in more meaningful ways than in the past, printed materials still carry the bulk of the load. Other materials are used and are in evidence, but more frequently as supplements to *the* text.

The writing style in most social studies materials used for instructional purposes is expository (explanatory or informative), not narrative. In history, particularly, the style often seems narrative, but this is more an impression and flavor than a fact. History, of course, is the unfolding of a story. But the goal of the writers is to impart information, and the goal of the reader is to receive such information and ponder it. Narrative and descriptive paragraphs are utilized, but only to introduce, illustrate, expand, or breathe life into an idea. Expository and definitional paragraphs are used most frequently.

Although social studies material used for instruction tends increasingly to emphasize major concepts, a concept is usually rather meaningless unless the reader is able to soak up enough support to defend it. For instance, to conclude from the textbook passage in Example 8.1 that *noise pollution is a serious problem, damaging physically and psychologically,* is an important concept; however, it is rather vacuous if the reader cannot supply some proof for the conclusion.

The task is not vastly different from that of reading science materials, except that social studies materials are usually not quite as "fact packed" and hence tend to be more redundant—a plus for the reader. On the other hand, major concepts and their supporting facts and/or examples are not always as visible in social studies materials as in science materials.

As in science, writing assignments can be used to reinforce and extend social studies learning, both of concepts and of writing styles. When students organize their ideas into an essay or piece of written discourse, they seem to remember and use the ideas more effectively. Also, practice in writing the patterns most frequently found in social studies texts and supplementary materials appears to result in reciprocal improvement—in writing and in reading.

Example 8.1[3]   The impact of noise on people's lives is both psychological and physiological. Many people find living in a noisy environment such as that found in almost every American city to be nerve-wracking at best. After describing a day in a city in terms of noise in a *Saturday Review* editorial, Norman Cousins concluded:

> Whether or not they realize it, the American people are waging unremitting war against themselves. The weapons are tranquility-smashers, and are fitted out with decibel warheads. They penetrate all known cranial barriers and the innermost core of an individual's privacy, impeding the processes of sequential thought, breaking down the sensibilities, and unhinging the capacity of serenity. The noise level is rising and the level of common sanity is falling.*

> While the effect of noise on sanity is not easy to measure, it is known that high noise levels damage hearing and in some cases result in deafness. Noise affects other parts of the body as well. Sudden noises such as sonic booms result in increased heart rates and disturbed sleep for many people. Some scientists have suggested that long exposure to high noise levels also speeds the aging process.

GRAPHICS   Graphics play an important role in many kinds of materials, but they are especially significant in social studies. They usually contribute additional information or serve to stress the importance of printed information in support of a major concept.

The reader must learn two major strategies in coping with the study-reading of graphics in social studies: (1) guided synthesis of graphic material with written material when the writers direct the reader to the graphic at a given point and (2) independent synthesis of graphic material when the writers do not refer to the graphic on a given page.

*Copyright 1962 by Saturday Review Co. First appeared in *Saturday Review*, December 8, 1962.

GUIDED SYNTHESIS

Social studies materials abound with pictures, maps, charts, tables, and graphs. At times, writers guide the synthesizing of the graphic information with the written information by directing the reader to a particular graphic at a specific point in the material. For instance, examine the map, its caption, and the written material in Figure 8.1.

Types of directed references to graphics differ from book to book and even within books. In Figure 8.1, first the writers ask the reader to glance at the map just to find out where Arabia is in relation to Europe; the writers expected the reader to return to the passage immediately. Teachers should help students realize that such references are useful, for they reinforce the verbal information and often ensure retention. A few directed lessons in using such references will often make the activity a habitual one.

The second reference to the map in this particular social studies textbook is more oblique than the first, but really more important. The writers suggest that the reader take a more careful look at the map. The key should be utilized. The teacher should also direct the reader to the caption *"Map Study,"* available in this specific textbook, to obtain additional information and/or to get assistance in using the map. Reading the first sentence and writing the answer to the first question are useful to the reader at this point. The remainder of the caption as well as part of the key will be useful later when the writers suggest that the reader turn back to the map "for the routes of the Crusades." This method of using the map for the development of more than one concept—amount of land conquered as well as routes of the Crusades—also gives the reader a preview of what is to come in the reading. Class time spent in helping students make use of such important graphics is bound to pay off in increased comprehension and retention.

INDEPENDENT SYNTHESIS

Unless instructors take the time to point out and to give practice in using graphics unreferred to by the writers, the graphics are frequently skipped when students are reading. And most of the time, in modern instructional materials, such graphics have significance. They are usually not placed on a page solely for aesthetic purposes; publishing costs are too high. These graphics serve several different purposes: (1) they expand an idea referred to in the running text; (2) they illustrate or exemplify a larger concept mentioned in the text; and (3) they summarize and organize related points stated on one or more pages. They always seem to reinforce what has been written, and frequently they add another dimension or provide supporting information to make a concept more understandable.

The map and diagram in Figure 8.2 are an example of graphics unreferred to by the authors but of great importance to the reader in providing significant

Figure 8.1   Guided Synthesis in the Social Sciences[4]

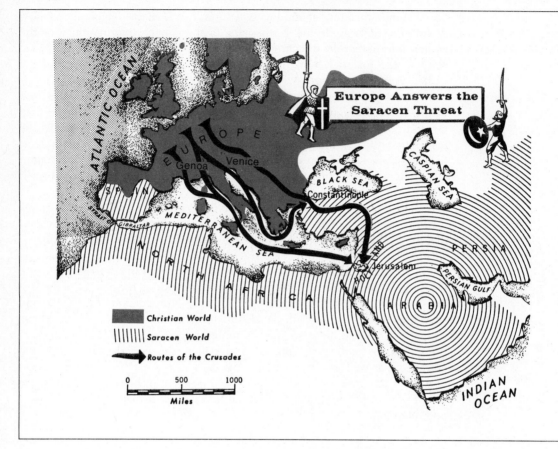

details in addition to a graphic summary of information discussed in the text.[5] Teachers must help students develop the habit of spending time with such graphics, for they act as reinforcers, organizers, and summarizers.

The graphs in Figure 8.3 are reprinted from one page of a social studies textbook.[6] Note that if a student does not know how to read a pie graph, a line graph, or a bar graph, he or she will lose a great deal of information. The text itself contains very little discussion of the concepts and details presented in the graphs. Students need to spend much time studying the graphs in order to understand the important information being offered. (See the activities at the end of this chapter for some directed procedures with such graphs.)

Students usually need direction in interpreting charts, tables, graphs, and time lines. Time should be spent in getting them used to looking at all graphics and then studying those that contribute additional or reinforcing information.

The circled lines on this map show you how the Saracens expanded their power into Africa and even into Europe. (1) Where was the homeland of Mohammed's followers? Trace the routes followed by the Crusaders to the Holy Land. Most members of the First Crusade traveled to the Holy Land by way of Constantinople. Later Crusaders followed the sea routes. (2) Name two Italian ports from which sea routes started.

The Saracens Threaten to Overrun Europe

About the year 600 a new religion, called *Islam* (or Mohammedanism), grew up in Arabia. (Find Arabia on the map. . . .) Just as Christianity is based upon the teachings of Christ, so Islam is based upon the teachings of a great religious leader named Mohammed. The Saracens in Arabia believed that the religion taught by Mohammed was the only true religion. They sent armies to conquer other people and force them to accept the religion of Mohammed. Soon they conquered all of North Africa and crossed the Strait of Gibraltar into Spain. For centuries the Saracens pushed hard against the Christians in Europe, threatening always to gain more territory. The map . . . shows how much land the Saracens conquered.

Source: *This is America's Story*, by Howard B. Wilder, Robert P. Ludlum, and Harriett M. Brown, pp. 19–20; copyright © 1972, Houghton Mifflin Company. Reprinted by permission of the publisher.

They should be directed to read and understand the caption first, since it normally explains, in general terms, what the graphic is attempting to do.

PRIMARY SOURCES Particularly in history, although also in other components of social studies, the use of primary and/or scholarly secondary sources is increasing. These are introduced sometimes as individual documents and/or excerpts interspersed with the running content of the usual textbook material. Such readings play an important role in the social studies curriculum, and students need to be guided to reading strategies for recognizing the uses of documents and for learning how to read them.

Figure 8.2   Independent Synthesis in the Social Sciences

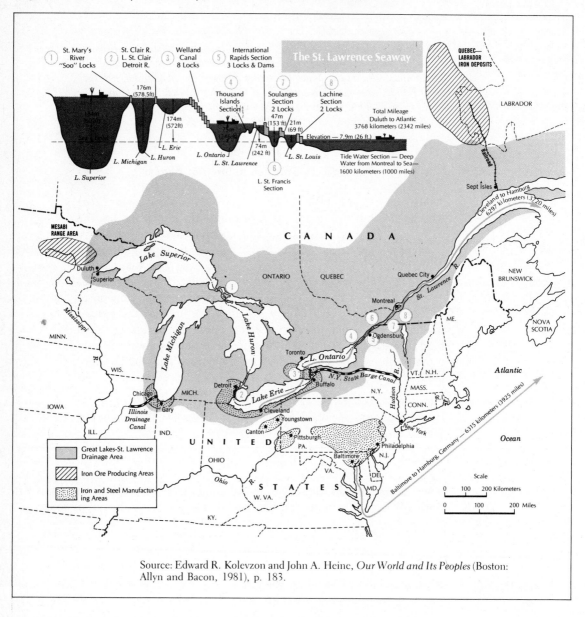

Source: Edward R. Kolevzon and John A. Heine, *Our World and Its Peoples* (Boston: Allyn and Bacon, 1981), p. 183.

Figure 8.3   Independent Synthesis in the Social Sciences

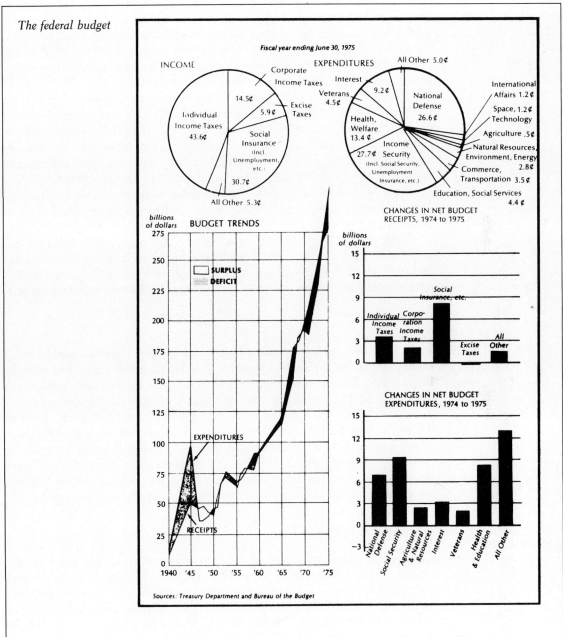

The federal budget

Source: William A. McClenaghan, *Magruder's American Government* (Boston: Allyn and Bacon, 1976), p. 339.

In the passage on noise pollution in Example 8.1, the writers used an excerpt from an article by Norman Cousins. Readers should be encouraged to zero in on such excerpts and should even be led to discuss why the writers included the excerpt rather than paraphrasing it. In this particular situation, the readers need to be guided to pick out the information in support of the *psychological* impact of noise presented by Cousins and to balance it with the paragraph by the writers on the *physiological* impact.

Even for good readers, some of the guidance may include a discussion of certain clauses and phrases used by Cousins well beyond the reading level of the book and the readers. *The weapons are tranquility-smashers, and are fitted out with decibel warheads* may contain figures of speech confusing to some readers. *Unremitting war, cranial barriers,* and *unhinging the capacity for serenity* are examples of phrases that might cause misunderstandings. Students are entitled to increase their independent competencies by receiving assistance from teachers, particularly when confronted by unusual uses of language.

The excerpt from a contemporary history text presented in Example 8.2 may not be the whole truth, yet it provides the reader with firsthand information and vivid description. It is also a prime example of material that many readers tend to overlook because it is more difficult to read than the surrounding text.

PATTERNS AND STRATEGIES

In my judgment, after reviewing a host of instructional materials used in social studies courses in junior and senior high schools, seven major text patterns surface: *topic development, enumeration, generalization, sequence, comparison or contrast, effect-cause,* and *question-answer.* Although other patterns are sometimes used, these seven appear to be the ones used most frequently. Four of the seven overlap those described in Chapter 7; however, enough differences within each pattern as used in social studies are evident; hence, each of the patterns is presented in this chapter. The explanations in Chapter 7 can serve as additional reinforcement, and vice versa. As in the previous chapter, patterns are explained, examples are given, and specific strategies are developed.

TOPIC DEVELOPMENT

Examples.   A topic names an area and is important as a focal point for the clustering of vital statistics. As indicated earlier, a topic differs from the concept of "main idea," with which it is sometimes confused. The topic is subsumed by the main idea; the function of a main idea is to present a full statement about the broadest and most significant message of the passage. Example: *noise pollution*—the topic; *impact of noise on people's lives is both psychological and physiological*—the main idea or major message of the writer. The topic development pattern is easy to recognize once readers are able to differentiate among specific facts, illustrations, and definitions often used in the development of the topic. Its purpose is not to develop a major idea or to emphasize relations but to present various kinds of information about a topic.

The topic development pattern is seldom, if ever, found in single paragraphs of social studies materials used for instruction. The topic is usually developed over a number of paragraphs or throughout the section of a chapter. It is infrequently used in textbooks, although it may be found in parts of geography texts. Its most common use is in reference materials, such as the excerpt in Example 8.3, from the science supplement of an encyclopedia.

Example 8.2* Captain John Smith waited many years before publishing his first report of Pocahontas' saving his life in 1607. He first described the incident in *Generall Historie of Virginia, New England and the Summer Isles*, published in 1624. He referred to himself in the third person (that is, as "he" or "him").

At last they brought him to Meronocomoco, where was Powhatan their emperor. Here more than two hundred of those grim courtiers stood wondering at him, as he had been a monster; till Powhatan and his train had put themselves in their greatest braveries. Before a fire upon a seat like a bedstead, he sat covered with a great robe made of rarowcun skins, and all the tails hanging up. On either hand did sit a young wench of 16 or 18 years, and along on each side of the house, two rows of men, and behind them as many women, with all their heads and shoulders painted red, many of their heads bedecked with the white down of birds; but every one with something; and a great chain of white beads about their necks.

At his entrance before the king, all the people gave a great shout. The queen of Appamatuck was appointed to bring him water to wash his hands, and another brought him a bunch of feathers, instead of towel, to dry them. Having feasted him after their best barbarous manner they could, a long consultation was held; but the conclusion was, two great stones were brought before Powhatan. Then as many as could laid hands on him, dragged him to them, and thereon laid his head, and being ready with their clubs, to beat out his brains, Pocahontas the King's dearest daughter, when no entreaty could prevail, got his head in her arms, and laid her own upon his to save him from death. Whereat the emperor was contented he should live.[7]

---

*From *Quest for Liberty* by June R. Chapin, Raymond J. McHugh, Richard E. Gross. Copyright © 1971, 1974 by Addison-Wesley Publishing Company, Inc.

Example 8.3[8]

Philippe Cousteau

Philippe Cousteau, the youngest son of famed oceanographer Jacques Cousteau, was born in Toulon, in 1940. He studied at the College de Normandie and at the Massachusetts Institute of Technology. As a youth he worked as a diver and photographer—he made his first Aqualung dive at the age of four—on his father's research ship, the *Calypso*. In 1965 he participated in and filmed an underwater experiment in which he and five other aquanauts lived 100 meters underwater for 28 days.

Philippe Cousteau filmed the Emmy-award-winning television series *The Undersea World of Jacques Cousteau* and coproduced with his father the television adventure series *The Cousteau Odyssey*. He and his father also coauthored *Sharks* (1969).

Philippe Cousteau died when a seaplane he was piloting capsized and sank off the coast of Portugal. He was a resident of Marina del Rey, California, and is survived by his wife and daughter.

Strategies.   The readers' tasks are threefold: first, they must, of course, recognize the topic; second, they must ascertain the organizational format of the supporting ideas; third, they must gather the ideas and relate them to the topic. This pattern is easily executed by most readers.

Step One: Recognition of Topic.   In most cases the topic is stated in a heading. Occasionally, particularly in geography and/or economics texts when features of several related countries (like the Scandinavian countries) are being cited one after the other, headings are not utilized; in this case readers must isolate the group of paragraphs pertaining to a particular country and find the topic in the introductory sentence of each group. Even when headings are given, however, the topic can be confirmed or checked by reading the introductory sentence(s).

When learning this strategy, the reader should be asked to name the topic and the reason why he or she chose it.

Step Two: Recognition of Organizational Format.   The reader needs to skim through the material to locate the organizational format—the method used to develop the topic. In Example 8.3 above, the first paragraph is roughly chronological, the second discusses Cousteau's accomplishments, and the third his death. Some knowledge of this structure helps the reader as he or she amasses the facts.

Step Three: Relationship of Supporting Ideas to Topic.   If the topic has been developed almost solely through the use of specific facts, key words should be extracted from each sentence as explained on pages 160–161 in order to accumulate all the important details. Then the details so accumulated should be listed below the topic. The reader should review the original material to check the accuracy of the organized notes.

Outcome. As already indicated, since the goal in this pattern is to amass information about a topic, a listing of notes is sufficient. The topic should be stated first, followed by a numbered listing of the facts. Although some sequence is evident in the Philippe Cousteau obituary, the order of events is not important here. Numbering the facts only serves as a structure for isolating pieces of information and as a visible aid for retention and review. Here is one student's note-making effort:

Philippe Cousteau

1.   Born in Toulon (France) in 1940.
2.   Youngest son of oceanographer, Jacques Cousteau.
3.   Studied at College de Normandie and MIT.
4.   As a youth worked as diver and photographer.
5.   Made first Aqualung dive at four.
6.   In 1965 participated in and filmed underwater experiment—lived with five other aquanauts 100 meters underwater for 28 days.
7.   Filmed Emmy-award-winning television series "The Undersea World of Jacques Cousteau."
8.   Coproduced with father the television series "The Cousteau Odyssey."
9.   Coauthored *Sharks* (1969) with father.
10.   Died in seaplane accident (probably in 1980, copyright date of book).

ENUMERATION

Examples. The enumeration pattern in social studies is very similar to the pattern used in science, except that it rarely deals with more than a few paragraphs. Most frequently, as in science, the topic is introduced immediately coupled to a stated number of subtopics. For instance, one might be introduced to a series of three paragraphs by the statement "There were three major causes of the War of 1812." The first cause might be developed in the first paragraph, the second in the next paragraph, and the third in the final paragraph of the group. Or one paragraph might list six subtopics (each numbered) introduced by the statement "The treaty stated several significant provisions:"

At times the pattern may not be as visible and may depend largely on headings to signify the subtopics, as in Example 8.4, from a U.S. history text.

Example 8.4[9]

Slavery Is Introduced

The year 1619 saw two important developments in Jamestown. In August, a Dutch ship brought 20 Negroes to Jamestown; thus, the first Negroes came to Virginia. Until the mid-1600's comparatively few Negroes were imported, and most of these were servants rather than slaves. In 1661, however, the Virginia legislature recognized slavery as legal. Soon afterwards, the Negroes became an important source of labor in the colony, and the number sold by Dutch slave-traders sharply increased. One hundred years after the founding of Jamestown, Virginia had some 12,000 Negro slaves.

Representative Government Begins

Also in 1619 the London Company made important changes in the government of Jamestown. A "general assembly" was to be held yearly; and the governor, his council, and two representatives from each of the settlements around Jamestown were to attend. This assembly was empowered "to make and ordain whatsoever laws and orders" it thought "good and profitable." The governor and his councilors were appointed by the London Company, but the town representatives, or *burgesses*, were elected by the colonists. This assembly, known as the House of Burgesses, held its first session in July, 1619, in the little church at Jamestown. From this simple beginning grew the practice of representative government in the American colonies.

Strategies.   The strategies are generally the same as those explained on pages 154–155: recognition of topic, recognition of subtopics, and organization of details related to a subtopic. The ways the strategies are implemented, however, are often different.

Step One: Recognition of Topic.   As in science, the readers must be alert to an opening statement that states the topic and gives the number of subtopics to be presented. From then on, the map for their reading strategy is laid out. They know that the topic is "major causes of the War of 1812" and that three causes will be stated; they realize that "the treaty" is the topic and several provisions will be named. In Example 8.4, the opening sentence promises "important developments" in Jamestown and indicates that there are two of them. Readers must relate the topic "important developments" to the total context of their reading and realize that the full topic is "important developments in the American colonies."

Step Two: Recognition of Subtopics.   Readers, once tuned in to the enumeration pattern, have little trouble locating subtopics, which are usually signaled by numbers or words (*first, next,* and so on) generally associated with a sequential progression. The difficulty, in coping with some social studies materials, is apparent in Example 8.4. The reader must realize that the headings for each of the paragraphs are the "two important developments." Indeed, this point is not clear, for the passage is written in a way that makes the reader first assume that there must be two important developments related to the introduction of slavery. As the first paragraph is studied, however, it becomes evident that the topic is developed through the use of chronological order; the whole paragraph is concerned only with the one development—the introduction of slavery. And as the second paragraph is read, it becomes evident that the writers are picking up the introductory statement, for they open the paragraph with "also in 1619. . . ." In addition, the heading and last sentence of the paragraph emphasize the second development.

Students should be given practice in locating such subtopics and relating them back to the topic, particularly when the subtopics are somewhat elusive. Directed guidance in doing this should increase comprehension, especially for the weak reader.

Step Three: Organization of Details Related to Subtopic. Once each subtopic has been located and understood, the reader should return to the first subtopic to read the details and/or illustrations. (In some cases the subtopics will not be further explained, illustrated, or defined; then, of course, this step is unnecessary.) Certainly in Example 8.4, once the readers recognize chronological order in paragraph one, the task is quite reasonable. Also, once students note that paragraph two is developed through an explanation of the "general assembly," the details about representative government can be accumulated with ease.

Outcome. Again, a simple written list of facts underneath the topic will suffice as proof of understanding, as an aid to understanding, and as a referent for future review. Here are one student's notes on paragraph one of Example 8.4:

Slavery Is Introduced in Virginia

1. August, 1619. Dutch ship brought first 20 Negroes to Jamestown.
2. Until mid-1600s. Few Negroes imported—most servants not slaves.
3. 1661. Virginia legislature recognized slavery as legal.
4. Soon afterward. Negroes became important source of labor and number sold by Dutch slave-traders sharply increased.
5. 100 years after founding of Jamestown. Virginia had some 12,000 Negro slaves.

See Chapter 7 for additional enumeration examples.

GENERALIZATION

Examples.   The generalization pattern is prevalent in social studies materials as well as in science and other subject areas that rely on the development of ideas across many passages. In social studies the generalization is most often found as a conclusion, a definition, or a broad informational statement. The generalization, whatever its form, is most important for the reader to locate and comprehend in this pattern of writing, but as already demonstrated on pages 158–163, it cannot stand alone. The reader must find "support" for the generalization. Usually the generalization is stated first, followed by the support— description, narration, facts, or illustrations—as in the following two excerpts. (A good example of a generalization in the form of a conclusion may be found on page 158).

Example 8.5[10]   Covert operations are different from espionage in that their main purpose is to influence a foreign situation without the source of the influence becoming known. Such operations may take the form of secretly financing, advising, or otherwise helping a group which is trying to overthrow an unfriendly foreign government. They may take the form of secret money subsidies or other assistance to a foreign political party or to a particular faction of a foreign labor movement, or student organization, or similar groups. They may take the form of psychological warfare—for example, the publication of an underground newspaper or the operation of a clandestine (secret) radio station which, according to the circumstances, may report the truth or spread unfounded rumors calculated to destroy morale or to mislead. They may take the form of an outright bribe of a foreign official to make a certain decision. They may take the form of infiltrating one or more secret agents into positions of power in a foreign government or any important foreign political, economic, or social group.

Example 8.6 is a short descriptive paragraph supporting a broad statement (generalization) with facts. Note that the last sentence of the paragraph reaffirms the statement introduced in the first sentence and reinforced in the second.

Example 8.6[11]   Over the years, the sickly boy developed into a vigorous man. Roosevelt became, in fact, a bundle of energy. He moved quickly, talked rapidly, laughed loudly, and cut the air with sharp, wide movements of his arms as he talked. He seemed to burst into rooms, not enter them. He seemed to shout, not talk. He seemed to run, not walk. Wherever Theodore Roosevelt was, there was plenty of action.

In the next excerpt, narrative and expository materials are used at the outset to provide support for a statement (generalization) made in the concluding paragraph. In this passage the reader has to use some critical thinking in order to make the full connection between the "story" and the generalization.

Example 8.7[12] The Africans were spread out thinly along the ridge as they watched the wagon train wind slowly through the valley, following the river. They had been following the train for a great distance, for drums had warned them that it was coming. Now their drums warned the people ahead of the train's approach. The Africans did not know who the people in the wagons were. They could see that the wagons were filled with strange furniture and tools. Large herds of animals followed the train.

All the wagons were driven by men and women with white skin. The men dressed in clothing which covered them almost completely, and the women wore dresses to their ankles. To the Africans all this seemed weird, for these white people had to be very uncomfortable in the hot sunshine.

It was the year 1836. At that time, the Africans could not know who these people were. They called themselves Boers. They were descendants of the Dutch settlers who had lived at the tip of southern Africa. After the British had taken over southern Africa in 1814, the Boers found life difficult under British rule. In 1836, they began what they called the "Great Trek." Thousands of them packed their belongings into wagons and moved into the interior looking for new lands and a new place to settle.

But the Africans who watched the train could not have known these people's story.

They only watched the endless train—wagon after wagon passing by. Probably, many began to wonder. How many wagons and how many people could there be? What do these people want? Why have they come? Where are they going?

In the years to come, the Africans learned that the people from the south wanted land. They wanted fertile land for farms that they could call their own. To the Africans, this would mean that these people were taking land from them.

All over Africa similar scenes took place. By the year 1900, all of Africa had been occupied by people from European nations. They had taken control of the continent and made the land their colonies.

Strategies. All the strategies described on pages 159–163 may be applied to similar social studies materials for students who need basic help in locating and understanding generalizations. For those who just need some brief guidance in recognizing the pattern so they may proceed independently, a few paragraphs should be analyzed in the following way.

Step One: Locate the Generalization.   One is often told that a generalization is *usually* the opening sentence of a paragraph and that its next most common position is at the end of a paragraph. Such a statement is false. In fact, good writers try hard not to write in such a formula-like, mechanical manner. Frequently, in the expository writing of social studies, the reader will find the heading, and/or the first sentence or two stating the generalization, but by no means habitually. In Example 8.5, the first sentence does state the generalization. In Example 8.6, the first two sentences and the last collaborate to form a generalization. In Example 8.7, the generalization is developed in the concluding two paragraphs and, as already suggested, depends on the reader's ability to evaluate and synthesize the various statements.

A method of locating the generalization in a passage is to scan the passage first in search of a broad and important statement. Scanning the covert operations excerpt in Example 8.5 and finding the repetitions of "they may take the form of . . ." should lead readers back to the first sentence. Likewise, in the Roosevelt example (8.6), the repetition of "he" at the beginning of so many sentences should carry the readers back to Roosevelt and the realization that his vigor, energy, and activeness are being developed. Granted, Example 8.7 is more difficult, but a perusal should enable readers to realize that a story is being told at first and that they must look to the generalization following the story.

Step Two: Classify the Generalization.   This step is brief but useful, as it provides a tool for accuracy in locating the supporting information. In Example 8.5, the generalization is a definition; in Examples 8.6 and 8.7, the generalizations are broad statements, as differentiated from the clear conclusion of the opening sentence of Figure 7.1 in the preceding chapter. Although the distinction between a broad statement and a conclusion is not always clear-cut, a conclusion always includes an aspect of opinion; the writer must prove her or his point. The broad statement is more an overall summary of pieces of information about a topic.

Step Three: Locate the Supporting Information.   Having found and classified a generalization, the reader is able to look for the kind of evidence that will support the type of generalization made. For instance, in the "conclusion" paragraph on page 159, the reader hunts for and lists the "proof." In Example 8.5, the student is able to note rather quickly that each "may take the form of " is an illustration to further explain the definition. In Example 8.6, the reader, having recognized the generalization as a broad, informational statement, seeks the descriptive details that make the statement viable. In Example 8.7, the readers must recognize that the story and the details about the coming of the Boers only assume significance as supporting information for a generalization about the takeover of Africa by people from European nations (some students will need much assistance with this passage).

Outcome. An outline is a good organized outcome for this type of reading, especially if students are asked to state the type of generalization made and the type of evidence used. Such an understanding of the writers' thinking should help readers as they proceed to other material using generalizations.

Constructing and writing an outline helps to organize thought and stimulate retention. The outline then serves as both a tool for review and a structured way of synthesizing one piece of information within a larger framework. Such outlines, however, need not conform to a formal outline format. They are most useful if they represent the pattern of writing found in the text. Here is one student's outline of the covert operations example:

Generalization

Main purpose of covert operations is to influence a foreign situation without source of influence becoming known. (The generalization is a definition.)

Evidence (illustrations of covert operations)

1. Secretly financing, advising, or otherwise helping a group to overthrow an unfriendly foreign government.
2. Secret money subsidies or other assistance to foreign political party or particular faction of foreign labor movement, student organization, or similar groups.
3. Psychological warfare (underground newspapers or secret radio station to either report truth or spread unfound rumors to destroy morale or mislead).
4. Bribe foreign official to make a certain decision.
5. Infiltrating secret agents into positions of power in foreign government or any important foreign political, economic, or social group.

SEQUENCE

Examples. Although the sequence pattern has been discussed with respect to science (Chapter 7), it takes on a different meaning in social studies. I was tempted to use the label *chronology* for the pattern in social studies, but there is sequential writing other than time order. Generally speaking, when reading this pattern in social studies, not as much precision (understanding each step in its appropriate sequence) is needed as in science. More attention is placed on using the pattern as a way of developing a larger idea. For instance, the sequence of events in Example 8.8 is important only as an illustration of the Amish and their relationship to the public schools. In Figure 8.4, the dates and times are useful only as markers for a group of events that lead to a specific outcome. In the examples cited on pages 169–171, the reader had to learn each step in exact order to understand the steps in a process or in an experiment.

The narrative passage in Example 8.8 was used as an opening illustration in an essay entitled "The Amish and the Schools." Such material is used frequently to set the stage and introduce a large concept further developed in the remainder of the section or chapter.

Example 8.8[13]   The Amish, both children and adults, seemed to be waiting. The adults sat quietly while the children worked on their lessons. Soon, a caravan of cars and school busses ground its way up the country road to the schoolhouse. A group of men left the cars, walked across the dusty playground and forced their way into the building. "This school is closed," said their leader, "and all of the students will have to come with us to the public school in town."

The words cracked through the room like a series of explosions. The Amish fathers prayed, although they did little else to stop the officials. Sobbing mothers and children began to sing "Jesus Loves Me." Some of the children, afraid, ran from the school to the cornfields, only to be chased by the men from town. Others had to be dragged, weeping and protesting, to the waiting busses. Finally, the school was empty of students, the bus engines started, and the caravan, with its load of unhappy children, started off for the school in town. In the leading car, one official turned to another and said, "Finally, that's over. We'll educate these kids, whether they like it or not." The parents, gathered in front of the Amish school, stood silently, watching the dust trail left by the churning wheels of the caravan slowly settle back to earth.

The excerpt in Figure 8.4 is part of a series of events describing space conquests of the United States. The pattern is chronological, a pattern commonly found in American and world history texts. As is also common in history texts, it reads like a story (narrative), but the essential purpose is to inform (expository).

Strategies.   In the sequence pattern the reader must learn to separate the static information from that which is a part of the developing sequence. For instance, in the example on page 170, students eager to place everything in a sequential order often use the opening statement, which is used to introduce the experiment, as step one. The temptation is even greater, however, with the more redundant social studies materials. In Example 8.8, there are many instances of descriptions that are not part of a sequence. "The words cracked through the room . . . ," which opens paragraph two, comprises an expansion of the last sentence in paragraph one. The *praying*, *sobbing*, and *running* are simultaneous

Figure 8.4   Studying a Chronological Sequence[14]

Preparations were now being made for the greatest effort of all, the flight of Apollo 11. The blast-off on this flight came on Wednesday, July 16, [1969]. Colonel Edwin E. Aldrin, Jr., of the Air Force, accompanied by Neil A. Armstrong, a civilian astronaut, descended on schedule in a lunar module to a flat, dry plain on the moon's Sea of Tranquility. It was then just past 4 P.M. on a Sunday, a time well calculated for maximum TV audience, and millions were transfixed at their sets watching the event. Some hours later, shortly after 10 P.M., Neil Armstrong slowly descended the ladder from the spacecraft and gingerly set his foot on the moon's grainy surface. "That's one small step for *a* man, one giant leap for mankind," he said. And Americans and others were too grateful for the universal rather than nationalistic spirit of this statement to wonder what was the difference between man and mankind, or why one got a small step and the other a giant leap.

Aldrin soon joined Armstrong for a brief walk and the collection of some rock samples. On Monday, after twenty-one hours and thirty-seven minutes on the moon, the mod-

NASA photo

ule blasted off, rejoining the spaceship and Lieutenant Colonel Michael Collins. On Thursday, July 24, the space voyagers splashed down in the Pacific right on schedule and were recovered by the *Hornet*.

events that followed the words of the officials—all a part of one step in the sequence.

Likewise in Figure 8.4, the chronological steps are intertwined with explanations—essential exposition but not always specific steps in time order. The reader must be able to comprehend that the explanations for a chronology of dates alone are completely meaningless.

As is true for other patterns, a skimming of the passage should result in a rough appraisal of the steps in the sequence. Once this is accomplished, the task is fairly simple. The reader needs to read and jot down each step, being sure to include all necessary information to make the step understandable. When this is completed, the final step is to ascertain the meaning of the sequence in terms of the major message the writers wish to convey.

Step One: Recognition of Steps. As in science, reading and rereading are essential activities to ensure that each step is located and to make certain that other vital information (not in a step) is retained. As students take notes it is useful to number each step. In Example 8.8, the *status quo* represented in the opening sentences could be considered a step, for it is the first event in a sequence of happenings. Words such as *soon* and *finally* help to pinpoint some, but not all, of the additional steps. Responses by students do not have to match the text—as long as a sensible sequence is noted—for some readers will consider two closely related acts as one step.

In the space sequence (Figure 8.4), the chronology is cued by references to dates and times following an introductory statement.

Step Two: Meaning of the Sequence. A sequence or chronology is rarely used in social studies material simply to present a series of steps. The pattern is usually illustrative for the purpose of supporting a larger concept. In the Amish passage (Example 8.8), the total narrative, in sequential form, serves as a "set" for the entire essay. As readers handle similar material, they need always to be aware that the sequence has a meaning beyond its structure.

Outcome. One outcome of a sequence that is chronological is a time line. The student can demonstrate understanding of the chronology of events by organizing the time line and heading it with a title that encompasses the reason for the chronological development. One student organized the time line shown in Figure 8.5.

See additional examples of the sequence pattern on pages 168–172 in Chapter 7.

COMPARISON OR CONTRAST

Examples. Comparison—the setting forth of similarities and differences—is a pattern used frequently in social studies materials. Contrast alone—the setting forth of differences only—is found less frequently, although individual paragraphs, often part of a larger comparison pattern, may be developed solely through contrast. The following excerpt is a good example of a comparison pattern (Example 8.9).

Example 8.9[15] In the 19th century, two widely differing schools of socialist thought emerged, the Utopian Socialists and the Marxians. The first group believed that public ownership of the means of production was a necessary goal for human happiness. However, they wanted to reach it gradually and peacefully, using democratic methods to make changes through the government. They believed in ballots, rather than bullets. They also felt that owners who had mines, factories or land taken away by the government should be paid for their property. People who have these beliefs today are called Socialists.

Figure 8.5   Outcome of a Sequence

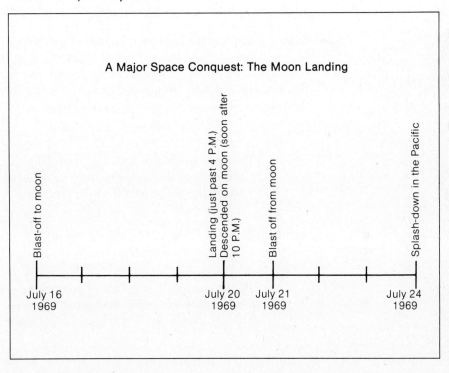

The second group, led by Marx, also wanted the government to take over all private property used to produce goods. However, their methods were to be very different. They thought that violence or revolution would be necessary because the owners of property would fight to hold on to it. No payment should be made to these owners who lost their property. Today, those who believe in these methods are called Communists. The Russian Communists are the heirs of Marx.

The excerpt in Example 8.10 is a succinct example of the contrast pattern.

Example 8.10[16]   Tribes differed in their basic ways of providing for themselves. Indians of the Southwest lived in villages and planted their corn and squash in orderly rows. Around the Great Lakes forest Indians hunted deer and small fur-bearing animals. On the Great Plains braves tracked the buffalo. In the Pacific Northwest plentiful supplies of salmon and other fish tempted Indians into their canoes and kept hunger away.

Strategies.   The comparison or contrast pattern is almost always signaled by writers through the use of introductory statements at the outset of the pattern. In Example 8.9, the reader knows he or she will be involved in reading comparison or contrast through the introductory words "two widely differing schools of . . . thought emerged. . . ." A quick scan by the reader immediately reveals that the rest of paragraph one deals with "the first group" and paragraph two is concerned with "the second group." The reader should begin by jotting down notes like those below on "the first group."

Socialists

1.   Public ownership of means of production.
2.   Gain public ownership gradually using democratic methods.
3.   Owners should be paid for their property.

Then notes should be taken on "the second group."

Communists

1.   Public ownership of means of production.
2.   Gain public ownership through revolution.
3.   Owners should not be paid for their property.

A perusal of the notes indicates to the reader that the pattern is comparison and that there is one similarity—the goal—but different ideas about how to achieve the goal.

In a contrast paragraph such as Example 8.10, the reader simply must search for the differences, as the writers open the paragraph with "tribes differed in their basic ways of providing for themselves." A listing of the four regions and of how the Indians differed in providing for themselves satisfies the purpose for reading.

See pages 168–169 for further examples and strategies related to the comparison-contrast pattern.

EFFECT-CAUSE

Examples.   Social studies materials are quite naturally prolific with the effect-cause pattern. A good part of the writers' concerns is to present events and positions followed by apparent reasons for the occurrence or the belief. The short excerpt in Example 8.11 depicts an event (the effect) and then states why it occurred (the cause).

In Example 8.12, the effect is not as clearly labeled as in the preceding example; but it is unfolded in the first paragraph, followed by a second paragraph of causes.

Example 8.11[17]   War, meantime, had broken out between the United States and Mexico. The main cause was a long standing dispute over where the southern boundary of Texas belonged. Americans were saying it lay along the Rio Grande, and the Mexicans were insisting that it belonged along the Nueces River.

Example 8.12[18]   While this is not the place to discuss the pros and cons of American policy in Southeast Asia, Americans should not have been surprised by Martin Luther King's stand. In opposing what he considered to be an imperialistic adventure and a war of colonial oppression, King was acting in the great tradition of Negro leaders throughout American history. Frederick Douglass, it will be recalled, had denounced the American war against Mexico; his son had ridiculed and protested the American war against Spain. And to a man of Dr. King's historical scholarship, the dangers to the struggle for Negro rights of continued American participation in the Vietnam conflict seemed clear.

First of all, no matter what the proclaimed intentions of the American government might be, American soldiers were fighting against a colored people as they had in the Philippines from 1898 to 1901; and that could only aggravate anti-Negro feeling domestically. Secondly, Negro troops who provided more than eleven percent of the American combat forces in Vietnam and suffered eighteen percent of the casualties might well ask themselves the same question that Private William Simms found unanswerable during the Philippine campaign. In the third place, militarism had always been the arch-enemy of tolerance and progress. After each of America's wars, there had been a reaction of more or less severe hysteria against all progressive movements, including the struggle for Negro equality. And finally (as Dr. King reminded his critics), he *had* received a Nobel Prize for peace, he *was* a citizen of the world as well as an American Negro, and he felt himself responsible to work for peace everywhere. From the viewpoint of history, it would seem that Dr. King had no need to apologize at all for his new position.

Strategies.   The effect-cause pattern is useful as a purpose setter for reading. Once the student recognizes the pattern, it is a relatively simple matter to amass the causes for a given effect. On occasion a cause or causes will be stated prior to an effect, but not often in social studies. Sometimes a given cause will turn into an effect for another group of causes. But in textbook materials, the effect-cause pattern is usually quite straightforward.

Two steps must be taken as strategies for this pattern. After skimming to be sure the pattern is effect-cause, the reader must (1) recognize the effect and (2) locate the cause(s).

Step One: Recognition of the Effect.   In short, simple materials, the effect is obvious and is presented at once. The reader has only to search for a cause or causes. In Example 8.12, readers have more of a job to accomplish. They must review mentally the background knowledge they possess about Martin Luther King and sift through all the statements in the first paragraph to conclude that the effect is King's position—opposition to continued participation in the Vietnam war.

Step Two: Location of Causes.   Certainly many statements can be effects standing by themselves without causes to substantiate them. The effect-cause pattern is present only if the causes follow the statement of the effect. The reader can ascertain this by asking the question *why*, for writers do not always state that "the causes of the effect will now be given."

Example 8.11 is somewhat unusual, for the writer actually states that he is going to present "the main cause." But, in addition, the question *why* provides double assurance that the effect-cause pattern is present. In Example 8.12, the question *why* asked after reading the first paragraph is bound to establish the effect-cause pattern. The writer also uses signal words—*first of all, secondly, in the third place*, and *finally*—to make sure that the reader locates the four causes.

QUESTION-ANSWER

Examples.   At first in my thinking, the question-answer pattern seemed subsumed by other patterns, for it can represent effect-cause, topic development, enumeration, and so on. But it is an important pattern prevalent in social studies materials used for instruction. It most often spans several paragraphs and is often utilized as the pattern for a total section of a chapter. For instance, in Example 8.13 the heading could be (and often is) a question; instead of "Why Strikes Take Place," the heading could have been "Why Do Strikes Take Place?" The rest of the section in the textbook (even beyond the two paragraphs cited, is used to answer the question. Several answers are offered.

Example 8.13[19]

WHY STRIKES TAKE PLACE

Why do strikes start? What issues cause them? One major cause of nearly all strikes is the demand for general wage increases. The rising cost of living seems always to diminish the purchasing power of the worker's dollar. To offset this trend, workers periodically seek new contracts with significantly higher wages. Employers, on the other hand, oppose large-scale wage increases, since their own costs have been rising, too. These rising costs, coupled with a larger payroll, severely reduce profits. Workers and employer cannot come to terms, so a strike results.

Job security is another root cause of strikes. Job security is protected in part by rules involving seniority and division of work. A worker who has held a job with a company for a long time is said to have *seniority*. A senior worker feels that he should have more and greater privileges than a more recently hired worker. He wants to have first choice of machine tools or of work stations. In slack times, when the company has to lay off some workers, the senior worker wants those with less seniority to be laid off before he is. Recently, union workers have been demanding job security in the form of a guaranteed annual wage. A guaranteed wage would assure the worker of adequate income throughout the year to support himself and his family.

Another pattern, exemplified in the segment below, is to raise a question structured as a separate paragraph followed by a paragraph or more containing the answer(s). This particular example from an American history text contains only one question and one answer.

Example 8.14[20] What contribution did miners make to the conquest of the western frontier?

The miner who trudged across mountains, desert, and plains in an endless search for precious metal found out what was in that expanse of territory west of the ninety-eighth meridian. At the middle of the nineteenth century Americans, despite the expeditions of Lewis and Clark and Zebulon Pike, knew little about the West. On maps much of it was labeled simply as "the Great American Desert." In the next few years, however, prospectors wandered over virtually every inch of the western frontier. By word of mouth and in diaries or letters they reported their observations, thus familiarizing the rest of the country with that vast area.

Strategies. Even though the question-answer pattern depends on other patterns in a cognitive sense, when it appears it should be treated solely as a question-answer pattern, for it is a great reading-study tool. Once a question is spotted, the reader's purpose is established—find the answer(s). The strategies are as simple as that!

The reader must always, however, be on the lookout for multiple answers. In Example 8.13, two answers are given for each question. (There are additional answers in the remainder of the text not reproduced here.) In Example 8.14, the reader gathers the single answer to the question as she or he reads; the author pinpoints the answer in the last sentence of the paragraph.

Outcome. The written response to a question-answer pattern should reflect the pattern. It could be set up in this way:

Question: What contribution did miners make to the conquest of the western frontier?

Answer: They familiarized the rest of the country with that vast area.

Or it could be written in paragraph form as in the following example by a student:

What contribution did miners make to the conquest of the western frontier? Over the years, in search of precious metal, they wandered throughout the western frontier. By word of mouth, or in their diaries and letters, they reported what they saw and thereby familiarized the rest of the country with the western frontier.

Writing the question and answer in paragraph form helped this student organize what she had read. She used composing as a learning tool in social studies.

4 W'S AND AN H

Newspaper and news magazine reading is an important part of many social studies classes. Pages 223–227 in Chapter 9 of this book are devoted to a discussion of such reading and of written reports based on articles read in newspapers and news magazines. Certainly in this mass media world it behooves the social studies teacher and/or special reading teacher to devote much attention to this kind of contemporary reading. The question pattern of *"Who? What? Where? When? How?* and sometimes *Why?"* should be utilized in student reports on news events.

RELATED ACTIVITIES

1.   Use an opaque projector to project the map and accompanying text in Figure 8.1. Have students perform the strategy of interrelating text and map. Then have them examine the map carefully and trace the routes of the Crusaders as suggested in the caption. Have students answer, independently and on paper, the two questions raised in the caption in addition to any you may want to generate.

2.   Follow up activity 1 with a map and caption plus interrelated text from a book being used by the students. Duplicate the material on a worksheet accompanied by questions for students to answer. Walk around the class or group and note individual responses. Assist with problems.

3.   Figure 8.3 provides samples of the major types of graphs. Directed lessons can be organized on the pair of pie graphs, the pair of bar graphs, and/ or the line graph. Questions should first be directed toward the facts prior to the relationships. For example, in reading the pie graphs, two *fact* questions might be: What part of each dollar is received by the government from individual

income taxes? What part of each dollar is spent by the government for national defense? A *relationship* question could be: What is the difference, as measured by parts of the dollar, between what the government takes in for social insurance and what it expends for income security? Similar follow-up activities need to be undertaken with material from the students' texts.

4. Turn to the section *Ten Tips for Reading Primary Sources* in Chapter 8 of Thomas and Robinson, *Improving Reading in Every Class*, third edition, 1982 (unabridged). The material may be duplicated for student use. A number of students find it useful to refer back to this excerpt after its introduction and review by the instructor.

5. Survey the reading students are expected to accomplish in the near future in their social studies materials. Select sample patterns of writing that occur most frequently and guide students in their use. You might want to begin with examples in this book, but you need to include the actual content the students will be coping with. Frequent reviews of materials they will be reading allows the introduction and reinforcement of all major patterns of writing prevalent in social studies materials.

6. For some students the overall strategy of comparison is useful in understanding writing patterns. Comparing *topic development*, for example, with *generalization* helps cement each pattern. For students who continue to confuse *enumeration* with *generalization*, try the following procedure: (1) Present several *topic development* patterns until students understand the idea of *topic*. (2) Introduce simple paragraphs presenting the *generalization* pattern until they are clear about the pattern and its difference from *topic development*. (3) Then present the *enumeration* pattern and pinpoint the concept of the enumeration statement "promising" information to come rather than offering information. (4) Present the three kinds of patterns and opportunities for students to differentiate among a number of examples.

SELECTED READINGS

Beyer, Barry K., and Anita Brostoff, eds. "Writing to Learn in Social Studies." *Social Education* 43 (March 1979):176–99.

Bullock, Terry L., and Karl D. Hesse. *Reading in the Social Studies Classroom*. Washington, D.C.: National Education Association, 1981.

Donlan, Dan. "Locating Main Ideas in History Textbooks." *Journal of Reading* 24 (November 1980):135–40.

Hash, Ronald J., and Mollie B. Bailey. "A Classroom Strategy: Improving Social Studies Comprehension." *Social Education* 42 (January 1978):24–26.

Lunstrum, John P., and Bob L. Taylor. *Teaching Reading in the Social Studies*. Boulder, Colo.: ERIC Clearinghouse for Social Studies–Social Science Education in collaboration with ERIC/RCS, IRA, and Social Science Education Consortium, June 1978.

Mehlinger, Howard D., and O.L. Davis, Jr., eds. *The Social Studies*, Eightieth Yearbook of the National Society for the Study of Education, pt. 2. Chicago: University of Chicago Press, 1981.

Preston, Ralph C. *A New Look at Reading in the Social Studies*. Newark, Del.: International Reading Association, 1969.

Shepherd, David L. *Comprehensive High School Reading Methods*, ch. 9. Columbus, Ohio: Charles E. Merrill, 1978.

Singer, Harry, and Dan Donlan. *Reading and Learning from Text*, ch. 12. Boston: Little, Brown, 1980.

Strang, Ruth; Constance M. McCullough; and Arthur E. Traxler. *The Improvement of Reading*, 4th ed., ch. 10. New York: McGraw-Hill, 1967.

Turner, Thomas N. "Making the Social Studies Textbook a More Effective Tool for Less Able Readers." *Social Education* 40 (January 1976):38–41.

NOTES

1. John Jarolimek, "The Social Studies: An Overview," in *The Social Studies*, Eightieth Yearbook of the National Society for the Study of Education, pt. 2, ed. Howard D. Mehlinger and O.L. Davis, Jr. (Chicago: University of Chicago Press, 1981), pp. 10–12.
2. James P. Shaver; O.L. Davis, Jr.; and Suzanne W. Helburn. *An Interpretive Report on the Status of Pre-College Social Studies Education Based on Three NSF-Funded Studies* (Washington, D.C.: National Council for the Social Studies, 1978).
3. Robert F. Madic and others, *The American Experience* (Reading, Mass.: Addison-Wesley, 1971) p. 658.
4. *This Is America's Story*, by Howard B. Wilder, Robert P. Ludlum, and Harriett M. Brown, pp. 19–20; copyright © 1972, Houghton Mifflin Company. Reprinted by permission of the publishers.
5. Edward R. Kolevzon and John A. Heine, *Our World and Its Peoples* (Boston: Allyn and Bacon, 1981), p. 183.
6. William A. McClenaghan, *Magruder's American Government* (Boston: Allyn and Bacon, 1976), p. 339.
7. June R. Chapin, Raymond J. McHugh, and Richard E. Gross, *Quest for Liberty* (San Francisco: Field Educational Publications, 1971), pp. 52–53.
8. Excerpt from Barbara Tchabovsky, "In Memoriam," in *Encyclopedia Science Supplement, 1981* (Danbury, Conn.: Grolier, 1980), p. 289. Reprinted with permission of the *Encyclopedia Science Supplement*, copyright 1981, Grolier Inc.
9. Richard C. Wade, Howard B. Wilder, and Louise C. Wade, *A History of the United States* (Boston: Houghton Mifflin, 1972), p. 28.
10. Pat M. Holt, *United States Policy in Foreign Affairs* (Boston: Allyn and Bacon, 1971), p. 116.
11. Wilder, Ludlum, and Brown, *This Is America's Story*, p. 564.
12. Yosef ben-Jochannan, Hugh Brooks, and Kempton Webb, *Africa* (New York: W. H. Sadlier, Inc., 1971), p. 9. Reprinted by permission.
13. William E. Gardner and others, *Selected Case Studies in American History*, vol. 2 (Boston: Allyn and Bacon, 1970), p. 187.
14. Clarence L. Ver Steeg and Richard Hofstader, *A People and a Nation* (New York: Harper & Row, 1977), p. 779.

15. Edward R. Kolevzon, *The Afro-Asian World* (Boston: Allyn and Bacon, 1969), p. 87.
16. Bernard A. Weisberger, *The Impact of Our Past* (New York: McGraw-Hill, 1972), p. 42.
17. Henry F. Graff, *The Free and the Brave* (Chicago: Rand McNally, 1968), p. 379.
18. Robert Goldston, *The Negro Revolution* (New York: Macmillan, 1968), pp. 228–29. Permission granted by Collins-Knowlton-Wing, Inc. Copyright © 1968 by Robert Goldston.
19. Bertram Linder, *Economics for Young Adults* (New York: W.H. Sadlier, 1971), pp. 166–67.
20. John E. Wiltz, *The Search for Identity: Modern American History* (Philadelphia: Lippincott, 1978), p. 328.

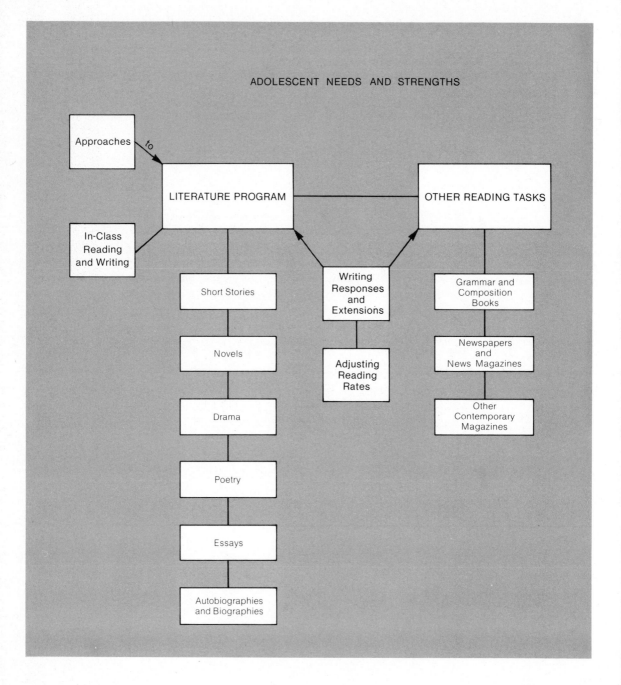

ADOLESCENT NEEDS AND STRENGTHS

Approaches — to → LITERATURE PROGRAM

In-Class Reading and Writing

LITERATURE PROGRAM — OTHER READING TASKS

Short Stories

Novels

Drama

Poetry

Essays

Autobiographies and Biographies

Writing Responses and Extensions

Adjusting Reading Rates

Grammar and Composition Books

Newspapers and News Magazines

Other Contemporary Magazines

9
English

In terms of reading and writing tasks, the teacher of English probably has the most difficult job of all. Students are expected to read the varied genres of literature in addition to reading newspapers and magazines and an English (grammar-composition) textbook. They are expected to learn to write well in many modes and for varied purposes. Students are frequently called on to read the directions and exercises in a variety of workbooks, in supplementary texts, and sometimes on work- or contract-sheets. In the reading of literature, there is an added task for English teachers: they are expected to develop appreciation of, and continuing interest in, the literature of America and of the world.

Such a smorgasbord of tasks calls for the development and refinement of many abilities in acquiring vocabulary, comprehending, and developing flexible reading rates. And, despite some popular opinion, most English teachers are not reading or even writing teachers; that is, they have not necessarily received more educational background related to reading and writing instruction per se than have science, social studies, or industrial arts instructors. In the past, and to some extent even at present, the invalid notion has existed that English teachers have the responsibility of teaching all the "reading and writing skills." In fact, they have all they can do to cope with such tasks in their own area. In addition to the varied tasks called for by the English curriculum, the curriculum usually taps aspects of thought, feelings, and behavior not common to other content areas. Since so much of the reading involves imaginative reading, the English teacher demands heightened conceptual awareness and deep interaction at the affective level.

THE LITERATURE PROGRAM

Simmons, Shafer, and West suggested that English teachers listen to what adolescents are saying and read what they write. Young people, through "underground" newspapers and magazines as well as free presses and other types of writing, have shown:

> . . . considerable dissatisfaction with school, with both the organization and content of the curriculum, with the grading system, with the "generation gap," and with the inability of high school

students to communicate satisfactorily with teachers, parents, and adults, with their attempts to find (like Studs Lonigan) a "place in the world they never made. . . ."[1]

The quest for the development of new English programs, using a variety of new techniques and new media to help promote the development of young people, is a necessary one. . . . You will never be able to know too much about their language, their unique identities, or their "secret places." You will need to know much about them to begin a quest with them for new alternatives in schools and in English as a school subject.[2]

The very ability that permits adolescents to "function in the world of the possible" enables English teachers to help heighten:

. . . awareness and comprehension of the forces that are helping to shape their present lives and that may, without their intelligent intervention, determine their futures—or at least the manner in which, as adults, they live their tomorrows.[3]

Elkins stated:

Perhaps the most important difference between the cognitive functioning of the child and that of the adolescent is that the child functions in the real world only while the adolescent can function in the world of the possible. . . .[4]

The adolescent's ability to go beyond the here and now means he also has the potential to think logically about people and situations that are not present. He does live in the present, as does the child, but he can also project into the future, which the younger child cannot do to any appreciable degree. . . .[5]

The ability of adolescents to hypothesize, categorize, make high-level abstractions, and introspect must be taken into account in the teaching of literature. Elkins suggested that the "sensitivity training" students obtain "through literature can be an initial motivating force for increasing cognitive abilities."[6]

Farrell mentioned just a few of the ways English teachers could "sensitize students to matters related to the past, the present, and the future—or, rather, possible futures."[7]

1.   *Using Media.* (a) By advanced reading of television guides, teachers can alert students to forthcoming programs that treat pressing issues. The programs can then become the subject of classroom discussion and of writing assignments. (b) Individualized reading assignments can be made in such periodicals as *Harper's, Atlantic, Saturday Review, The New Republic, New York Review of Books, American Scholar,* and *Daedalus.* Students can share their reading through small-group discussions and panels. Writing assignments

might vary in length from the paragraph to the term paper. Discussion of controversial issues could lead to further research and debates. (c) Students could use tape recorders to interview grandparents and other older acquaintances about changes they have observed during their lifetimes. Portions of the tapes could be shared in the classroom, and tapes could be exchanged for home listening. (d) Photographs in family albums might be shared for what they reveal about the process of aging and about changes in manners and styles. Discussion and writing could follow.

2. *Exploring the Effects of Media.* Students could discuss or describe in writing how life in America would differ if each of the following were eliminated: airplanes; quadraphonic and stereophonic records, tapes, and systems; television sets; radios; automobiles; telephones; computers; cameras. Out of such explorations, students should begin to sense how media pervasively affect the values, organization, and commitments of a nation.

3. *Projecting One's Life.* Students can be given the following kinds of assignments: (a) Assume that you are seventy years old. Your twelve-year-old grandchild has written asking you to describe the most important events in your life. Write your response. (b) Assume that you are seventy-five years old and that you have kept a diary. Share your entries describing how you spent a typical day at ages thirty, fifty, and seventy-five.

4. *Role Playing.* Students are given the following kinds of assignments: (a) Assume that you have decided to campaign for mayor. Write a statement describing what you intend to do to improve your city if you win. (b) Assume that you are a medical doctor who has three patients with terminal kidney cancer. You have available only one machine for dialysis. Discuss your criteria for choosing which patient shall live. (c) Assume that thousands of starving children in India and Bangladesh can be adequately fed if Americans are willing to cut by 10 percent the amount of meat they eat. You are put in charge of a campaign to persuade your fellow citizens that they must make sacrifices so that others may live. Outline the methods of persuasion you would use in your campaign.

5. *Writing Scenarios.* Students can be given the following kinds of assignments: (a) Describe in chronological order the national and international events that lead to a banning of all nuclear weapons in 1995. (b) Describe in chronological order the events that lead to India's being economically self-sufficient by the year 2000.

6. *Using Literature.* (c) Students can read and discuss various forms of speculative fiction—dystopian and utopian literature, sci-

ence fantasy and science fiction—for the imaginative insights into the future such literature offers. Classes might be broken down into small groups, each of which is encouraged to develop its own American Utopia. (b) Students can read and discuss multiethnic literature so that they may come to appreciate and honor life styles and values that differ from their own. (c) Students can read and discuss literature that shows humans living in harmony with, or alienated from, nature. Such literature might include poems of the English nature poets, prose and poetry from the oral tradition of native Americans, and essays of contemporary figures like Joseph Wood Krutch, Edward Hoagland, and Loren Eiseley. Students should come to understand that persons who exploit nature not only risk their peace of mind: they jeopardize the continuance of the human race.[8]

Many English programs today are based on an elective system, so some of the problems of *how to organize* may not always be as serious an issue as in the past. An elective course on black literature, for example, will undoubtedly cross genres, but the question of chronological versus thematic approach must still be faced. In all probability, the teacher will choose a thematic approach, since chronology postpones contemporary areas of concern for too long a time. In general, the chronological approach is not successful with high school students.

The topical or thematic approach seems most suitable for the adolescents of today. Simmons, Shafer, and West suggested "self-identity" as a crucial theme for adolescents and indicated that there is plenty of literary material available for developing the theme. They also listed ten other "literature-centered units" that they felt have great potential appeal for high school students: (1) alienation; (2) the black experience; the deferred dream; (3) appearance versus reality; (4) literature and war; (5) the "God is Dead" concern; (6) individualism versus conformity; (7) man and nature; (8) the generation gap; (9) the world of the future; and (10) initiation.[9]

Donlan illustrated a participation guide built around multiple texts. The following chart is taken from his article delineating the readings he chose for tenth and eleventh graders involved in a unit called "Survival."[10]

Group Reading Selections for "Survival" Program

	A *(easy reading)*	B *(hard)*	C *(moderately difficult)*
Short Fiction	*The Day of the Bullet* by Stanley Ellin	*Flowers for Algernon* by Daniel Keyes	*An Occurrence at Owl Creek Bridge* by Ambrose Bierce

	A *(easy reading)*	B *(hard)*	C *(moderately difficult)*
Drama	*The Hitch-Hiker* by Lucille Fletcher	*Emperor Jones* by Eugene O'Neill	*The Lottery* (play version) by Shirley Jackson
Poetry	*The Mate* by James Stokely	*Auto Wreck* by Karl Shapiro	*On the Move* by Thom Gunn
Novel	*Call of the Wild* by Jack London	*Lord of the Flies* by William Golding	*Old Man and the Sea* by Ernest Hemingway
Nonfiction	*My Well-Balanced Life on a Wooden Leg* by Al Capp	*A, B, and C: The Human Element in Mathematics* by Stephen Leacock	*A Bush Pilot's Deadly, Daily Game* by Don Moser

Irrespective of the unit organization, there are valid reasons for focusing attention on, learning reading techniques for, and studying the genres of literature in the secondary school. With sensitive and individualized instruction, students who have not developed the habit of turning to literature for enjoyment may do so. Those who do turn to literature for enjoyment may be introduced to a wider menu. In both cases perceptive instruction aimed to increase understanding will foster appreciation. As Sterner said:

> It is perfectly possible to read a story with genuine enjoyment even though there is not full understanding. But only with increased understanding of the vocabulary, style, and structure can there be a genuine appreciation of the worth of a story, a complete recognition of the author's aim and of his success in attaining it.[11]

Generally speaking, the generalization Sterner formulated for a story is applicable to all genres of literature; therefore, the instructional procedures used for each genre must be carefully considered since the desired student goals are identical. The suggestions discussed and listed over the next several pages are focused, inasmuch as possible, on organizational approaches and reading/writing techniques as differentiated from other literary concepts fully within the knowledge and domain of the English teacher.

Maturity Levels for Genres. A given literature program should be started with selections chosen to meet the maturity levels of the readers. In a still valuable curriculum bulletin on reading in grades 7, 8, and 9 (suitable for the upper grades also), stages of maturity of interest were suggested, as listed on page 212. Teachers were urged to help students progress from one level to the next.

Incident, action, adventure

The humorous situation

An interesting character

The clever plot that sustains interest by its shifting situation

The strange background of living conditions into which the reader is immersed

The fantasy story where the reader deliberately says, "Let's pretend"

The mystery to be solved

The gripping mood that is developed

The significance of the social problem that confronts the reader[12]

Readiness for Genres.   In addition to maturity of interest, the experiential backgrounds, abilities, goals, and language faculties of the prospective readers must be taken into consideration. Choice of reading selections should be made by both teacher and students. Instructors may often narrow the range of choice for specific purposes—to emphasize a genre, to introduce a time period, or to meet certain student needs—but readiness to undertake the reading, as understood by students and teacher, must be a strong factor.

When one or more selections have been chosen, the instructor should be prepared to devote further time to readiness for those aspects of the reading not within the overall backgrounds of specific students. A pertinent example is the choice of *Romeo and Juliet* by a small group of students who know about the story line and its possible relevance to them, but do not realize the problem they will run into when they attempt to read Shakespeare's English. If the group is to read the play at that time (and it might be more satisfying to hear and/or see a performance), much readiness for understanding and appreciating the language must be built (see Chapter 3).

Individualization.   The traditional pattern of having a complete class read a given selection together at the same time is usually unsatisfactory, for all students are never at the same stage of readiness. Discussions and/or compositions growing out of the reading of a variety of selections are more interesting than those based on a single reading. Each student is able to make an independent contribution rather than searching for some way of avoiding complete repetition.

The traditional reasons for having a whole class read the same selection at a given time are (1) that certian selections will be covered by all students, and (2) that students will learn how to study particular genres of literature by concentrating together on a specific work. Should a teacher want students to understand the author's message in an essay or a short story, or the poet's message in an epic poem, there is no reason why small groups and/or individuals could not choose selections from a limited list developed by the teacher and possibly the students. The success of the lesson lies not in the reading of a given selection but in the ability to understand the writer's message. Shared discussions citing a variety of selections enhance understanding in addition to heightening enjoyment.

Should an instructor want students to learn how an author prepares steps leading up to the climax of a short story, students will gain a more complete picture by discussing and/or writing about several short stories rather than just one. As an added bonus, the individualization of such instruction increases appreciation, since students view a variety of patterns to choose from as they turn to independent reading.

An instructor who wishes the entire class to share one literary experience might prepare the class for viewing a movie, filmstrip, or television production. The class might also listen to a recording, although there is more homogeneity in the viewing-listening situation than in listening alone. Certainly, for a number of students, there is more homogeneity in these other modes than in written symbols. If the teacher feels strongly about using one selection for the entire class, as a place to start from prior to individualization, a selection should be chosen that is within the reading ability of at least most of the poorer readers in the group. All students should be informed that the selection is being used only for introductory and demonstration purposes.

SHORT STORIES

A short story involves selected incidents, some type of plot, and usually an opposition of interests. It is a compressed view of a segment of fictitious life, although the characters and events may be based on actuality. A short story has no rigid form or given length.

An interesting method of introducing the short story to a class is to (1) have small groups and/or individuals choose from a restricted list; (2) ask students to read the stories not only for enjoyment and understanding but also to ascertain the characteristics of a short story; or (3) have students share the contents of the stories with the total class as they also contribute to a list of the characteristics of a short story. This method will help students begin to develop strategies for reading short stories, such as the three suggested below.

1. "There is no waste in the short story. Everything is omitted that is not absolutely essential. The tale plunges into action immediately. Many incidents are left unmentioned. . . . Only those events are presented that are required to advance the story."[13] Readers, therefore, are required to use their imaginations and infer much of the necessary background from minimal clues. Hence readers must be prepared to interact with the author and fill in missing pieces as they read. Teachers will need to assist some readers by encouraging them to guess and to use their imaginations. Students can best learn to make these moves with the encouragement of teachers who do not mind errors. Only as students make errors in judgment and analyze them will they be able to approach the next short story with a sense of security.

2.   The beginning segments of a short story seem particularly difficut because not enough of a cumulative effect has yet developed to be of aid to the reader.[14] Readers should, especially when dealing with short stories on new or strange topics, read the beginning slowly and thoughtfully. They may want to read the introductory segments more than once. It is helpful to try to link the "new" or "strange" concepts to past experiences, realistic or vicarious. Instructors can help students by discussing those aspects of the beginning of the story that bother them, if they wish, prior to their completing the story. Instructors are frequently able to facilitate the reading by reminding readers of background experiences that connect with the ideas presented in the introductory pages of the short story.

3.   In some short stories the language is not the language of the reader, and without assistance, particularly in those beginning segments, students may flounder through the total experience. For example, consider these seventy-eight words contained in the opening sentence of "The Legend of Sleepy Hollow":

> In the bosom of one of the spacious coves which indent the eastern shore of the Hudson, at that broad expansion of the river denominated by the ancient Dutch navigators the Tappan Zee, and where they always prudently shortened sail, and implored the protection of St. Nicholas when they crossed, there lies a small market-town or rural port, which by some is called Greensburgh, but which is more generally and properly known by the name of Tarry Town.[15]

Many students left alone with that opening sentence would not want to go on and would not be able to process the information. Help is certainly needed with the overall picture as well as guidance in figuring out such a lengthy description. In the first subordinate clause, students should be able to perceive the picture if they understand the use of *bosom*, the meaning of *spacious coves*, and the rather picturesque notion of *indent*. The next clause, ending in *Tappan Zee*, is particularly difficult, for a prepositional phrase is intruded between the verb and its object; students may not be sure of the meaning of *denominated*. The next two clauses (beginning with *and where* and ending with *crossed*) must be looked at as two actions and hence students should concentrate on the verbs. They may, however, need help with the meaning of *prudently*, the meaning of the term *shortened sail*, and the whole concept of *implored the protection of St. Nicholas*. Quite an undertaking—and without guidance the whole short story can be a gruesome experience for some students.

Elkins felt that literature units should begin with the short story because students' attention can be captured with its brevity. She also suggested that the short story allows the teacher to plan for the heterogeneity among students. Particularly for "those not as academically inclined," one could provide a variety of brief experiences focusing on the sequences of events. Elkins also indicated that the short story is conducive to divergent thinking. Finally, she stated that teachers could build from the simple to the complex and also match stories with students since there is such an abundance of short stories to choose from.[16]

NOVELS

Simmons, Shafer, and West chose the novel as an opener for a unit because they felt that students were more accustomed to the narrative form and not plagued with some of the problems created by the brevity of short stories.[17] The novel is not only longer than the short story but usually takes more of an unhurried look at a number of characters involved in several subplots that eventually interrelate with the major plot. The following list of strategies from Simmons, Shafer, and West's *Decisions about the Teaching of English* may best be developed by having small groups of students select novels that seem to appeal to them from an intensive or extensive bibliography:

1. Recalling the characters as they reappear in the story
   a. Remembering something of their characteristics
   b. Keeping from confusing them with one another

2. Recalling the stage in the plot where the thread was broken, and connecting it with its resumption

3. Keeping the sub-plots mentally separated

4. Recognizing by the middle of the story, the relationship of the sub-plots to the main thread

5. Following the motives of the characters and recognizing their influence on later events

6. Making a mental condensation of the entire story in the form of a very brief summary

7. Recognizing the problem (if any), the climax, and the final resolution or solution of the story

8. Discussing with classmates the characters, their motives, the events, the problems, etc. at intervals during reading, and after the novel is completed

9. Evaluating the novel
   a. Individual phases
   b. As a whole[18]

DRAMA

In a play, aside from the directions, the playwright has the characters speak for themselves without interference of description, narration, or explanation. Reading a play is therefore difficult. The only clues are provided by the dialogue, so readers must use both auditory and visual imagination. Some people call the written play simply a blueprint for performance. On the other hand, the reading of a play without benefit of performance does permit individual interpretations and individual pacing on the part of the reader. Each experience— the reading and the viewing of a performance—probably contributes to the reader's appreciation of drama.

Simmons, Shafer, and West pointed out that it is most important for students to have a clear, graphic picture of the setting before the play begins. They suggested the reinforcement approach:

> Do with settings what you should do with just about every component of a play: *use several reinforcement activities for the silent reading.* Discuss the setting with them. Draw it on the board. Have them sketch it on a piece of paper. Show them a photograph or model of one exactly similar if it is available (don't knock the old Globe Theater model!). If you have slides or filmstrips of the setting, parts of the play, or the entire play, use it as reinforcement. Remember, a play was written to be *seen.* Students who have trouble visualizing are really in a tough way when asked to read this genre.
>
> The reinforcement approach, through oral and audiovisual activities, is needed throughout the study of dramatic selections. Much oral reading of parts can be helpful, and stop the reading occasionally to ask them and their classmates about various aspects of the lines. Don't forget that a character in a play is using facial expressions, gestures, and movement while he is speaking. Also, there may at times be simultaneous activity on stage during the lines; other characters may be moving about, coming and going, making side comments, and reacting kinetically to what is being said. Most of this action is never stated in print, so *somebody—you—*must indicate its occurrence and significance. [19]

Some students may enjoy reading a play on their own without having to be responsible for performing in it. They should be permitted to do so. At other times, a small group might want to read a play together and put it on for the class or for themselves. Whatever the approach, the instructor will want to help students "tune in" to the particular type of dialogue used by the playwright by giving as much individual attention as possible to students who have difficulty with it.

In addition to contending with the nature of the dialogue, the most important other reading strategy students need assistance with is learning to make inferences from the dialogue. They must be able to infer character traits, feelings, and motives from the dialogue, as well as action and movements of the characters on stage. Inferences must also take the form of visualizing characters and settings as well as "audizing" conversations, especially at critical moments. [20]

POETRY

More than any other genre of literature, beautiful poetry can be destroyed by minute analysis. And, even worse, students who might have been captured by a rhythmic tale, a mood, or a magnificently expressed idea are turned away from poems—perhaps forever. Teachers, fearful of "turning off" their students, often avoid poetry or allow students to interpret given poems in any way they desire. Certainly there is latitude for interpretation, but real appreciation does not develop unless poems are understood. The major reading strategy is to help students understand each poem.

Without analyzing each four to eight lines, students can learn to read ballads and longer story poems in much the same way as they approach short stories and novels. Once they have, with the instructor's aid, learned something about the nature of the times in which the poem is set, the language patterns used, and the types of figurative language employed, they can read to enjoy, understand, and appreciate the story. Lyric poetry, aimed at the creation of a mood, is more difficult to understand, for the reader must make a number of inferences. However, here again it is unnecessary to read and interpret on a line-by-line basis. Students need to become used to the use of figurative language in creating moods that do not tell a story.

Simmons, Shafer, and West presented some convincing reasons for the problems teachers have in leading their students to read poetry:

1. Poetry does not necessarily tell a story but often develops abstract ideas and propositions concerning human experience.

2. Unlike the junior novel, there is little or no transitional or junior poetry.

3. The form or structure of poetry is unrelated to the reading experiences of most adolescents.

4. Word order in sentence structure is often very different from the langauge experienced and anticipated by young readers.

5. Ease of understanding is sharply reduced when unusual words, dialects, and historical allusions appear in critical places and are of prime importance to the poet's purpose.

6. Use of historical and mythological illusions, unclear or unknown to the reader, may cause lack of communication and/or reduction of the force with which the poet wishes to communicate specific ideas.

7. Figurative language, of course, is the cause of comprehension problems for all but the most sophisticated of readers.[21]

In light of these reasons for problems, it behooves the instructor to take a lot of care and time in preparing students for reading poetry. Certainly for particular students, the choice of poetry to be read is of tremendous importance. Chesler offered four criteria for the selection of poems that "are appropriate for students who need to learn how to read a poem."[22] The first criterion, *understandable on a literal level*, was operationally defined as students being able to follow "the poem's thought flow or narrative movement without considerable reliance upon the teacher or a dictionary."[23] Chesler suggested that if the poem was suitable but several vocabulary problems existed, those words should be defined in advance unless they could be inferred from context.

Chesler's second criterion was that students needed to be able to *feel* a poem "by connecting it to a personal experience, undergone directly or vicariously."[24] He suggested that teachers might need to help students (through trips, in-class presentations, other media, class discussion) make "the connection between their world and the vision presented in the poem under consideration."[25] The third criterion was that of the *appearance* of the poem. Chesler felt that meaning should be conveyed clearly through visual as well as auditory means. His fourth criterion was *sound appeal*. He indicated that the acutely trained ears of students could be used to help them read the poem in terms of meaning and aesthetic unity.

Since, as indicated earlier, figurative language is so prevalent in poetry and causes so many problems, time should be taken in class to assist young people in understanding the whole area of metaphor. Students enjoy working with figurative language if the instructor begins with their own language. The daily conversation of teenagers is filled with metaphor. Once students learn that figurative language is a way of communicating that they use constantly, the figurative language of the poetry they are to read will not seem so forbidding.

ESSAYS

Essays have not been treated with enough importance in the English curriculum. Along with short stories, they are of particular significance to a developing reader in the secondary school, for contemporay magazines and newspapers stress these forms of writing. Newspaper editorials and many featured columns are essays in the truest sense.

Elkins pointed out that:

Although the essay is the genre in which the author speaks directly to the reader, students are frequently unable to approach the essay and converse with the author on his terms. They need a wealth of observational, conversational, and research experiences either in preparation for reading the essay or as a follow-up. These experiences enable students to comprehend the essence and importance of the essay and to share the process through which the essayist arrived at his point of view. The same process may lead them to a view that is opposite from the essayist's. Appropriate concrete experiences with the genre will develop an ability to handle essays on an abstract level.[26]

An essay usually focuses on a single subject and expresses the point of view and personality of the writer. Essays are not exhaustive and have no set form. They may be impersonal, autobiographical, or narrative in nature. Since essays are so varied in nature and range from simple to quite complex, they are excellent vehicles for individualizing instruction. Specific essays can be matched to the interests, needs, or abilities of particular students.

Three strategies are of specific importance for the reader of essays:

1. Be aware that the essay is written from the author's point of view. Consider this as the ideas are processed. Try to read between the lines and decide how the author arrived at his or her opinions.

2. Suspend judgment until all the evidence is in. Try to retain the information gained without reacting to each idea. Aim at full understanding of the point of view.

3. Attempt to evaluate what has been said by the author in comparison to your own views and biases—a difficult task. Strive to look at the comparison as objectively as possible prior to accepting or rejecting, partially or fully, the views of the author. (See pp. 106–107.)

AUTOBIOGRAPHIES AND BIOGRAPHIES

An autobiography is an account of one or more individual lives written by the subject(s); a biography is such an account written by someone other than the subject(s). Although they are nonfiction, autobiographies and biographies are bound to be slanted by the perceptions and knowledge of the writers. They are usually written in narrative style with a conscious selection and shaping of the material.

Readers should be guided to proceed with the reading of autobiographies and biographies in a different frame of mind from that created for the reading of a novel. The temptation is to read the narrative in much the same way. But the reader needs to remember that the plot in an autobiography or a biography is human nature. This genre—as differentiated from a memoir, which focuses on outward events—turns the focus on penetrating analyses of human motives and emotions. The reader should come away from the reading experience with a fairly comprehensive portrait of the subject.

Students should be able to create outlines, summaries, and even pictures of the personality they read about. They should be able to answer classmates' questions in regard to the nature of that particular human being.

Readers of autobiographies and biographies should also be helped, through sound questioning, to recognize the author's prejudices, biases, and attitudes. The reader capable of abstract thought will heighten his or her own understanding and appreciation by perceiving the philosophy of life reflected through the events, behaviors, and thoughts expressed in the autobiography or biography.

RESPONSES TO LITERATURE

It seems imperative that emphasis be placed on individual responses to literature rather than on the sharing of facts or the development of a literature program containing selections everyone must read at a given time. A literature program that places great value on having all students read and analyze certain books and selections placed in some rigid sequence across the grades appears to be on its way out. There still are, however, some stout defenders of Shakespeare for all and "The Rime of the Ancient Mariner" for many. Such a position seems incongruous with the needs of adolescents to respond to and interact with those issues and themes of relevance to them. In the minds of some students, classics are developed because they are handed down from one English teacher to another.

Some classics may be suitable for some students at specific times; grade level does not dictate that readiness. And other students may never be ready to read the original versions of particular selections deemed as "musts." Books and shorter selections of various types, sometimes classics and sometimes contemporaries, should be chosen from a master list developed by students and teachers. The master list, possibly organized by grade level but preferably not, should provide a variety of literary experiences suitable to the reading abilities, needs, and interests of the prospective readers. Should a teacher want groups of students within the classroom to select a common work for group discussion, the list can be narrowed for that specific purpose. The list should have a great deal of flexibility so titles may be added and deleted when desirable.

A secondary school literature program that makes contact with students considers the nature of the learner, the background from which he or she comes, the purposes of the learner, and the nature of the task to be performed. An exciting literature program encompasses all types of media—films, filmstrips, recordings, television, live dramatization—in addition to books. The content of such programs must be subject to fairly rapid change in relation to the needs, backgrounds, and interests of the school population. A literature program that remains stagnant and rigid may be a potent force in defeating the development of lifetime readers.

Teachers need to help students respond to literature in many ways so that the literary world becomes a wonderful place for them. Certainly instructors must help students understand what the authors are saying and how they are saying it, but foremost and uppermost, teachers should encourage diverse and imaginative responses built on the interaction *that* student had with *that* author. "Encouraging students to explore and respond openly and honestly, rather than merely to parrot back what the teacher has said, is the aim of the response-centered approach."[27]

It is my belief—based on teaching and observation—that students are able to contribute to oral discussions in greater depth and with more organization if they write their responses in advance. In this respect, the written composition or notes serve as an advance organizer for the discussion.

Donelson and Nilsen suggested that under most conditions students need thinking time prior to responding. They added:

> The only questions that can be asked and answered in rapid fire order are those to which students already know the answers. At the beginning of a discussion these may serve to refresh memories and to insure that the class is starting from the same factual base, but even very simple-sounding questions may have very complex answers. It sometimes helps if during a discussion, the questioning begins at a concrete or factual basis and then moves progressively toward the abstract. [28]

IN-CLASS READING

Means concluded, after nine years of experimentation, that tenth, eleventh, and twelfth graders who were allowed to select their own books and were given time in class for silent reading tended to go on to read extensively. [29] He organized individualized reading classes that met daily for a class hour. The major non-reading activity was a ten- to fifteen-minute conference with the teacher when a book was completed. No book lists or formal book reports were used; students had complete free choice. Assistance in selection was given only on request.

The most widely read books during the nine years were: (1) *Animal Farm*, (2) *Catcher in the Rye*, (3) *Grapes of Wrath*, (4) *Lord of the Flies*, (5) *Of Mice and Men*, (6) *Old Man and the Sea*, and (7) *The Stranger*. During the last four years of the study the following popular titles appeared: (1) *Catch 22*, (2) *Love Story*, and (3) *Tell Me That You Love Me Junie Moon*. The five most popular authors over the nine years were Steinbeck, Hesse, Salinger, Vonnegut, and Brautigan.

Simmons, Shafer, and West suggested that silent classroom reading could be organized in several ways, in terms of kinds of responses desired:

> One way is to assign questions to be considered *before* the reading begins. This has both the advantages and disadvantages of limiting the reader's perspective on his material. It can also give clear direction to whatever reaction activity follows the reading period.
>
> For a more individualized approach, response requirements can be provided each student as he finishes the material in question. When the student finishes his reading, the teacher can provide reaction assignments best fitted to his ability. This approach allows the teacher to discuss with each student the nature of whatever responsibilities he is assigned. For the teacher who is aware of the

reading abilities of his students and who has prepared a wide variety of questions aimed at varying levels of reading achievement, this approach can pay rich dividends.

Reading can be assigned with no reaction requirements at the outset. Once the reading has been completed, questions of various kinds can be asked. This strategy allows each student to consider a variety of matters pertaining to the material he has just read. When conducting any subsequent reaction sessions, the teacher must be careful to allow individual impressions to be voiced. Tactful guidance of the reaction period is an important dimension of assigning reading without asking for specific responses. The discussion can be structured or unstructured.

Variety in in-class activity can also be achieved by developing materials to be read by the students. The teacher can assign all students the same text, or he can assign different texts to different groups, or he can assign individual texts to individual students. The procedure can also be varied by asking various individuals to approach their reading with different purposes in mind.

We see, then, that silent reading activities have much potential for diversification. In-class reading can help the teacher and student to work together more closely on ideas found in the material assigned, and a good deal of variety can be injected into the assignments. [30]

OTHER READING TASKS

In addition to what has been defined as literature, the student in English class is responsible for reading and study in grammar and composition texts and any other materials whose purposes are solely to inform, explain, and/or convince. One hopes that the English instructor is also guiding students in reading parts of newspapers and contemporary magazines, for these are the kinds of reading tasks that the greatest number of adults will turn to most frequently during their lifetimes.

GRAMMAR AND COMPOSITION BOOKS

The grammar-composition-language textbook is used in different ways by different teachers in various schools. Sometimes it functions as a basic text, read and studied in page-by-page order; more often, instructors have the book used as a reference tool and an assignment source. Whichever technique is utilized, if the book is used, students should receive some guidance in coping with it. Each group of writers and each publishing company utilizes a different format, but usually there is a consistent, recognizable pattern in a given text.

English texts are particularly valuable as reference tools both in directed grammar assignments and in helping students with their compositions. Few students turn to this type of text on their own, however, unless the instructor has previewed the books with them, talked about their importance, and conducted at least a few directed lessons using one or more of such texts as a base. Students who become accustomed to using English texts as a reference source have found a tool that fosters independence.

Example.   English textbooks are largely expository in nature, although introductions and examples are frequently written in narrative discourse—particularly at the junior high level. As in a mathematics textbook, the material is quite evenly distributed among the development of concepts, the development of principles, and problems to solve (normally in the form of exercises). A large number of paragraphs are definitional. Since there are so many details to explain and define, numerous types of typographical aids are used to call attention to important concepts.

In Figure 9.1, eighth-grade students are being introduced to sentence structure. Students are clued in to the important concepts through the use of boldface print and the "language strip." These aids, as well as the overall format, are used throughout the book.

Strategies.   Although most composition-grammar books do not necessarily make fascinating reading for most students, the writing style is direct, simple, and operational. Once students get used to the patterns of writing, they should have no problems reading additional pages. In Figure 9.1, students might be guided through the following steps a few times until they can proceed independently. Of course, those students who are already independent need little or no guidance, whereas some students may need help through many lessons before feeling secure enough to proceed on their own.

Step one: The title is the topic. What does it mean?

Step two: Read the first one or two paragraphs for help in clarifying the topic.

Step three: Study the Language Strip.

Step four: Answer as many of the questions as you can through your study of the Language Strip. Then, look for assistance in the remaining material, not including APPLICATION.

Step five: Be sure you understand all the concepts before proceeding to APPLICATION. Ask the instructor about a specific problem.

Step six: Read the directions carefully. Complete the APPLICATION.

NEWSPAPERS AND NEWS MAGAZINES

Most surveys of the reading habits of adults indicate that newspapers and magazines are still read daily by a large proportion of the population. According to Barth:

Figure 9.1   Studying Sentence Structure[31]

BASIC SENTENCES

The Rule for Basic Sentences

Before you begin, think about the word *rule*. What meaning does it have for you? In your investigation of language, *rule* will have another meaning. It will mean "restating something that you already know."

Now think about the term *basic sentences*. This term describes certain kinds of sentences from which all other English sentences can be made.

Keep these meanings for *rule* and *basic sentences* in mind as you study the three basic sentences in the Language Strip.

1. How many parts does a basic sentence have?
2. What is the subject called? The predicate?
3. What is another way of writing **Noun Phrase**? **Verb Phrase**?
4. We can say that a basic sentence may be written as **NP** followed by **VP**. In the rule at the bottom of the Language Strip, what does **S** stand for? What does → stand for? What does + stand for?
5. Read the rule, translating the abbreviations and the symbols into the words they stand for.

Language Discovery   Basic sentences may be written as a noun phrase followed by a verb phrase. The rule for basic sentences is written:

$$S \rightarrow NP + VP$$

Application   Write the rule that describes how all basic sentences are written. Space out the rule so that your paper is divided roughly into two columns. Then write each of the basic sentences given below, putting the **NP** in the **NP** column and the **VP** in the **VP** column.

1. The students planted some pines.
2. Trash spilled from the containers.
3. The campgrounds had one vacancy.
4. My room is small.
5. Louise read her horoscope.
6. We jumped across the puddles.
7. No one had an umbrella.
8. The messenger waited for an answer.
9. The suitcase was empty.
10. Cats roam the alleys.

Source: Jerome Martin and Dorothy C. Olson, *Patterns of Language* (New York: American Book, 1974), p. 34. Reprinted by permission of D.C. Heath and Company.

There are over 62,000 magazines (11,296 newspapers) published in the United States, with an average monthly circulation of over 238 million. . . . Though more books are being sold now than ever before, more people also buy *TV Guide* than buy *Reader's Digest*, the top two mass circulation magazines in the U.S.[32]

Johnson[33] and others stress the value and importance of using newspapers in the classroom for a number of reasons: (1) The material is inexpensive and yet offers an opportunity to deal with the contemporary scene and a variety of reading strategies. (2) Since textbooks and other printed materials used for instruction go out of date so quickly, the newspaper serves as a way of dealing with the present and checking on the present validity of textbook material. (3) Newspaper units can be interesting to learners as well as nonthreatening to poor readers. (4) As pointed out by Cheyney, "one major emphasis should be that of developing students' analytical and critical reading skills."[34]

In reading the reporting of "facts" in a newspaper (versus clear editorial writing), the well-known formula of using specific questions *(Who? What? Where? When? How?)* seems to work for most articles. Usually the questions can be answered in the first paragraph or two. Note that in both items cited from two different newspapers in Example 9.1, the reader can use the strategy of *Who? What? When?* and come away with clear answers.

Example 9.1
1. The Chicago Teachers Union and the Board of Education reached tentative agreement yesterday on a contract that reportedly includes a 5 percent pay raise for teachers.[35]

2. Tentative agreement was reached Thursday between the Chicago Teachers Union and the Board of Education on a contract that calls for about a 6.5 percent salary increase.[36]

Where? was not stated precisely, although it is evident that events took place in Chicago. *How?* was subsequently answered in the second paragraph of one of the articles, although not until much later in the other. Nevertheless, the strategy of raising the *4W* and *1H* questions as an aid for getting quick information from a newspaper article is useful. The remaining paragraphs of an article usually give more details related to the questions and sometimes may answer "Why." At any rate, students should be prepared to ask "Why," should the information be present.

But a far more important strategy must be employed. As "factual" reporting has become more difficult to ascertain in both newspapers and news magazines, the reader must attempt to separate what appears to be fact from what appears to be opinion. It does seem as though it is fact that the Chicago Teachers Union and the Board of Education reached tentative agreement about a contract having to do with a salary increase; but the percentage of raise is questionable since one source states 6.5 and the other says 5. Further checking is necessary.

Students must be helped to develop the following concepts in reading newspaper reports of "fact" and summaries in news magazines:

1. Writing something down or printing it does not make it true. Approach all news writing with a questioning mind.

2. Verification of what is read should be accomplished by checking a number of other reliable sources.

3. Cognizance should be taken of the editorial policy of the publication, for "facts" can sometimes be subtly changed by a word here and there loaded with bias or emotion.

4. The reader should attempt to hold personal bias in abeyance while reading the news. Try to obtain the writer's message before evaluating it.

When reading editorials, the reader knows that the writer is trying to persuade and/or take a particular stand; in fact, although all editorials cannot qualify as literature, the editorial is really another kind of essay. In this case it becomes imperative for the reader to withhold judgment and attempt to understand the message, including the writer's bias. Once the message is understood, readers can rebut from their fund of knowledge and emotions as well as by finding editorials that reflect opposing ideas. If readers can be encouraged to read and listen to as many news sources as possible, they will at least hear and read a variety of opinions, particularly in light of the numerous and serious problems confronting society today. Teachers can best encourage such activities by asking students to report on an issue only after having read and/or listened to two or more sources concerned with the same issue.

Readers should approach editorials with the following questions:

1. What is the issue?

2. What side of the issue is essentially represented here?

3. What specific evidence is given to support that side?

4. Is there any evidence apparent in this editorial to support another side?

5. How does the writer show a bias? Are particular words or patterns of writing used that accomplish this? What are they?

Readers of newspapers and news magazines should be encouraged to write the answers to the *4W* and *1H* questions in a well-organized paragraph or two. One way of having students learn to report succinctly but thoroughly is to have them publish their own newspaper. Shuman, in discussing the results of such a project, reported:

Through their preparation, students have worked together harmoniously toward a common goal. They have learned something about proofreading as well as about writing. They have come to appreciate some of the complexities of putting together a coherent, balanced product, working against a deadline and within quite absolute space restrictions. Apathetic students have become enthusiastic contributors and valuable critics. The entire project has added new zest to many English classrooms.[37]

OTHER CONTEMPORARY MAGAZINES

Whether it be *Sports Illustrated* or *Seventeen*, the reader will need to apply survey techniques by using the tables of contents and thumbing through the varied offerings in each magazine. Readers should be helped to develop this strategy, for they will not have the time, generally, to read the entire magazine. And, especially as they emerge into the world of work or enter a university, they must be selective in order to choose readings that will interest them or that will be essential for a given purpose.

Some magazines are purely informational; others may include full-length novels, short stories, essays, and so on. Since magazines are read by many, are easily obtainable, are more up to date than books, are relatively inexpensive, are easy to transport, and relate to varied interests and occupations, the English instructor should spend class time helping students learn to use them and to become accustomed to using them. More time spent in developing broad and critical newspaper and magazine readers will, in the long run, develop a better overall citizenry than the inordinate amount of time sometimes concentrated on one or two pieces of literature.

WRITING AS A TOOL OF STUDY

Aside from the use of writing as a response to literature or as a creative endeavor, writing may be used "as a tool for exploring a subject."

It is only when students begin to write on their own that the implications of new knowledge begin to be worked through and . . . that they really come to know the material.

This is because writing can be a powerful process for discovering meaning rather than just transcribing an idea that is in some sense waiting fully developed in the writer's mind. Our language provides a whole panoply of devices that not only convey our meaning to others, but help us develop the meaning for ourselves. These devices take many shapes: they include the buts and the ands and the althoughs that relate one set of information to another; they include the basic syntactic relationships of subjects and objects and predicates; and they include structural devices that underlie larger stretches of discourse—time sequence in narrative, or generalization and supporting detail in exposition.[38]

Although writing has been stressed in this volume as a responsibility of each teacher in each classroom, it is in the English classroom that much of the initial learning and emphasis must be generated. Students need direction in writing research reports (see Chapter 5 in Thomas and Robinson[39]). They need continuing experience in writing in the expository and argumentative-persuasive modes (see pages 91–92 and 109–110 in this volume). They need to be helped to place a great deal of emphasis on planning and organizing prior to writing (see pages 83–84 in this volume).

READING RATES

Rates of reading have received little attention in earlier chapters, for, in the main, study-reading of expository materials does not demand a great deal of rate flexibility. Yes, there is some flexibility related to the nature of the material and the purpose for reading, but that has been touched on in discussing pre-viewing (pp. 73–75) and in pointing out the need to read at a very slow pace in mathematics and in the physical sciences. Social studies materials, written in a narrative style, may be read a little faster, but generally the reader wants to proceed slowly enough to digest and weigh the information.

Reading instruction in the English class appears to be an appropriate place for considering a variety of reading rates, as the purposes for reading and the varied nature of the materials necessitate adjustments in thinking speed. Some of the strategies suggested in this chapter and introduced in English class may indeed be reinforced in functional situations in other content areas as well. The English instructor should plan to make use of some materials from other content areas to demonstrate differences in rates of reading and to help pave the way for transfer of training.

The nature of the task (type of material and purpose for reading it) should be considered as a student embarks on a study or reading mission. In addition to readiness procedures discussed in Chapter 3, readers should be encouraged to think about the probable reading rates needed to best accomplish a given task. Some directed practice in adjusting rates to the task at hand will help to develop a flexible reader who learns to slow down and speed up in relation to need.

The bulk of instructional materials used in classrooms is read (studied) at rather slow rates (100 to 250 words per minute); the slowest rates, as has been indicated, would probably be used with math and some science materials. The "lighter" the reading matter becomes and the less complex the purpose, the faster will be the rate normally. (Those students who are "stuck" at one plodding or rapid rate for all materials and all purposes are especially in need of direct guidance.) Light or easy fiction read purely for entertainment, not analysis, might be read anywhere up to 500 words or so per minute. Beyond 500 to 550 words per minute, skimming probably takes place where only partial ideas are gained in an attempt to get the general drift of the material. Scanning, or speeding through material until you locate a particular item, may be extremely fast—perhaps 1,000 words per minute or more.

Any one of the rare categories may be improved with practice. The only limitations imposed are the varied natures of the tasks, our rate of thinking or comprehension, and the physiological boundaries of our visual apparatus. Many advocates of speed reading appear to consider skimming the normal reading act for all materials. I cannot accept this idea and heartily recommend that schools inspect several longitudinal follow-up studies of commercial agencies prior to "buying" some type of package program that promises that all students will be reading at rapid rates. It would seem more advantageous to develop programs that improve reading comprehension with accompanying flexibility of rate for many students as they accomplish reading and study tasks throughout the curriculum.

Mendelsohn has spoken of speed reading as:

> . . . analogous to jetting to utopia. Passengers tend to arrive prior to knowing why they came or what they are looking for. As absurd as such an excursion might be, it has surely been undertaken and is in fact underwritten daily in many . . . school classrooms. Approval for such a directionless voyage comes every time a teacher awards unqualified praise for the student who heads the chart for the most library books devoured, or with the teacher who rewards those who can scan and emerge with appropriate responses to a comprehension quiz.[40]

A few suggestions follow that emphasize the development of flexibility of reading rate in relation to three factors: (1) the nature of the learner, (2) the purpose for reading, and (3) the difficulty of the material for a given learner. Each learner's ability to make adjustments in rates of reading should be evaluated in advance of assignments. (Note the informal tests in Thomas and Robinson.[41]) The suggestions for instruction below may also be used as evaluation tools.

FLEXIBILITY STRATEGIES

1. Have students read two different editorials in the same newspaper. Tell them that you expect retention of all significant details in one, but merely the gist of the other. It is interesting sometimes to have half the group read one editorial for one purpose and the other half read the same editorial for the other purpose. Ask for free, written response. After collecting the papers, discuss the processes they used. Have them realize the differences in approach and rate.

2. Time students while they read a simple short story for its theme. Then time them while they read another simple short story to find a description of the main character. Check on results and then discuss approaches and rates.

3. Contrast the time spent on finding the facts in a math problem and in a short narrative poem.

4.   Teach scanning on at least two levels of complexity. First, help students scan to find a specific answer to a specific question. Discuss possible key words to search for. Point out that this may be done at rapid-fire speed without reading most of the words until the reader arrives at a possible key word—then he or she slows down to read the answer. If the answer is not provided, scanning begins again. Second, guide students in finding the answer(s) to a question when the answer is broader and key words do not equate exactly with the words in the question. Scanning is still rapid, but the reader is on the lookout for more possible wordings of the answer(s).

For example, at level one a question might be: "When did Ghana gain its independence?" In scanning, the reader will be on the lookout for *independence* and dates. At level two a question might be: "What types of species might be found living in the valley?" In scanning, the reader will need to realize that there may be many possible answers scattered throughout the material.

5.   Although learners have been skimming if they have used previewing techniques, they can learn to skim for other reasons. One very important reason is to decide whether or not a given piece of material contains what they need. Concentrated practice on this type of selective skimming is useful throughout life. Have students locate an article in a magazine and read through it rapidly as they would do with the preview technique. Then they should decide whether they want to read it or whether it contributes to information they seek. In an ensuing discussion they should indicate why they read or did not read the article.

6.   Have students graph their reading purposes and rates over a three-day period as they deal with their various assignments in all classes plus any reading they do on their own. Schedule the time to have students exchange graphs and discuss the need for flexibility.

USE OF INSTRUMENTS

In some English classrooms, or more often in adjacent "reading labs," instruments are utilized to help students increase their rates of reading. The two types described below are used most frequently.

Reading Pacers.[42]   While pacers produced by different manufacturers vary, with all pacers a cover, a bar, or a beam of light moves down the page, pressuring the student to increase his rate. A dial controls the speed of the descending occluder or light beam.

Pacer training is motivational for some students and profitable for a number, as long as vocabulary and comprehension are already adequate. If not, until such inhibiting factors are removed, forcing such training may be harmful. In one reading laboratory a young man was in tears about his performance on the pacer. He was being forced to "read" faster and faster when he did not understand what he was reading.

Controlled Reading Techniques. In addition to the functions of the pacer, controlled reading devices force specific left-to-right eye movements. Such techniques are used in connection with films or filmstrips. Probably the most popular of these techniques is the filmstrip approach used in the Controlled Reader (for four to fifteen students) or the Controlled Reader Jr. (for one to three students) produced by EDL-McGraw-Hill. Morris . . . cautioned that students should be grouped for such training on the basis of reading achievement levels and rates of reading with comprehension.[43]

RELATED ACTIVITIES

1. Vaughan, Estes, and Curtis suggested an activity for developing conceptual awareness as a way of stimulating the thinking process.[44] The activity is valuable as a way of having students synthesize into a meaningful conceptual unit much of the bits and pieces of information (and inferences) they make during the reading of a literary work. The authors presented the following two-steps for constructing a concept guide:

    a. Analyze the reading passage to determine the major concepts the students should acquire. List each in a word or, at most, a phrase. These words and phrases will comprise Part II of the guide.

    b. Reread the passage and select statements that underlie the major concepts chosen for emphasis. These statements, plus any distractors you might use, will comprise Part I of the guide.[45]

The authors used a sample guide based on *A Patch of Blue*. The teacher chose the major concepts for Part II: prejudice, love, intolerance, sincerity, fear. For Part I they listed ten true-false statements. Examples: "*Niggers is black*. You want to have a *black friend?*" or "Without *tolerance* there can be *no friendship*."

Responses should be argued in class with references back to the text.

2. McKenna found that even eighth graders could be turned on to *Hamlet* by taking the following steps:[46]

    a. He paraphrased large portions and interspersed segments of the actual play throughout the retelling. As he indicated:

> Since my intent was to recapture in part the effects of both drama and poetry, I chose passages which best exemplify these qualities and which could, with little injury, be set against a background of prose.[47]

    b. He paraphrased, commented on, or deleted "obsolete or unusually difficult expressions."[48]

c. He devoted a total of nine school days to *Hamlet*. The first two were used for readiness activities; the middle five were used to explore small portions of each of the five acts; the last two days "were given to class discussion of the questions posed by the drama."[49]

An example of one of the passages and its prose accompaniment follows:

News reaches Hamlet of the ghost's appearance.

Hamlet's thoughts were then interrupted by the approach of his good friend, Horatio, and two guardsmen. The three of them bore some very strange news. It seemed that for several nights a spirit had appeared at the edge of the palace, and the men on guard had become both alarmed and bewildered. They had asked Horatio to accompany them this night, and he too had seen the ghostly shape of an armed man and agreed with the guardsmen that it closely resembled Hamlet's father.

HORATIO.   As I do live, my honored lord, 'tis true,/ And we did think it writ down in our duty/ To let you know of it.
HAMLET.   Indeed, indeed, sirs, but this troubles me./ Hold you the watch tonight?
GUARDSMEN.   We do, my lord.
HAMLET.   Armed, you say?
GUARDSMEN.   Armed, my lord.
HAMLET.   From top to toe?
GUARDSMEN.   My lord, from head to foot.
HAMLET.   Then saw you not his face?
HORATIO.   Oh yes, my lord, he wore his beaver up.
HAMLET.   What, looked he frowningly?
HORATIO.   A countenance more in sorrow than in anger.
HAMLET.   Pale, or red.
HORATIO.   Nay, very pale.
HAMLET.   And fixed his eyes upon you?
HORATIO.   Most constantly.
HAMLET.   I would I had been there.
HORATIO.   It would have much amazed you.

The figure, you will recall, was armed, which in those days meant that it appeared wearing metal armor. Thus, Hamlet was right to suspect that the men had not actually seen its face. But their reply that its steel visor (the "beaver") was up was sufficient to explain. The group agreed that it would be best for Hamlet to accompany them to the castle's fringe on the following night.

Perhaps the spirit was looking for the prince. Perhaps it would even speak.[50]

McKenna reported a tremendous reaction from students. They were impatient to move on from chapter to chapter of the scenario; they stated opinions and suggested alternatives. "Even the most reticent suddenly found their voices and made their views known."[51]

3. Epstein taught and refined skimming and scanning, as well as critical reading strategies, through a unit on newspaper (or news magazine) reading published during the first week of each of his students' lives.[52] Students answered such questions as:

    a. Who were the leaders of government on your birthday? Are any of these people living today? What are they doing now?

    b. Look at the sports section. Have the sports played on your birthdate changed at all? Do players receive the same fees? Have various leagues changed? Do teams still play in the same cities? How did your favorite team do on your date of birth?

    c. Shop for a car. What features were being offered? What was the list price of the car you liked? Do any of the cars advertised no longer exist? Are there any cars advertised today which were not advertised on your date of birth? Have sales pitches changed at all?

    d. Study the employment section of the paper and locate a job or profession that you might consider. What salary was offered? What were working conditions like? How did salary and conditions compare with today's job offers? Do you see any listings in the current paper that didn't exist on your birthdate? Were there any jobs that were restricted to men only which are today open to members of both sexes?[53]

4. Encourage students to read and/or report on their reading in a variety of ways. Approaches should differ from individual to individual and from time to time. In addition to the approaches below, turn to pages 308 to 309 in Chapter 12 of this book.

    a. Develop a reading "pack" on a favorite topic (poetry, tennis, science fiction). Use the pack to entice other students.

    b. Draw and describe in depth a favorite or detested character from something that has been read—without reporting on the entire reading selection.

    c. Prepare a series of slides illustrating the important events in a selection.

d. When possible, write and present a television scenario based on something that has been read.
e. Read up to this point (predetermined by instructor) and then write the answers to these questions: "(1) What has happened to this point? (2) What effect has the action had on the people involved? (3) What do you think will happen next?"[54] Now finish reading the selection. How valid were your predictions?

SELECTED READINGS

Burton, Dwight L. *Literature Study in the High Schools*, 3rd ed. New York: Holt, Rinehart and Winston, 1970.

Cheyney, Arnold B. *Teaching Reading Skills Through the Newspaper*, Reading Aids Series, edited by Charles T. Mangrum. Newark, Del.: International Reading Association, 1971.

Dale, Edgar. "How to Read a Newspaper." *The News Letter* (College of Education, Ohio State University) 33 (March 1968).

Elkins, Deborah. *Teaching Literature: Designs for Cognitive Development*. Columbus, Ohio: Charles E. Merrill, 1976.

Finder, Morris. "Teaching to Comprehend Literary Texts—Drama and Fiction." *Journal of Reading* 17 (January 1974):272–78.

Graves, Michael F.; Rebecca J. Palmer; and David W. Furniss. *Structuring Activities for English Classes*. Urbana, Ill.: National Council of Teachers of English, 1976.

Hillocks, George, Jr. "Toward a Hierarchy of Skills in the Comprehension of Literature." *English Journal* 69 (March 1980):54–59.

Johnson, Laura S. "The Newspaper: A New Textbook Every Day." *Journal of Reading* 13 (November 1969):107–12, 164; and pt. 2, 13 (December 1969):203–5, 240–45.

Kaplan, Ruth. "The Writing-Reading Approach in English." In *Fusing Reading Skills and Content*, edited by H. Alan Robinson and Ellen Lamar Thomas, pp. 108–13, 205–14. Newark, Del.: International Reading Association, 1969.

Painter, Helen W., ed. *Reaching Children and Young People Through Literature*. Newark, Del.: International Reading Association, 1971.

Purves, Alan C., and Richard Beach. *Literature and the Reader*. Urbana, Ill.: National Council of Teachers of English, 1972.

Reading, Grades 7–8–9: A Teacher's Guide to Curriculum Planning, Curriculum Bulletin No. 11 (1957–58 series). New York: Board of Education of the City of New York, 1959.

Sailer, Carl. "Building Reading Skills via Reading the Newspapers." In *Reading and Realism*, edited by J. Allen Figurel. Newark, Del.: International Reading Association, 1969.

Sargent, Eileen E. *The Newspaper as a Teaching Tool*. Norwalk, Conn.: The Reading Laboratory, 1975.

Simmons, John S.; Robert E. Shafer; and Gail B. West. *Decisions about the Teaching of English*. Boston: Allyn and Bacon, 1976.

Smith, Ruth B., and Barbara Michalak. *How to Read Your Newspaper*, 2nd ed., and *Teacher's Manual*. New York: Harcourt Brace Jovanovich, 1978.

Taubenheim, Barbara W. "Erikson's Psychological Theory Applied to Adolescent Fiction: A Means for Adolescent Self-Clarification," *Journal of Reading* 22 (March 1979):517–22.

Teaching with Newspapers. (Newsletter published by the American Newspaper Publishers Association Foundation.) The Newspaper Center, Box 17407, Dulles International Airport, Washington, D.C. 20041.

NOTES

1. John S. Simmons, Robert E. Shafer, and Gail B. West, *Decisions about the Teaching of English* (Boston, Mass.: Allyn and Bacon, 1976), p. 43.
2. Ibid., p. 45.
3. Edmund J. Farrell, "Forces at Work: English Teaching in Context, Present to Perhaps," in *The Teaching of English*, the Seventy-Sixth Yearbook of the National Society for the Study of Education, ed. James R. Squire (Chicago: University of Chicago Press, 1977), p. 338.
4. Deborah Elkins, *Teaching Literature: Designs for Cognitive Development* (Columbus, Ohio: Charles E. Merrill, 1976), p. 12. Reprinted by permission of the author.
5. Ibid., p. 15.
6. Ibid., p. 13.
7. Farrell, "Forces at Work," p. 338.
8. Ibid., pp. 338–40.
9. Simmons, Shafer, and West, *Decisions*, pp. 76–77.
10. Dan Donlan, "Multiple Text Programs in Literature," *Journal of Reading* 19 (January 1976):314. Reprinted with permission of the author and the International Reading Association.
11. Lewis G. Sterner, *Favorite Short Stories* (New York: Globe, 1967), p. 17.
12. *Reading, Grades 7–8–9: A Teacher's Guide to Curriculum Planning*, Curriculum Bulletin, no. 11, (1957–58 series) (New York: Board of Education of the City of New York, 1959), p. 163.
13. Ibid., pp. 165–66.
14. Nathaniel Shapiro, "Critical Reading of a Short Story: An Introspective–Retrospective Study" (Doctoral dissertation, Hofstra University, 1974).
15. Washington Irving, "The Legend of Sleepy Hollow," in *Classic American Short Stories*, ed. Theodore W. Hipple (Boston: Allyn and Bacon, 1977), p. 1.
16. Elkins, *Teaching Literature*, pp. 67–68.
17. Simmons, Shafer, and West, *Decisions*, pp. 78–81.
18. *Reading, Grades 7–8–9*, p. 169.
19. Simmons, Shafer, and West, *Decisions*, pp. 81–82.
20. *Reading, Grades 7–8–9*, pp. 176–78.
21. Simmons, Shafer, and West, *Decisions*, pp. 83–86.

22. S. Alan Chesler, "Integrating the Teaching of Reading and Literature," *Journal of Reading* 19 (February 1976):361.
23. Ibid.
24. Ibid., pp. 361–62.
25. Ibid., p. 302.
26. Elkins, *Teaching Literature*, p. 245.
27. Kenneth L. Donelson, "Changing Content in the English Curriculum: B. Literature," in *The Teaching of English*, the Seventy-Sixth Yearbook of the National Society for the Study of Education, ed. James R. Squire (Chicago: University of Chicago Press, 1977), p. 162.
28. Kenneth L. Donelson and Alleen P. Nilsen, *Literature for Today's Young Adults* (Glenview, Ill.: Scott, Foresman, 1980), p. 376.
29. Harrison J. Means, "Nine Years of Individualized Reading," *Jounral of Reading* 20 (November 1976):144–49.
30. Simmons, Shafer, and West, *Decisions*, pp. 289–90.
31. Jerome Martin and Dorothy C. Olson, *Patterns of Language* (New York: American Book, 1974), p. 34.
32. Rodney J. Barth, "Using the Media to Improve Reading," *Journal of Reading* 19 (February 1976):427.
33. Laura S. Johnson, "The Newspaper as an Instructional Medium," in *Teachers, Tangibles, Techniques: Comprehension of Content in Reading*, ed. Bonnie S. Schulwitz (Newark, Del.: International Reading Association, 1975), pp. 76–82.
34. Arnold B. Cheyney, *Teaching Reading Skills Through the Newspaper*, Reading Aids Series, ed. Charles T. Mangrum (Newark, Del.: International Reading Association, 1971), p. 4.
35. Connie Lauerman, "5 per cent Pay Hike Reported: Tentative Teacher Pact OKd," *Chicago Tribune*, January 18, 1974, sec. 1, p. 3.
36. Lillian Williams, "Teachers' Tentative Pact: 6.5% Raise," *Chicago Sun-Times*, January 18, 1974, p. 3.
37. R. Baird Shuman, *Strategies in Teaching Reading: Secondary* (Washington, D.C.: National Education Association, 1978), pp. 90–91.
38. Arthur N. Applebee and others, *A Study of Writing in the Secondary School*, Final Report NIE–G–79–0174 (Urbana, Ill.: National Council of Teachers of English, September 1980), p. 142.
39. Ellen L. Thomas and H. Alan Robinson, *Improving Reading in Every Class*, 3rd ed. (Boston: Allyn and Bacon, 1982), chap. 5.
40. Leonard R. Mendelsohn, "Jetting to Utopia: The Speed Reading Phenomenon," *Language Arts* 54 (February 1977):120.
41. Thomas and Robinson, *Improving Reading*, pp. 203–6; abridged version, pp. 171–74.
42. Thomas and Robinson, *Improving Reading*, p. 220.
43. Helen F. Morris, *EDL Controlled Reading Skill Development*, Teacher's Guide (Huntington, N.Y.: Educational Developmental Laboratories, 1976).
44. Joseph L. Vaughan, Thomas H. Estes, and Sherry L. Curtis, "Developing Conceptual Awareness," *Language Arts* 53 (November/December 1975):1141–44, 1153.
45. Ibid., p. 1143.
46. Michael McKenna, "Shakespeare in Grade 8," *Journal of Reading* 19 (December 1975):205–7.
47. Ibid., p. 206.
48. Ibid.
49. Ibid.

50. Ibid., pp. 206–7.
51. Ibid., p. 207.
52. Ira D. Epstein, "What Happened on the Day You Were Born?" *Journal of Reading* 20 (February 1977):400–2.
53. Ibid., pp. 401–2.
54. Simmons, Shafer, and West, *Decisions*, p. 64.

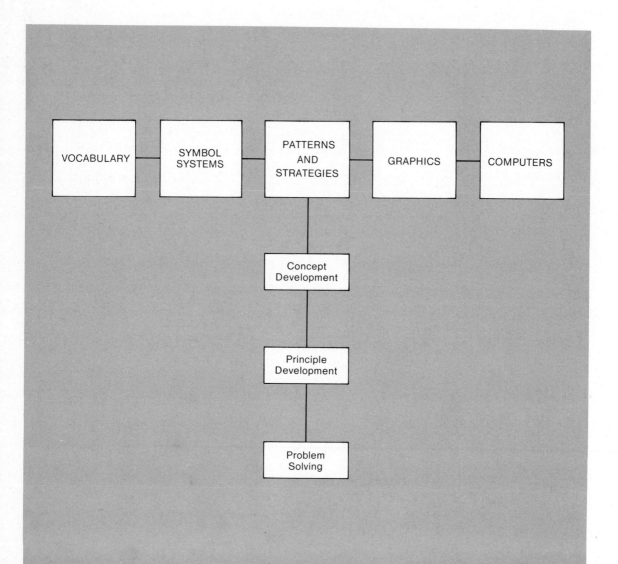

10
Mathematics

The field of mathematics, educationally speaking, appears to be in somewhat of a state of confusion. As Roark said, "It just seems like the whole field has fallen apart, and no one knows how to put it together again."[1] We "have entered a period of renewed questioning of the school mathematics curriculum,"[2] with some concern for *what* to teach but with major concern for *how* to teach.

Elementary algebra and general mathematics are the most popular courses, followed not so closely by geometry and advanced algebra. All the other math courses in the secondary school are much more sparsely attended.[3] Saunders suggested that mathematics courses be directed toward the real-life needs of students.[4] McGarvey proposed:

> We might restructure our curriculum thematically, each course developed about a particular mode of mathematical reasoning. We might offer a course, for example, that taught both algebraic and geometric topics and emphasized the concept of generalization in mathematics. Or we might offer a course in inductive reasoning or a course in deduction. The central theme of our secondary curriculum might be mathematics' constant movement from the empirical to the abstract.[5]

Whatever movement the mathematics curricula take, it seems inevitable that teachers will rely strongly on a basic mathematics textbook for the introduction and/or reinforcement of the introduction of concepts and principles, as well as for a source of multiple examples and problems to be solved. The reading and study of mathematics, comparable to some aspects of the reading and study of chemistry and physics, are focused essentially on the development of specific concepts and principles. A good part of a mathematics textbook is devoted to explaining and defining particular terms that stand for certain ideas or concepts. These terms must be explicitly understood if the reader is to comprehend the principle (generalization) growing from the development of concepts. Therefore, offering students the bulk of a teacher's guidance in the reading and solving of mathematical problems should be avoided. Students must be helped to understand the concepts and principles from which the problems emerge. In this light it would seem that strategies for reading and studying math must concentrate on patterns of presenting concepts and principles as well as on solving mathematical problems.

A student who learns how to solve a given problem but has not learned how to independently solve others that involve similar concepts and principles is in trouble. In order to achieve some independence in the successful reading of mathematics, a student should receive guidance in coping with the exceptionally heavy and specialized vocabulary load, the integration of symbol systems, the variety of graphics, and the major patterns of writing utilized by textbook writers.

VOCABULARY

Although general vocabulary strategies were discussed in Chapter 5, additional discussion of the vocabulary of mathematics is essential. Much time and space are allotted to the explication and definition of concepts in instructional materials; students must be prepared to understand—to understand well enough to put the concepts to immediate use. These concepts are communicated through language units. As Henderson said:

> It is difficult to distinguish between teaching a concept and teaching the meaning of a term or expression which designates the concept. A teacher does about the same thing when he teaches a concept of an ellipse, for example, as when he teaches what the term *ellipse* means. Hence it is not profitable pedagogically to distinguish between these two activities. . . .[6]

There is, of course, no point at all in attempting to make any distinction between concept and language unit when a student is studying an assignment; the language unit stands for the concept without the mediation of the teacher.

Since concepts must be put to rather immediate use in formulating principles and then in solving problems, precision is essential. That is, synonyms or descriptions that approximate meaning are not functional; meanings must be exact so that they can eventually be used in mathematical computations. Some writers have concluded that context clues are therefore useless in math. But such is not the case. In mathematics more than in any other subject area, the meanings of language units are carefully and precisely dealt with *in context*. Learners must become aware of the most frequent techniques used for helping them derive precise meaning.

As discussed and illustrated on pages 122 to 123, the context clue, a statement of meaning, is a forthright statement used to elucidate the meaning of a language unit the writers feel might be misconstrued or might be unknown to the reader. In mathematics, writers start with the assumption that the reader has not met the language unit before and it is their task and obligation to make the concept absolutely clear—and functional.

By far the most frequent context clues used in mathematics texts are statements of meaning through formal definition. Usually the definition is preceded or followed by examples and/or description. Many times graphics are used to support verbal description and examples. Frequently the language unit being defined is printed in italics or, on occasion, boldface type. At times, in a particular book, there will be a consistent method of setting each definition apart from the rest of the text—in a box, italics, boldface, color, or a list at the end of the chapter. Most often clusters of interrelated concepts are defined at one time.

In Example 10.1, for instance, the author defines the word *degree* and

---

Example 10.1[7]

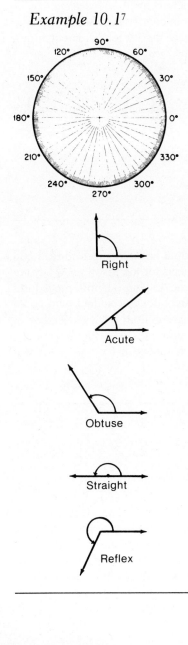

Right

Acute

Obtuse

Straight

Reflex

KINDS OF ANGLES

The *degree*, indicated by the symbol "°", is the unit of measure of angles and arcs. A degree is 1/360 part of the entire angular measure about a point in a plane. If a circle is divided into 360 equal parts and lines are drawn from the center to these points of division, 360 equal central angles are formed, each measuring 1 degree. Each of the corresponding 360 equal arcs also measures 1 degree. The degree (°) is divided into 60 equal parts called *minutes* (symbol '). The minute (') is divided into 60 equal parts called *seconds* (symbol "). When a ray turns from one position to another about its fixed endpoint, one complete rotation is equal to 360°.

A *right angle* is one-fourth of a complete rotation; it is an angle whose measure is 90°.

An *acute angle* is an angle whose measure is greater than 0° but less than 90°.

An *obtuse angle* is an angle whose measure is greater than 90° but less than 180°.

A *straight angle* is one-half of a complete rotation; it is an angle whose measure is 180°. The two rays that form a straight angle extend in opposite directions along a straight line that passes through the vertex.

A *reflex angle* is an angle whose measure is greater than 180° but less than 360°.

the related words *minutes* and *seconds*. He defines by verbal explanation accompanied by a clear graphic. The graphic becomes particularly important as a reference point since the author continues to explain the five types of angles—the goal to begin with. Note that each defined angle is paired up with a clear graphic to further clarify meaning.

Figure 10.1 is illustrative of a clear definition of one concept broken down into its specific forms. The author of the text has clarified meanings by examples, clear statements, and comprehension questions to cement knowledge.

Less frequently the appositive form is used in combination with some type of definition or example. In Example 10.2, note the use of statement in apposition in collaboration with a definition of the symbol.

Example 10.2[8]   The symbol $\sqrt{}$, called a *radical sign*, is used to designate the *non-negative square root* of a number. Thus,

$$\sqrt{4} \;=\; 2,$$
$$\sqrt{\%_{16}} \;=\; \tfrac{3}{4}$$
$$\sqrt{0} \;=\; 0.$$

Since precision is important, students should be encouraged to read and reread slowly when meeting definitions of concepts for the first time. They are usually not repeated. It might be wise to help some students establish procedures for studying and storing key concepts.[9] Obviously, for the student who could not remember or immediately review the precise definitions given earlier of *congruent, plane, rigid motion, similar,* and *dilation,* understanding of the theorems that follow the introductory paragraph shown in Example 10.3 will be nil.

Example 10.3[10]   In this section, we shall show that if two triangles are congruent, in the same plane, then one can be moved onto the other by rigid motion. Then we shall show that if two triangles are similar, then one can be moved onto the other by a rigid motion, followed by a dilation.

Having students paraphrase definitions in writing is a useful technique. Some students find paraphrasing of such condensed information difficult, but once they are able to use their own words as well as the words of the author in an adequate "re-explanation" of the meaning, they really do understand.

Another helpful means of understanding and retaining definitions is to answer questions about them in writing—as in Figure 10.1. Writing a definition or answering questions in writing about a definition has more value for helping to internalize the meaning than does group oral response.

Figure 10.1 Studying a Math Concept[11]

ENDORSING A CHECK

Before a check can be cashed, it must be endorsed on the back. An *endorsement* is the signature of the person to whom the check is written. It guarantees that the person endorsing the check will pay the amount of the check if the bank on which it is written refuses payment. There are three types of endorsements:

With endorsement A anyone with check in hand can cash it—even someone who finds a check lost by the endorser.

With endorsement B only Juana Rivera can cash the check. When Juana cashes the check, she must also endorse it under Brad's name.

With endorsement C the check cannot be cashed at all but can only be deposited in Brad's bank account.

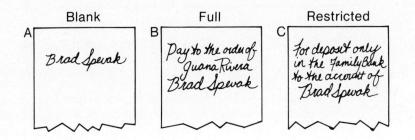

Blank   Full   Restricted

Exercises

1. To whom is the check written that is endorsed by Brad Spevak?
2. Does an endorsement indicate who wrote the check?
3. Suppose the above check "To the order of" Brad Spevak was written by Michael Steele against his account in the Home Bank. He has a balance of only $19.48.

Since the check is for $23.40, the Home Bank refuses payment. With Endorsement A who must now pay $23.40 to the person who cashed the check? With endorsement B who must pay?

4. With Endorsement B if Juana Rivera does not pay the $23.40, must Brad pay the amount?

Source: Francis G. Lankford, Jr., *Consumer Mathematics* (Boston: Allyn and Bacon, 1981), p. 186.

SYMBOL SYSTEMS

Reading appears to be easier when one symbol system at a time is used, at least for the majority of readers. In mathematics, of course, it is impossible to use one symbol system at a time. In basic mathematics, words, numerals, and signs are intertwined; from algebra on, the reader must contend with words, numerals, signs, and letters. In addition, the interrelationships among the symbol systems must be understood and eventually utilized to solve problems.

When an instructor is trying to help students understand concepts, principles, and problems that undoubtedly contain elements of more than one symbol system, some time should be spent on directing their attention to the various symbols. Effort placed on careful observation and thought about the different symbols, prior to concentrating on what the total statement says and means, can be profitable for a number of students. In the problem in Example 10.4, which utilizes three symbol systems, attention should be directed toward $2,828.51, *bale weighed 775 pounds*, $28.625 *per hundred pounds*. Some students tend to overlook dollars and cents signs, while others frequently forget about a number because it is written out (hundred) rather than expressed in arabic numerals. In this particular problem, a few students may need to have their attention called to the 5 in *$28.625*.

Example 10.4[12]   How many bales of cotton were bought for $2,828.51, if each bale weighed 775 pounds and cotton sold for $28.625 per hundred pounds?

In Example 10.5, a student must be able to read the words of a definition and understand how they interrelate with the mathematical symbols, letters, and numbers. The student must then be able to put it all together in solving specific problems related to the definition.

Another way of helping students focus on the meaningful interrelationships among symbol systems is through oral reading. Although oral reading is often overused and misused (see page 308), it is a useful tool when attention needs to be concentrated on an area, particularly if the given area causes difficulty for the student. Seemingly, the very act of verbalizing gives some help in the process of clarification. This type of oral reading—to help students focus with accuracy on the interrelationships among the symbol systems—should be very much like the oral reading that is recommended for proofreading—unit by unit—*but with active thinking taking place.*

For instance, in Example 10.4, a reader might read silently, "How many bales of cotton were bought for . . ."—and then read $2,828.51 out loud, being sure to note the *comma* indicating thousands, the *dollar sign* denoting dollars, and the *decimal* denoting cents. The reader would then read aloud the fact that a "bale weighed 775 pounds . . . cotton sold for $28.625 per hundred

Example 10.5[13]

VOLUME OF A SPHERE

The volume of a sphere is equal to $\frac{4}{3}$ times pi (π) times the cube of the radius.

Expressed as a formula it is $V = \frac{4}{3}\pi r^3$. Sometimes the formula $V = \frac{\pi d^3}{6}$ is used when the diameter is known.

Exercises

1. Find the volumes of spheres having the following radii:
   a. 5 in.   b. 21 cm   c. 8¾ in.   d. 2 ft. 6 in.

2. Find the volumes of spheres having the following diameters:
   a. 18 in.   b. 49 mm   c. 2⅝ in.   d. 6 ft. 5 in.

pounds." Oral emphasis would then be on the weight of a bale, the accurate reading of $28.625, and per hundred pounds. Oral emphasis on "per hundred pounds" will often suffice to help the careless reader realize that *hundred* is in reality a number that must be considered.

For some students it may be necessary to isolate specific troublesome signs and symbols for directed practice until they feel they can recognize them anywhere. Looking at individual parts of formulas, for example, and discussing them with emphasis on meaning often clarifies the whole idea of formulas (or certain formulas) for a number of learners. For instance, a thoughtful talking through of the opening sentence in Example 10.5 should serve to isolate difficulties and clarify the relationships. At that point, the formula should seem reasonable and clear. Some discussion of the third sentence in that example is necessary if the student is to complete successfully both exercises 1 *and* 2.

GRAPHICS   Graphics, particularly in the form of figures, are used with great frequency in mathematics. They are often used to illustrate visually that which is being explained verbally; the reader must learn to move back and forth from print to figure. Figures are found as introducers, reinforcers, and integral segments of concepts, principles, and problems. Under no condition can the learner afford to skip or skim over a figure; the figure must be "read" and "reread" with care.

In Figure 10.2 the learner must use both the figure and the statement in order to solve the problem. Although the term *figure* is utilized rather generally in many texts to refer to most graphics, some texts distinguish among figures (geometric figures), diagrams (usually line drawings), graphs, tables, and charts. Figures and diagrams are most frequently integral parts of explanations and

*Figure 10.2   Using a Graphic to Solve a Math
                Problem*[14]

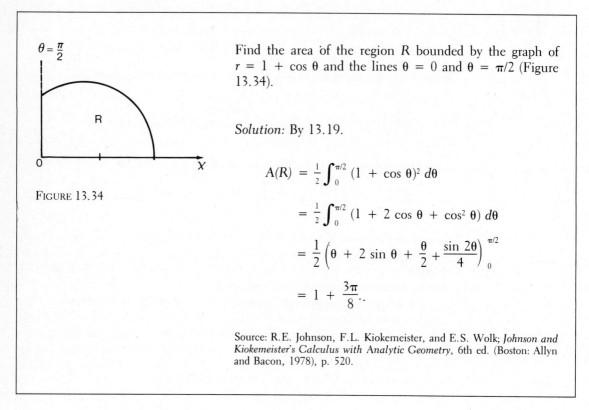

$\theta = \frac{\pi}{2}$

R

0   X

FIGURE 13.34

Find the area of the region R bounded by the graph of $r = 1 + \cos \theta$ and the lines $\theta = 0$ and $\theta = \pi/2$ (Figure 13.34).

Solution: By 13.19.

$$A(R) = \frac{1}{2} \int_0^{\pi/2} (1 + \cos \theta)^2 \, d\theta$$

$$= \frac{1}{2} \int_0^{\pi/2} (1 + 2 \cos \theta + \cos^2 \theta) \, d\theta$$

$$= \frac{1}{2} \left(\theta + 2 \sin \theta + \frac{\theta}{2} + \frac{\sin 2\theta}{4} \right) \Big|_0^{\pi/2}$$

$$= 1 + \frac{3\pi}{8}..$$

Source: R.E. Johnson, F.L. Kiokemeister, and E.S. Wolk; *Johnson and Kiokemeister's Calculus with Analytic Geometry*, 6th ed. (Boston: Allyn and Bacon, 1978), p. 520.

problems; graphs, tables, and charts are often used as supporting evidence.

At other times, particularly in junior high school materials, exercises are organized around graphs, tables, and charts to teach students how to use them and to illustrate the role they play in mathematics. A reasonable amount of study time should be spent on graphs, tables, or charts whose formats and functions are unknown to students so that they may become independent users of such graphics. The example in Figure 10.3 is a page from a junior high school mathematics textbook that helps learners reinforce and utilize their knowledge of reading graphs. In questions 14 through 16, the writers extend and further reinforce this knowledge by having students prepare independently a frequency distribution table, a histogram of the frequency distribution, and then a frequency polygon. Guided activities of this type make for effective and efficient use of the graphics of mathematics.

*Figure 10.3   Using a Graphic with Guided
Activities*[15]

Refer to the following graph to answer Exercises 8 through 13.

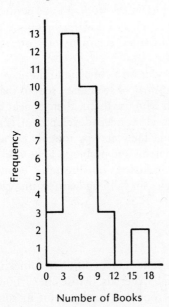

Number of Books

*Number of Books Read by Each Member of
Class 8–309 During the Summer*

8. Why is a histogram used to picture this data?
9. Give the frequency of each interval.
10. Which interval has the greatest frequency? the least?
11. How many pupils read 10–12 books? 13–15 books?
12. If a pupil read 8 books, in which interval would his score be recorded?
13. Can you tell exactly how many pupils did not read any books at all? Explain.

Mrs. Green recorded the number of days that each member of her home room class was absent during the month of January as follows:
0, 1, 2, 3, 4, 0, 2, 2, 0, 0, 4, 1, 1, 3, 3, 0, 0, 2, 0, 3, 3, 5, 2, 0, 2, 0, 2, 2, 0, 4

14. Make a frequency distribution table of the above data, showing absence for 0 day; 1 day; 2 days; 3 days; 4 days; 5 days.
15. Draw a histogram of the frequency distribution.
16. Draw a frequency polygon of the above data.

Source: Helen K. Halliday and others, *Contemporary Mathematics* bk. 8 (New York: William H. Sadlier, 1970); p. 386.

PATTERNS AND STRATEGIES

There are probably a number of ways that one could view the patterns of writing in mathematics. By its very nature the written material must be presented in small units—a very different writing style than is usual in other major subject matter areas. Often the small units interrelate—particularly in developing concepts and principles—but frequently they are entities, as in the writing of problems. It does not seem very profitable for the student to be confronted with a multitude of small patterns to look for, such as following directions, sequence, comparison, and so on, as they are but small segments of more meaningful writing patterns.

In my judgment—assisted by Henderson's conceptual framework[16]—and after surveying and studying a large number of secondary school mathematics textbooks and working with the students who use them, there appear to be three major patterns of writing in mathematics: (1) concept development, (2) principle development, and (3) problem solution. They occupy roughly equal space in most math textbooks, with example problems and problems to be worked having a slight edge. The three patterns are discussed and illustrated below with attention concentrated on specific strategies for helping learners unlock the ideas within each pattern of writing.

CONCEPT DEVELOPMENT

Examples.   The concept development pattern takes different forms in different situations and in different instructional materials. Most often, however, the concepts being developed are set off from the regular print in some way—boldface, italics, color, or boxed. And, of course, the purpose within the concept development pattern is to clarify and make functional one or more concepts that can then be used in viewing principles and/or solving problems.

The following examples are representative of two ways in which the concept development pattern occurs. Each can be approached through a similar set of strategies; the outcome must be functional comprehension of the concept.

Example 10.6 is obviously at a simpler level than Example 10.7. Three interrelated concepts are developed through explanation, activity, and questions. In Example 10.7, one overall concept is introduced (the magnetic compass), but attention is concentrated on the three operational aspects of the concept (true course, magnetic course, and compass course).

Strategies.   Undoubtedly a number of teachers and students have worked out successful strategies for approaching the study of concepts in mathematics. On the other hand, there are many students who rarely meet success on their own until they have been taught a specific group of strategies. For these students in particular the following procedure has proven useful: (1) study the heading; (2) read the definition(s); (3) reread the definition(s); (4) read the explanatory information and graphic(s); (5) reread when necessary; and (6) reread the definition(s).

Example 10.6[17]

THE DIAMETER

1. In circle *K* the endpoints of $\overline{CB}$ are on the circle and $\overline{CB}$ passes through *K*, the center of the circle. Line segment *CB* is called a *diameter* of circle *K*.

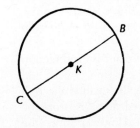

> A line segment that has both endpoints on the circle and passes through the center of the circle is a diameter of the circle.

2. Use a compass to draw a picture of a circle with center A. Draw several diameters. Measure the length of each diameter with a ruler. How do the diameters compare in length?

> All diameters of the same circle are equal in measure.

3. What point do all the diameters of a circle have in common? How many diameters do you think a circle has? Why?

> For any circle the set of diameters is an infinite set.

Step One: Study the Heading.   Most concept development sections of instructional materials have headings. A student should be taught to stop and think about the heading: "What do I think it is saying? What do I know about the topic? Can I make an educated guess about what it means?" Some time spent in thought, even if the topic is quite unknown or complex, will set a purpose for the ensuing reading.

Step Two: Read the Definition(s).   Students should locate and read silently the definition(s), *boxed* in Example 10.6 and *discussed* in the second and third paragraphs of Example 10.7.

Example 10.7[18]

THE MAGNETIC COMPASS

When navigating an airplane by chart and compass, called *dead reckoning*, the navigator frequently determines the compass course from the true course and the true course from the compass course.

The *course* of an airplane is the direction in which it flies over the earth's surface and is expressed as an angle. It is called the *true course* when it is measured clockwise from the true north (North Pole). However, since the compass needle points to the magnetic north, the pilot must correct his true course reading. This correction is called *magnetic variation* or *variation* and the corrected course reading is called the *magnetic course*. This variation is designated as west variation when the magnetic north is west of the true north and as east variation when the magnetic north is east of the true north. The variation for any locality may be found on aeronautical maps.

Since the metal parts of the airplane affect the compass, the magnetic course reading must be corrected. This corrected course reading is called the *compass course*. The correction caused by the magnetism of the plane is called *deviation* and is designated east or west.

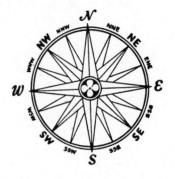

The following angular equivalents in degrees may be used for the given directions:

North (N.) = 0°
Northeast (N.E.) = 45°
East (E.) = 90°
Southeast (S.E.) = 135°
South (S.) = 180°
Southwest (S.W.) = 225°
West (W.) = 270°
Northwest (N.W.) = 315°

Step Three: Reread the Definition(s).   The student needs to be helped to develop the habit of rereading the definition(s). Rereading will serve to cement understanding for those who appeared to comprehend on the first reading, and it should help those who did not understand completely the first time. Students should be encouraged to reread out loud parts that do not seem quite clear; oral rereading of difficult ideas often assists understanding. The rereading also helps to fix the definition(s) in mind, which lends purpose to the next step.

Step Four: Read the Explanatory Information and Graphic(s).   Students should read slowly and carefully—to digest each step as it is offered—bearing in mind how the steps are leading to the definition(s). In coping with Example

Example 10.7 (continued)

To *find the magnetic course from the true course*, add west variation but subtract east variation.

To *find the compass course from the magnetic course*, add west deviation but subtract east deviation.

To *find the compass course from the true course*, first change true course to magnetic course, then to compass course. (See page 389.)

To *find the magnetic course from the compass course*, subtract west deviation but add east deviation.

Find the compass course if the true course is 125°; variation, 7° W.; and deviation, 2° W. (See page 390.)

$$
\begin{array}{r}
125° \text{ true course} \\
+ \quad 7° \text{ west variation} \\
\hline
132° \text{ magnetic course} \\
+ \quad 2° \text{ west deviation} \\
\hline
134° \text{ compass course}
\end{array}
$$

Find the true course if the compass course is 54°; variation 11° W.; and deviation, 50° E.

$$
\begin{array}{r}
54° \text{ compass course} \\
+ \quad 5° \text{ east deviation} \\
\hline
59° \text{ magnetic course} \\
- \quad 11° \text{ west variation} \\
\hline
48° \text{ true course}
\end{array}
$$

Answer: True course is 48°.

To *find the true course from the magnetic course*, subtract west variation but add east variation.

To *find the true course from the compass course*, first change compass course to magnetic course, then to true course.

10.6, readers should turn to the circle and note the label K immediately after reading the phrase "*In circle K . . .*" before proceeding. Then they should go on reading, "*the endpoints of* $\overline{CB}$ *are on the circle . . . ,*" turning back to note the endpoints on the circle itself. Readers should continue to read, "*and* $\overline{CB}$ *passes through K, the center of the circle.*" Then they ought to view what they have read by attending to the drawing of the circle. (Students should proceed in similar fashion through the explanations of the three definitions, stopping to execute the activities called for and answering the questions asked either to themselves, in writing, or in oral discussion.)

In Example 10.7, particularly because of the density of detail, the reading needs to be slow and accurate. Readers should be sure of the differences among the definitions before attempting to read and figure out the methods of computation. The boxed illustrations of sample problems are useful for clarification. Students should be directed to go through the steps of each sample problem as an aid to understanding and later completion of subsequent problems they must solve.

Step Five: Reread When Necessary.   It is not always necessary to reread the explanatory material. For instance, few students would need to reread the material in Example 10.6 to understand the definition fully. But a number might want to reread all or portions of Example 10.7 to be certain of their understanding, particularly since this material is succinct and the learner is expected to emerge with the ability to work problems related to the three ideas. Oral reading of parts and checking back to earlier reference sources (including the instructor) may be necessary.

Step Six: Reread the Definition(s).   The definition(s) should be reread for the purpose of certifying accuracy and completeness of comprehension. The learner should now be quite sure that the concept(s) can be put to use in understanding principles and/or solving related problems.

Step Seven: Write the Definition(s).   For some students writing the definition(s) in their own words—to some extent—helps with the internalization of the meanings. This step is optional. For instance, it is probably much more useful for Example 10.7, with its greater verbosity, than for the succinct definitions in Example 10.6.

PRINCIPLE DEVELOPMENT

Examples.   A principle in mathematics is a generalization growing out of a series of concepts. A principle may be labeled in different ways—postulate, theorem, proposition, law, rule, axiom—with various shades of meaning, but all are rather formal statements of mathematical truth or assumed truth. Very frequently a principle is stated both in words and in an equation or formula. Capital letters, color and/or boldface, and italic type are usually used to express the principle itself or to label its existence.

Principles must be understood if problems are to be solved. Usually principle development patterns of writing utilize problems with stated solutions as illustrations of the statement of the principle. Most often such illustrations follow immediately after the statement of the principle, but occasionally an illustration is cited prior to the formal statement of the principle. In all cases, after the statement of the principle or a group of principles plus illustrations, problems based on the principle(s) are posed for the student to solve.

Example 10.8, dealing with the law of cosines, is from a basic algebra text. Read through it and the example that follows before turning to the study strategies.

LAW OF COSINES

Example 10.8[19]

We have seen that we can solve an oblique triangle if two of the given parts are a side and its opposite angle by using the Law of Sines. But the third and fourth cases listed in Section 11–2 do not contain these opposite parts. To develop a usable formula for these two cases, consider the following: Place any oblique triangle so that one vertex is at the origin and one side lies along the positive x-axis (Fig. 1). This is purely a matter of convenience and results in no loss of generality. For our purposes

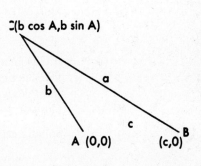

A may be either acute or obtuse. Use the distance formula to find a. To eliminate the radical, we must find the value of a^2. Then,

$$a^2 = (b \cos A - c)^2 + (b \sin A - 0)^2$$

$$= b^2\cos^2 A - 2bc \cos A + c^2 + b^2 \sin^2 A$$

This may be written $a^2 = b^2(\cos^2 A + \sin^2 A) + c^2 - 2bc \cos A$

Recall that $\sin^2 A + \cos 2A = 1$

Then $\qquad\qquad a^2 = b^2 + c^2 - 2bc \cos A.$

This formula expresses one side of a triangle in terms of the other two sides and their included angle. We can express each side of the triangle according to this pattern:

$$a^2 = b^2 + c^2 - 2bc \cos A$$

$$b^2 = a^2 + c^2 - 2ac \cos B$$

$$c^2 = a^2 + b^2 - 2ab \cos C$$

Putting this in words we state the **Law of Cosines.**

Example 10.8 (continued)

Example 10.8 (continued)

Theorem

The square of any side of a triangle is equal to the sum of the squares of the other two sides diminished by twice their product times the cosine of the included angle.

Since we started with any oblique triangle this theorem includes all possible oblique triangles. Just as a matter of interest, what would happen to

$$c^2 = a^2 + b^2 - 2ab \cos C$$

if C were a right angle? What is cos 90°? How much is $2ab \cdot 0$? Then we have the statement with which you are very familiar: $c^2 = a^2 + b^2$. *In other words, the Pythagorean Theorem may be considered as a special case of the Law of Cosines.*

Solving each of the above expressions for the cosine of the angle, we have

$$\cos A = \frac{b^2 + c^2 - a^2}{2bc}$$

$$\cos B = \frac{a^2 + c^2 - b^2}{2ac}$$

$$\cos C = \frac{a^2 + b^2 - c^2}{2ab}$$

Here we have the angles of a triangle expressed as functions of the three sides. Thus, the Law of Cosines enables us to do two things:

1. Find the third side of a triangle given two sides and the included angle. Having done this, we can find the other two angles by the Law of Sines, thus completing the solution of the triangle.
2. Find the angles of a triangle given the three sides.

Example 1

In $\triangle ABC$, given $a = 10$, $b = 15$, $c = 60°$. Find c.
Solution:
Since the given parts are two sides and the included angle, use the Law of Cosines.

$$c^2 = a^2 + b^2 - 2ab \cos C$$
$$c^2 = 100 + 225 - 2 \cdot 10 \cdot 15 \cdot \tfrac{1}{2}$$
$$c^2 = 175$$
$$c = 13 \text{ (to the nearest integer)}$$

Example 2

In $\triangle ABC$, given $b = 12$, $c = 20$, $A = 120°$. Find a.

Solution:

Again, two sides and the included angle. Hence, Law of Cosines.

$$a^2 = b^2 + c^2 - 2bc \cos A$$
$$a^2 = 144 + 400 - 2 \cdot 12 \cdot 20(-\tfrac{1}{2})$$
$$a^2 = 784$$
$$a = 28$$

Example 3

In $\triangle ABC$, given $a = 7$, $b = 13$, $c = 8$. Find B.

$$\cos B = \frac{a^2 + c^2 - b^2}{2ac}$$

$$= \frac{49 + 64 - 169}{2 \cdot 7 \cdot 8} = \frac{-56}{112} = -\tfrac{1}{2}$$

Is it significant that cos B is negative?

$$B = 120°$$

Example 4

In $\triangle LMN$, $l = 3$, $m = 7$, $n = 5$, find Cos N.

Solution:

Replace a, b, c, C by l, m, n, N respectively in

$$\text{Cos } C = \frac{a^2 + b^2 - c^2}{2ab}$$

$$\text{Cos } N = \frac{l^2 + m^2 - n^2}{2lm}$$

$$= \frac{9 + 49 - 25}{42} = \frac{33}{42}$$

In Example 10.9, explaining the rule of Pythagoras, care is taken to develop the principle systematically since many of the students using the refresher math text from which the excerpt has been taken have had prior problems with mathematics. Following this example are study strategies for principle development that refer back to both this example and the example about the law of cosines.

Strategies. Although Examples 10.8 and 10.9 are organized somewhat differently, the reader is confronted with the same tasks—understanding the principle and learning how to apply it. Essentially the same strategies may be used in

Example 10.9[20]

RULE OF PYTHAGORAS*

An important mathematical principle used in finding distances by indirect means is the hypotenuse rule, sometimes called the rule of Pythagoras. It expresses the relationship of the sides of a right triangle. A right triangle is a triangle having a right angle. The side opposite the right angle is called the *hypotenuse*. The other two sides or legs are the *altitude* and *base* of the triangle.

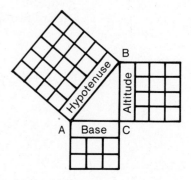

The area of the square drawn on the hypotenuse illustrated in the diagram is 25 square units and is equal to the sum of the areas of the squares drawn on the altitude and base (16 square units and 9 square units respectively). This is the rule of Pythagoras. It is usually stated as: *the square of the hypotenuse is equal to the sum of the squares of the other two sides.* As a formula this relationship is expressed:

$$h^2 = a^2 + b^2$$

h representing the hypotenuse, *a*, the altitude, and *b*, the base.

If any two sides of a right triangle are known, the third side may be found by the Pythagorean relation expressed in one of the following simplified forms:

$$h = \sqrt{a^2 + b^2} \qquad a = \sqrt{h^2 - b^2} \qquad b = \sqrt{h^2 - a^2}$$

In each case the square root is used because to determine the length of the side of a square when its area is known, the square root of the area must be found.

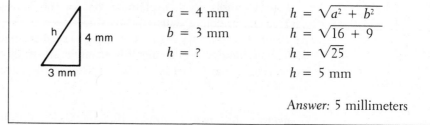

Find the hypotenuse of a right triangle if the altitude is 4 millimeters and the base is 3 millimeters.

$a = 4$ mm $h = \sqrt{a^2 + b^2}$

$b = 3$ mm $h = \sqrt{16 + 9}$

$h = ?$ $h = \sqrt{25}$

                 $h = 5$ mm

Answer: 5 millimeters

*Pythagoras, a Greek mathematician, lived about 550 B.C.

Find the altitude of a right triangle if the hypotenuse is 20 centimeters and the base is 12 centimeters.

$h = 20$ cm $a = \sqrt{h^2 - b^2}$

$b = 12$ cm $a = \sqrt{400 - 144}$

$a = ?$ $a = \sqrt{256}$

                     $a = 16$ cm

Answer: 16 centimeters

Find the base of a right triangle if the hypotenuse is 39 feet and the altitude is 15 feet.

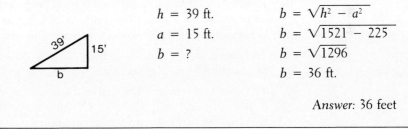

$h = 39$ ft. $b = \sqrt{h^2 - a^2}$

$a = 15$ ft. $b = \sqrt{1521 - 225}$

$b = ?$ $b = \sqrt{1296}$

                     $b = 36$ ft.

Answer: 36 feet

Practice Problems

1. Find the hypotenuse of each right triangle with the following dimensions:

Altitude	12 m	8 cm	60 km	33 ft.	180 m	136 yd.
Base	9 m	15 cm	25 km	56 ft.	112 m	255 yd.

2. Find the altitude of each right triangle with the following dimensions:

Hypotenuse	13 mm	35 cm	89 ft.	53 km	219 ft.	325 m
Base	5 mm	28 cm	80 ft.	45 km	144 ft.	165 m

3. Find the base of each right triangle with the following dimensions:

Hypotenuse	25 cm	87 m	73 mm	91 yd.	153 ft.	477 km
Altitude	24 cm	63 m	48 mm	84 yd.	72 ft.	252 km

Example 10.9 (continued)

Example 10.9 (continued)

4. By rule of Pythagoras and by actual measurement:
    a. Find the diagonal (line segment joining opposite corners) of a rectangle 8 cm long and 6 cm wide.
    b. Find the diagonal of a square whose side measures 7 m.

5. What is the shortest distance from first base to third base if the distance between bases is 90 ft.?

6. How high up on a wall does a 25-foot ladder reach if the foot of the ladder is 7 feet from the wall?

7. A child lets out 60 m of string in flying a kite. The distance from a point directly under the kite to where the child stands is 36 m. If the child holds the string 1.5 m from the ground, how high is the kite? Disregard any sag.

8. An airplane, flying 252 kilometers from town A due west to town B, drifts off its course in a straight line and is 39 kilometers due south of town B. What distance did the airplane actually fly?

9. Two poles, 34 ft. and 48 ft. high respectively, are 75 ft. apart. What is the distance from the top of one pole to the top of the second pole?

10. The escalator between the first and second floors of a store measures 28 ft. vertically and 25 ft. horizontally. How many feet are you carried when traveling from the first to the second floor?

---

studying both examples and, in fact, most principle development patterns of writing. The following approach appears to be satisfactory for many students: (1) study the heading and introductory material; (2) read the principle; (3) reread the principle; (4) read illustrations and sample problems; (5) reread, compute, write, and/or draw as needed; and (6) reread the principle.

Step One: Study the Heading and Introductory Material.   When a heading and introductory material are present, students should be encouraged to stop and think about this initial information. They may find they know more than they supposed at first glance; they will also now be ready to read with a purpose—to confirm their thinking, to fill in missing ideas, or to learn something quite new.

Step Two: Read the Principle.   In Example 10.8, the principle is called both a law and a theorem. First the **law** is written mathematically and then it is stated in boldface words as a **theorem**. In Example 10.9, the **law** is discussed informally, then presented mathematically, and finally stated in italicized words. Writers and/or publishers usually use boxes, a good deal of white space, italics, and color or black boldface print to make the principle stand out from the rest of the text.

Students need to read the principle carefully, including the supporting information, which almost always includes (a) the principle written as an equation or formula, (b) alternative and/or simplified ways of writing the equation or formula, and (c) sometimes necessary additional information.

Step Three: Reread the Principle. Frequently the primary reading of a principle results in limited understanding, so more thinking time is necessary. Rereading the principle and thinking through chunks of it at a slow pace usually helps comprehension. Paraphrasing is useful for some students. Learners need to emerge from this second reading of the principle with enough understanding to follow the writers' illustration(s) of how the principle operates. Instructors may sometimes find it necesssary to work with individual students on the reading of complex principles. Help with new uses of words, words new to the student, or specific interrelationships of words may make the difference between success and failure in the steps that follow.

Step Four: Read Illustrations and Sample Problems. In both examples, students must read the illustrations—the figures and the mathematical representations of the principle—and relate them back to the principle. In addition, the sample problems cited for each example should be carefully studied and related back to illustrations and principles. Instructors should carefully guide this type of activity whenever students demonstrate some lack of understanding. Time spent in giving such assistance usually saves time in the long run, for students learn to study subsequent introductions of principles with greater care.

This step is important for its clarification of the principle. Students should be helped to realize that they need this complete understanding prior to attempting the solution of problems on their own. In Example 10.8, students learn how to solve several expressions for the cosine of the angle, are told of two specific uses of the Law of Cosines, and are then given the opportunity to work their way through four problems with solutions. In Example 10.9, the Pythagorean relation is expressed in three simplified forms, the student is cautioned about the need to find the square root of the area, and three clear problems with solutions are presented.

Step Five: Reread, Compute, Write, and/or Draw as Needed. With pencil in hand and scratch pad or paper handy, the illustration(s) should be reread and computed even though the computation is more or less a copy of what is evident. This kind of activity sometimes cements the principle much better than does reading alone.

Step Six: Reread the Principle. Rereading the principle is an important step because it serves as a final check on understanding. If there are still questions at this point, the instructor will want to step in and help students individually. Once a student understands the principle and knows how to make use of it, he or she is then ready for the inevitable next activity—solving a group of problems by making use of the principle.

PROBLEM SOLVING

The solving of problems, especially word problems, is usually cited by students as the most complex and troublesome part of mathematics. The reason is easy to understand, for it is in the area of problem solution that the reader is normally called upon to function quite independently. With concept and principle development patterns of writing, the instructor is often a guide or, indeed, may present the material verbally with the help of a chalkboard prior to the textbook reading. And also, of course, the answers to problems (procedures and results) are what students are held accountable for.

There is little question that fast-paced reading does not belong in mathematics, particularly in the reading and study of problems. The wise reader of problems makes many regressions, right-to-left eye movements, to ponder over something he or she was not certain of or to check on the accuracy of a language unit that does not seem to equate with what was read subsequently. Whether the problem is a word problem in general math or in algebra or a problem in another area of mathematics, *deliberate, careful, thorough study* is rule number one.

The emphasis in the strategies that follow is not on *how to solve problems*, but on *how to read and study problems* so that they may be solved. These strategies are, in my judgment, among the best in the existing literature on the topic. Students should be given the opportunity to try several sets of strategies. Johnson and Rising cautioned about having "problem solvers get stuck because they have fixed on a single procedure or approach."[21]

Cooney, Davis, and Henderson, in *Dynamics of Teaching Secondary School Mathematics*, presented a detailed discussion of maxims to "serve as guidelines for teachers in helping students solve problems." The following points cover their list of maxims and supporting major points:

1. Make sure students understand the problem.
    a. Do the students understand the meanings of the terms in the problem?
    b. Do the students take into consideration all the relevant information?
    c. Can the students indicate what the problem is asking them to find?
    d. Can the students state the problem in their own words? If appropriate, can the students explain the problem in terms of a sketch?
2. Help students gather relevant thought material to assist in creating a plan.

     a. Assist the students in gathering information by having them analyze the given conditions (and sometimes the assumed solution).

     b. Help students obtain information by analyzing an analogous problem.

     c. When students have become discouraged by pursuing an unproductive approach, help them view the problem from a different perspective.

3. Provide students with an atmosphere conducive to solving a problem.

4. Once students have obtained a solution, encourage them to reflect on the problem and the means of solution.

     a. If possible have students verify solutions that have not been established deductively.

     b. Encourage students to seek and present alternate ways of solving a problem.

     c. Challenge students to investigate variations of the given problem.[22]

Word Problems in General Math. The following problem and steps were taken from Thomas and Robinson; the steps are particularly useful strategies for reading and studying word problems. Students reading math problems must always bear in mind that they are not concerned with a "story line" but with the solution of a problem that may be generalized to other similar problems.

Example 10.10[23]   So far this year Johnny Bench has 13 hits for 37 official times at bat. Later if he has a great day and goes 5 for 5 in today's game, by how many more points will his batting average increase?*

> *Step 1: Read the problem thoroughly, asking, "What is this all about?"* Size up the problem situation. Is there a word you don't know? Now is the time to check up on its meaning. A single word left unknown—a slip-up because of one unclear meaning—may make the rest of your efforts ineffective.
>
>   The student's thinking should run something like this: "The problem is all about batting averages and comparing two of them." If the student does not know what "he goes 5 for 5" means, he or she must find the definition before proceeding further. Of course, students should have the

Example 10.10 (continued)

---

*Richard Muelder, University of Chicago Laboratory School mathematics teacher and former chairman of the mathematics department, devised the baseball problem and helped apply the sequence of steps to it.

Example 10.10 (continued)

background information that batting averages are decimal fractions between zero and one, rounded to three places.

Step 2: Reread the problem, asking, "What am I to find here?" Make sure you understand precisely what the problem asks for. The student should think, "I need to figure two batting averages—one for Bench's present record and a second after today's game. Then I'm to figure the increase."

Step 3: Ask yourself, "What facts are given?" What information is already supplied you in the problem? Make jottings. The student might think, "I know the number of Bench's hits and times at bat right now, and I know that he adds 5 to each of them in today's game."

Step 4: Plan your attack. Read the problem through once more, asking, "What processes will I use?" or "What formulas will I need?" Plan the steps you'll take in finding what's required. Continue to make jottings.

The student's thinking should run something like this: "I must divide the total times at bat into the number of hits to find the batting average. First, I'll divide 37 into 13 so that I can get Bench's first average. Then I must add five to each of these in order to learn his new record. Then I must divide 18 by 42 to determine Bench's new average. And last, I must find the difference between his first and his second average."

Step 5: Estimate the answer. Ask yourself, "What would a reasonable answer be?" The student might possibly estimate something like this: "Both 13/37 and 18/42 are batting averages over .333 but under .500. So their difference will be less than ½."

Step 6: Carry out the operations. Now carry out the planned operation. Hopefully, the student will obtain, as an answer, an increase of .077 in Bench's average.

Step 7: Check your work. Compare the answer you arrived at with your estimated answer. Go back to the original problem and check your results against the conditions of the problem. See if your answer fulfills those conditions.

No one can bat over 1.000. Thus, if the student gets the spectacular increase of over 3.300, something is wrong! Check by asking, (1) Was my error caused by a single error in arithmetic? or (2) Did I misunderstand the problem?

The example and series of steps suggested by Shepherd are reprinted slightly adapted in Example 10.11. Here is another good set of strategies for reading and studying a word problem.

Example 10.11[24]   1. *Read* it slowly and carefully. Picture the scene or situation in your mind.

2. *Reread* the last sentence—decide what is asked.

3. *Reread* the entire problem—determine the facts given to work with.

4. *Determine* the process to use.

5. *Estimate* the answer—judge reasonableness of estimate.

6. *Compute*—For example, these steps would be followed for the following problem:

Mr. Stone bought a new sewing machine for his wife. The store asked him to make a down payment of 20%. If the cost of the machine was $160.00, how much was the down payment?

a. The situation:	Mr. Stone is buying his wife a sewing machine and he must make a specified down payment.
b. What is asked:	How much is the down payment?
c. Facts given:	The sewing machine cost—$160.00. Down payment must be 20%.
d. Process:	Multiplication to compute the size of the down payment.
e. Estimate:	A little more than $30.00 (20% of 100 is 20.00; 20% of 50 is 10.00).
f. Compute the problem:	20% of 160.

Word Problems in Algebra. As shown, slightly adapted, in Example 10.12, Strang and Bracken contributed an interesting approach to the reading and study of a word problem in algebra reported to them by a teacher.

Example 10.12[25]   Two automobiles start at the same time from towns 330 miles apart and travel toward each other. If one averages 30 miles an hour and the other averages 25 miles an hour, in how many hours will they meet?

The first impulse of many students upon reading a verbal problem is to get panicky. Where does one start? One way to allay this fear is to point out that very few mathematical problems can be solved by one quick reading. All we can hope to gain the first time we read the problem is the general idea. The subsequent readings must be more deliberate. During the second reading we can select all the active forces which appear in the problem and list them on the right side of our paper. If the nature of the problem alters any of these forces, we must list the altered form also.

Example 10.12 (continued)

·*Example 10.12 (continued)*

From the second reading we glean three important factors:

rate of speed of first auto

rate of speed of second auto

distance traveled.

On our third reading we must supply the numerical and symbolic description for each of these factors. We must also determine what our unknown is to be. If the unknown is not immediately apparent, it will unfold as the result of the process of elimination as we fill in the data for all our factors. This leads us to:

30 m.p.h. = rate of speed of first auto

25 m.p.h. = rate of speed of second auto

x = number of hours traveled

330 miles = distance separating automobiles

We now have the elements but lack perception of the entire problem. Let us read again (fourth reading) with an aim of gaining this understanding and setting up an equality. This is the crux of the problem. The teacher may help by asking such questions as, "Have you ever seen a similar problem?" or "What are all the plausible relationships you can think of?" Insight must arise at this point. In this problem it is the recall of the formula that distance is equal to the rate multiplied by the time. It is wise at this insightful moment to estimate the probable answer in order to confirm our understanding and to serve as a safeguard against a mechanically defective solution.

	Solution		*Check*
$30x + 25x = 330$		$30\,(6) + 25\,(6) = 330$	
$55x = 330$		$180 + 150 = 330$	
$x = 6$		$330 = 330$	

One more cautious reading must be made in which each detail of the preceding steps is carefully checked. It is here that the "careless" mistake is found. The mathematical "check" only verifies the mechanical manipulation of the preceding information. The verbal check verifies the correct interpretation of the information.

The flow chart in Figure 10.4, designed by Richard Muelder, is reprinted from Thomas and Robinson. It illustrates how to set up a problem with one variable.

Figure 10.4   *Flow Chart: Setting up a Problem
              with One Variable*[26]

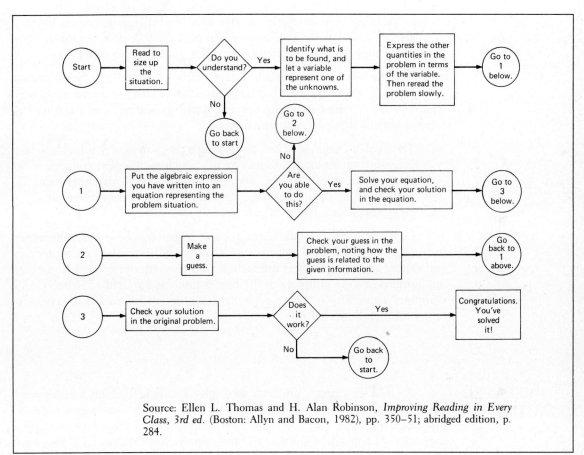

Source: Ellen L. Thomas and H. Alan Robinson, *Improving Reading in Every
Class, 3rd ed.* (Boston: Allyn and Bacon, 1982), pp. 350–51; abridged edition, p.
284.

COMPUTERS   Norris pointed out that the analytical thinking and problem-solving ability
              needed in math is enhanced by the computer.[27] He also indicated the practical
              need of equipping citizens with the ability to program and use computers, as
              they are fast becoming common aspects of many jobs, learning situations, and
              household tasks.

                   From the viewpoint of writing and reading tasks, the computer presents
              a number of challenges. Students who engage in programs must learn to follow
              directions precisely as they run a program and as they compose responses to the
              program. And, as Norris stated:

Computers provide feedback to the programmer that is unlike the information we give our students. Syntactical errors are highlighted almost instantaneously. There is never any doubt about intentions or meaning. The computer accepts only what it is programmed to accept, and nothing else. Students must learn to follow the rules, and if they don't, the computer provides immediate feedback.[28]

Students who write programs are, of course, involved in a type of composing activity useful to math but equally useful in learning a type of activity related to the writing-composing process. Reading, writing, and thinking become intertwined as part of the total process.

The analysis required to test and debug a program is very valuable. One must understand the structure of a problem in order to provide an adequate set of test data. Trying to decide why the machine did what it did instead of what you wanted it to do is a very worthwhile experience in analytical thinking.[29]

Computer literacy would seem to be an important object of mathematics instruction. Students need to learn computer *capabilities* (what a computer can and cannot do through direct interaction with computer programs), computer *applications* (a wide sampling of the way computers are used in society), and computer *algorithms* (introduction to the notion of algorithm and its representation through flow charts).[30]

RELATED ACTIVITIES

1. Use an opaque projector to display Example 10.1 on a screen and guide students through the reading. Have students note that *degree* must be clarified before they can move on. Clarification should take place through a discussion of both the definition and the portrayal on the graphic. Then have students read each definition of an angle and, together, inspect each graphic. Once they seem to understand, remove the material and ask students to draw the types of angles as you define each. An alternate approach is to have students define each angle from drawings executed on the chalkboard by individual students. In addition to, and/or in place of Example 10.1, choose similarly organized materials from texts used by the students.

2. Find a definitional pattern leading up to a simple equation in the textbooks you are using. Help students understand that the authors are leading them toward an equation by first defining the main concept. Have students execute the steps of a problem using the equation to be sure they understand the concept.

3. If the appositive form, as shown in Example 10.2, is used often in the texts your students are utilizing, point out some and have students find

others. Be sure they comprehend the meaning in appositive form through written paraphrase, drawing, or written application in a problem. Placing attention on the form will cause students to be on the lookout for such meanings as they read on their own.

4. When explanatory material is dense with concepts that are not explained at that moment, even though defined earlier, review them prior to problem-solving activity. Don't leave the definitions at the verbal level if it is possible for students to sketch the concept or relationship of concepts. If at the verbal level, try to help students express the meaning in their own words. Choose both kinds of explanations and use them as examples. Then have students search for their own "challengers" to bring before the group. Example 10.3 can be used for this purpose in appropriate situations.

5. Figure 10.3, or your choice of an example like it, is a useful way of assisting students to realize the importance of knowing definitions and using a graphic to perform functional math activities. Figure 10.3, may be used on an opaque projector, and an overhead projector can be utilized with a suitable example or two of your own represented on transparencies.

6. Select a dense passage from an appropriate math text and demonstrate the six strategies to be used in understanding a group of related concepts as a prelude to problem solving. (Examples 10.6 and 10.7 may be projected if suitable.) Repeat the process a few times, assisting the students. Review the process from time to time, particularly when a group of complex concepts is presented. When possible review the steps with individual students who are having problems linking understanding of concepts to problem solving.

7. Demonstrate the six strategies for principle development in much the same way you worked with concept development described in activity 6. Use Examples 10.8 and 10.9 if suitable.

8. Select pertinent problems from class texts on which to practice problem-solving procedures. Take the time to help students work out their own schemes. Offer several ways of proceeding (as suggested in the chapter) and try to have students develop the plan(s) most effective for them. Renew emphasis on problem-solving techniques with each unit until students put them to use automatically.

SELECTED READINGS

Bell, Frederick H. "Posing and Solving Verbal Problems." *Mathematics Teacher* 73 (December 1980):652–56.

Cooney, Thomas J.; Edward J. Davis; and K.B. Henderson. *Dynamics of Teaching Secondary School Mathematics.* Boston: Houghton Mifflin, 1975.

Earle, Richard A. *Teaching Reading and Mathematics.* Reading Aids Series. Newark, Del.: International Reading Association, 1976.

Geeslin, William E. "Using Writing about Mathematics as a Teaching Technique." *Mathematics Teacher* 70 (February 1977):112–15.

Henderson, Kenneth B. *Teaching Secondary School Mathematics.* What Research Says to the Teacher, no. 9. Washington, D.C.: National Education Association, 1969.

Henrichs, Margaret, and Tom Sisson. "Mathematics and the Reading Process: A Practical Application of Theory." *Mathematics Teacher* 73 (April 1980):253–57.

Krulik, Stephen. "To Read or Not to Read, That Is the Question!" *Mathematics Teacher* 73 (April 1980):248–52.

Lees, Fred. "Mathematics and Reading." *Journal of Reading* 19 (May 1976):621–26.

Ley, Terry C.; Loren L. Henry; and Robert E. Rowsey. "Eighth Graders' Performance in Reading and Computing for Science-Related Word Problems." *Journal of Reading* 23 (December 1979):222–28.

Lovelace, Terry L., and Conrad K. McKnight. "The Effects of Reading Instruction on Calculus Students' Problem Solving." *Journal of Reading* 22 (January 1980):305–8.

O'Mara, Deborah A. "The Process of Reading Mathematics." *Journal of Reading* 25 (October 1981):22–30.

Pachtman, Andrew B., and James D. Riley. "Teaching the Vocabulary of Mathematics through Interaction, Exposure, and Structure." *Journal of Reading* 22 (May 1978):241–44.

Riley, James D., and Andrew B. Pachtman. "Reading Mathematical Word Problems: Telling Them What to Do Is Not Telling Them How to Do It." *Journal of Reading* 22 (March 1978):531–34.

Shepherd, David L. *Comprehensive High School Reading Methods*, 2nd ed., ch. 11. Columbus, Ohio: Charles E. Merrill, 1978.

Singer, Harry, and Dan Donlan. *Reading and Learning from Text.* Boston: Little, Brown, 1980, chap. 14.

Thomas, Ellen L., and H. Alan Robinson. *Improving Reading in Every Class*, 3rd ed., ch. 11. Boston: Allyn and Bacon.

NOTES

1. Anne C. Roark, "Mathematics: Fundamental Changes Ahead," *Chronicle of Higher Education* 15 (May 1978):3–4.
2. Craig McGarvey, "Mathematics and Miseducation: Toward the Next School Curricula," *Mathematics Teacher* 74 (February 1981):93.
3. James T. Fey, "Mathematics Teaching Today: Perspectives from Three National Surveys," *Mathematics Teacher* 72 (October 1979):492.
4. Hal Saunders, "When Are We Ever Gonna Have to Use This?" *Mathematics Teacher* 73 (January 1980):7–16.
5. McGarvey, "Mathematics and Miseducation," p. 94.
6. Kenneth B. Henderson, *Teaching Secondary School Mathematics*, What Research Says to the Teacher, no. 9 (Washington: National Education Association, 1969), p. 7.
7. Edwin I. Stein, *Fundamentals of Mathematics* (Boston: Allyn and Bacon, 1980), p. 402.
8. Richard E. Johnson, Lona Lee Lindsey, and William E. Slesnick, *Algebra*, 2nd ed. (Reading, Mass.: Addison-Wesley, 1971), p. 458.

9. See Ellen L. Thomas and H. Alan Robinson, *Improving Reading in Every Class* (Boston: Allyn and Bacon, 1982), p. 39, abridged edition, pp. 32–33.

10. Edwin E. Moise and Floyd L. Downs, Jr., *Geometry*, 2nd ed. (Reading, Mass.: Addison-Wesley, 1971), p. 616.

11. Francis G. Lankford, Jr., *Consumer Mathematics* (Boston: Allyn and Bacon, 1981), p. 186.

12. Mary P. Dolciani and others, *Modern School Mathematics: Pre-Algebra* (Boston: Houghton Mifflin, 1970), p. 330.

13. Stein, *Fundamentals of Mathematics*, p. 459.

14. R.E. Johnson, F.L. Kiokemeister, and E.S. Wolk, *Johnson and Kiokemeister's Calculus with Analytic Geometry*, 6th ed. (Boston: Allyn and Bacon, 1978), p. 520.

15. Helen K. Halliday and others, *Contemporary Mathematics*, bk. 8 (New York: William H. Sadlier, 1970), p. 386.

16. Henderson, *Teaching Secondary School Mathematics*, pp. 6–16.

17. Halliday, *Contemporary Mathematics*, bk. 7, p. 367.

18. Edward I. Stein, *Stein's Refresher Mathematics* (Boston: Allyn and Bacon, 1980), pp. 389–90.

19. Myron R. White, *Fundamentals of Algebra*, Course 2 (Boston: Allyn and Bacon, 1972), pp. 310–12.

20. Stein, *Refresher Mathematics*, pp. 407–9.

21. Donovan A. Johnson and Gerald R. Rising, *Guidelines for Teaching Mathematics* (Belmont, Calif.: Wadsworth, 1972), p. 246.

22. Thomas J. Cooney, Edward J. Davis, and K. B. Henderson, *Dynamics of Teaching Secondary School Mathematics* (Boston: Houghton Mifflin, 1975), pp. 246–72.

23. Thomas and Robinson, *Improving Reading in Every Class*, 3rd ed. pp. 349–50 (abridged edition, pp. 282–84).

24. David L. Shepherd, *Comprehensive High School Reading Methods* (Columbus, Ohio: Charles E. Merrill, 1978), pp. 288–89.

25. Ruth Strang and Dorothy Kendall Bracken, *Making Better Readers* (Boston: D. C. Heath, 1957), p. 255.

26. Thomas and Robinson, *Improving Reading in Every Class*, 3rd ed., pp. 350–51 (abridged edition, p. 284).

27. Donald O. Norris, "Let's Put Computers into the Mathematics Curriculum." *Mathematics Teacher* 74 (January 1981):24–26. Copyright 1980 by the National Council of Teachers of Mathematics. Used by permission.

28. Ibid., p. 26.

29. Ibid.

30. Thomas P. Carpenter and others, "The Current Status of Computer Literacy: NAEP Results for Secondary Students," *Mathematics Teacher* 73 (December 1980):669.

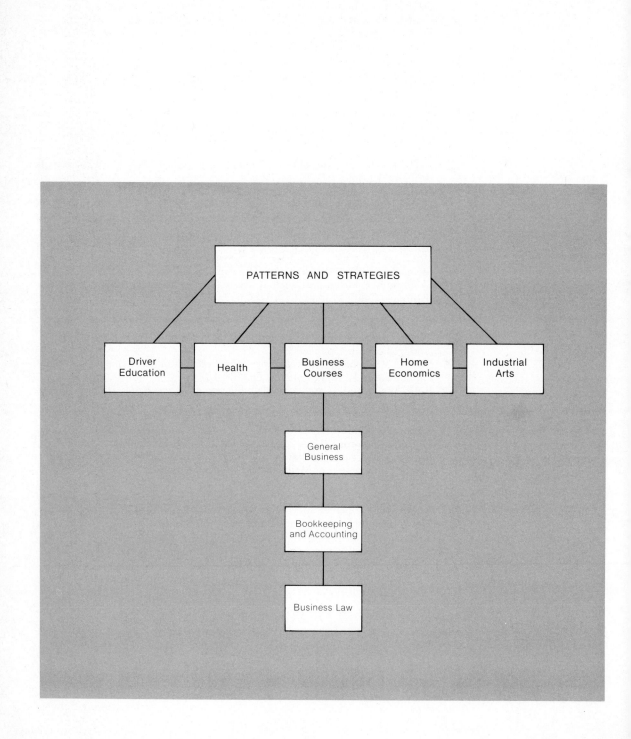

11
Additional Important Subjects

Since the processes of reading and writing are so intertwined with the study of any content area, all teachers who use reading and writing as study tools must give some guidance to their students. Business subjects and foreign language courses are certainly dependent upon the writing, reading, and study abilities of students. Other courses involve reading and study in varying amounts. Some, such as physical education, usually include few or no reading assignments, although a physical education instructor can certainly play a role in helping students "turn on to reading." In an article entitled "Reading Improvement in the Gymnasium," Maring and Ritson build a case for integrating reading and writing with physical education.[1] All teachers, depending on opportunities and relationships with students, are able to guide students toward books and periodicals in their areas that may whet appetites, improve performance, and help to develop lifetime readers and writers (see Chapter 12).

In this chapter, emphasis is placed on reading and study in *business courses*, *driver training*, *health*, *home economics*, and *industrial arts*. The Selected Readings section at the end of the chapter is longer than usual, for it includes reports that make suggestions or indicate procedures for reading and study in other subjects not discussed in this chapter.

BUSINESS COURSES

GENERAL BUSINESS

The topics handled in general business courses include getting a job; career information; coping with daily business needs related to spending, saving, and investing money; budgeting; consumer protection; and information about available consumer services. A few general business textbooks are available, as well as an increasing number of supplementary reading materials devoted to specific aspects of general business. The difficulty levels of the materials range from extremely simple to very complex, depending on the nature of the tasks.

Two types of reading are called for: (1) reading the regular text plus graphics to gain information about a topic, and (2) reading and learning how to fill out a variety of forms used in daily life. Students usually need guidance in both.

Examples.   In Figure 11.1, the reader is asked to read a sequence of events related to the routing of a check, from writing it to charging it to the writer's account. Students may use the graphic as reinforcement for the text.

Strategies.   Although the writing pattern in Figure 11.1 is clearly the presentation of steps in a process, there are no key terms (such as first, then, finally) that clue the reader into spotting each step. The reader should be led to discover that the title is a distinct clue and the opening sentence "promises" that the reader will be dealing with the intermediate steps. The opening sentence acts as a broad, general summary of the process. Readers should be cautioned to read the intermediate steps sentence by sentence with the understanding that more than one step may be named in a given sentence. For instance, the first sentence at the beginning of paragraph two names two steps: (1) Mr. Smith received the check. (2) Mr. Smith deposited the check in his bank. The graphic confirms what has been read.

A number of paragraphs in general business texts are definitional and act to define technical terms, often printed in italics. Definitions are usually developed through straight explanation and examples. Many other paragraphs are explanatory and develop a variety of topics usually introduced by a heading or title. (See pages 91–92 and 109–110.)

Some materials on the market today provide instruction in filling out forms necessary for living in our complex society. Figure 11.2 is an example of such a form. Students should be introduced to the concepts and practices of credit plans and should then be presented with a sample form. If the material does not insist that the student read and actually cope with the sample form, the instructor should so insist. The concepts should be cemented, for merely reading about them does not help most students when they must actually fill out such forms. The secondary school must assume the responsibility for ensuring that students can handle such realistic tasks.

When first approaching a form, the instructor should assume that students know nothing about it. All students should have an actual or reproduced copy of the form to be filled out. The teacher should closely guide the reading and writing, and each student's work should be carefully checked. Students should have the opportunity of filling out similar forms with or without teacher assistance until they are proficient. The same kind of instruction—carefully guided to independent—should be followed for all important forms.

BOOKKEEPING AND ACCOUNTING

Bookkeeping and accounting textbooks present many reading hazards for students. Much guidance by the instructor is needed whether or not the text is used page by page as a textbook or as a reference tool. Even more than in mathematics and science, what is being read is immediately operational. Students must interrelate several symbol systems, learn to understand specialized

*Figure 11.1   Reading a Text and a Graphic in a
General Business Course[2]*

THE CHECK CLEARING PROCESS

From the time a check is first written by a depositor until it is returned to the depositor several weeks later, it will usually have passed through a number of hands. Assume that Anne Jones has a checking account in Bank A, Boston, Massachusetts, and that on January 10, 19—— wrote a check on her account for $25 payable to Arthur Smith, New York City.

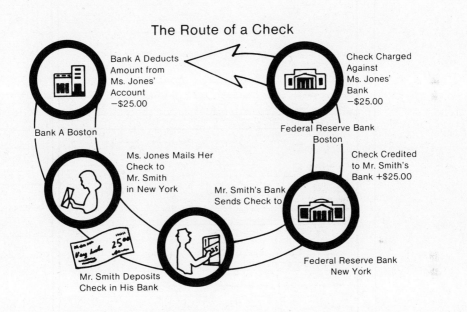

The Route of a Check

Mr. Smith received the check in the mail from Ms. Jones on January 12 and deposited it in his bank in New York City. Mr. Smith's bank will send the check to the Federal Reserve Bank in New York. The Federal Reserve Bank in New York will, in turn, send the check to the Federal Reserve Bank in Boston, the district in which Ms. Jones' bank is located. The Federal Reserve Bank in Boston will charge the check against the balance of Bank A, Boston, and then return the check to Bank A, where Ms. Jones' account is actually kept. Bank A, Boston, will charge the check against Ms. Jones' checking account and return the check to her.

Through this type clearing process checks are routed from bank to bank each day in sizable batches.

Source: Hobart H. Conover, Bertha Wakin, and Helene L. Zimmerman, *General Business for Today's World* (Boston: Allyn and Bacon, 1977), pp. 265–66.

Figure 11.2 Reading a Form in a General Business Course[3]

SEARS, ROEBUCK AND CO. INDIVIDUAL CREDIT ACCOUNT APPLICATION

APPLICATION TO BE COMPLETED IN NAME OF PERSON IN WHICH THE ACCOUNT IS TO BE CARRIED.

COURTESY TITLES ARE OPTIONAL PLEASE PRINT

☐ MR. ☐ MRS. ☐ MISS ☐ MS. ____ First Name ____ Initial ____ Last Name

Mailing Address if Different than Residence Address

Residence Address (Street) (Apt. #) City State Zip Code

Phone No: Home ____ Phone No: Business ____ Soc. Sec. No. ____ Age ____ Number of Dependents ____ (Excluding Applicant)

Are you a United States citizen? ☐ Yes ☐ No If NO, explain immigration status: ____

How Long at Present Address ____ Own ☐ Rent-Furnished ☐ Rent-Unfurnished ☐ Board ☐ Monthly Rent or Mortgage Payments $ ____

Name of Landlord or Mortgage Holder ____ Street Address ____ City and State

Former Address (if less than 2 years at present address) ____ How long ____

Employer ____ Street Address ____ City and State

How long ____ Occupation ____ Net Income $ ____ (Take Home Pay) Monthly ☐ Weekly ☐

Former Employer (If less than 1 year with present employer) ____ How long ____

ALIMONY, CHILD SUPPORT, OR SEPARATE MAINTENANCE INCOME NEED NOT BE REVEALED IF YOU DO NOT WISH TO HAVE IT CONSIDERED AS A BASIS FOR PAYING THIS OBLIGATION.

Alimony, child support, separate maintenance received under: ☐ Court order ☐ Written agreement ☐ Oral understanding Amount $ ____ Monthly ☐ Weekly ☐

Other income, if any: Amount $ ____ Monthly ☐ Weekly ☐ Source ____

Name and Address of Bank ____ Savings ☐ Checking ☐ Acc't No. ____

Name and Address of Bank ____ Savings ☐ Checking ☐ Acc't No. ____

Previous Sears Account ☐ Yes ☐ No ____ At What Sears Store do you usually shop? ____ Account No. ____ Is Account Paid in Full ☐ Yes ☐ No Date Final Payment Made ____

Relative or Personal Reference not living at above address ____ (Name) (Street Address) (City and State) (Relationship)

CREDIT REFERENCES (Attach additional sheet if necessary.) List all references (Open or closed within past two years)

Charge Accounts Loan References Bank/Store/Company Address	Date Opened	Name Account Carried in	Account Number	Balance	Monthly Payments

Authorized buyer ____ First Name ____ Initial ____ Last Name ____ Relationship to applicant

Authorized buyer ____ First Name ____ Initial ____ Last Name ____ Relationship to applicant

THE INFORMATION BELOW IS REQUIRED IF: (1) YOUR SPOUSE IS AN AUTHORIZED BUYER OR (2) YOU RESIDE IN A COMMUNITY PROPERTY STATE (ARIZONA, CALIFORNIA, IDAHO, LOUISIANA, NEVADA, NEW MEXICO, TEXAS, WASHINGTON) OR (3) YOU ARE RELYING ON THE INCOME OR ASSETS OF ANOTHER PERSON, INCLUDING A SPOUSE OR FORMER SPOUSE, AS A BASIS FOR PAYMENT.

Name of spouse ☐ / Name of former spouse ☐ / Name of other person ☐ ____ Address ____ Age ____

Employer ____ Street Address ____ City and State ____

How long ____ Occupation ____ Soc. Sec. No. ____ Net Income $ ____ (Take Home Pay) Monthly ☐ Weekly ☐

Name and Address of Bank ____ Savings ☐ Checking ☐ Acc't No. ____

Name and Address of Bank ____ Savings ☐ Checking ☐ Acc't No. ____

THE PERSON ON WHOSE INCOME OR ASSETS YOU ARE RELYING AS A BASIS FOR PAYMENT MUST SIGN BELOW, HOWEVER, YOUR SPOUSE NEED NOT SIGN IF YOU RESIDE IN A COMMUNITY PROPERTY STATE OR IF YOUR SPOUSE IS AN AUTHORIZED BUYER.

SEARS IS AUTHORIZED TO INVESTIGATE MY CREDIT RECORD AND TO VERIFY MY CREDIT, EMPLOYMENT AND INCOME REFERENCES. X ____ (Signature of person on whose income or assets applicant is relying.) Date ____

(FOR OFFICE USE ONLY) 810 National Rev. 11/81 PLEASE PRINT

Name / Address / City State / Zip / 4th Line Address / Interviewer ____ Date / Investigator ____ Date / PSAS File

Date Opened / Approved Line of Credit / Date / Authorizer / SC ☐ / MCP ☐

ACCOUNT NUMBER / Store Stamp / ☐ Employee / X Reference ☐ MCP ☐ SC ☐ Other / ISSUED: SC Cards / MCP Identifications / NO. / DATE

NOTICE: SEE REVERSE SIDE FOR IMPORTANT INFORMATION

Courtesy of Sears, Roebuck and Co.

meanings for a multitude of words and phrases, read directions with precision, and be able to use what has been learned in solving realistic problems.

Example.   The most common pattern of writing consists of three stages: (1) explanation of a concept, (2) illustration of the concept, and (3) related problems to solve. In some texts the stages are sequential for each concept. In other texts, as represented by the excerpt from a beginning accounting text in Figure 11.3, only the first two stages are presented as a unit. In this case, the third stage—related problems to solve—follows at the conclusion of the chapter; sometimes additional problems are included at the end of the book.

Strategies.   Students who are exhibiting some difficulties in bookkeeping and accounting may well be having reading and study problems. Especially for these students, instructors need to take time to guide their reading in the textbook until they do better independently. In fact, all students may need this guidance, particularly when they are facing a new or especially complex assignment. To many students, bookkeeping and accounting present the same kinds of difficulties encountered in passages from math and the physical sciences. There is more to be gained through guiding the silent reading of the material, interspersed with discussion and explanation plus performance of the operations, than through the assignment of unexplained material to be read independently for a test or recitation.

For the type of material illustrated in Figure 11.3, the following steps are helpful for the student: (1) study the title, the subheadings, and the graphic(s); (2) survey the printed material; (3) study the explanation of the concept; (4) study the illustration of the concept and the accompanying graphic(s); (5) complete one or two related problems with teacher guidance; and (6) complete one or two related problems independently.

Step One: Study the Title, the Subheadings, and the Graphic(s).   Students should tap their own resources at the outset by realizing what they already know about what is stated in the title and subheadings and what they see in the graphic(s). Time taken in looking through these parts of the material will increase efficiency in study. At first some students may need directed progression through this step.

Step Two: Survey the Printed Material.   Prior to careful study, the printed material should be surveyed for three purposes: (a) to get an overall idea of content, (b) to pinpoint any terms the student is uncertain about, and (c) to note the organization of the material. This step is vital, for it aids students in establishing a readiness for purposeful reading. In addition, knowledge of how the material is organized—first the explanation of the concept and second the specific illustration of the concept—facilitates comprehension and encourages retention.

If students find terms they are uncertain of, they should be directed to

Figure 11.3 Writing Pattern in an Accounting Text[4]

CASH PAYMENTS JOURNAL

A special journal in which only cash payments transactions are recorded is called a cash payments journal.

Form of Cash Payments Journal

The cash payments journal used by Sunrise Art Center is shown [below]. This five-column cash payments journal has special amount columns for transactions that occur frequently. For example, Sunrise Art Center makes frequent payments to creditors. Thus, there is a special amount column for Accounts Payable Debit. Transactions that do not occur often, such as the monthly payment of rent, are recorded in the General columns.

Journalizing Cash Payments in a Cash Payments Journal

All cash payments made by Sunrise Art Center are recorded in the cash payments journal. The source document for each cash payment is a check stub in the checkbook.

Most cash payments are for (1) expenses, (2) cash purchases, (3) payment of creditors, (4) withdrawals of cash by the owner, and (5) payroll transactions. Examples of entries for these transactions are shown in the illustration below.

CASH PAYMENTS JOURNAL — PAGE 16

	DATE		ACCOUNT TITLE	CHECK NO.	POST. REF.	1 GENERAL DEBIT	2 GENERAL CREDIT	3 ACCOUNTS PAYABLE DEBIT	4 PURCHASES DISCOUNT CREDIT	5 CASH CREDIT	
1	1977 Dec.	1	Rent Expense	243		500 00				500 00	1
2		1	Purchases	244		210 00				210 00	2
3		5	McGuire Art Company	245				252 00		252 00	3
4		7	S. G. Justin, Drawing	246		450 00				450 00	4
5		7	Employees Income Tax Pay.	247		78 60				165 00	5
6			FICA Tax Payable			86 40					6
7											7
8											8
9											9
10											10

Cash payments recorded in a five-column cash payments journal

On Line 1 is an entry to pay the rent for December, 1982. On Line 2 is an entry for a cash purchase. Line 3 shows a payment on account to a creditor. Line 4 shows a cash withdrawal. Lines 5 and 6 show the deposit for payroll liabilities. These entries are similar to the ones made for the same transactions in the combination journal.

Source: Robert M. Swanson and others, *Century of Accounting* (Cincinnati, Ohio: South-Western, 1977), pp. 429–30.

use the context around the terms to figure them out before turning to another source for assistance. In the example, students who do not remember the term *source document* from prior work will need help from the instructor or another source, as the term is not fully explained through the context. In bookkeeping and accounting, so many terms used in everyday conversation and nontechnical reading—*journal, entry, recorded*—have specialized meanings that it behooves the teacher to place attention on such language units more than once in order to ensure retention of the specialized meanings.

Step Three: Study the Explanation of the Concept. The concept, of course, should be cemented in the reader's mind prior to proceeding to the illustration of the concept. Careful, slow silent reading of the first four paragraphs in the example should result in an understanding of the concept. If discussion demonstrates that there are hazy areas, readers should be directed back to particular sentences for silent or oral rereading and should then be held responsible for explaining what they had misunderstood.

Step Four: Study the Illustration of the Concept and Accompanying Graphic(s). Students should focus on the illustration of the concept to see how it is put to work in a practical situation—always true of reading in bookkeeping and accounting at the secondary school level. In the example, readers will turn to the graphic as they follow the explanation in the concluding paragraph. If students can explain the graphic and relate it back to the major concept in the initial paragraph, they have succeeded—at least in verbal understanding.

Step Five: Complete One or Two Related Problems with Teacher Guidance. Although the textbook often introduces other concepts before posing problems to be solved, it is wise (particularly with poor readers) to turn to one or two problems in the book or to teacher-designed problems. Immediate application of what has been learned, under guidance, is an important step for the reader, particularly for one who has been having difficulties.

Step Six: Complete One or Two Related Problems Independently. Students (especially those who have been having reading problems) should be encouraged to work on one or two problems themselves *without* teacher guidance. Then they should bring the results to the instructor. Usually, except for small calculation errors, this action results in success and cements understanding. Also such successful application permits the reader to turn to the next concept with more confidence.

BUSINESS LAW

Example. Texts in business law are comparatively easy to read in contrast to bookkeeping and accounting textbooks. Essentially they follow the pattern of

(1) presentation of a problem or situation, and (2) explanation of the problem or situation, sometimes with examples, but mainly expository in nature. Example 11.1 is representative.

Strategies. The pattern in Example 11.1 is quite typical. In some texts the opening problem might consist of the description of a situation without the question, but essentially texts are composed of problems, answers, and review problems. The reader should read the problem once for the overall idea and then again to be sure all important ideas are understood. The answer should be studied in the same way. It will prove profitable to make notes at this point, as the reader must go on to a series of questions and answers in a chapter.

Example 11.1[5]

WHAT IS INSURANCE?

Problem 1

The Jones family consists of Mr. and Mrs. Jones and their two young daughters. Mr. Jones is employed regularly and earns $9,000 per year. The family owns the home it occupies and an automobile. Mr. Jones is uncertain of the future. He feels that the family may suffer if he should suddenly become ill and be unable to work. He also fears that a fire may damage their home and cause considerable loss. What advice would you give Mr. Jones?

Before studying the insurance contract and the various kinds of insurance which people may buy, it is important to understand the purpose behind insurance. Everyone constantly faces risk. A serious accident or ill health may disable one for a long time and prevent his making a living. Death may remove the family breadwinner. Fire may destroy homes and personal belongings. An automobile accident may involve considerable financial loss. Insurance, of course, cannot prevent these risks from becoming realities. The best it can do is soften the blow when it falls by providing a money payment—*indemnity*—to make up for what was actually lost. That is the real purpose of insurance—protection against financial loss. In other words, buying insurance transfers the risks to someone else, usually an insurance company organized for that purpose. The reason an insurance company is able to assume these risks and to compensate in case of loss is that the company does the same thing for many persons and receives contributions from each one. These contributions are sufficient to cover the losses of a few contributors.

Insurance may be defined as a contract whereby one party, for a consideration, agrees to indemnify another for specified losses.

Since Mr. Jones in Problem 1 would be financially unable to cover his risks with his own funds, he should take out insurance to provide for his family in case of emergency.

Eventually the reader will confront review problems to answer and will want to refer back to the notes.

Essentially the reading task in business law is not complex. There are numerous terms that may be new to the reader, but these are normally explained in context, as *indemnity* was. Note making plays an important role, since there is much information to retain. Notes made in some type of outline form, as demonstrated on pages 155, 156, 167, 187, 189, 193, and 198, are most useful.

DRIVER EDUCATION

Driver education has become an increasingly popular and important elective in the secondary school curriculum. Reading and study, in addition to practical instruction, are necessities, because students must learn a great deal of information both to pass the driver's test and to become efficient, effective drivers. In addition to drivers' manuals, there are a number of textbooks on the market that are quite readable even though they are packed with facts. A good deal of the writing is in the second person, addressed directly to the reader, as in Figure 11.4.

Examples.   Since so much information is crammed into a book, the writing style is often a little choppy. Readers proceed from one subheading to another without much transition, although related topics are grouped together. Occasionally terms are introduced without explanation, but generally the terminology is familiar to most readers. Pictures, diagrams, and charts are used widely. The passage in Figure 11.4 is an example of the most frequently used writing style. The excerpt in Figure 11.5, written in the third person, represents the writing style included in about one-third of a typical textbook. Along with it is one of the types of graphics used often. Many of the other graphics in a typical text are diagrams of essential driving maneuvers.

Strategies.   Readers of the excerpt in Figure 11.4 have four tasks: (1) read and think about the title and the two introductory paragraphs, for they point out the importance of the nine imperative statements that follow; (2) study the photographs and caption, which further emphasize the significance of the nine statements; (3) read and reread the nine statements, being certain that each action is understood; and (4) read and respond to the three sets of questions (the third set may require further research).

The four tasks are somewhat applicable to other readings in driver education, for one frequent writing pattern is introductory material written in the third person followed by actions or rules written in the second person. Particularly in the section dealing with the actions, some students will need assistance with technical and some nontechnical vocabulary. Students should feel free to approach the instructor for help with such words as *position, stability, dusk,* and/or *reflectors.* In Figure 11.5, *low blood-alcohol levels, impaired, consump-*

*Figure 11.4   Second-Person Writing Style
in a Driver Education Text*[6]

PROTECTING THE BICYCLIST

A bicyclist may get in a driver's way because of the great difference between the speed of cars and bicycles. Also, riders can maneuver their bicycles so quickly that they may surprise a driver.

Remember that many young bicycle riders are unskilled and uninformed about traffic problems. Others seem to dare car drivers to hit them. All are poorly protected and completely dependent upon the skill and courtesy of the motorist.

How to Protect the Bicyclist
1 Check the position and stability of the rider.
2 Adjust the speed of your car as necessary.
3 Check oncoming traffic, the traffic behind you, and your path around the bicycle.
4 Make it easy for other drivers to see the bicycle and adjust.
5 Tap your horn gently well in advance, when overtaking cyclists unaware of your presence. Avoid startling the rider.
6 Pass carefully when a safe opportunity arises.
7 Be sure to signal turns when in front of a cyclist. A right or left turn cuts across his path and could upset him.
8 Watch for cyclists when you open the street-side door. Also watch for them if you stop a few feet away from the curb and open the curbside door to let someone out. Often a door is flung open right in the face of a passing cyclist.
9 Watch at night or at dusk for cycles without lights or reflectors. Though these are required, you will always find some foolhardy riders without them.

1.   Outline a driver's procedure in approaching and passing a bicycle.

2.   Give at least five of the ways for a motorist to protect bicyclists. Why should the motorist protect them?

3.   Do traffic laws in your state apply to bicyclists? To motorcyclists? Why is this necessary?

Source: From *Let's Drive Right*, 5th edition by Maxwell Halsey, Richard Kaywood, and Richard A. Meyerhoff. Copyright © 1975 Scott, Foresman and Company. Reprinted by permission.

*Figure 11.5   Third-Person Writing Style
in a Driver Education Text*[7]

OUNCES OF ALCOHOL	BLOOD-ALCOHOL CONCENTRATION	DRIVING SYMPTOM
 (1 oz.)	.02	Bad driving habits appear
 to (2-3 oz.)	.05	Takes risks—loss of skill
 to (5-6 oz.)	.10	Physical and mental ability impaired —legally "under the influence"
 to (7-8 oz.)	.15	All physical and mental skills affected —unmistakably drunk
 to	.40	At this stage, most drivers have passed out

The relationship of blood-alcohol content to driving.

Even at low blood-alcohol levels, one's ability to make driving judgments such as, "Shall I pass or not?" or "Shall I drive or not?" is impaired. In fact, one may feel more confident than normal in making these decisions. This false confidence makes consumption of more than one drink per hour a risky undertaking.

There is evidence to indicate that recently acquired judgments and knowledge are the first to be affected by alcohol. Given two persons with equal tolerance to alcohol, the driving of the one with the least amount of driving experience will be more affected than the driving of the more experienced one.

Intermediate Effects of Alcohol

Five drinks in the span of one hour bring the average individual to a blood-alcohol level of about .10 percent. Eight drinks will bring him to a blood-alcohol level of about .16 percent. At .16 percent many drinkers become dazed and dizzy. At .20 percent one's frontal vision is shortened by approximately 30 percent, speech is slurred, and hearing becomes affected. It is dangerous to drive a car when one is in the .05 and above percent blood-alcohol range.

Advanced Effects of Alcohol

In the .25 to .40 percent blood-alcohol level range, physical control is largely lost. Speech and hearing are seriously affected. Some persons become unconscious in this range. A level of .50 percent could be lethal, but death also can occur at lower levels.

Source: Duane R. Johnson and Joseph G. Pawlowski, *Tomorrow's Drivers*, pp. 39–40. Copyright © 1974 by Houghton Mifflin Company. Used by permission.

tion, tolerance, and *intermediate effects* are some of the terms that might need clarification. At any rate, driver education instructors should become familiar with the vocabulary strategies discussed in Chapter 5.

Figure 11.5 is similar to the kinds of reading tasks asked often in science and social studies (see Chapters 7 and 8). Students should be led to read the first two paragraphs as "stage-setters" for the *evidence* to be presented. They should be helped to make use of subheadings, graphics, and captions to add to and reinforce what they are reading in the running text. Particularly at the beginning of a course and/or when introducing a new chapter or unit in the text, instructors should spend time in helping the students practice the kind of study that makes use of all the aids available. Students who are made conscious of the aids and who are given directed guidance in using them usually become better readers.

HEALTH

Textbooks concerned with health vary considerably. Texts and other instructional materials designed for seventh and eighth grades tend to be less "fact-packed" than those slated for the senior high school. Some materials are almost completely written in the second person (often easier reading for the poorer reader), whereas others emphasize factual reading written in the third person. Most vary in level of difficulty. A readability formula executed on a senior high health textbook must include a multitude of samples to result in any type of fair "readability" estimate.

Strategies.   Examples from health texts follow in Figures 11.6 and 11.7. The example in Figure 11.6 is from a seventh-grade text and deals with a common topic, pollution—in this case, air pollution. In order to cope with this material, the reader must become accustomed to paragraphs that present explanations and also raise unanswered questions—questions to be answered in the reader's mind. Although the pattern seems simple, it is difficult to get used to. The reader must be sure he or she understands the facts clearly before dealing with the question(s). The questions are useful as devices to help the reader apply knowledge accumulated through this particular reading as well as through other life experiences. The instructor may want to incorporate writing into the lesson by having the student select one of the questions as the topic for a written paragraph.

Students should also be taught how to read the graphics. The photograph and its caption simply add to the overall concept, but the chart adds very specific information. Students should be helped to "read" the chart by using it to write answers to such specific questions as: "What are the two major sources of all air pollution?" "What are the parts of polluted air?"

In Figure 11.7, students should be directed to use the heading—a question—to find the answers. Students can use the question as the introduction to a paragraph they write that goes on to answer the question. The instructor, however, will want to raise some additional questions after viewing the students' paragraphs. It may, for instance, be necessary to clarify the difference between *carcinogens* and *cocarcinogens* or to explain *why* carbon monoxide is the most dangerous gas in cigarette smoke or *how* dangerous nicotine is. This type of study interaction—combining student responsibility for individually answering with questions to the group—will result in increased understanding.

The instructor will want to spend some time with the graphic to help students understand its importance. It is clearly more important for its overall impression than for the details. Students need assistance in making such discriminations with graphics.

HOME ECONOMICS

Although a major part of the work in home economics consists of laboratory activities, reading assignments are frequently made in texts and other materials. Poor readers who turn to home economics as a shelter from other areas, where reading is more prevalent, are often shocked when they are confronted with difficult reading assignments. Home economics teachers need to be careful about the worksheets they design, for condensed explanations and directions frequently cause problems for poor and inaccurate readers. Textbooks in this area, in general, do not provide glossaries or much contextual aid for figuring out both technical and nontechnical terms.

In addition, home economics teachers should encourage and guide carefully any type of written assignment—even responses on worksheets. Students need to be taught how to write in the patterns of home economics; English teachers do not know enough about the discipline to accomplish the job. And, in fact, the very writing of recipes and other directions reinforces learning; the writing of coordinated paragraphs stimulates organization, which will, indeed, carry over into expertise in home economics.

Examples. As in a number of other content areas, writing style varies from easy to complex and, at times, from third to second person. Sometimes the pattern is explanation of a concept, as in Example 11.2, or of a specific object, as in Example 11.3. Frequently the pattern consists of suggestions or things to do, as in Example 11.4.

Other writing styles common in home economics are seen in recipes and directions on packaged mixes. Thomas and Robinson provide explicit examples of these, along with strategies for coping with them.[13]

Strategies. In Example 11.2, the heading that names the topic was printed in violet in the original text and hence stood out. Topic headings appear to be prevalent in home economics materials; therefore, the reader needs to be trained to be wary of merely looking for supporting information. In reality, the headings

Figure 11.6   Writing Pattern in a Health Text[8]

Smog-filled San Francisco. An inversion layer created a tight lid of air that prevented smoke and polluting fumes in the downtown area from escaping. The Bettman Archive, Inc.

Air Pollution

Another resource which is affected by man's increasing population and progress is air. *Air pollution* is one of the most noticeable problems affecting the environment today. In what ways, do you think, is air pollution affecting man and other living things?

of topics seem to function mainly as separators of one section from another, not as carriers of the essential message. For instance, the major message in Example 11.2 is that *the body does not store vitamin C for long; hence, we need to have a source of vitamin C daily.*

On the other hand, in Example 11.3 the heading "*Modacrylics*" serves its purpose as a clustering point for all the information about it. The good reader can easily cope with both types of headings once he or she is made aware

Generally, air pollution comes about because of the need to make and operate more things for more people. To make more electricity, to heat more houses, and to operate more motor vehicles, more fuels must be burned. These fuels include coal, natural gas, oil, and gasoline. The burning of such fuels causes harmful chemicals to enter the air. What other causes of air pollution can you think of? Why, do you think, has man allowed the air-pollution problem to come about? What, do you think, are some things that might be done to help prevent and control air pollution?

Parts of Polluted Air and Some of Their Sources

Parts	Sources
Carbon monoxide	Motor vehicles (cars, trucks, buses, planes, etc.) and power plants and other industries that burn fuels
Sulfur oxides	Power plants and other industries
Hydrocarbons	Motor vehicles and power plants and other industries
Nitrogen oxides	Motor vehicles and power plants and other industries
Particulates (soot, dust, ashes, etc.)	Power plants and other industries, motor vehicles, and refuse burning

Source: John T. Fodor and others, *A Healthier You* (River Forest, Ill.: Laidlaw Brothers, 1980), pp. 191–92.

of the differences through guided practice. The poor reader will need more of the teacher's attention, however, for both. Examples 11.2 and 11.3 contain a number of terms, technical and nontechnical, that are unexplained and may be unknown—*adrenal glands, adrenal cortex, secrete, hormones, cholesterol, saturated, compounds,* and *affinity,* to name a few. Much of the information in Chapters 7 and 8 of this volume should be applied to these kinds of reading-study assignments in home economics.

Figure 11.7   Studying a Text and a Graphic in a Health Course[9]

WHAT DOES CIGARETTE SMOKE CONTAIN?

Smoke formed by a burning cigarette contains more than five hundred different materials. Many of these are known *carcinogens*; that is, they cause cancer. Others are *cocarcinogens*. This means they may be harmless in themselves, but they help to increase the harmful effects of carcinogens.

More than 90 percent of cigarette smoke is made up of twelve gases that are known to be health hazards. The most dangerous gas in cigarette smoke is carbon monoxide. In the body, carbon monoxide takes the place of some of the oxygen in the blood. The heart must work harder to circulate blood so that all body tissues get the necessary amounts of oxygen.

Cigarette smoke also contains nicotine, the material that causes an intense desire to smoke. Nicotine is a stimulant. Cigarette smoking causes blood pressure to go up and heart rate to increase. Taken in large doses, nicotine can be poisonous. For example, 60 milligrams of nicotine taken all at once will cause the respiratory system to stop working. Death could occur. This is the amount of nicotine a person would receive by smoking twenty cigarettes all at once.

When the particles in cigarette smoke are cooled, they form a brown, sticky material called *tar*. The majority of known carcinogens in cigarette smoke are found in tar. Tar builds up in the body, along the air passages leading to the lungs and in the lungs themselves. A pack-a-day smoker inhales about one full cup of tar each year.

Source: Marion B. Pollock, Candace O. Purdy, and Charles R. Carroll, *Health: A Way of Life* (Glenview, Ill.: Scott, Foresman, 1979), p. 232.

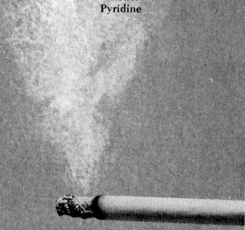

Compounds judged most likely to contribute to health hazards of smoking

Carbon monoxide
Nicotine
Tar

Compounds judged as probable or suspected contributors to health hazards of smoking

Acetaldehyde
Acetone
Acetonitrile
Acrolein
Acrylonitrile
Ammonia
Benzene
2,3-Butadione Butylamine
Carbon dioxide
Cresol (all isomers)
Crotononitrile
Dimethylamine
DDT
Endrin
Ethylamine
Formaldehyde
Furfural
Hydrocyanic acid
Hydrogen sulphide
Hydroquinone
Methacrolein
Methyl alcohol
Methylamine
Nickel compounds
Nitric oxide
Nitrogen dioxide
Phenol
Pyridine

Some of the harmful materials that have been identified in cigarette smoke are shown here. They include nicotine, a liquid used as the poison in insecticide sprays; hydrogen cyanide, a poisonous gas; formaldehyde, used as a strong disinfectant and a preservative; ammonia, a strong-smelling gas; and carbon monoxide, a poisonous gas also found in automobile exhaust.

BODY STORAGE OF VITAMIN C

Example 11.2   The reserves of vitamin C stored in the body are quite small. The largest amount is stored in the adrenal glands. When these glands (the adrenal cortex) secrete hormones, there is a sharp lowering of vitamin C and cholesterol in them. Smaller amounts are stored in the brain, the liver, and other glands and organs, and in the hemoglobin of the red blood corpuscles.

Vitamin C is absorbed from the small intestines and circulates to every tissue, so that each cell can use it to make the collagen that helps hold cells firmly together. When the body tissues and reserve depots are saturated, the excess is at once excreted in the urine as water and through the lungs as carbon dioxide. One cannot get too much vitamin C. The excess you eat at breakfast is disposed of before lunch (in less than four hours).

This is the basis for the recommendation that we have a source of vitamin C daily. Even better, distribute the foods that contain this nutrient among all three meals in the day.

You can understand, then, why breakfast skippers are likely to have a day's diet that is too low in vitamin C. Though we still have much to learn about this vitamin, we know enough now to improve the quality of life.[10]

Modacrylics

Example 11.3   Modacrylic fibers have many of the characteristics of acrylics, but they are a combination of acrylonitrile and one or more vinyl compounds. Modacrylic fabrics melt at fairly low temperatures, but they do not readily support a flame. Their affinity for dyes varies, and some fabrics tend to mat and pill more than others. Modacrylics are used mainly in fur-like fabrics for outer garmets.[11]

Example 11.4   *Washing time* is also important. Washing time for cottons and linens (ordinary sheets, tablecloths, etc.) is eight to ten minutes unless the clothes are badly soiled, then an additional five minutes may be necessary.

Delicate fabrics should not be washed for more than three minutes, and *woolens never more than a minute or two after a ten-minute soaking in suds.* The rinse water must be the right temperature for woolens and the period of agitation cut to a minimum.

A *fabric conditioner* may be used on synthetic and wash-and-wear fabrics, and a *chlorine bleach* may be used on white cottons and linens that do not have special finishes. *Never use chlorine bleach on silk or wool.*[12]

Although Example 11.4 contains some difficult terms, it is constructed for easy reading. A few students might have trouble with the sentences that contain more than one admonition; if so, they should read one part of the sentence at a time orally and explain its meaning. The italics make it clear that this writer is emphasizing specific points.

INDUSTRIAL
ARTS

Unfortunately, much of the reading in industrial arts is complex. Explanations of concepts, formulas, and procedures are frequently hard to follow, and little attempt seems to have been made to define technical and difficult nontechnical words in any consistent manner. One has to be an able abstract thinker to contend with books on design drafting, and even following directions in basic shop manuals seems complex.

Some industrial arts instructors do not use textbooks even for reference because of the high readability levels. On the other hand, avoidance of this kind of reading may seriously handicap students who want to pursue vocations in these areas. One method used by instructors is to organize worksheets, but even these must be very carefully constructed, keeping in mind the reading abilities of the group. Industrial arts teachers need to guide students in the reading of worksheets as well as in the reading of textbooks and related materials. Time spent in readiness procedures and vocabulary development (Chapters 4 and 5) are particularly significant in helping students cope with complex, but often necessary, reading materials.

Examples.   The first two examples are taken from a junior high school textbook on basic electricity. The third is from a senior high text on drawing and planning. Note that although the excerpt in Example 11.5 is by no means simple reading, it is elementary in contrast to Example 11.6 (from the same text).

The authors of the book from which Figure 11.8 was taken have attempted

Example 11.5

Atomic energy can be used to generate electricity. In the atomic power plant the atomic reactor produces a tremendous amount of heat, resulting from the fissioning atoms of the nuclear fuel. This heat, as in the conventional thermal power plant, is used to change water to steam to rotate steam turbines, which, in turn, rotate the electric generators. Here, too, scientists are seeking ways to bypass the wasteful heat cycle by transforming atomic energy directly to electrical energy.[14]

*Figure 11.8   Studying a Text in an Industrial
             Arts Course*[16]

Section 1: Unit 14

**MAKING A WORKING DRAWING WITH
TWO VIEWS**

What would a working drawing of a rolling
pin look like? Fig. 14–1. If you used three
views what would you see? Yes, the front view
and the top view would be exactly alike. Often
it is not necessary to have three views for a
good working drawing. This is almost always
true of cylindrical shapes. Fig. 14–2. Many
other objects can be drawn to show all needed
information with only two views.

Points to Remember

1.   Always make the most distinctive
view the front view. For example, suppose
you are making a working drawing of the top
of a footstool or small table. Fig. 14-3. You
need only two views—one to show its shape
and one to show the thickness. Fig. 14-4.
Since the circular shape is the most important, this should be made the front view.

2.   Draw a top or side view, whichever
is best, as the second view. Fig. 14-4. Sometimes it is more convenient to use the top
view and sometimes the side view is best.

3.   Whenever possible use only two
views even though three could be drawn. It
is often a waste of effort and space to show
the third view. This is especially true of wood-
working drawings. For example, nothing new
could be learned by making a side view of this
small wall shelf. Fig. 14-5. All the information you need for making it is shown on the
front and top views.

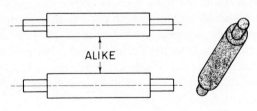

14–1.   *Two views of this rolling pin are alike. A
two-view drawing, then, is all that is
needed.*

14–2.   *A cookie jar like this would require only
two views. With a note, only one would
be necessary.*

Source: John L. Feirer, *Drawing and Planning,* 3rd ed., revised by John R. Lindbeck
(Peoria, Ill.: Chas. A. Bennett, 1975), pp. 99–100.

Example 11.6   The value of the *R-C* **time constant** may be calculated from the following formula:

$$t = C \times R,$$

where **t** is the time in seconds, *C* is the capacitance in farads, and *R* is the resistance in ohms.

Example

What would be the *R-C* time constant of a series circuit containing a 0.001-microfarad capacitor and a resistor of 50,000 ohms?

$$t \text{ (seconds)} = 0.000,000,001 \text{ farad} \times 50,000 \text{ ohms,}$$
$$t = 0.000,05 \text{ second, or } 50 \text{ microseconds.}$$

Answer

The *R-C* time constant is employed in many electronic applications where a very small, accurate time interval is desired. The proper interval is obtained by using appropriate resistors and capacitors.[15]

---

to write as simply as possible; nevertheless, much guidance is necessary if accurate execution is desired.

Strategies.   Although Example 11.5 contains many terms that some readers will find difficult, it is well organized and typical of a small portion of the writing found in the instructional materials used in industrial arts classes. It begins with a generalization and then contributes supporting evidence. Students should be guided to look for such generalizations and then for the facts subsumed under it. The pattern is used not only with paragraphs but with series of paragraphs, as exemplified by writing patterns in many other content areas. (See pages 151–172 and 184–202 for examples.)

Example 11.6 poses a real threat for some readers. When this type of reading is first met, instructors should provide much time to help students develop study approaches. Some of the suggestions cited on pages 260–265 will be useful. The following study steps have been helpful for a number of industrial arts students: (1) read the entire passage for the general idea; (2) reread the formula and the explanation of it; (3) reread the example; and (4) reread the entire passage.

Step One: Read the Entire Passage for the General Idea.   The first reading of such technical material should be for the purpose of "viewing the forest before noting the individual trees." The survey will help students focus on the components of the passage and the way the passage is organized. The job seems a little less formidable when the reader sees that there is first a formula and then an example that clarifies and makes the formula useful. The reader also realizes what the general idea of the passage is, especially when (as in the examples) attention is focused on the generalization or conclusion at the end of the passage. Many readers need teacher guidance with this step before they can make it on their own.

Step Two: Reread the Formula and the Explanation of It.   At this time readers should concentrate only on understanding what the formula says. They should be sure that they can figure out the formula through the explanation. Again, with some formulas direction by the instructor might be essential for some readers.

Step Three: Reread the Example.   This rereading should be for the express purpose of being sure that the example makes sense as an illustration of the formula. It can also help in clarifying any hazy notions about the formula.

Step Four: Reread the Entire Passage.   To clarify any uncertainties and/ or to check understanding, it is wise to reread the total passage. The readers should be certain that they comprehend the formula, the example and its answer, and the generalization or conclusion at the end of the passage.

In Figure 11.9, the student must be careful not to jump to the *figures* without carefully reading the text. Students must learn to interrelate text reading with the reading of the figures. (See further suggestions for this in Chapter 8, pages 179–181.) A useful technique is to have students write—as much as possible in their own words—the drawing steps they need to follow. Having them then execute their own drawings is, of course, the final step. Instructors should help students with some of the technical vocabulary and should probably make the assignment more specific for their particular students.

RELATED ACTIVITIES

1.   In general business courses, in reading laboratories and reading classrooms, as well as in other content area classrooms, students should have the opportunity to read and fill out the multitude of forms that are likely to besiege them. Such important communication materials belong in the school as important reading-writing activities; coping with them should not be left to chance. Students can role play at times if it helps them to better face the task when it actually confronts them. For example, if a credit account application is brought to class, students can work in teams. One student can be the person representing the store, and the other student can be the person applying for a credit card. The store representative should attempt to help the applicant fill out the form. When both are confused, the instructor should be available as consultant. If the form is so confusing that all have trouble, the students should be actively encouraged to contact the store and suggest specific simplifications.

*Figure 11.9   Reading Figures in an Industrial
             Arts Course*

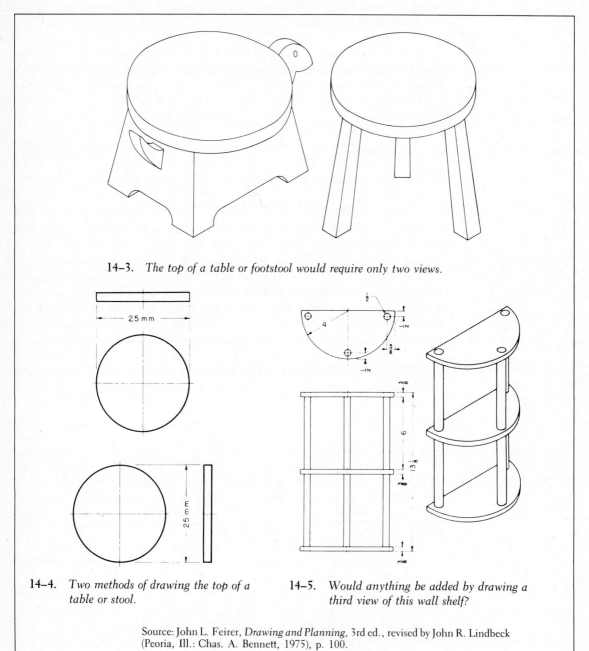

14–3.   *The top of a table or footstool would require only two views.*

14–4.   *Two methods of drawing the top of a table or stool.*

14–5.   *Would anything be added by drawing a third view of this wall shelf?*

Source: John L. Feirer, *Drawing and Planning*, 3rd ed., revised by John R. Lindbeck (Peoria, Ill.: Chas. A. Bennett, 1975), p. 100.

2.   The seven steps suggested for reading bookkeeping and accounting texts should be practiced with a common passage and graphic to begin with. Some students find initial success if the passage is short and reproduced on a worksheet. Once the group has worked together on the procedure and questions have been ironed out, try letting individual students work on passages themselves, moving through the six steps at their own pace. Be sure, though, to provide suitable problems for steps five and six. The problems must fit the explanation in the reading and not introduce other concepts—old or new.

3.   Show the chart in Figure 11.5 on a screen, using an opaque projector, and have students learn how to read a chart. First, have them read the caption and discuss it in relation to what they should expect to find in the chart itself. Second, have them read each heading and relate the information to the caption. Third, have them overview the chart in order to realize that columns one and two present information from smallest to largest amounts. In doing this the students will, of course, also realize the relationship between the two columns. Fourth, have them read each horizontal line across the three columns to get all the basic information. Fifth, have them summarize the information gained.

4.   Apply steps one through four on pages 290–291 suggested for certain kinds of reading in industrial arts to material facing the students. Take each step slowly and be sure to get feedback from students for each step. For example, after completing step two, students should be able to explain the formula to you so it is letter clear; if it is not, they need to repeat step two—sometimes with your help.

SELECTED READINGS

ART

Erickson, Robert D. "The Art Room Collection." In *Fusing Reading Skills and Content*, edited by H. Alan Robinson and Ellen Lamar Thomas, pp. 89–96. Newark, Del.: International Reading Association, 1969.

————, and Ellen Lamar Thomas. "Art Class Book Collection Promotes Better Reading." *Journal of Reading* 12 (February 1968):333–36.

Thomas, Ellen L., and H. Alan Robinson. *Improving Reading in Every Class*, 3rd ed., unabridged, ch. 17. Boston: Allyn and Bacon, 1982.

BUSINESS EDUCATION

Ahrendt, Kenneth M., and Shirley S. Haselton. "Essential Reading Skills in Bookkeeping." *Journal of Reading* 16 (January 1973):314–17.

Carter, R. Carlos, and Doris Dingle. "Coping with the Language Arts Dilemma," *Journal of Business Education* 55 (October 1979):8–15.

Haehn, Faynelle. "Let's Have a 'Read-In' in Typewriting." In *Fusing Reading Skills and Content,* edited by H. Alan Robinson and Ellen Lamar Thomas, pp. 69–74. Newark, Del.: International Reading Association, 1969.

Harrison, Lincoln J. "Teaching Accounting Students How to Read." *Journal of Business Education* 35 (January 1960):169–70.

Holder, Birdie M. "Vary Writing Instruction with Group Writing Format." *Business Education Forum* 33 (January 1979):22–24.

House, Forest W. "Are You Solving the Reading Problems in Bookkeeping?" *Business Education World* 33 (February 1953):291–92.

Hulbert, Jack E. "Effective Business Writing." *Business Education Forum* 34 (February 1980):20–24.

Lynch, David. "Help Your Students to Express Ideas More Concretely." *Business Education Forum* 34 (April 1980):17–19.

Musselman, Vernon A. "The Reading Problem in Teaching Bookkeeping." *Business Education Forum* 14 (December 1959):5–7.

Robinson, Richard D.; John Carter; and Don B. Hokanson. "Business Teachers Are Reading Teachers." *Journal of Business Education* 44 (February 1969):201–2.

Schultheis, Robert A., and Kay Napoli. "Strategies for Helping Poor Readers in Business Subjects." *Business Education Forum* 30 (November 1975):5–13.

Shepherd, David F. *Comprehensive High School Reading Methods,* pp. 305–20. Columbus, Ohio: Charles E. Merrill, 1978.

Sumner, Mary. "Teaching Reading Skills in Business Classes." *Business Education Forum* 34 (December 1979):20–22.

Thomas, Ellen Lamar, and H. Alan Robinson. *Improving Reading in Every Class,* 3rd ed., ch. 13. Boston: Allyn and Bacon, 1982.

Todd, Mavis M. "Learning to Write for the Reader." *Business Education Forum* 34 (May 1980):17–18.

Wood, Jerry L. "Reading and Typewriting." *Journal of Business Education* 40 (December 1964):109–11.

FOREIGN LANGUAGES

Bialystok, Ellen. "The Role of Conscious Strategies in Second Language Proficiency." *Modern Language Journal* 65 (Spring 1981):36–42.

Cooper, Thomas C. "Sentence Combining: An Experiment in Teaching Writing." *Modern Language Journal* 65 (Summer 1981):158–65.

Duncan, Helen M. "Reading a Foreign Language." *Modern Language Journal* 45 (January 1961):17–19.

Finstein, Milton. "Reading Skills and French." In *Fusing Reading Skills and Content,* edited by H. Alan Robinson and Ellen Lamar Thomas, pp. 67–68. Newark, Del.: International Reading Association, 1969.

Hendrickson, James M. "The Treatment of Error in Written Work." *Modern Language Journal* 64 (1980):216–21.

Preston, Ralph C. "Give the Student Tips on How to Get the Most from Foreign Language Books." In *Improving Reading in Secondary Schools: Selected Readings,* edited by Lawrence E. Hafner, pp. 401–3. New York: Macmillan, 1967.

Reiss, Mary-Ann. "Helping the Unsuccessful Language Learner." *Modern Language Journal* 65 (Summer 1981):121–28.

Sacks, Norman P. "Some Aspects of the Application of Linguistics to the Teaching of Modern Foreign Language." *Modern Language Journal* 48 (January 1964):7–17.

Schulz, Renate A. "Literature and Readability: Bridging the Gap in Foreign Language Reading." *Modern Language Journal* 65 (Spring 1981):43–53.

Seibert, Louise C., and Lester G. Crocker. *Skills and Techniques for Reading French*. Baltimore: Johns Hopkins Press, 1958.

Strang, Ruth, and Dorothy Kendall Bracken. *Making Better Readers*, pp. 256–62. Boston: D.C. Heath, 1957.

Strang, Ruth; Constance M. McCullough; and Arthur E. Traxler. *The Improvement of Reading*, 4th ed., pp. 365–69. New York: McGraw-Hill, 1967.

MUSIC

Shepherd, David F. *Comprehensive High School Reading Methods*, pp. 345–48. Columbus, Ohio: Charles E. Merrill, 1978.

Strang, Ruth, and Dorothy Kendall Bracken. *Making Better Readers*, pp. 267–71. Boston: D.C. Heath, 1957.

Strang, Ruth; Constance M. McCullough; and Arthur E. Traxler. *The Improvement of Reading*, 4th ed., pp. 375–77. New York: McGraw-Hill, 1967.

Thomas, Ellen Lamar, and H. Alan Robinson. *Improving Reading in Every Class*, 3rd ed., unabridged, ch. 16. Boston: Allyn and Bacon, 1982.

Tirro, Frank. "Reading Techniques in the Teaching of Music." In *Fusing Reading Skills and Content*, edited by H. Alan Robinson and Ellen Lamar Thomas, pp. 103–7. Boston: Allyn and Bacon, 1969.

Wulffson, Don L. "Music to Teach Reading." *Journal of Reading* 14 (December 1970):179–82.

PHYSICAL EDUCATION

Maring, Gerald H., and Robert Ritson. "Reading Improvement in the Gymnasium." *Journal of Reading* 24 (October 1980):27–31.

Metcalf, James. "Teaching Writing in Physical Education." *Journal of Physical Education and Recreation* 50 (1979):38.

Patlak, Sanford. "Physical Education and Reading: Questions and Answers," *Fusing Reading Skills and Content*, edited by H. Alan Robinson and Ellen Lamar Thomas, pp. 81–88, 201–4. Newark, Del.: International Reading Association, 1969.

Strang, Ruth, and Dorothy Kendall Bracken. *Making Better Readers*, pp. 278–79. Boston: D.C. Heath, 1957.

Thomas, Ellen Lamar. "Books Are the Greatest." *Journal of Reading*, 12 (November 1968):119–24.

————, and H. Alan Robinson. *Improving Reading in Every Class*, 3rd ed., ch. 18; (abridged ed., ch. 15). Boston: Allyn and Bacon, 1982.

Turner, Bud. "PE Journal." *Journal of Physical Education and Recreation* 48 (1977):56–57.

VOCATIONAL EDUCATION

Carney, John J., and William Losinger. "Reading and Content in Technical-Vocational Education." *Journal of Reading* 20 (October 1976):14–17.

Ciani, Alfred J., and Donald E. Hogue. "How to Help Industrial Arts Students with Reading." *Industrial Education* 65 (October 1976):32–33.

Conroy, Michael T. "Questions to Ask About a Textbook for Students with Reading Difficulties." *Industrial Education* 69 (February 1980):21–23.

————. "Reading and Following Printed Directions." *Industrial Education* 69 (March 1980):24–28.

Derby, Thomas L. "Informal Testing in Vo-Ed Reading." *Journal of Reading* 18 (April 1975):541–43.

Ferrerio, Anthony J. "Try Industrial Arts and Vocational Education for Retarded Readers." *Industrial Arts and Vocational Education* 49 (February 1960):19–20.

Frederick, E. Coston. "Reading and Vocational Education." In *Fusing Reading Skills and Content*, edited by H. Alan Robinson and Ellen Lamar Thomas, pp. 145–50. Newark, Del.: International Reading Association, 1969.

Incardone, Peter. "Help! I Can't Read." *VocEd* 53 (December 1978):51–52.

Johnston, Joyce D. "The Reading Teacher in the Vocational Classroom." *Journal of Reading* 18 (October 1974):27–29.

Levine, Isidore N. "Solving Reading Problems in Vocational Subjects." *High Points* 12 (April 1960):10–27.

Luparelli, Augustus N. "A Reading Program for Vocational Classes." *VocEd* 56 (June 1981):31–32.

Mangieri, John N. "We Can Help Students with Poor Reading Skills." *Industrial Education* 61 (November 1972):45–46.

Nieratka, Ernest; Irene Peachy; and Ed Ryne. "Reading and the Vocational Student." *Industrial Education* 64 (October 1975):26, 28.

Pearson, Herbert, and Ellen L. Thomas. "If Your Classes Have Trouble Reading Instructions . . ." *Industrial Education* 63 (October 1974):22–23.

Sanacore, Joseph. "Effective Use of the Industrial Arts Textbook." *Man/Society/Technology* 35 (May/June 1975):264–65.

Shepherd, David L. *Comprehensive High School Reading Methods*, pp. 321–40. Columbus, Ohio: Charles E. Merrill, 1978.

Strang, Ruth, and Dorothy Kendall Bracken. *Making Better Readers*, pp. 271–78. Boston: D.C. Heath, 1957.

Strang, Ruth; Constance M. McCullough; and Arthur E. Traxler. *The Improvement of Reading*, 4th ed., pp. 369–75. New York: McGraw-Hill, 1967.

Szymkowicz, Dorothy. "Home Economics and Reading." In *Fusing Reading Skills and Content*, edited by H. Alan Robinson and Ellen Lamar Thomas, pp. 62–66. Newark, Del.: International Reading Association, 1969.

Thomas, Ellen Lamar, and H. Alan Robinson. *Improving Reading in Every Class*, 3rd ed., ch. 12. Boston: Allyn and Bacon, 1982.

Wilson, Mildred. "Teaching Reading in Home Economics." *Pennsylvania School Journal* 121 (September 1972):22–23, 59.

Young, Edith M., and Leo V. Rodenborn. "Improving Communication Skills in Vocational Courses." *Journal of Reading* 19 (February 1976):373–77.

NOTES

1. Gerald H. Maring and Robert Ritson, "Reading Improvement in the Gymnasium," *Journal of Reading* 24 (October 1980):27–31.
2. Hobart H. Conover, B. Bertha Wakin, and Helene L. Zimmerman, *General Business for Today's World* (Boston: Allyn and Bacon, 1977), pp. 265–66.
3. Courtesy of Sears, Roebuck and Co.
4. Robert M. Swanson and others, *Century 21 Accounting* (Cincinnati, Ohio: South-Western, 1977), pp. 429–30.
5. From *Business Law* by George Getz, 4th ed., p. 246; © 1972 by Prentice-Hall, Inc., Englewood Cliffs, N.J.
6. Maxwell Halsey, Richard Kaywood, and Richard A. Meyerhoff, *Let's Drive Right*, 5th ed. (Glenview, Ill.: Scott, Foresman, 1975), p. 151.
7. Duane R. Johnson and Joseph G. Pawlowski, *Tomorrow's Drivers* (Chicago: Rand McNally, 1974), pp. 39–40.
8. John T. Fodor and others, *A Healthier You* (River Forest, Ill.: Laidlaw Brothers, 1980), pp. 191–92.
9. Marion B. Pollock, Candace O. Purdy, and Charles R. Carroll, *Health: A Way of Life* (Glenview, Ill.: Scott, Foresman, 1979), p. 232.
10. Ruth Bennett White, *Food and Your Future* (Englewood Cliffs, N.J.: Prentice-Hall, 1972), p. 129.
11. Hazel Thompson Craig, *Clothing: A Comprehensive Study* (Philadelphia: J.B. Lippincott, 1973), p. 254.
12. Ibid., p. 281.
13. Ellen L. Thomas and H. Alan Robinson, *Improving Reading in Every Classroom*, 3rd ed. (Boston: Allyn and Bacon, 1982), ch. 14.
14. Abraham Marcus, *Basic Electricity*, 3rd ed. (Englewood Cliffs, N.J.: Prentice-Hall, 1969), p. 286.
15. Ibid., p. 179.
16. John L. Feirer, *Drawing and Planning*, 3rd ed., revised by John R. Lindbeck, (Peoria, Ill.: Chas. A. Bennett, 1975), pp. 99–100.

Part D
EPILOGUE

Chapter 12, "Lifetime Readers and Writers," focuses on a goal or product but also emphasizes process. Probably no one would disagree that the outcome of instruction should be utilization of what has been learned. Without citizens who can read and write in order to make decisions, weigh arguments, solve problems, and use leisure time intelligently, a nation is in trouble. In Chapter 12, total school involvement is stressed as the broad means of helping students become lifetime readers and writers. In addition, specific techniques and suggestions are offered to accomplish such a goal. These techniques and suggestions are applicable in any classroom.

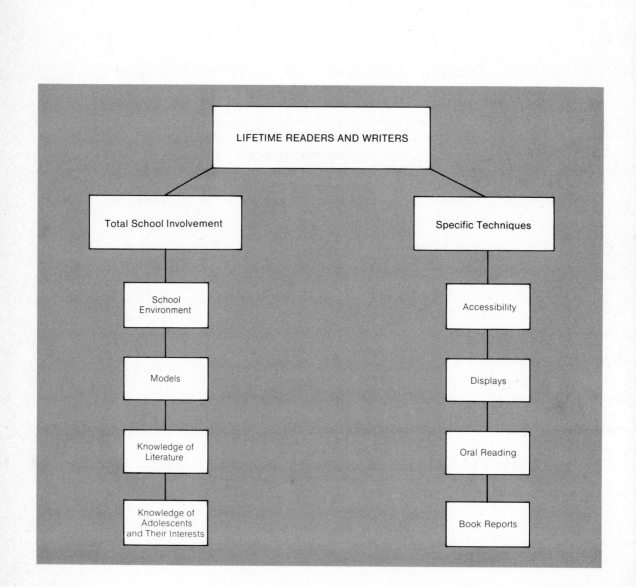

12
Lifetime Readers and Writers

Reading-writing programs fail if strategies are learned but only put to use when forced upon learners by external pressures. A secondary school that graduates a high percentage of able readers and writers should also be graduating "turned-on" readers and skilled writers. Such goals are not impossible if the faculty is composed of committed readers and writers. The graduates will be grateful all their lives!

Granted that the form of reading materials may change and is changing—we may be able to sit at home and punch a button that will permit us to read and view material of our choosing on a television screen. Granted that micro-computers will provide miscellaneous and relatively inexpensive ways of composing and reading. Granted that a library collection may be contained in a small box of microfiche. But, in one way or another, the need and desire to read and to write will continue, albeit in new forms.

There seems little question that reading and writing are vital parts of everyone's daily life—driving, shopping, using consumer products, filling out a variety of forms, and so on. They can also be vital parts of life for helping to find out how-to-make it, how-to-play it, and how-to-learn about it. These are important tasks students need to accomplish. Teachers should be assisting students to learn to use reading and writing for these purposes.

Instructors should also be guiding students to make use of various other media to satisfy these informational tasks. Although the other media are valuable, most students, once presented with many opportunities to search for information needed for specific tasks, turn back to reading for its flexibility. That is, students can turn to the reading at will. They can reread. They can undertake the reading in a variety of places, for books are easily transported.

The same advantages accrue to readers who become infatuated with reading for pure enjoyment, for escape, for learning more of the world around them, and for enjoying language. These are the readers we teachers hope to develop. We have a chance of doing so if we recognize the need for turning to both kinds of independent reading—the essential and the delightful. As adults gain more and more leisure time, their need to read will increase rather than decrease. They will learn many other ways of utilizing and enjoying their leisure, but many will want to turn to the solitary, individual act of reading—of choosing their own paths into the world of yesterday, today, and tomorrow.

Unfortunately, only a small percentage of people who know how to read have turned to reading for edification and enjoyment beyond school-required reading assignments. Newspapers, and to some extent magazines, are read widely, even with competition from other media, but there are relatively few readers of books. Book sales have increased, but this is probably because lifetime readers are reading more books now than before rather than because the number of book readers has increased.

It seems essential that secondary school teachers turn their attention to the vital task of developing lifetime readers and writers. High school teachers often bemoan the fact that students do not turn to reading or writing, but the very teachers who moan, often precipitate the problem themselves through inactivity or very little activity in these areas.

Suggestions for the development of lifetime readers and writers follow.

TOTAL SCHOOL INVOLVEMENT

ENVIRONMENT FOR READING AND WRITING

Throughout its halls, rooms, and offices, a school building must reflect the importance of reading and writing in each person's life. Students and staff members should be able to find out about a new book, a new collection, or a new filmstrip. Students should be acquainted with various kinds of journals, with features of certain newspapers, and with new uses for old books. Students should be stimulated to watch bulletin boards for displayed compositions on interesting topics by fellow students. Correspondence between students in the school and either students in other lands or interesting characters in the community provides interest and motivation. Facsimiles of primary documents—particularly related to American history—interest students and also emphasize the importance of composition. Obviously one person cannot make a school building live and breathe reading and writing; displays, notices, and information ought to be coordinated by a central, but changing, committee of students, staff members, and parents.

Traditionally, the high school has been amazingly negligent in these vital areas. Faculties cannot continue to lament the fact that students do not turn to reading and writing when they themselves do not create the atmosphere that will make students want to do so. The secondary school principal must assume a key role in this team effort. If the principal will spearhead such activity (including serving on the coordinating committee), the school environment will become a reading-writing environment. Numerous principals do not realize how important it is for them to "get the ball rolling," to maintain active interest, and to praise the efforts of the personnel involved.

The school must also attempt to play a role in developing an environment for reading and writing within the home. Without doubt this is a more difficult task and in many instances a hopeless one. But junior and senior high schools, generally speaking, have made little effort in this direction. Parents need to be helped to learn that reading materials within the interest and achievement levels of their children ought to be easily accessible in the home and attractively displayed whenever possible. Parents ought to be helped to realize that Aunt Tillie's presents of soberly bound classics that sit on the shelf are not the books that will appeal to many of their youngsters. Parents ought to be helped to understand that in the home, just as in the school, a reading atmosphere is created only with effort, only by providing those reading materials that satisfy adolescent needs, questions, and interests. They need to be helped to learn that encouraging writing and praising the adequate-to-excellent writing of their teen-agers will stimulate further writing and provide their children with a gift of unmeasurable importance.

MODELS TO EMULATE

Too often we teachers talk and preach too much; we fall short as examples. Here is an area in which adolescents are searching for models, and too infrequently do they find them among their teachers or parents. All teachers must be readers and writers. They must be readers of literature above and beyond what has to be read to function in the role of teacher. There is no acceptable excuse for teachers "not having the time to read"; they must read. Indeed, if they expect students to use writing, they too must write and make their writing visible. The biology teacher is not only a specialist in biology; he or she is a teacher who shares equal responsibility with the English teacher and the French teacher for developing lifetime readers and writers. Here, too, is an area in which the physical education teacher should assume a vital role—getting students to realize that, although the physical education teacher does not teach reading or writing skills often, he or she is nevertheless very much interested in reading and writing and in helping students turn to these activities.

All teachers should carry to school each day the books they are currently reading for enjoyment or information. They should make these books visible to their students. Whenever they have an idle moment, they might try to do some of this kind of reading rather than, for example, grading papers. Probably they ought to plan periods of time in class when the students would see them turn to a book to finish a page or chapter. The teacher might sometimes share the book with students, just as they often expect students to share books with them. If a teacher has written a short story or poem, the composition—even in an early draft—can be shared with students. They are often good critics and can help improve drafts. Ideas for stories and essays should also be discussed with students. Students need to feel active interest in and enthusiasm for writing and reading, and the visible model is most important.

Whenever feasible, teachers ought to chat with parents about their being models to emulate. Too many parents "konk out" in front of the television set, happy to become passive after a hard day's work. The activity may be pleasant, but if they are concerned about their children's lifetime reading and writing habits, they ought to spend some time making their reading and writing activities visible to their offspring. They should share what they are reading and writing—not necessarily by means of a family reading circle, but through a variety of informal techniques, many of which teachers could discuss with parents. At PTA meetings and in school visits, more time spent on techniques of developing lifetime readers and writers will pay greater dividends in the long run than some of the topics now handled.

KNOWLEDGE OF LITERATURE

Simmons, Shafer, and West pointed out that adolescents "exhibit low interest in topics such as didacticism, moral-religious themes, community life, and literary form—to mention only a few."[1] They emphasized teacher enthusiasm as an important factor in promoting adult themes but suggested that teachers "should have some background in popular literature for adolescents . . . ."[2]

> Most well-written works on the teenage situation focus on one meaningful factor: the *process of becoming.* The concept of initiation into adulthood can be found in literary works of all genres, from various eras, and on all levels of subtlety. Teachers would do well to keep abreast of books that portray the adolescent situation. They can provide an effective mirror through which early adolescents can view themselves while taking their initial look at literary selections.[3]

All teachers need to be familiar with the adolescent and adult literature related to their particular fields and, when possible, with contemporary literature on an even broader base. If students are to become lifetime readers, it is most important to have persons whom they respect available to guide them in selection. The teacher who is well read in terms of adult literature should also be acquainted with adolescent literature: transitional and junior novels, magazines for adolescents, and expository and biographical books written particularly for junior and senior high school students. Knowledge of such literature and efforts to chat with adolescents about their literature will very often be a potent force in the development of lifetime readers.

If at all possible, secondary school teachers ought to take a course in adolescent literature if they have not taken one in the past ten years. The books available today are plentiful and often magnificent. Although teachers will want to review some of the classics, they will also be delighted with contemporary writing by sensitive authors who are conscious of the needs of adolescents. The secondary school teacher who has no time for a course at this point should read as widely as possible and keep up with the book reviews—both in the Sunday editions of newspapers and in numerous other sources where careful annotations of books are available.

KNOWLEDGE OF ADOLESCENTS
AND THEIR INTERESTS

Carlsen, a highly respected and knowledgeable authority concerned with the teenager and reading, stated that "teenagers' book choices indicate that they use reading in a personal if not therapeutic way."[4] He went on to say:

> Perhaps the central concern of adolescents is the search for identity. A teen's physical self and emotional reactions are no longer the familiar, comfortable fit they were in childhood. Relationships with parents and friends have undergone sudden changes. The state of aloneness may be faced for the first time. Some teenagers have the uncomfortable feeling that others are watching and judging them. Others recognize for the first time that they have an inner life, and their thoughts seem unique and troubling. They may experiment with roles and attitudes, as expressed in clothing, hair styles, and deliberately selected behavior patterns. In attempting to come to terms with self, the teen talks endlessly to friends or siblings. It has been said that teen love is intensely conversational, not so much for communication as to discover self.
>
> In the search for identity the young use books, particularly fiction and biography, as a main source of information. Through them they try on different roles, and sometimes discover people like themselves whom they can observe handling their lives. This may not be a proper use of literature, but it is a phase that teenagers must go through if they are to keep reading. Unless the books they read offer them experiential encounters, most will be turned off reading.
>
> The developmental tasks facing the adolescent represent experiences in dealing with human relations, dealing with the inner self, and dealing with vocation.[5]

A good deal of research in the area of reading interests indicates that, within the developmental needs facing all adolescents, girls and boys do show some difference in preferences, which tend to become more obscure as boys and girls become mature, adult readers. Boys overwhelmingly prefer male protagonists in outdoor settings, engaged in realistic physical action. Girls are somewhat more catholic in their tastes, but they do show some preference for female protagonists and activity that is more closely linked to thinking and feeling than to doing.[6]

During early adolescence (grades 5 through 8 or 9) the following types of literature are generally most popular: animal stories, adventure stories (mainly among boys), mystery stories and tales of the supernatural, sports stories, stories of contemporary adolescent life in other countries (especially among girls), home and family life stories (girls), slapstick humor, settings in the past (girls), and fantasy (girls more often than boys). During middle adolescence (grades 9 and 10) interests deepen and often change direction: nonfiction adventure, historical novels, mystical romances (girls), and stories of adolescent life. In late adolescence (eleventh and twelfth grades) students turn to adult material but still also read books written for teenagers in relation to the following areas: search for personal values, themes of social significance, strange and unusual human experiences, and transition to adult life.[7]

Teenage writing is also, of course, related to adolescents' search for identity and to their interests. Armed with some knowledge of teenagers and their interests, and with specific knowledge about the youngsters in a given classroom, the teacher can help students organize their experiences prior to putting those ideas down on paper. As is true for nearly all of us, students will write best about ideas drawn from their own experiences—real and/or vicarious.

SPECIFIC TECHNIQUES

ACCESSIBILITY

Every secondary school should have a school library. Junior and senior high schools without libraries should make every effort to engage some type of service that will make books accessible to students. But often books are not accessible to students even when a fine collection is kept in a central high school library. Too often high school libraries are occupied all day with study halls or classes in "library science." If we are to encourage students to develop lifetime reading habits, they must have access to a library when they need it. They must be able to meander through many kinds of reading collections. They must have the time to select and evaluate.

Students must also, of course, know school librarians who are not store-keepers of books but active consultants. A student should be able to get from a school librarian not just assistance in finding information related to a course activity, but assistance in choosing materials for personal reading needs. In addition, the librarian should be getting into classrooms and talking about new books related to various subject fields. The librarian ought to visit English classes, for example, to talk about new books related to the problems of adolescents, or science, math, and home economics classes to discuss new journals and books related to these areas. Too often such departments as math or home economics are not contacted about books and journals that may relate to their areas. Very often students are not informed of the variety of materials available.

Every high school classroom should have its own library collection. These books and related materials should be catalogued and distributed by the central library so that everyone can make use of them; and a collection should not stay in a given classroom more than a few weeks. The librarian and teachers can decide how long they want the collections and what kinds of materials they want in them. Students should be able to withdraw books from the classroom collection. In a class on problems of American democracy, for example, there should be a changing collection related to the ongoing work in the course. In order to have an effective collection, the librarian and the teacher should work with a reading consultant to be certain that the levels of materials are varied enough for the abilities within the class.

An increasing number of communities are concerned about what should or should not be accessible in a school. The question of censorship is far from being resolved. On the one hand, we have such a rational statement as this: "Censorship leaves students with an inadequate and distorted picture of the ideals, values, and problems of their culture."[8] On the other hand, Hogan points out:

> The uncomfortable truth is that we are all censors. The difference is that when . . . teachers practice censorship, we call it "book selection." . . . When we make selections for classroom use or recommendations for library acquisitions, we take several variables into account. We think about (1) the budget, the available funds; (2) the level of difficulty and/or sophistication of the materials; (3) the accuracy, the scholarly and professional respectability of the materials; (4) the narrowness of focus vs. the breadth of appeal; (5) the transactional relationship between our schools and the communities that support the schools.[9]

Parents have a right to question what their youngsters are reading and writing, but educators—as the professionals—have a right to defend choices for the greater good of their young citizens. Each school or school district should have a well-organized plan and policy in regard to book selection as well as procedures for handling censorship efforts.[10]

DISPLAYS

Along with the classroom collection, a few books should be attractively displayed so that students will be drawn to them. High school classrooms are sometimes rather cold places; one way of warming them is to have a small corner devoted to displays of literature related to the subject area. Attractive displays do not necessarily entail a great deal of time and effort. For example, when a dust cover is put on a bulletin board, it is possible to mount it on a piece of bright poster paper at an angle, securing a three-dimensional effect by pinning the fly leaves under and pushing the cover up. A shadow box can be made from any cardboard box and can be decorated and thumbtacked to the bulletin board to feature the book of the week.

Such displays are usually most appealing if they focus on a specific interest. If the teacher has learned something about the interests of the students, he or she can put up a short-term display dealing with the specific interest of a small group within the class. Permanent displays are not nearly so effective as short-term displays that concentrate on specific themes: "for girls only" for a couple of weeks, or "man in a flying machine" for another period of time. Many students remain with a given interest for a long period of time, but others can be weaned away by attractive displays made by teachers who know adolescent interests and literature.

Students' compositions can be displayed in attractive ways too—with their permission. If compositions are graded through holistic scoring or trait analysis (see pages 54–57), rather than detailed analyses with red pencil, and are displayed for specific purposes, students will feel encouraged to become part of such displays. Essays, poems, stories, and reports can be grouped together because they relate to a specific topic being discussed or a particular interest area, or even used as a preorganizer for a discussion to ensue.

ORAL READING

Oral reading in the secondary classroom has a role to play. But it should not be used for instructional purposes when each student in turn reads a paragraph or two aloud. This technique serves to make reading a rote, mechanical activity rather than an endeavor to unlock meaning. There are times, however, when prepared individuals may read their own compositions or excerpts from other materials to the class or to a group for their information or enjoyment. At these times the preparation must be excellent so that the reception is excellent. Those who are listening must also be well prepared.

Oral reading by the teacher should be done frequently in high school classrooms. If the teacher is an effective reader, this technique helps students to appreciate the flavor and meaning of good literature. There are also excellent recordings by professional readers that can be used to advantage in many subject-matter classrooms.

BOOK REPORTS

One sure way of encouraging the reluctant reader to remain reluctant is through the use of stereotyped book reports. High school students ought to be given the time and the opportunity to read books of their own choosing without reporting to teachers. The mimeographed sheet, used every three, four, or six weeks, on which the student must record the chief characters, a summary, and personal reactions will certainly work toward defeating lifetime reading interests. If there is to be a report, a variety of alternative techniques are available. Some students like to tell about their books in class; others prefer an individual conference with the teacher; and still others can be drawn out informally by a few questions. On the other hand, some students enjoy writing book reports but should be given freedom in the method they choose. Here are some other possibilities:

1. Give an imaginative sales talk to interest others in reading a given book or group of books.

2. Audiotape a book report that individuals can play back at will. (This is particularly good for the student who fears the class oral presentation.)

3. Write a book blurb with accompanying illustration (optional) for a book jacket.

4. Contribute to a classroom file of summaries and reactions to books through file cards, a class book, or a cumulative folder on a given book.

5. Write a letter recommending a book to a friend.

6. Write a book review for a class, school, or town newspaper.

7. Write a set of questions for others to answer after they have read a given book.

8. Write a new ending or section for a book because of dissatisfaction with what has been presented or because an alternative ending or additional scene might be interesting.

9. After several people have read the same book, the group can interact and share reactions and their varied conceptions of what the author had to say.

10. When somewhat similar books have been read or a TV or movie version of a book has been viewed, comparisons can be drawn.

DEFEATING LIFETIME READING INTERESTS

Piercey and Obrenovich wrote an article entitled "If Kids Don't Hate to Read by the Time They Get to High School, Here Are Some Suggestions to Help Them (hate to read, that is)."[11] I was so taken with it and its message that I hastened to obtain permission to use large chunks of it here. The article was a superb combination of drawings and words, some of which are presented in Figures 12.1 and 12.2 on pages 310–311.

SELECTED READINGS

Barmore, Judith M., and Philip Morse. "Developing Lifelong Readers in the Middle Schools." *English Journal* 66 (April 1977):57–61.

Beyard-Tyler, Karen C., and Howard J. Sullivan. "Adolescent Reading Preferences for Type of Themes and Sex of Character." *Reading Research Quarterly* 16, no. 1 (1980):104–20.

Carlsen, G. Robert. *Books and the Teenage Reader: A Guide for Teachers, Librarians, and Parents*, 2nd rev. ed. New York: Bantam Books, 1980.

Ciani, Alfred J., ed. *Motivating Reluctant Readers*. Newark, Del.: International Reading Association, 1981.

Donelson, Kenneth L., and Alleen P. Nilsen. *Literature for Today's Young Adults*. Glenview, Ill.: Scott, Foresman, 1980.

Erickson, Robert D. "The Art Room Book Collection." In *Fusing Reading Skills and Content*, edited by H. Alan Robinson and Ellen Lamar Thomas, pp. 89–96. Newark, Del.: International Reading Association, 1969.

Figure 12.1   How to Help Kids Hate to Read

Source: Dorothy Piercey and Michael Obrenovich, "If Kids Don't Hate to Read by the Time They Get to High School, Here Are Some Suggestions to Help Them (hate to read, that is)," *Journal of Reading* 16 (January 1973):306. Reprinted with permission of the authors and the International Reading Association.

Figure 12.2   How to Help Kids Hate to Read

HOUSE DETENTION CLASSES IN THE LIBRARY. What better way to have them turn their backs on books?

WHEN YOU CATCH A STUDENT HIDING HIS OWN BOOK IN THE TEXTBOOK, MAKE A FEDERAL CASE OF IT. Ridicule him, hold up the book (or newspaper or magazine) for his peers to see, tsk-tsk, roll your eyes — anything to make him feel ashamed.

—EPILOGUE—

From a middleclass, male, high school junior comes this mouthful:

I hate to read because:

1. There are no good books in the class and the ones that are good are too hard to read for anyone in the class.

2. We never get a chance to read. We're promised some reading time at the end of the class but never get it.

3. The teacher talks and teaches to us like we are kindergarden (sic) students.

4. If I want to read a book from home it has to be one that I hadn't already read. Even if I had forgotten all about it.

5. We have to increase the reading pacer by 25 wpm. each day and it goes way to (sic) fast.

6. The teacher complains that I'm not listening because I don't no (sic) what we're doing when I can't hear her.

7. When I'm trying to read she starts talking to someone and it disturbs me so I can't do it.

8. When we use the tape recorder I can't understand a single thing they say and I can bearly (sic) hear them.

9. If you ask or tell the teacher something she explains something else and then wonders why you don't understand some things.

10. She would help a lot of kids if she spent a little time working individualy (sic), but it never comes across her mind to do so.

And thereby hangs a fail.

Source: Dorothy Piercey and Michael Obrenovich, "If Kids Don't Hate to Read by the Time They Get to High School, Here Are Some Suggestions to Help Them (hate to read, that is)," *Journal of Reading* 16 (January 1973):309. Reprinted with permission of the authors and the International Reading Association.

Gentile, Lance M., and Merna M. McMillan. "Why Won't Teenagers Read?" *Journal of Reading* 20 (May 1977):649–54.

Hatcher, Thomas C., and Lawrence G. Erickson, eds. *Indoctrinate or Educate?* Newark, Del.: International Reading Association, 1979.

Isaacs, Mary Ann L. "Adolescent Literature: Gleaning from the Abundance." *Journal of Reading* 22 (April 1979):654–56.

LiBretto, Ellen V., ed. *High/Low Handbook: Books, Materials, and Services for the Teenage Problem Reader.* Ann Arbor, Mich.: R.R. Bowker, 1981.

Patlak, Sanford. "Physical Education and Reading: Questions and Answers." In *Fusing Reading Skills and Content,* edited by H. Alan Robinson and Ellen Lamar Thomas, pp. 81–88. Newark, Del.: International Reading Association, 1969.

Piercey, Dorothy, and Michael Obrenovich. "If Kids Don't Hate to Read by the Time They Get to High School, Here Are Some Suggestions to Help Them (hate to read, that is)." *Journal of Reading* 16 (January 1973):305–9.

Shapiro, Jon E., ed. *Using Literature & Poetry Affectively.* Newark, Del.: International Reading Association, 1979.

Simmons, John S.; Robert E. Shafer; and Gail B. West. *Decisions about the Teaching of English,* pp. 49–106. Boston: Allyn and Bacon, 1976.

Smith, Joseph A. "A Survey of Adolescents' Interests: Concerns and Information." *Adolescence* 15 (Summer 1980):475–82.

NOTES

1. John S. Simmons, Robert E. Shafer, and Gail B. West, *Decisions about the Teaching of English* (Allyn and Bacon, 1976), p. 61.
2. Ibid.
3. Ibid.
4. G. Robert Carlsen, *Books and the Teenage Reader: A Guide for Teachers, Librarians and Parents,* 2nd rev. ed. (Bantam Books, 1980), p. 12. © 1967, 1971 by G. Robert Carlsen. Reprinted by permission of Harper & Row, Publishers, Inc.
5. Ibid., pp. 12–13. Copyright © 1967, 1971 by G. Robert Carlsen. Reprinted by permission of Harper & Row, Publishers, Inc.
6. Ibid., adapted from pp. 34–35.
7. Ibid., adapted from pp. 36–41.
8. Kenneth L. Donelson and Alleen P. Nilsen, *Literature for Today's Young Adults* (Glenview, Ill.: Scott, Foresman, 1980), p. 459.
9. Robert Hogan, "Censorship in the Schools," in *Dealing with Censorship,* ed. James E. Davis (Urbana, Ill.: National Council of Teachers of English, 1979). Cited by Holly O'Donnell in "Who's Being Protected—the Books or the Students?" *Journal of Reading* 24 (March 1981):538.
10. Donelson and Nilsen, *Literature,* pp. 414–15.
11. Dorothy Piercey and Michael Obrenovich, "If Kids Don't Hate to Read by the Time They Get to High School, Here Are Some Suggestions to Help Them (hate to read, that is)," *Journal of Reading* 16 (January 1973):306, 309.

Name Index

Subject Index